W9-CCY-589

Jews in the Modern World

VOLUME

TWO

Jews
in the
Modern
World

Edited by
JACOB FREID

Twayne Publishers, Inc.   New York

Library of Congress Catalog Card Number: 61-15671

MANUFACTURED IN THE UNITED STATES OF AMERICA BY
UNITED PRINTING SERVICES, INC.
NEW HAVEN, CONN.

CONTENTS

PART III

ART AND LITERATURE

In a former generation, it was generally assumed that representational art had been unknown among the Jews before the Age of Emancipation, because of their over-literal interpretation of the prohibition in the Ten Commandments: "Thou shalt not make unto thee any graven image, or any likeness of anything that is in heaven above or that is in the earth beneath or that is in the waters under the earth." There were, of course, certain periods in Jewish history when this injunction was minutely obeyed, and Jews would not tolerate even in their homes any representation, however crude, of any living thing. But recent archaeological discoveries in Palestine and elsewhere have made it clear that this attitude did not prevail universally, or at all times. There were more liberal interludes, when the interpretation of the biblical passage was conditioned by the ensuing verse: "Thou shalt not bow down to them, nor serve them," implying that the prohibition extended only to the creation of graven images *for worship*. At such times, representational art was used with relative freedom for decorative or illustrative objects—occasionally even for purposes closely associated with divine worship, or in the synagogue itself.

CECIL ROTH, *The Jews in the Renaissance*

INTRODUCTION

by JACOB FREID

ARE WE ON THE EVE OF AN AMERICAN-JEWISH CULTURAL RENAISSANCE?

What can be said in assessing the pros and cons of American Jewish life, in attempting to project the significant trends into the future, and in trying to determine how they will influence the next generation? Is there sufficient basis for a tentative, if not a definitive answer to the question "Is creative Jewish living possible in America?"

That there are debits—here discussed—to balance off the assets on the communal ledgers of contemporary Jewish life in America is conceded; that the dire predictions of the Israeli critics in Part IV's Israel-Diaspora dialogue deserve sober, searching examination is not denied. Yet despite dissatisfactions at home and demurrers abroad the answer must be affirmative.

Uncertainty, indefiniteness, and flux are the characteristics of the present time of transition for American Jewry, while at the same time it is in the midst of a cultural and creative ferment and expression in the arts and literature. The extent and equality of this flowering of Jewish creativity as indicated in Part II, are sufficient to claim that our artists, writers and musicians are on the eve of a renaissance in the lively and fine arts.

The Literary Supplement of the London *Times*, which ranks among the important sections in world literature, devoted a comprehensive essay by Theodore Solataroff in its special issue of "The American Imagination" to "A Vocal Group, the Jewish Part in American Letters."[1] The critic considered the "emerg-

---

[1] November 6, 1959. The essayist considers the main quality of Jewish writing today "is its creative energy rather than its focus, and its tendency to flow outward to the American rather than inward and backward to the Jewish."

ence of American-Jewish writing as a decisive force in American letters" to be a significant and formidable development.[2]

The foremost American-Jewish literary critic and anthologist, Harold Ribalow, has been able to put together three collections of short stories which mirror a diversified cross-section of Jewish life as expressively reflected by modern Jewish authors.[3] Apart from the fact that these stories are entirely representative, savory in emotion, effervescent and sympathetic with Jewish warmth and humor, evocative and penetrating in their depiction of tragedy—their impressively demonstrated realities are that: American-Jewish stories are being written for and published in good number in America's finest literary magazines; they are written with "a skill and fluency that stamp them as outstanding examples of the short story as an art form";[4] they are written by successful and established authors as well as new writers recently risen to prominence on the American literary scene; these stories offer sensitive, mature and accurate insight into the role of the Jew in American national life. Not only are these anthologies a tribute to the editorial skill of Mr. Ribalow, they are an irrefutable proof of his contention, based on their published evidence, that the quantity and quality of the Jewish contribution to American letters is impressive, and that American Jews together with non-Jews who before World War II were supremely indifferent to Jewish writing, today are facing up to Jewish issues and problems in America.

No community can be negated or consigned to future Toynbee-esque oblivion as a fossil on a neglected shelf of Jewish and American life and letters, which is so exuberant, prolific and talented in its virile creativity. If its Israeli doomsayers do not, the London *Times* nonetheless does consider American-Jewish letters of sufficient stature to be afforded special treatment in

---

[2] *Ibid.*

[3] *This Land, These People* and *These Your Children*, Beechhurst Press; *The Chosen*, Abelard-Schuman. Among the contributors are Charles Angoff, Nelson Algren, Herbert Gold, Ben Hecht, Albert Halper, Shlomo Katz, Arthur Miller, Budd Schulberg, James Yaffe, Bernard Malamud, Isaac Rosenfeld, Irving Kristol, Meyer Levin, Irwin Shaw.

[4] Harold Ribalow, "Image of the Jew in Literature," Philadelphia *Jewish Exponent*, December 4, 1959.

its literary section. The successors to the proletarian writers of the thirties, in their concern with and expression of Jewish themes, have achieved an artistic peak of Jewish creativity in America during the past decade, never before reached in the United States.[5] As Ribalow discusses the "startling metamorphosis" of the Judaism of creative American Jewish writers in his essay, it is evident that there has emerged in the United States a body of fiction by and about Jews which offers useful insights into the patterns of Jewish living in America. They are a hope and a challenge for a similarly meaningful metamorphosis in the Judaism of American Jewry.

The Jewish best seller is also an established fact of American publishing today. Harry Golden's *Only in America* and *For 2¢ Plain* reached the front ranks as best sellers and were followed by a third, *Enjoy! Enjoy!*, which was bought by the delighted droves who were the happy partners of a love match with the two earlier collections of Golden words and wit.

According to *Publisher's Weekly*, Herman Wouk's *This Is My God*, despite both pro and con reviews, went past the 100,000 sales mark. This is remarkable for a book which is a popular and simple retelling of the Jewish holidays, their meaning and significance, the Jewish faith and how it evolved.

Meyer Levin's *Eva*, a novel which also received mixed reviews and related the grim tale of how a Jewish girl survived the Nazi genocide blueprint, similarly climbed the best seller heights with sales of 31,000 within a few short weeks after publication. Apart from its literary qualities, the sociologist must be impressed by the fact that *Exodus* by Leon Uris sold almost a half million hardcover copies and over one and one half million copies in its paperback edition. This is one of the most fabulous gold strikes in publishing history. The significant fact is that the numbers of sales of this and other books discussed in Ribalow's essay here, cannot be accounted for by the American Jewish reading public alone. Apparently Jewish books, and books about Jews and Judaism are being read in ever greater numbers by non-Jews. The Jew in fiction, like the Jew in suburbia, Ribalow believes, has become an accepted

---

[5] Ribalow, "Introduction," *The Chosen*, op. cit., p. 9.

figure. He is accepted by all readers, Gentile and Jewish alike.[6] And with the non-Jews reading avidly about their Jewish American citizens, Jews themselves are picking up more and more books on Jewish subjects.

Further, the books themselves fill a need and appeal to a large number of people. If Harry Golden's work isn't exclusively Jewish, his tone and tempo are. His readers feel good when they read him. They are suffused in a "Golden" glow for humanity brewed of nostalgia, humor, wit, counsel and insight. So it goes. The swastika painters who erupted in a flurry of activity in the wake of a Christmas 1959 daubing of a Cologne synagogue by two young neo-Nazis, cannot obliterate the fact that the American atmosphere has changed. Jewish writers are "accenting the positive,"[7] and publishers are acknowledging that their rising charts signify that Jews are Americans other Americans want to know about. If Israeli intellectuals are too intent upon pronouncing its doom to see that the intended corpse is very much alive and creatively expressive, then their unwillingness to admit that the reports of the patient's demise—as in the case of Mark Twain—are grossly exaggerated, must be attributed to myopia, not to empirical observation.

The fact that Alfred Werner finds a constantly increasing body of American Jewish painters and sculptors and handicraftsmen whose art merits serious critical reviews at frequent intervals is additional evidence. His essay indicates the extent and quality of American Jewish creativity in the fine arts, synagogue architecture and the crafts. Jewish scholars, intellectuals and social scientists also are producing essays, studies and non-fiction books of merit.[8]

In the eighteen centuries following the abortive Bar Kochba uprising, Jews, dispersed into the lands of Europe, Asia and Africa, spoke the language of the people among whom they lived. Aramaic in the ancient and medieval worlds from the

[6] Ribalow, "The Jewish Best Seller," *American Zionist*, January, 1960.
[7] *Ibid.*
[8] *The Jews: Social Patterns of an American Group*, edited by Marshall Sklare, The Free Press, 1958, in its thirty-three essays, is important and substantial evidence of the range and interest by social scientists in American Jewry.

Babylonian exile to the Spanish expulsion, and Yiddish in the medieval and modern worlds, were the most important languages of dispersion.

Menahem Boraisha outlined the story of the development and growth of Yiddish into a language of the theatre, journalism and of original literary creation. A half-century ago Yiddish was the dynamic, creative cultural medium and language of some twelve million Jews living in virtually every part of the globe. But though it is represented by a distinguished and significant literature, including works of world stature which have been translated and achieved fame in other languages, most of its reading and writing constituency has been destroyed by Hitler or silenced by the rulers of the Soviet Union.

While Yiddish is waning outside of its vibrant Latin-American centers, Hebrew is flowering in Israel. Meyer Waxman outlines "The Story of Hebrew" and relates the "miracle" of the renaissance of the Hebrew language in this generation. He traces the continuity, development and growth of Hebrew from earliest times to the present, and indicates the Haskalah movement to be the herald of the modern Hebrew revival of the last eighty years in the land of its birth. For the American public, Hebrew today is sampled in a sprinkling of English translations such as the Israel Argosy anthologies, and in selected novels and non-fiction titles. Dr. Waxman's list of modern Hebrew writers is not meant to be all-inclusive. It does, however, indicate the outpouring of creative Hebrew literature and serious writing in our times.

First-rate Jewish periodicals are published reguarly in the United States as ready vehicles for the secular and religious scholar, the intellectual and the creative writer.[9] The excellence of these bi-weekly, monthly and quarterly magazines is not

---

[9] Among these are the Bi-Weekly and Monthly magazines: *Commentary* (AJ Committee), *Congress Bi-Weekly* (AJ Congress), *Jewish Frontier* (Labor Zionist Organization), *National Jewish Monthly* and *Jewish Heritage* (B'nai B'rith), *Jewish Spectator;* the Quarterlies: *Chicago Jewish Forum, Jewish Social Studies* (Conference on Jewish Social Studies), *Judaism* (AJ Congress), *Midstream* (Theodor Herzl Foundation); Religious: *American Judaism* (Reform), *Orthodox Jewish Life, Conservative Judaism* and *United Synagogue Review* (Conservative), *Reconstructionist* (Jewish Reconstructionist Foundation), *Tradition* (Rabbinical Council of America).

duplicated by the communal newspapers. There is a prolific Anglo-Jewish press of weeklies published in virtually every major community. Apart from the *National Jewish Post and Opinion*, these concentrate on local and Israeli news plus some syndicated features and the news services of the Jewish Telegraphic Agency and the Seven Arts Syndicate. Among the best of these are the Boston *Jewish Advocate*, the Newark *Jewish News*, the Philadelphia *Jewish Exponent*, the Detroit *Jewish News*, the Denver Intermountain *Jewish News*, the Chicago *Jewish Sentinel*, the Miami *Jewish Floridian*.

There is no community publication comparable to the London *Jewish Chronicle*, or analagous in the Jewish field to either the *Christian Science Monitor*, or as a paper of record, to the New York *Times*.

Inhibited by lack of funds, Gabriel Cohen of Indianapolis, Indiana, publisher of the *National Jewish Post and Opinion*, has never been able to achieve for the Jewish community a genuine national channel of communication such as secular Jewish publisher, Adolph Ochs of Chatanooga, Tennessee, and New York, through the New York *Times* with its national and worldwide corps of expert correspondents, was able to achieve for both New York and the national community through his paper of record, or as Erwin Canham achieved for the nation's readers in general and his church in particular with the *Christian Science Monitor*.

As in the case of these two esteemed national newspapers, independence, quality of reportage and analysis, and freedom from venal, vested interests or pressure group corruption are essential. When it was founded after World War II, the Office of Jewish Information of the American Jewish Congress and the World Jewish Congress hoped to provide a listening-post intelligence service for Diaspora Jewry of daily observation and reports by able correspondents throughout the lands of dispersion, by reporting communal events, trends, portents and problems concerning the Jewish community's social, political, economic and demographic status, and its cultural, educational and religious life. Here again funds were lacking.

At present, American-Jewish journalism is represented mainly by intramural community house organs and social gazettes and calendars. There is not what Philip Klutznick, former president of B'nai B'rith, called a "vital national Jewish publication." The often distinguished writing that is the hallmark of the literate periodicals is largely absent in the Anglo-Jewish press.

The daily pulse beat of Jewish life, with its nuances of unique and common meaning and portent, is lacking in the United States and in other countries. Only Israel is projected to a good extent in Zionist publications, news dispatches, correspondents' reports and articles.

Such a national newspaper may have to wait for the millennium of an organized Jewish community in America. The overall lack of unity and disorganization is reflected in the press projection of its communal life. Instead of meaningful focus, we are given shapelessness; instead of purpose, pointlessness; instead of the intellectually gifted, Jewishly insightful journalistic light that illuminates, a nebulous haze. There is understanding of this lack and a concern to remedy it. Perhaps here also a maturing community will respond as the Council of Jewish Federations and Welfare Funds did in setting up a Jewish cultural foundation.

CHAPTER SIXTEEN

STORY OF JEWISH ART

by ALFRED WERNER

In one of his canvasses the Jewish painter, Marc Chagall, shows an old bearded Jew resting wearily by the roadside on his flight from his oppressors. All the old man has rescued from destruction is a large *Torah*, which he holds tenderly, as though it were his child. The motif is convincing; it appears quite natural that from the drama of flight a Jewish artist should select for emphasis not human emotion and turbulent action but an idea. Jews traditionally tend to regard themselves as primarily the "People of the Book." Unfortunately, the strong predilection the Jews have shown throughout the centuries for moral and religious speculation has somewhat obscured Jewish achievement in other creative realms, especially in the arts. Moreover, it has repeatedly been claimed that the Jews have been less gifted in the arts than have other people.

Some basis for this claim originates in the popular notion that the Second Commandment actually forbids sculpture and painting: "Thou shall not make unto thee a graven image, nor any manner of likeness of anything that is on heaven above, nor that is in the earth beneath, nor that is in the water under the earth."

Prohibitions like this are to be found in other religions as well. It is known that early Christian theologians objected to sculptures and paintings, in which they believed they saw dangerous tendencies toward idolatry. Mohammed, too, was suspicious of artists, probably because he regarded them as endowed with supernatural powers and thus as possible competitors with God's creative powers; and Moslem theologians banned both painting and sculpture.

With all its apparent rigidity, the Second Commandment leaves such branches of art as architecture and the so-called applied arts completely untouched. Besides it should be remembered that the Lawgiver goes on to say: "Thou shall not bow unto them nor serve them," thus primarily forbidding the creation of such forms as could be worshipped in the manner of the pagans. It is true there were times when the danger of a lapse into heathenism was so great that zealous men like the Prophets condemned *all* display of art rather than risk any disintegration of the faith. However, as the Palestinian archaeologist, Sukenik, has pointed out, there were long periods of laxity in enforcing the biblical prohibition.

Likewise, in the Diaspora some rabbis looked askance at any attempts to introduce objects of art into the ghetto, such as adorned Christian houses of worship and Gentile homes. As far as the Middle Ages were concerned, the historian David Kaufmann maintained that while some of the rabbinical dicta forbade the presentation of works of art, as did some church edicts, "one need not claim . . . that Judaism abhorred all beauty." Kaufmann asserted that the alleged bias of the Synagogue against art was "a myth which the proofs of literature and of the preserved art objects have long ago dispelled."

Indeed, it would be difficult to imagine an entire people blind to physical beauty or to assume that the Jewish soul had exhausted itself in what Matthew Arnold called its message of "conduct" and "obedience to the word of the Lord." It is generally overlooked that the very Book of Exodus which contains the Decalogue with its prohibition of certain forms of art also includes a detailed description of the beauty of the Tabernacle, that portable sanctuary which served as a place of worship for the Israelites during their travels through the wilderness. Moreover, the Book of Exodus refers to the artists in glowing terms. The Lord, according to the text, appointed Bezalel and Oholiab to construct the Tabernacle. Bezalel is said to have possessed the skills "to work in gold, and in silver, and in brass, and in cutting of stones for setting, and in carving wood" and to have had as well the gift of weaving in many different colors.

Whatever the actual beauty of the Ark, the seven-branched

Candelabrum, the carpets and the other parts of the Tabernacle may have been, the description in Exodus of the artist as a God-inspired being is proof of the high esteem in which the artist was held by the Israelites. Significantly, the term *haham*, sage, is used in the Bible for the first time with reference to the builders of the Tabernacle. It is no less interesting to note that the rabbinical literature of the post-biblical era ascribed to Bezalel a knowledge of construction exceeding even that of the wisest of all men, Moses.

Many utterances in favor of art can be found in the literature of the Diaspora. The Talmud, for example, explains the biblical words: "This is my God and I will adorn Him" through the following admonition:

> Make a beautiful *sukkah* in His honor, a beautiful *lulab*, a beautiful *shofar*, beautiful *tzitzith* and a beautiful Scroll of the Law and write it with fine ink, a fine reed . . . and wrap it about with beautiful silks."

This same attitude toward beauty and the arts is seen in the exhortation of the fourteenth-century Spanish-Jewish philosopher, Profiat Duran:

> The House of Learning should be beautiful and pleasing in structure. This increases the desire for learning, and strengthens the memory because the viewing of pleasing forms and beautiful reliefs and drawings rejoices the heart and strengthens the mind.

To be sure, the kind of art that was officially accepted by our ancestors was basically of a religious nature. This is not surprising if one remembers that, in its inception, the art of all peoples was essentially religious (although additional motifs may have been present). However, among the Israelites there also developed a purely secular art, even though it never played as paramount a role as in ancient Greece or Rome. There were architects and craftsmen who built and decorated the palaces for kings and men of wealth.

In the Diaspora, Jews supplied the non-Jewish market with products of their skills. As a people, neither the ancient Hebrews, the children of the ghetto, nor the modern Jews have ever been immune to beauty. It is significant that to this very day the pious Jew is supposed to recite certain benedictions on seeing various objects of beauty, thus thanking God for having created them for men to enjoy.

But is there such a thing as *Jewish* art? The modern brand of nationalism was unknown in ancient times; it was religion, not nationality or race that separated the Israelites from their neighbors. Hence, Jewish art in ancient Palestine, and subsequently in the other regions of the Mediterranean world where Jews settled in large numbers, distinguishes itself from the art of other peoples through specific religious motifs, generally related to the ritual purpose of the individual art object, rather than through any national style. Devoid of any chauvinism, King Solomon borrowed the artist Hiram from the King of Tyre to help him with the building of the Temple; some of the artists who participated in executing the impressive murals of the ancient synagogue at Dura Europos, Syria, covering the walls with scenes from the Old Testament, may have been non-Jews. In more recent times, Christian artists have occasionally been commissioned to produce Jewish ritual objects which now, to the unbiased observer, appear to be "genuinely" Jewish.

There was much of "Jewish art" in the Middle Ages, art in a style different from that of the country in which the Jews were living. Forced segregation and frequent persecution had isolated the Jews within the larger communities and had influenced their feeling and thinking, though the spirit of the outside world often pierced even the thickest ghetto walls. However, when in the era of emancipation these walls came tumbling down, the artists of Jewish origin assimilated themselves so quickly to the spirit and the demands of the non-Jewish world that they became, and were recognized as German, French, Dutch, Swedish masters, and not as Jewish artists. Accordingly, the term "Jewish art" in the narrowest sense is applied correctly only to religious art and to some of the works by those twentieth-century artists who, in the wake of the Jewish renaissance, have become aware of Jewish national values and have expressed the distinctive emotions and strivings of their own people.

We still know very little of Hebraic art in ancient times and of Jewish art in the Middle Ages, though infinitely more than the experts knew a generation ago.

Recent discoveries in and around Palestine prove beyond any doubt that (a) the references to ancient Hebrew art found in the Bible as well as in the works of such writers as Josephus Flavius are based on facts, and (b) that this art was somewhat different from that of other Western Asiatic peoples. King Solomon probably was not boasting when he mentioned the "skillful men that are with me in Judah and in Jerusalem, whom David my father did provide," i.e., a body of court artists, assembled by David. Nor does the Bible exaggerate, to judge by recent excavations, where it relates that when the Israelites were forced into captivity, the Babylonian victors took along "the craftsmen and the smiths a thousand." Hosea's scornful exclamation, "Israel hath forgotten his Maker and builded palaces"; Isaiah's observation, "Everyone worshippeth the work of his own hands, that which his own fingers have made"; and Ezekiel's outbursts against a chamber in the Temple of Jerusalem where "every detestable form of creeping thing and beasts" was to be found will now be read with greater interest, for they seem to indicate that there may have been relatively as many art objects in Jerusalem as existed in Athens or Alexandria.

Indeed, the excavations in the Holy Land, while confirming the literary reports, convey only a faint picture of the wealth of art that must have existed at least since the reign of the Kings. At Megiddo the remains of imposing administration buildings and stables, probably belonging to the architecture of King Solomon's era, were unearthed. Carefully hewn stone palaces and other buildings were found there and elsewhere, with such remnants of outer ornamentations as the attractive capitals of pilasters. As for interior decorations, beautifully made small ivory tablets were found in Samaria. While the subjects depicted on them, such as deities, animals and trees, show Egyptian influence, the inscriptions are often in Hebrew or

Aramaic. Limestone and bronze lamps, faïence vessels, silver basins and other attractively executed domestic utensils suggest a certain sophistication on the part of the owners.

Unfortunately there is no trace left of Solomon's Temple, and nothing but a fragment of a wall (today known as the Wailing Wall) of the Second Temple, built by King Herod. The palaces and castles of the Maccabees seem to have been destroyed completely. However, archaeologists unearthed a considerable number of Jewish coins, minted from the Maccabean period (middle of second century B.C.E.) up until the short-lived revolt of Bar Kochbah (132-135 C.E.). While the coins of other ancient nations generally bear the images of emperors and military leaders, of animal sacrifices and records of war and conquest, these Jewish coins show, in addition to Hebrew inscriptions, such peaceful Jewish motifs as *lulab* and *ethrog*, utensils like amphora, ampula, *omer* cups, trumpets and lyres, the *menorah*, and the Temple at Jerusalem. Also, we have additional proof of the flexible interpretation of the Second Commandment, since some of the ancient Palestinian seals bear strikingly realistic representations of various animals in addition to Hebrew inscriptions.

After the destruction of the Temple at Jerusalem (70 C.E.) synagogues were built throughout Palestine. Even before that period synagogues had existed in various parts of the ancient world. The ruined walls of some of the ancient synagogues have been preserved, as well as some of their beautiful mosaic floors. At Beth Alpha in Palestine the mosaic pavement shows a variety of subjects, such as the story of the sacrifices of Isaac, zodiacal signs and numerous ceremonial objects. The mosaic pavement of an ancient synagogue in Transjordania, dug up from beneath the remains of a Byzantine church, tells the story of the Flood with superb craftsmanship. The most interesting and beautiful monument of ancient Jewish art, however, was unearthed in the 1930's by an expedition conducted by Yale University in cooperation with the French Academy of Letters. This was the aforementioned synagogue of Dura Europos, Syria (third century C.E.), which contains many murals retelling biblical stories from the Patriarchs to King Solomon with nobility of spirit and admirable skill.

The influence exerted by Jewish art upon early Christian culture has been noticed only recently. It was the Jews who designed the synagogue as the meeting place of worshippers rather than as the dwelling place of the deity, thus influencing the architectural structure of the church. More importantly, Judaism influenced early Christian art in turning away from the natural to the supernatural, and in presenting subjects of transcendental rather than of material significance. Early Christian artists also often copied Old Testament models; Jesus, for instance, was often portrayed by the catacomb artists as holding a rod—obviously based on Jewish representations of Moses striking the rock with his rod.

The Middle Ages are commonly held to have ended with the discovery of America. For the Jews they continued, practically speaking, until the French Revolution razed the medieval ghetto walls and gave the Jews full civil rights. This was hardly an era in which the arts could flourish freely among the Jews. Moreover, in most European countries the Jews were excluded from virtually all occupations but trading and moneylending, and the guilds and crafts were closed to them. Nevertheless, certain skills were handed down from father to son throughout the centuries, in strict observance of the talmudic admonition that a Jewish father ought to teach his son a trade, "for if one does not do so, it is like teaching him robbery." In fact, medieval Jews in some crafts equalled or even excelled their Christian and Mohammedan colleagues. Significantly, quite a few objects of medieval art, originally attributed to some anonymous non-Jewish master, have recently been re-classified as specimens of Jewish art. A typical example is the famous "Islamic" carpet in Berlin's Kaiser Friedrich Museum, the woven design of which was later recognized as depicting *Torah* shrines.

Arts and crafts flourished among Jews only in those regions where for long periods there was little or no oppression, such as Spain, Italy, Greece, Poland, and various Mohammedan lands in Asia and Africa. Even in ancient times Jews had been famous for goldsmithing, and ancient writers praised one of their outstanding achievements—a golden mountain with trees and

animals, surrounded by a grapevine—a work presented by the
Judean King Aristobul II to Pompey, who placed it in the
temple of Jupiter Capitolinus in Rome. Apparently the Jews
retained this kind of skill, for as late as 1415 Pope Benedict XIV
forbade Jewish smiths to manufacture Christian ceremonial objects, such as goblets and crucifixes. (The same bull, incidentally, barred Jews from binding any Christian books mentioning
the name of Jesus or of Mary). Jews must have been excellent
workers in metal, for the fourteenth-century English poet,
Chaucer, who was hardly a friend of the Jews, in describing
a coat of mail praises it as

. . . a fyn hawberk
. . . al ywrought of Jewes werk.*

Jews minted coins for the Merovingian dynasty in France,
as well as for some Arab rulers. For one caliph they made
costly silks and flags decorated skillfully with Arabic slogans,
emblems and other adornments. The Venetians drew inspiration
from the works of the Jewish glass blowers in Tyre. Fine glass
with inlaid gold figures was produced by Jews in Alexandria.
The sixteenth-century Jewish historian, Solomon ibn Verga, speaks
of Jews in Persia "who can work the windows of the King so
finely in wood and stone, it is as though they were made of
gold and silver." Jews were famous dyers, lace makers, and
cartographers. Even in the German lands where Jews were
subjected to frequent pogroms, Jewish artistic productiveness
was never completely stifled. Jewish book binders were held
in such high esteem that in 1458 a Jew bound several books
for the city council of Nuremberg—the same Jew, incidentally,
who wrote and illuminated the beautiful and costly *Haggadah*
that is now kept at the Hebrew Union College in Cincinnati.
In 1490 the city of Noerdlingen commissioned a Jew to bind
the city records.

* "The Tale of Sir Thopas," in *The Poems of Chaucer,* ed. F. N. Robinson (Boston: Houghton Mifflin, 1933), p. 199.

EDITOR'S NOTE: This may have been said in ridicule. See Kölbing,
Englische Studien, II, 510.

There were Jewish painters and sculptors in Catholic Spain, not only converts to Christianity, but also professing Jews who did altar paintings for churches and individuals. In 1480, only a few years before the expulsion edict, the Queen of Spain forbade the painting of holy Christian subjects by Jewish or Mohammedan artists. There exists also a cryptic reference to a Jewish painter, Marlibrun (Meir le Brun), who seems to have lived in Billingsgate, London, in the latter half of the thirteenth century. Considered the foremost artist of his time, he was commissioned by King Edward I to paint a picture of the Virgin for All-Hallows Church, Barking, in London. The picture (which is not preserved) was a great attraction for the faithful, who made pilgrimages to the shrine in order to view it, and for a long period it was regarded as one of the sights of London.

Regrettably, only scanty records of some medieval Jewries are preserved, leaving their artistic activities entirely in the dark; in particular, the number of Jewish art objects produced prior to the sixteenth century that have come down to us is, unfortunately, small. As for the old synagogues, a few built in the Romanesque, Gothic, Renaissance, or Moorish style were preserved because, at one time or another, they had been converted into churches like the one in Trani, southern Italy, built in 1247 by a Jewish architect, or the beautiful synagogues in Toledo, Spain, one of which (now the church Santa Maria la Blanca) is believed to have been built by a Jew because of certain features of its style. The oldest synagogue in Central Europe, that of Worms, built in the twelfth century, was destroyed by the Nazis in November, 1938.

Distinctly Jewish designs are to be found on tombstones, some dating back to the sixth century in Spain; while the oldest known specimen in the Rhine district, Germany, is the one in Mayence, dated 1064. The work of Jewish carvers, they contain Hebrew inscriptions and quite often bear family coats-of-arms and animal figures symbolic of the name of the deceased carved on the stones. Tombstones of the *kohanim* (priests) are often marked with a carving of the hands as extended in the priestly blessing, while those of the Levites bear an ewer as symbol of their office in the Temple, that of serving the priests.

In general, the Sephardim used richer decorations on the tombstones than were used by the Ashkenazim.

While it is difficult to identify any marked Jewish style in art objects made for secular purposes, and often for the non-Jewish customer, there existed, apart from the carving of tombstones, a large field where genuinely Jewish talent could display itself: Jewish religious art for synagogue and home. Anyone who wishes to get an idea of the wealth of fine Jewish ceremonial objects that were to be found all over Europe ought to study the "Tentative List of Jewish Cultural Treasures in Axis-Occupied Countries," compiled by the Research Staff of the Commission on European Jewish Cultural Reconstruction (printed as a supplement to *Jewish Social Studies*, Vol. VIII, No. 1). It lists the names of more than seven hundred libraries, museums, and private collections, both Jewish and non-Jewish, many of which contained not only valuable Jewish books' and documents, but also costly specimens of Jewish religious art. How much of these treasures was destroyed by the Nazis is unknown. (How many artists of talent perished, and what true works of art were to remain unborn, we shall never know). Fortunately quite a few treasures of this kind survive in British and Russian museums, as well as in Israel. In this country, a fair idea of the development and scope of Jewish pre-emancipation art can be obtained from the collections in the Jewish Theological Seminary of America in New York, in Cincinnati's Hebrew Union College, in Chicago's Jewish People's Institute, and in the Section of Historic Religious Ceremonials in the Smithsonian Institute.

The *Torah* was the focal attraction for Jewish artists in the Middle Ages. It was written—and sometimes illuminated—by special scribes (*sofrim*). In Moslem countries, especially among the Karaites, the text was often written in Arabic script. There exists a marked difference between the illuminated Hebrew Bibles of the East, and those of western Europe. The former contain only decorative patterns; no human beings or animals are portrayed but there are representations of the Tabernacle. In the West, however, the prohibition of the Second Commandment was less strictly observed by the scribes. There is in London a thirteenth-century French Hebrew Bible written on the finest vellum, with forty miniatures painted on a thicker parchment. It is lavishly provided with initials illuminated in gold, and with full-page miniatures showing Abraham welcoming the three angels, the passage of the Israelites through the Red Sea, David playing the harp, and other biblical scenes. They show a resourcefulness and skill found only among the best specimens of contemporary French art and are probably the work of a Jew because the interweaving of the text with the pictures required a considerable knowledge of Hebrew. Also in London is the famous Farhi Bible, with its beautifully ornamented pages; the artist, Elijah ben Abraham Benveniste, a Provençal, began to work on it in 1366 and spent sixteen years on this complicated task. It is interesting to note that there even exists a manual of the art of illuminating manuscripts written in Portuguese, but in Hebrew characters, by Abraham ben Judah Ibn Hayim during the latter part of the thirteenth century.

While great skill was devoted to illustration and adorning the *Torah,* the other Hebrew books were not neglected. It was especially the *Haggadah* that lent itself to illustration. The most famous of all medieval *Haggadoth* is probably the one named after the city of Sarajevo, Bosnia, where it was rediscovered. As the *Haggadah* was not used in the synagogue but at home, whatever religious restrictions might have been imposed on the artist could be brushed aside more easily, and this was certainly the case with the illustrator of the Sarajevo *Haggadah* who retells so charmingly the story of the Bible from the Creation up to the exodus from Egypt. Incidentally, it has been noted that a comparison of the illuminated Hebrew Bibles and *Haggadoth* with the frescoes at Dura Europos reveals the fact that not only did many of the subjects illustrated in that ancient synagogue reappear in the pages of the medieval Hebrew manuscripts, but that they are also treated there with a similarity that is striking.

The invention of printing at first did not diminish the beauty of the Hebrew books, as woodcuts and metal engravings of the highest caliber replaced the work previously done with pen and brush. It was only the mass production of more recent times that permitted the issue of drearily unattractive prayer-books, *Haggadoth,* and so forth. However, since the 1930's successful attempts have been made to restore beauty to our Holy Books—an excellent example is the richly adorned *Haggadah* illustrated by Arthur Szyk.

After the reading in the synagogue, the Book of Books was put into the *Torah* mantle, which was generally of silk or velvet, often beautifully embroidered by skillful and pious women of the congregation. Of the same quality was the *Torah* curtain (*parochet*). Pointer (*yad*), crown (*Keter Torah*) and breast-plate (*tas*); and the other holy articles used in connection with the *Sefer Torah* were made of fine gold or silver. Equally attractive were the ceremonial objects used outside the synagogue. The traditional Jewish home of means had a pair of silver candlesticks, used when the Sabbath was being ushered in, a row of silver wine cups, an eight-branched *menorah,* a spice holder used for *habdalah* on Saturday night, small silk or velvet bags containing the *tefillin,* often wrought with the design of the Shield of David, and a silver *mezuza* on the door post. *Hallah* cover and *habdalah* plate, *ethrog* box, *hanukkah* lamp, *seder* plate, *moror* dish, *matzoh* cover, *haroset* saucer and spoon are some of the other utensils used in the celebration of Sabbath and holidays. There are many old beautiful *tallesim* still to be found, and occasionally an old *mizrah,* hung on the eastern wall of the home. Some of these items may be several centuries old and mirror German or Italian Renaissance style blended with the much older traditional Jewish forms, but it is hard to tell which of them were made by Jewish, and which by non-Jewish craftsmen. Be that as it may, Jewish religious art as exhibited in ceremonial objects does not lag behind contemporary Christian ecclesiastical art in persuasiveness and beauty.

There is now little or nothing left of one distinctive branch of Jewish art, namely, Polish synagogal architecture, the work of simple seventeenth- and eighteenth-century carpenters and masons. There were stone synagogues that looked like veritable fortresses and were in fact the first line of defense of the frontier villages against the enemy. Then there were the extremely graceful—though highly combustible—wooden synagogues, surrounded with galleries and covered with curved roofs slightly reminiscent of Chinese pagodas. Many of these synagogues were lavishly decorated with polychrome murals in which the Jewish folk artist gave free rein to his imagination. He decorated the walls with paintings of musical instruments, the signs of the zodiac, candelabra, palm leaves, geometrical figures, bounding deer, griffons, all manner of fantastic flora and fauna, and naïve visions of Jerusalem. One of the most famous of these folk artists, Eliezer ben Shelomo, called Sussmann, who lived in the eighteenth century, painted the interiors not only of Polish synagogues, but also of some in southern Germany. Externally modest, these structures showed a wealth of internal splendor. Sussmann, who used luminous reds and blues and skillfully interwove Hebrew inscriptions as decorative motifs, was probably one of the greatest Jewish folk artists of his era. The polychromatic murals Sussmann made for the small synagogue of Horb have survived in the Bamberg municipal museum. It is feared that the early Polish synagogues, spared during World War I, fell victim to the holocaust of 1939-1945.

Even before the Emancipation Era opened the art schools and art galleries to gifted Jews, a considerable number of Jews had managed to penetrate the glittering world of secular art, though not without having first submitted to baptism. Take only Ercole de Fideli (originally Salomone de Sesso, about 1465-1518) who made a magnificent sword for Cesare Borgia that has been called "Queen of Swords"; or the seventeenth-century Francesco Ruschi, the son of a converted Jewish physician, about whom an Italian art historian wrote recently: "He breathed new life into all the younger generation"; or the famous English portrait painter, John Zoffany (1722/23-1810), the son of a Jewish cabinetmaker from Prague. However, these and many other talented artists who abandoned all ties with Jews and Judaism hardly belong in any history of Jewish art save, perhaps, by way of a footnote.

In some countries by 1800, in others a few decades later, society reluctantly stopped demanding from Jews what Heinrich Heine ironically called the "entrance ticket to civilization," namely, baptism. However, it was assumed that the Jewish man of genius would gratefully bow before the new deity, nationalism, and would try his best to become a full-fledged Englishman, Frenchman, German, Dutchman, and so forth, entirely stripped of his Jewish heritage. It is not surprising that many were willing to pay the price.

Between 1840 and 1962 hundreds of gifted Jewish artists have come into the limelight, and it is difficult not to be overwhelmed by the torrent of creative impulse they set loose. If these artists generally yielded to the dominant culture, they also frequently revenged themselves on it, by unwittingly undermining its nationalism. By a strange irony of fate many a Jewish artist—whether musician or writer, painter or sculptor—who had divested himself of his parental heritage, took the road toward universalism, a dominating motif in Judaism. Modern Jews were foremost among those who attacked the sovereignty of race and place, of local and provincial art. They demanded a creative art representing enlargements of experience on the universal human plane. In Paris, the mecca of vanguard art, Jewish immigrants from eastern Europe were instrumental in creating a modern French art that is more universal in its appeal than it is nationalistically French. On the other hand, there was the danger that this universalist trend might lead to a loss of the artist's own vital experience, to a loss of selfhood, and around 1900 a reaction set in, coinciding with, if not influenced by, the new movement of Zionism, as many a Jewish artist became aware of the value of his own group's life, lore and tradition.

Of the hundreds of painters, sculptors, etchers, engravers, and architects of Jewish origin who have risen in Europe and America since the French Revolution, we shall emphasize only about a dozen—those who exerted a great influence upon the development of art. Some of them were not unaware of the spiritual bonds linking them with Israel; others were entirely alienated from their group. In any case, the works of these masters have completely destroyed the misconception that Jews cannot paint, sculpt, or build.

Jews were leaders in the fight against the romantic and historical schools of the early part of the nineteenth century, guiding the rebellion in behalf of realism, plein-air painting and the understanding of the social importance of art. Josef Israels (Netherlands, 1824-1911) forsook the traditional way, being one of the first painters to free his palette from the influence of the dark studio and to execute his studies in the open air. Long before the term "social significance" was coined, he was probably the first person to enter into the spirit of the people, to go to the humble fisherman in a little village for inspiration without any sense of patronage, amusement, or charity—the first to paint their sorrow and grief. Israels also painted many Jewish subjects such as *A Son of the Old People,* showing a sad old-clothes dealer sitting before his modest shop, *A Jewish Wedding, The Old Scribe,* and others. Their realism lifts these striking Jewish pictures high above the idealistically stilted canvases of an Eduard Bendemann (*The Mourning Jews of Babylon*), or the saccharine, sentimental genre paintings of Moritz Daniel Oppenheim (*The Old Talmudist Hearing His Grandson's Lesson*) that have been imitated by dozens of mediocre artists to this day.

Camille Pissarro (France, 1831-1903) has much in common with his Dutch colleague, Israels. He was one of the founders of the Impressionist School which endeavored to represent nature in a shimmer of light, and atmosphere by means of tiny vibrating brush-strokes. Although he left us many masterly portraits and figure subjects, he was principally a landscape painter. Israels went to the fishermen; Pissarro discovered the peasants and the village, faithfully portraying scenes which had hitherto been despised and neglected. Painted in the act of performing their chores, these peasants have none of the superimposed grandeur with which the non-Jew Millet, for example, endowed his characters. Alluding to the biblical grace and calmness prevailing in his great contemporary's canvases, the realist Pissarro remarked: "While Millet is biblical, I am a Jew," thus stressing his heritage and his search for the unvarnished truth. In his later years Pissarro became a faithful chronicler of the "luminous vibration" of the streets and boulevards of Paris.

Max Liebermann (Germany, 1847-1935), the dean of German impressionism and naturalism, also contributed toward democratizing art. Following in the footsteps of Israels, he painted Dutch landscapes and people. At Amsterdam he was attracted by the colorful scenes in the ghetto where Rembrandt had lived and worked. Simplicity and sincerity were his outstanding qualities, and it was inevitable that a man who painted such ignoble subjects as peasants working in a potato field or an old woman watching goats would not be a *persona grata* in the pseudo-romantic art world of the Kaiser's Germany. Eventually he became famous throughout Europe and was called to paint the portraits of some of the outstanding persons of his era—portraits notable for their realistic vigor and almost brutal frankness.

While Israels, Pissarro and Liebermann adhered to naturalism, the three outstanding twentieth-century painters of Jewish origin are protagonists of expressionism and surrealism. The former term has been used to describe the work of artists who reject the mere imitation of the outer world of reality for the expression of an inner world of feeling and imagination; surrealism rests in the belief in the omnipotence of the dream and its apparent illogicalities. The expressionist Amedeo Modigliani (Italy-France, 1884-1920) did not portray the photographic truth when he painted the customers of the cheap *bistros* of Paris, where he spent most of his life. Behind their "distorted" faces there is all the sensuality of their nature, magically penetrating the outer shell. An alcoholic and drug addict, Modigliani died in poverty in the prime of life, known only to a few connoisseurs. Today his paintings, which he sold for a few francs, are almost priceless.

With his friend, Modigliani, Chaim Soutine (Lithuania-France 1894-1943) shared a filthy garret in Montmartre. Even more strongly than "Modi" he saw the dread, the frenzy of persons and things beneath the surface, the wretchedness of the baker boy, the uneasiness of the school girl, the gusty wind tossing the branches and foliage of the old tree. He omitted details and used strong, sensuous, almost orgiastic colors. It is that contrast between the contorted, "unnatural" forms and the realistic, life-stressing colors that contributes to the mystical character of his work.

The critics did not overlook the Hebraic strain in Soutine's work, although the subject matter was not Jewish. "From his race" one of them wrote, "he inherits the sadness, but he transforms it, and to its tragic resignation he desperately reacts, ravaging the world and abandoning it like a piece of metal, twisted and fused by the flames." His colleague, Marc Chagall (Russia-France, 1889-   ), a forerunner of surrealism, also inherited the sadness of Israel, but he transformed it into an all-embracing pity, comradeship with suffering, loyalty to the persecuted—that is, into love. Judaism, as he experienced it in his home town, was a strong source of inspiration to him. But it is of secondary importance that he chose to paint, time and again, Jewish figures and motifs. The spirit of his paintings and etchings is pervaded with an optimism that would seem to some a more genuinely Jewish trait than Soutine's despair.

While Chagall is the dean of French *avant-garde* painting, Max Weber (Russia-United States, 1881-1961) was the Nestor of American modernists. Under the gripping influence of Cezanne he became a foe of academic formulas. Some critics prefer his exquisite landscapes and still lifes; others his presentations of workers and, especially, of orthodox Jews. A great spiritual beauty emanates from these groups of—according to superficial aesthetics—unattractive Jewish patriarchal types, joined in the study of the Law. Weber caught the ecstasy of their facial expression, the exultation of their uninhibited gestures.

Jews entered the field of sculpture with such eminent artists as the Russian Marc Antokolski and the American Moses Ezekiel, who achieved fame in the latter part of the nineteenth century but whose realism, once admired, now appears to us as being too studied and too detailed. Not yet sufficiently appreciated is the work of Enrico Glicenstein (Poland, Italy, United States, 1870-1942) who was primarily a sculptor but who also mastered brush, crayon, and etching needle. His primitive vigor, his directness, impatient of all unnecessary details and aimed solely at the utmost expressiveness of gesture, action, and movement give to his work the impression of massiveness and simplicity, indicative of great sculpture. He was the sculptor of his people; all their hopes and fears are revealed in his powerful lines. His *Messiah,* who, with a sorrowfully bent head awaits the day of awakening, is not a heroic conqueror but a sufferer who knows the tragedy of the world.

Glicenstein's sculptures have often been compared to works by African Negroes because of their almost aboriginal strength. The work of Jacob Epstein (United States-England, 1880-1959), is even less conventional. Many spectators have been flabbergasted by his disregard for the accepted canons of beauty and by his frank anatomical realism of details, particularly in his highly controversial and allegedly blasphemous statues: *Consummatum Est* (representing the dead Christ after the descent from the Cross), *Adam, Genesis* (inspired by the idea of a pregnant woman), *Jacob and the Angel,* and others. The three-ton statue of Adam shocked the anti-Darwinists, for Adam looks like a headless gorilla beating his chest. However, Epstein's adversaries failed to notice that Adam's head is thrown back to indicate that, to quote an art historian, Adam had already received the breath and the spirit of God. The versatile artist was also noted for his portrait busts of famous men and women, and of children.

Those who resent Epstein will probably react to the works of Jacques Lipchitz (Lithuania-France, 1891-   ) even more strongly. The "sculptor of the abstract" was first deeply impressed by the so-called Cubist movement which reduced all objects to geometric forms. Later he developed a style of his own, working out a technique of simplifying forms, as he regarded it the sculptor's task to translate the laws of human anatomy into organic sculptural terms rather than into their naturalistic equivalent. Under the impression of the Nazi pogroms, Lipchitz created a group, *David and Goliath.* Lipchitz' creations in stone, bronze, iron clay and even wire, considered "crazy" by the superficial onlooker, require deep study, for they are a true mirror of our revolutionary times, reflecting the struggle between the forces of the past and those of the future.

In the field of architecture, several Jews were pioneers in

the modern movements. The nineteenth-century American Jew of German origin, Dankmar Adler, is credited with the revolutionary phrase, "Form follows function." The aim of Adler, and of his more widely known non-Jewish associate, Louis Sullivan, was "realistic architecture, based on well-defined utilitarian needs." In Germany, the protagonist of the new style was Alfred Messel (1853-1909). He gave to all of his buildings a simplicity and directness, a purity of style that many claim has been surpassed by no one of his age in any country. He eliminated everything unnecessary, depended wholly upon simplicity and proportion, and used ornament only where lightness and grace were needed. When he used ornament, it was alive and new and not an adaptation or copy of much-used classical or Renaissance forms. His most famous creation is the impressive Wertheim department store in Berlin, a pioneering work in its field.

One of the best known twentieth-century architects was Erich Mendelsohn (Germany, 1887-1953), who learned a great deal from the Dutch Jew, Michael de Klerk. The famous Einstein Tower at Potsdam near Berlin, an elegant building designed along expressionist lines to symbolize the great scientist's achievement, was his work. Between 1919 and 1933 Mendelsohn designed many commercial buildings in Germany, especially the famous Schocken Department Store in Chemnitz. Later he went to Palestine where he built, among other things, the Government Hospital in Haifa, the Hadassah University Medical Center, and the Anglo-Palestine Bank in Jerusalem. He also constructed many houses in England and the United States. Mendelsohn, who was greatly interested in concrete and steel construction, always stressed the close bond that should exist between buildings and natural environment.

Interest in the manifestations of a specific Jewish spirit in the realm of art is a rather recent phenomenon. One of the first scholars to occupy himself with them was, peculiarly, not a Jew but the eighteenth-century Protestant, Tychsen, who published a study of illuminated Hebrew manuscripts (1778). When, in the pursuit of his studies, he approached Jewish scholars for help, they admitted that they themselves knew nothing of the subject. The nineteenth-century German-Jewish scholar, Leopold Zunz, probably was the first eminent Jew to start exploring the field of Jewish art. Interest in the subject was stimulated by the Anglo-Jewish Historical Exhibition (London, 1887), and its elaborate catalogue constitutes a landmark in the early development of Jewish art historiography insofar as it contains the first detailed listing of objects of Jewish ecclesiastic art and various Jewish antiquities. Still, it was not until the first decade of the twentieth century that Jewish art was emphasized, when young protagonists of Zionism, like the philosopher Martin Buber and the etcher and engraver Ephraim Moses Lilien stressed the appreciation of artistic values as a wholesome element in Jewish life.

It was a non-Jew, the dean of Polish painters, Jan Matejko, who remarked to Maurycy Gottlieb, when this young gifted student expressed his intention of devoting himself to Polish historical painting: "My son, you are a Jew; you cannot weep on the graves of Polish kings; leave it to others." Gottlieb followed the advice and his canvas *Praying Jews on the Day of Atonement* (1878) constitutes one of the first artistically successful attempts made by a Jew to portray non-biblical Jews realistically. As time went on, more and more Jewish painters showed interest in Jewish subjects. Referring to the aforementioned masterpiece by Josef Israels, *A Son of the Old People* (1889), Hermann Struck, a noted German-Jewish etcher and engraver, remarked: "The sad eyes of the old dealer, gazing off into the distance, personify, even as the whole physiognomy does, all the pains and sorrows, the utter resignation of the Jewish people through all the centuries—and perhaps also a ray of hope for a better future. One can justly say of this picture that a non-Jewish painter could never have painted it. . . . When the spirit of the [non-Jewish] milieu overcomes this Jewish spirit the artist ceases to be a Jewish artist or his work to be Jewish art. When, however, as in the case of Israels or Hirszenberg, the Jewish soul is stronger than the influences of the accepted land or of the artist's birth, then his work can really be called Jewish art."

The Hirszenberg referred to above is the Pole, Samuel Hirszenberg 1865-1907), who was one of the few real Jewish artists of his generation, that is to say, he was both a genuine Jew and a genuine artist. The devices with which he created unforgettable moods are simple. Take his famous *Yeshivah* picture, for instance. A few young talmudic students are sitting at their open books in the gloom of the *Beth Hamidrash*. What conveys a special charm to the painting is the peculiar light—the early streaks of dawn penetrating through the window panes, competing with the tremulous light of the waxen candle. No melodramatic design is used in his famous *Golus* painting either, yet the impression of the sad group of Jews tramping wearily over the seemingly endless expanse of snow is indelible.

Lack of space prevents us from more than mentioning—in alphabetical order—those Jewish artists in Europe and the United States who, at one time or another, devoted themselves to Jewish subjects. They include, in addition to those already mentioned, the following painters, etchers and engravers: Jankel Adler, Max Band, Uriel Birnbaum, Hyman Bloom, Joseph Budko, Isak Friedlander, A. Raymond Katz, Isidor Kaufmann, Jack Levine, Mané-Katz, Abraham A. Manievich, Zygmunt Menkes, William Meyerowitz, Maxa Nordau, Abel Pann, Leopold Pilichowsky, William Rothenstein, Boris Schatz, Lazar Segal, Jacob Steinhardt, Lesser Ury, Abraham Walkowitz, Jacques Zucker; and sculptors: Naoum Aronson, Benno Elkan, Aaron Goodelman, Chaim Gross, Minna Harkavy, Nathaniel Kaz and Chana Orloff.

It is rather easy to find artists of Jewish origin who have never cared to discover, by means of the brush, the etching needle, or the chisel, the *terra incognita* of the Jewish soul. The opposite extreme is rather rare, namely, cases like that of the Russian Jew, Issachar Ryback, who actually suffered from a feeling of guilt whenever he contemplated his still lifes and decorative pieces, for with him, whose parents had perished in a pogrom in the Ukraine, the "Jewish theme" was a kind of obsession. At the same time, there have been critics—both Jews and anti-Semites—who felt that they could read identifiable "Jewish" characteristics into any contribution to art made by any Jews. They claimed that whatever a Jewish artist puts on canvas, whether it be a still life painting, a landscape, a portrait or a nude, is intrinsically Jewish because the artist's approach, his very emotions, are "Jewish."

The middle road, however, between the extremes of full-fledged assimilation and exaggerated Jewish chauvinism in the field of art is shown by the late Hebrew poet, Hayim Nachman Bialik who, in an essay, clearly defined what he considered to be the rights and duties of the genuine Jewish artists:

> We ask that they themselves should be in our midst, that they should sit and stand and walk there; we claim the total stream of their vigor and the flow of their lives; we want them as they are, with all they have sinned and with all that they have made good, with their errors and sins. . . . We shall not demand any Jewish topics from them; let them work as it pleases them, but only in our midst, in our territory, within our realm, so that their faces are directed toward us and their eyes are upon us. Beyond that we lay down no conditions at all. They should dwell with us, that's enough. Man himself, as a vessel, containing the sum of life, is the most precious property of the nation. Each of them shall pour the vessel of his life into the stream of the nation and augment its power. If the fruit of their spirit comes to us from without, from beyond the fence, we do not gain enough from it to earn a livelihood. It lacks the material with which to build up our life.

When Bialik settled in Palestine in 1924, he found there a Jewish population of only 120,000 souls, yet its art had already shown amazing fecundity. In particular, the new-old country was an ideal testing ground for modern architecture. After World War I, Richard Kauffmann began building numerous agricultural settlements, schools, and sanatoriums—simple but attractive, taking into consideration the character of the landscape and climatic conditions without sacrificing the streamlined beauty. The Bezalel School, founded by Boris Schatz at Jerusalem in 1906 for the purpose of teaching arts and crafts, was reorganized in 1935 by Josef Budko in order to educate young students to a new sense of functionalism of form and material, and to make them draw their inspiration from the scenery of the country, from the appearance of its peoples, their folklore, their religious traditions, their daily occupations and festivals. In 1931, the mayor of Tel Aviv, Dizengoff, founded the Tel Aviv Museum in which there are an impressive number of Israeli artists represented by many talented works of art.

How did life in Palestine affect the artists? "Only in Palestine can there be a Jewish art," one of them wrote. "Golden hills, turquoise skies, beating rain, dryness, heat, Mediterranean-washed shores . . . the rhythm of *halutzim* songs, the scent of freshly turned furrows, harvests, grape-laden vines, sacred stones, a new spirit, a new awakening, individuals born or bred on Palestinian soil, a consciousness of the past, an awareness of the present, an enthusiasm for the future—these and more, subtly blended with the latent talents of individuals, begin to serve as a palette upon which a Jewish art will eventually mix its colors."

The best known of the artists who profited by the special mood of Israel is Reuven Rubin, a lyrical painter who caught the brilliant surface color of the country. Isaac Frenkel, Moshe Mokadi and Menahem Schmitt made numerous stage settings for the Hebrew theatres, Habima and Ohel; Anna Ticho used crayon, pencil or pen-ink; Joseph Zaritzki, water colors, to give expression to the strange and over-powering beauty of the Israeli landscape.

Whither Jewish art? All we know is that the tragedy that befell Jewry and the entire civilized world in the years of disaster did not leave untouched the minds of those Jewish artists who survived; nor did the energetic life-and-death struggle for Jewish nationhood and national happiness fail to impress many of the younger Jewish artists of our time. It seems to be the task of the Jewish artist—who reckons with an understanding public—to make full use of the reservoir of strength to be found in the lives and letters of his people, without forgetting his obligations toward humanity in general. Thus it follows, as Herzl, in his prophetic novel, *Old-Newland*, has the president of the Jewish Academy say:

We are in duty bound to increase Beauty and Wisdom upon the earth unto our last breath. For the earth is ourselves. Out of her we come, unto her we return. Ecclesiastes said it, and we today have nothing to add to his words: "But the earth shall endure forever."

POSTSCRIPT 1962

Looking at an early work, an artist will often feel no longer satisfied with it, noting with a more mature eye mistakes that he has made years before. But he is not likely to destroy this work, as it represents a milestone on his road toward self-improvement—a true sample of an earlier stage of development.

The writer is in an even less enviable position, for he cannot repudiate a work once published even if he would like to do so; he cannot possibly pick up the thousands of copies distributed by the publisher. As for *Story of Jewish Art,* if I were today commissioned to write a pamphlet of the same length on the same theme—the creation of works of art and architecture by Jews throughout the millennia—I would write an essay very different from the one I penned sixteen years ago. I would especially have chosen a different title, such as *The Jew and the Plastic Arts.* For I am now more reluctant to use the term "Jewish art" in referring, for instance, to the contributions of men like Pissarro or Modigliani, which belong in the category of French Impressionism and *Ecole de Paris* expressionism, respectively, and are neither dedicated to Judaism (as are ritual objects) nor indicative of any specific Jewish spiritual experiences of the artist.

I am, nevertheless, willing to let the text stand as it is, for it constitutes a pioneer effort, being the first popular summing-up of the subject to appear in English, and the first in pamphlet form. However, many things have happened in the intervening years, many names have been added to the ranks of Jewish practitioners of art, and some of the people then living have since passed away. Hence, an attempt must be made to deal briefly with changes and omissions in order to make this essay useful to a new group of readers.

One of those who passed away was the architect, Eric Mendelsohn, who died in San Francisco in 1953, having designed in the United States (to which he had come as a refugee in 1941), a series of strictly functional, yet very impressive large synagogues, and the Maimonides Health Center in San Francisco (which, by dissolving the entire front into balconies, avoided the usual grim and dismal appearance of hospitals). In 1959, the sculptor Jacob Epstein died in London, five years after having been knighted by the Queen of England. Obituaries stressed the importance of Sir Jacob as a liberator of sculpture from stifling traditionalism.

Many of the men and women who achieved national or even international fame by 1962, were not yet widely known sixteen years ago. Among these was a Hebrew writer who called himself Ben-Zion, and who turned to painting fairly late. His first one-man show, in 1948, at New York's Jewish Museum, was already characterized by boldly expressionist transfigurations of biblical episodes and other Jewish themes. Several artists who were prominent in the "Social Realism" movement of the 1930's, turned to Jewish motifs only after having been aroused by the suffering of Jews under Hitler. Among these is the master draftsman, Ben Shahn, who was inspired by the stories of Sholom Aleichem and the wisdom of the Book of Zohar. While these two are now over sixty, the sculptor Elbert Weinberg, born in 1928, represents several young American Jewish artists who discovered Judaism as an aesthetic inspiration. His bronze group, *Procession*—four figures in long priestly garments linked together by the concept of Jewish worship—was acquired for the sculpture garden of the Jewish Museum.

After the last war, the United States experienced a mass return to religion which resulted, among other things, in the building of thousands of churches and synagogues, mostly in suburban areas. Whereas the synagogues built prior to World War II were, on the whole, pretentious imitations of Egyptian, Moorish, Byzantine or Gothic buildings that were arbitrarily adapted to the requirements of Mosaic worship, the new temples are generally simple, functional edifices of quiet dignity. Prominent among the architects to specialize in the creation of these temples is Percival Goodman. To ornament the buildings with abstract or semi-abstract design, the new congregations often turned to noted artists, such as the painters Adolph Gottlieb, Abraham Rattner, Anton Refregier and Robert Motherwell (the last two non-Jews), and the sculptors Herbert Ferber, Ibram Lassaw, Seymour Lipton and Nathaniel Kaz. The traditional wing of American Jewry approved the introduction of abstract art, arguing that, in addition to being more akin to Judaism than figurative art, it was also more productive of an austere sacred atmosphere than realistic art, which was bound to distract the worshipper. To fit the new steel-framed synagogues of simple brick or cement, new ritual objects devoid of unnecessary detail and mainly concerned with the proper relationships of purpose, material, and form were replacing the over-decorated pseudo-Baroque utensils of the past. Noted for his fine work in this branch of art is the silversmith, Yehudah Wolpert who, prior to his residence in the United States, was a teacher in metal work at Jerusalem's New Bezalel Academy.

Back in 1946, nobody believed that there would be a revival of the *École Juive* of Paris which had flowered from ca. 1910 (the year young Chagall arrived in Paris) to the dispersal and partial destruction of French Jewry by the Nazi invaders three decades later. In the Nazi period, dozens of Jewish artists, such as the painter Adolphe Feder and the sculptor Moise Kogan, had been deported and killed. In 1943, Soutine had died a natural death, after an unsuccessful operation. Chagall, Lipchitz, Mané-Katz and others had found refuge abroad, while a few (among them Soutine's compatriot and close friend, Michel Kikoine) had managed to hide from the Nazis in France itself.

After the war, all of the survivors were in their fifties or sixties, and only a minority returned to Paris. But in the course of years, a new *École Juive* grew up. It is composed of young French-born Jews—such as the figure painter, engraver, ceramicist and stage-designer Gabriel Zendel, and the son of Kikoine, an abstract painter who signs his canvases "Yankel"; ref-

ugees such as the etchers Johnny Friedlander and Abram Krol,
and the Polish-born painter who signs his work "Maryan"; immigrants from French North Africa (among them the leading
abstract painter, Jean-Michel Atlan); and young men and
women from the United States and Israel who had originally
come to study art and subsequently decided to settle in Paris.

In *Story of Jewish Art*, I was forced to omit, for lack of space,
reference to several artists who had spent the better part of
their lives in Paris, especially the Bulgarian-born painter of
the female nude, Jules Pascin (1885-1930) and three important
sculptors, Ossip Zadkine, and the brothers Naum Gabo and An-
toine Pevsner (both leaders in the Constructivist movement).
Of Anglo-Jewish artists, I mentioned only Jacob Epstein and
William Rothenstein, yet there are others who have made
niches for themselves in the house of British art: for instance,
in the nineteenth century, the Pre-Raphaelite Simeon Solomon,
who died in abject poverty after a dissolute life; and in our
century Mark Gertler, Jacob Kramer, Bernard Meninsky, David
Bomberg, Barnett Freedman and Isaac Rosenberg (the last-
named, who was killed in World War I, was also prominent
as a poet).

Of Israeli artists mentioned in my pamphlet, Schmitt, who
changed his name to "Shemi," died in 1951. A mere listing of
all the nearly five hundred professional artists currently (1962)
working in Israel would, alone, fill pages. Hence, I must confine myself to naming several painters who have recently won
distinction beyond the borders of their country, especially Mordecai Ardon (who for some time directed the Bezalel School
of Art and is now heading the Arts Division of the Israel Min-
istry of Education and Culture); Marcel Janco, who had been
one of the youthful founders of the Dada movement, and is
now the mayor of the artists' village of Ein Hod; and the *sabra*
(Palestine-born) Moshe Castel who, from expressionist renderings of Safed and its people moved to pure abstraction. A
leading sculptor was Zeev Ben-Zvi (1904-52).

In 1946, I quoted an artist who wrote enthusiastically: "Only
in Palestine can there be a Jewish art." Yet by 1962, no single
"Israeli art concept" had emerged, and Israel's younger gen-

eration of artists is far less "Jewish" than their elders who had
grown up in the ghettos of eastern Europe. Those under forty
follow one of the numerous abstract styles that have evolved
in post-war Paris and New York. On the other hand, those who
are leaning toward representationalism, are often reminiscent of
the "regional" school of America, or the "Social Realism" that
flourished here in the thirties and was fostered in Mexico by
Diego Rivera and his associates.

Whither Jewish art? Whither Israeli art? Bezalel Schatz, it
now seems, was mistaken in his notion that a national art could
be created by an act of will-power—and in the twentieth century
at that. Today, frontiers have lost their former importance.
Ours is an age of internationalism, and the arts are the spear-
head of a general trend to erase unessential geographic differences. Nevertheless, a flavor of national, religious, racial or geographic separateness is likely to remain—non-aggressive, non-
exclusive, enjoyable like the varied offerings of the seasons, or
the pleasures appropriate to each age of Man.

CHAPTER SEVENTEEN

THE STORY OF YIDDISH

by MENACHEM BORAISHA

I

Among no other people has the national language become so holy as has the Hebrew language among Jews. To Jews, Hebrew is the "loshon hakodesh," the "sacred tongue." It is the language of the Creator and his hierarchy of angels. It is the language of the Torah, in which each separate word, each letter, is full of revelations and hidden meanings. This sanctification of the national language served to safeguard it against contamination or extinction, for no other people in all the world's history has lived, written and functioned in so many languages as have the Jews.

According to talmudic tradition, one of the reasons for the redemption of the ancient Israelites from Egyptian bondage was the loyalty they maintained to their own language. This would indicate that in the Egyptian "ghetto" Hebrew was the common and familiar speech. From the time the Israelites settled in the Promised Land until the destruction of the First Temple, there is no record of any alien tongue competing with Hebrew. During the period of the Second Temple, however, the picture changes. The populace speaks a Hebrew-Aramaic dialect. Later, the assimilated aristocratic circles speak Greek, while only the loyal heirs of the ancient traditions remain faithful to the Hebrew tongue.

After the collapse of the Bar Kochba uprising the use of Hebrew had evidently declined so considerably that the sage Reb Meier was compelled to declare that "whoever of the inhabitants

of the Holy Land recites the three prescribed daily prayers in
the Hebrew tongue is certain of his place in the world to come."
This was in the Holy Land itself. A later midrash declares that
when God gave the Torah to the Jews he revealed himself not
in one language but in four—Hebrew, Latin, Arabic and Aramaic. Other talmudic passages praise the beauty of Greek. Since
the Jews were already dispersed throughout the neighboring
countries and spoke the languages of those countries, it was
undoubtedly expedient to "legalize" them.

During the succeeding eighteen hundred years, with Jewish
migration into all the countries of Europe, Asia, and Africa,
the Jews spoke the language of the people among whom they
dwelt. In some of these languages, notably Greek and Arabic,
they were the authors of important works. In the modern world,
there is hardly a single civilized speech which has not been
the medium for the expression of Jewish creativeness. But Jews
did not merely accept or adopt the language of the people
among whom they lived; in some cases they *adapted* it; they
moulded it to their own needs, they refashioned and shaped it,
they transformed it into another, more intimate, more *Jewish*
speech. There have been several such languages during the
long course of Jewish history. Only two of them, however, have
managed to gather into themselves enough of the life, the wisdom and the spirit of the people to become important instruments of culture and, together with Hebrew, builders and guard-
ians of the structure of Jewish history. These two languages were
Aramaic, which flourished from the time of the Babylonian exile
until the Spanish period, and Yiddish, which began in approximately the twelfth century and has survived to the present day.

After the Babylonian exile the speech of the Jewish people
was Aramaic. In order to avoid making the Torah a closed book
to the common man, it became necessary during the Sabbath
readings of the Scriptures to translate every verse of the original
into the common speech. Later a written *Targum*—literally
"translation"—was introduced and it became compulsory to read
the Aramaic translation after the reading of the Hebrew text.
("Twice the text, once the Targum.") The custom was retained
for a long time in the Arab countries as well, even after Aramaic

had ceased to be the speech of the people. It is in Aramaic that
most of the Talmud was edited. The *Zohar,* the classic system
of Jewish mysticism, was written in Aramaic at the end of the
thirteenth century. The *kaddish,* as recited by mourners throughout the centuries and today, is in Aramaic; the same is true of
the hymns sung by the orthodox at the Sabbath table.

It is not unlikely that the teachers of the people deeply resented having Aramaic accorded a position of equality with
Hebrew. But this first people's language to be fashioned from
a borrowed tongue triumphed over all opposition; today the student who wishes to study the Talmud and the Zohar in the
original must master Aramaic. The second of the great popular
Jewish languages, Yiddish, has had to travel a more difficult
road. It has faced a constant struggle to hold its position; and
the fight is not yet over.

II

The Yiddish language began to develop in the Rhine provinces of Germany between the tenth and twelfth centuries. Out
of the language of that period and region the Jews fashioned
a speech which departed further and further from its original
sources until it began to live a wholly independent life of its
own. This development was natural. At first Hebrew words
were introduced into the German of the period; they dealt with
religious life, with domestic matters, and with trade. The original German words themselves were Judaized in their syntax,
and the sentence structure adapted to a Jewish conformation.
As a result of the frequent contact between Jews in various
countries, foreign words were introduced. Following the east-
ward migrations to Poland and Russia, new words were assimilated into popular usage, while the people themselves created
a wealth of new terms to express particular details of their
material and spiritual life. The teacher whose job it was to
interpret the Bible for the children, the rabbi who was required
to adjudicate all kinds of problems, the merchant who had to
carry on business correspondence, the artisan who needed terms
to designate tools and materials of his trade, the mother who

beguiled her child with story and song, the boy and girl pour-
ing out their young love—each of these made their contribution
to the language and helped to shape and enrich it. There were,
besides, the historic memory of the people, the images and
word-usages of the Bible and the Talmud; the disasters that befell the people, the hardships of daily life; all of these found
expression in new inventions, idioms, word forms and word com-
binations. Thus there was gradually formed a language which
encompassed the whole life of a people, its Torah, its customs,
its sorrows and cares, its wisdom and wit.

But from its first fumbling steps Yiddish encountered the opposition of the religious aristocracy. This opposition arose from
the fact that, from the very beginning, Yiddish became the
road to secular life, to amusement and relaxation. Through
it there were brought into the Jewish home the street songs
and love songs, and especially the sentimental romances of
knights and heroes which were popular among the Christian
population. The rabbis looked with strong disapproval on the
language of "women and idlers and common folk," but they
had to sign a truce with it, just as, centuries before, the spiritual
leaders in Palestine had found it necessary to make peace with
Aramaic.

But alien song and story could not be allowed exclusively to
stir the imagination of the common people, and thus religious
songs in Yiddish began to come into existence. There are examples of such songs dating from the fourteenth century, and,
in the same period, a translation of the Book of Esther, indicating that parts of the Bible were translated into Yiddish at that
early date. The first printed edition of the Scriptures in the
original Hebrew appeared at the end of the fifteenth century,
and by 1544 there appeared a translation of the Pentateuch
into Yiddish. From that time on, the number of religious works
in Yiddish increased. Original Jewish epic works appeared, such
as the famous "Epic of Samuel," competing with the Christian
romances. Yiddish became a language of original literary creation, not merely a spoken tongue into which other original works
had to be rendered. The prestige of the language grew even
greater with the rise of Hasidism at the end of the eighteenth

and the beginning of the nineteenth centuries. This democratic-religious movement, which sought to raise the lot of the common man through religion and which captured the imagination of half the Jewish population of Europe, became a powerful stimulus to the growth of the language.

It was in the same period that Yiddish encountered its second formidable opponent—German enlightenment and assimilation. In the eyes of the champions of enlightenment—they were later the founders of the movement for religious reform—the Jews had long ceased to be a people and were merely a religious group, Germans of "Mosaic persuasion." Their political program demanded that they rid themselves of everything that had to do with Jewish mass culture and identify themselves with national German culture. To them, Yiddish was nothing more than a "corrupt German," a "bastard jargon." It was not until many generations had passed and a science of philology had developed that serious scholars, Christian as well as Jewish, were able to study the language without prejudgment and to reach the conclusion that modern Yiddish and modern German were separate and independent languages which stemmed from a common source.

The denial of Yiddish by the German-Jewish proponents of assimilation was taken over by the leaders of the Haskalah (enlightenment) movement in Austrian Galicia, Poland, and Russia. But here, where Jews lived in large masses, the assimilationists were unable to stifle the language—as had been done in Germany. On the contrary, in eastern Europe the Haskalah movement itself had to conform to the folkways of the people and instead of hindering, it actually helped in the development of the folk tongue. Whoever sought to reach the people had to use the people's speech and, with the growth of a written Yiddish literature, there came a recognition of the individuality, richness, and beauty inherent in the language. There were those who, under the influence of the German school of thought, sought to "purify" and "correct" the language, attempting to substitute for it a type of elegant Judaeo-German. But those who remained rooted in the people sought in the masses the true riches of the folk tongue.

In the second half of the nineteenth century, secular education, within the framework of a *numerus clausus,* had become fairly widespread among the Jews in Poland and Russia. Jewish youth was seized by an irresistible urge for education and secular knowledge which the revolutionary and democratic movements supported and strengthened. The last decade of the nineteenth century witnessed the political organization of the Zionist as well as the Jewish socialist movements which were then maturing. This development awakened and released tremendously strong currents of folk energy. A large class of intelligentsia appeared—political leaders, teachers, writers, publicists, novelists, poets. The first Yiddish newspaper had appeared as early as 1686 in Amsterdam, Holland. Later attempts were made to issue Yiddish periodicals at various periods and in various countries—Romania, Galicia, and Poland. In the 1890's Yiddish weeklies and special literary publications appeared. The press grew. Traveling theatrical troupes toured the continent. Books without number began to pour from the presses, some of inconsequential value, others of considerable importance and literary worth. By the end of the century the great classical Yiddish writers—Mendele Mocher Sforim, Sholem Aleichem, Yitzchock Leibush Peretz—were known beyond the borders of Russia and Poland. At the opening of the twentieth century there was a large Yiddish daily press with a circulation in the hundreds of thousands, a significant literature which had found translation into other languages, a theatre with a repertoire of original folk plays, and the beginning of the scientific work of collecting folk songs, folk tales and folk idioms, and of research in the language and its history—all to the end of establishing Yiddish as an instrument and treasure of Jewish culture.

III

In the years since the 1880's America has played an important role in the diffusion of Yiddish culture.

There were Yiddish-speaking Jews in America even before the beginning of the vast wave of pogroms in Russia in 1881 and 1882. As early as 1872 there were in New York twenty-nine synagogues where the newly-arrived Russian Jewish immigrants could hold services according to their old customs. They spoke Yiddish in their homes and sent their children to *heders* where teachers translated portions of the Scriptures into Yiddish. Between 1870 and 1880 an additional 41,000 emigrants came to the United States from those countries, but with the outbreak of the pogrom wave in 1881 the influx of immigrants began to swell. In addition to the emigrants from Russia and Poland, Yiddish-speaking Jews came from Austria, Galicia and Romania. From 1881 to 1908 the United States received more than 1,800,000 Jewish immigrants from eastern Europe.

As a result of the pogroms a new type of Jewish immigrant came to the United States. To the vast stream of petty traders, merchants, artisans and workers, there was now added the intelligentsia—Russian revolutionists who had returned to their Jewishness as a result of the pogroms, or who were compelled to flee from Tsarist oppression. To compete with the earlier rabbis, shochtim, and teachers who were the acknowledged heads of the orthodox masses, there now came new leaders, younger men with socialist ideas and ideals. Their goal was to lead the struggle against the vicious exploitation of the immigrant masses, to organize them into labor unions and to propagate the principles of socialism among them.

The new wave of immigrants found in the United States a fairly well-established community with a newspaper of its own, *Die Yiddishe Gazetn*, an orthodox periodical which began to appear as a weekly in 1874. In 1883 it became a daily newspaper and changed its name to *Yiddishes Tageblatt*. Nor was this the only orthodox newspaper in the field. It is interesting to note that the United States had a daily Yiddish paper twenty years before Russia, where *Der Freind* first appeared in 1903. The newly-arrived young socialist generation began to look for ways and means of publishing a paper to reflect their own ideas. They succeeded in 1886. The readers of the paper were the members of the clubs and societies which had already been formed. Four years later, *Die Arbeiter Zeitung* appeared and in 1892 the literary journal, *Zukunft*, a monthly which is still in existence. In 1894 the socialist *Abendblat* was published;

in 1897 it was changed over to the *Forwarts*, the best entrenched of the Yiddish newspapers of today and the one with the largest circulation.

Though the majority of the newspapers of the period did not last long, by 1900 there were ninety Yiddish weekly and daily publications issued in the United States, a number which illustrates the force of the drive to establish a Yiddish press and the intensity of the need for it. The publications were of all shades, radical as well as orthodox. The orthodox element was no less militant than the radical; what followed was a spirited struggle in the columns of the papers between the two currents in Jewish life.

There was a large public, however, which sought in the printed word not information on the social and political events of the day, but pure entertainment. Workers, tired after a long day in shop and factory, peddlers back from knocking at countless doors, businessmen and housewives—all sought relaxation, escape into another and more pleasant world of phantasy. This flight from reality was offered by the writers of the long and fanciful romances which were printed in sections and sold by the thousands. Some of them were free renderings of popular novels from other languages, others were "original" creations. Up to 1900 approximately sixty-five such works were issued. The titles indicate their general character—*The Indian Prince, The Black Hand, the Count of Monte Cristo, Cleopatra, The Revenge of a Dead Man, The Imprisoned Woman, Unhappy Amelia,* etc. The success of romances such as these was so great that the newspapers, orthodox as well as radical, had to make use of them. The custom of serializing one or more novels of this kind became so deeply entrenched in the Yiddish press that even now it would be practically impossible for the press to get along without them. The number of such works printed and serialized up to the present time amounts to well over a thousand.

The credit for having developed Yiddish literature of high caliber in the United States must go not to the orthodox but to the radical, secular press. The experience of the Jewish radicals in the New World was identical with that of the leaders of the enlightenment in Russia. In this country, too, Yiddish was for them at first merely a means for popularizing various fields of knowledge and spreading ideas of social justice. But once they began to write the language and make use of its flexible vocabulary and rich idioms, there began to emerge a feeling for the language for its own sake. The generation of intelligentsia which came to the United States at the end of the nineteenth century included a number of creative young writers in whom the longing for the Old World as well as the drama of life in the New became sources of literary inspiration. Some of them were not even aware that in Europe a rich Yiddish literature was being created; they began to write in Yiddish because that was the demand of the new environment into which they had been transplanted. Others among those who came to the country were writers who had already begun their careers in the old country. The socialist poet and brilliant journalist Morris Winchevsky had already won a wide reputation before he came to the United States, but his contemporaries, I. Bovshover and David Edelstadt, and especially the famous poet, Morris Rosenfeld, developed and became known in this country. It should be noted in passing that the translations of the latter's poems into English, German, and Russian were the first examples of Yiddish poetry to find their way into world literature. Abraham Cahan, dean of these Jewish journalists, began his Yiddish writing career in the United States. The same is true of Jacob Gordin, novelist and dramatist, whose more serious works helped to raise the level of the Jewish theatre. The novelist—and later drama critic—B. Gorin, began his writing career in Europe, while the novelists and dramatists, Leon Kobrin and Z. Libin, first began to write in the United States. The folk-poet Eliakim Zunser and Abraham Goldfaden, the founder of the Yiddish theatre, came to this country with already well-established reputations.

The subject matter of the short stories, novelettes and long novels, poems, and plays came from the Old World and the New. There were stories of life in the old country, stories of families separated as a result of the wave of overseas immigration; there were stories of parents whose Americanized children were leaving hearth and home; there were stories of life in the sweatshops and factories, of cruel exploitation, of homesickness, of conflict between husband and wife, stories of young love—all of these themes were dealt with in Yiddish literary composition. The tendency of the radical press, naturally enough, was to make its literary creations informative and promote the ideas of social justice. Yiddish literature served this goal to a considerable extent; this was especially true in the case of Yiddish poetic writing. But with time there came a greater understanding and a sounder appraisal of works based on purely human and psychological themes. Toward the close of the nineteenth century the Yiddish-speaking public in the United States became aware of the emergence in Europe of a new and more dynamic Yiddish literature. It was a period in which the movement of political Zionism intensified the natural nationalist feelings which had always existed in the masses. From Europe came such writers as the poet and publicist, A. Liessin (Avrom Valt) and the dramatist and novelist, Dovid Pinski, both socialists and both fervent nationalists. Later came Dr. Chaim Zhitlovsky, one of the leaders of the Russian socialist-revolutionist movement and a man of enormous erudition, who declared open warfare against the assimilationist tendencies among the Jewish socialists in America. The arrival of such notables meant a continuous enrichment and release of the intellectual and artistic energies of the Yiddish intelligentsia.

A Yiddish theatre developed parallel with the Yiddish press and literature. The first attempt to establish a Yiddish theatre in New York took place in 1882. Its repertory was a conglomerate one. Among the productions were Goldfaden's historical operettas, a type of romantic Jewish heroic epic, and his satiric folk comedies, as well as home-made melodramas which were not far removed from the long and trashy novels and chronicles of the period. A decided advance was made in the theatre in 1891 with the performance of Jacob Gordin's "Judaized" classical works, such as *The Jewish King Lear, Sappho,* etc., and original dramas of Jewish life. Talented Yiddish actors and actresses began to arrive in the country and the number of theatres in New York, as well as in the other large cities, began to increase. The growing movement culminated in the establishment of the Yiddish Art Theatre in 1916.

The beginning of the present century saw the Yiddish press branch out in new directions. In 1903 there appeared the orthodox daily, *Morgen Journal,* and in 1905 the radical, but already nationalist, *Wahrheit.* About thirty years later the *Morgen Journal* took over and incorporated the *Yiddishes Tageblatt* and in 1919 the *Warheit* was absorbed by *Der Tag.* The Chicago *Yiddisher Courier* had been in existence since 1887. Daily newspapers were established in Philadelphia and Cleveland, and weekly journals appeared in other cities. Professional, literary and political weeklies also began to appear. In addition to the mass of popular scientific literature there began to appear translations of serious works, particularly in the fields of economics, sociology and history. Publishers issued the writings of European and American Yiddish writers. Around 1915 the Yiddish press had a circulation of more than 600,000, and readers many times that number. The Yiddish press was by far the most important single force in helping the immigrant to integrate himself into the New World environment.

IV

At the time of World War I, Yiddish was the language of about 12,000,000 Jews in all parts of the world. It encountered strong opposition in the assimilationist movement in Russia and Poland, but its dynamism as an instrument of culture rose so steadily that even its staunchest opponents had to yield to its superior force. Yiddish faced an additional challenge in the renascence of Hebrew which paralleled the upsurge of Zionism. The Hebraists regarded the maturing language of the masses as a powerful rival. But this opposition stemmed from political leaders of the movement rather than from the Hebrew writers. The fathers of Yiddish literature, Mendele Mocher Sforim and I. L. Peretz, as well as the great national Hebrew poet, Hayim Nachman Bialik, and later Zalman Shneour, Aaron Zeitlin and many others, wrote in both languages. It can be said that the influence of classical Hebrew on Yiddish literary style was matched by the influence on Hebrew writing of the living idioms of the Yiddish speech.

Yiddish experienced its greatest trials in the United States. Never in its 700-year history did the language encounter such formidable opposition as developed here.

The first Jewish immigrants into the United States—after the Sephardim—were the German Jews. They brought with them their ideas of religious reform and the ideology of German assimilationism, and these they immediately applied to the American Jewish scene. Together with other assimilationist concepts and attitudes they exhibited a contempt toward Yiddish as a "jargon." For many years after their arrival they held fast to their "pure" German. At the time when the mass immigration of Jews from Russia and Poland began, the German Jews were already well established economically and socially. They were not only the major employers of the new immigrants but also the philanthropists and cultural leaders. They considered it their duty to Americanize the newcomers as quickly as possible, and although in such institutions as the Educational Alliance in New York the brilliant Zionist folk orator Zvi Hirsch Masliansky was a regular speaker, the tendency of such institutions was to wean the masses away from Yiddish quickly and effectively.

Following the assimilationism of the German Jews came the assimilationism of the socialists, who established, organized, and led the labor movement among the Jewish masses. It is true that the speech, press, pamphlets, and books of the socialists were Yiddish, but this was only a temporary stopgap. In those years the socialists carried on a campaign against all forms of Jewish tradition; their argument was that nationalism in general must be eradicated and that the Jewish problem would be solved only in a socialist society. It followed that there was no need for the perpetuation of Yiddish as a language in such a society.

But the mightiest of the forces which threatened to engulf Yiddish completely was the totality of American civilization and in particular the public school. These found a useful partner in the indifference of the Jewish masses to the perpetuation of Jewishness in their children. At the present time, with a large network of Jewish educational institutions and organizations, a good number of Jewish children are still growing up without any sort of Jewish education. In the period under discussion the situation was much worse. The orthodox still sent their children to heders and Talmud Torahs, but orthodoxy itself grew impressively weaker. The rest of the Jewish population which had divorced itself from Jewish traditions left the shaping and moulding of its children to the civilization of the country. There was another factor which completely negated the order and continuity of Jewish family life—the child, growing up in the school and on the street, with English as his native tongue, became the psychological tyrant of the home; and the "greenhorn" parents surrendered the hegemony of the family mores to their "American" children.

The compelling force of religious tradition was still strong enough to induce the parents to force some of the ancient Hebrew into the child, especially for a son's *Bar Mitzva*. But there was no similar attitude toward Yiddish. Yiddish was spoken in the home and the various organizations and *landsmanschaften*, but for the children the little Yiddish they managed to pick up from their parents or grandparents sufficed; for them Yiddish was simply another of the old and outmoded curiosities which their parents had brought with them from the old country. At the best it served a sentimental need—it was not a real necessity.

Even on the lips of the parents the speech began to lose its original purity. It was to be expected that in the New World the language should incorporate into itself new words and constructions stemming out of the American scene; the same development was true of the American language in relation to the original English of Great Britain. For example, most of the immigrants came from small towns where many aspects of modern living were unknown—bathtubs, running water, electricity, etc. As a result, dozens of alien words found their way into Yiddish speech—*sink, icecream, car, ferry, subway, laundry, shop, quarter, lime, baseball, pushcart*—with only minor changes of inflection and intonation. Other words were "Judaized"—

alrightnik, dresskes, mufn (move), *vutn* (vote), *pedlen*. The constant use of English by the children in the home had the effect of compelling the parents to abandon many Jewish words and expressions and substitute their English equivalent. The same phenomenon operated among other ethnic groups in the country. The most significant change, however, was the fact that a section of the press, as well as speakers at meetings and rabbis in their pulpits, adapted themselves to the new manner of speech of the masses and talked and wrote in what they referred to as "plain Yiddish." Thus the attack on the language was carried on from within as well as from without.

Gradually a "resistance" movement arose. "Plain Yiddish" was not the language of the important poets such as Morris Rosenfeld, A. Liessin, Yehoash (S. Bloomgarden), or of the important novelists, dramatists, and journalists. The revolution of 1905 in Russia and the wave of pogroms and cruel reaction that followed brought a new class of intelligentsia to the United States. For the group of Jewish revolutionaries of the beginning of the century, Yiddish was more than a language for enlightening the masses; it was the language which summoned fighters to the barricades, the language of the people's revolutionary songs, the language of a people's renascence, of Sholem Aleichem and Peretz. It was more national, more Jewish, than it had been on the lips of the socialist intelligentsia of the 1880's. It already had the strength to carry the fight beyond the sweatshop and economic exploitation; it could fight against assimilation, too. Together with the revolutionary youth there also came a young literary generation which had been reared under the influence of European literature and which brought with it the aspiration for creative and linguistic perfectionism. Fed by the traditions of the Yiddish classicists, they sought to advance their art to match the standards of world literature. It took a long time before the "old guard" of Yiddish writers accepted these new contenders, but writers such as Dovid Pinski, A. Liessin and critics such as Joel Entin, M. Leontiev, and others welcomed them with open arms.

V

Under the influence of these new forces the opposition to
linguistic assimilation began to assume concrete form. Plans
were developed for the establishment of Yiddish schools for
children. In December 1910, the first such school was opened
by the Labor Zionist movement in New York; the children
attended it after the regular school day. The school called itself
"national-radical"; the curriculum omitted religion and religious
instruction and concerned itself with Yiddish language and literature, Jewish history, Hebrew, contemporary Jewish life, and
music. Similar schools were opened in 1911 in Rochester and in
1912 in Chicago, Milwaukee, and Sioux City. By 1918 there were
eighteen such schools in the country. The same year saw the
establishment of the Sholem Aleichem Folks Institute whose
schools were purely Jewish-Nationalist in character without any
political coloration. The Arbeiter Ring, the fraternal order
which was under the influence of the socialist movement and
the *Forwarts*, opened its own school in this same year.

The opening of the first Arbeiter Ring School was the cul-
mination of a long struggle in socialist circles between the old
ideological and linguistic assimilationists and the Yiddish-
minded socialists of the new generation. It was a struggle between the old and the new—and the new triumphed. Not that
the "old guard" abandoned its position; it fought for its ideas
of "complete integration" as do the present-day assimilationists
of the upper and middle classes. But the newly opened schools
satisfied the longing for a Jewish content in the life of the average Jew. The schools had to be supported by the parents themselves, which required work, organization, and financial sacrifice. This investment by the parents was repaid by the Yiddish
which the children brought home, by the holiday celebrations
which the schools instituted, and by a varied program of Jewish
activities in the Yiddish tongue. The school became a Jewish
hearth at which the elders were able to warm themselves, and a
center of spiritual life for the secular Jew, just as the temple and
synagogue were for the religious Jew. From 1918 to 1940 the
number of schools of various types grew to more than three

hundred. A demand for text books and experienced teachers arose as new problems in education presented themselves. Teachers' seminaries were established, publishing houses were formed, children's magazines and pedagogical journals were published—an entire cultural movement which served the schools and through which tens of thousands of people were steeped in a Jewish life arose.

World War I brought to the United States a number of Jewish writers with established reputations. Among them was the great humorist Sholom Aleichem, who had fashioned a glistening literary instrument out of the folk speech; the lyric novelist, Avram Raisin; the novelist, Sholom Asch, who already enjoyed a worldwide reputation; the dramatist, Peretz Hirschbein; the master of the novelette, L. Shapiro; the Hebrew-Yiddish novelist and dramatist, I. D. Berkovitch. In the first year of the war *Der Tag* was founded, a newspaper which undertook to be the organ of the nationalist Jewish intelligentsia. Among the journalists and publicists on its staff were Professor Yitzchok Isaac Hourwitch; Dr. K. Forenberg; A. S. Saks; the theoretician of labor Zionism, Nachman Syrkin; the banner bearer of Yiddishism, Dr. Chaim Zhitlovsky; the brilliant essayist, Dr. Avram Koralnik. Later there was the distinguished publicist and literary critic, Samuel Niger. The high standard of Yiddish journalism which *Der Tag* initiated compelled other papers to follow suit. To the recognized and familiar journalists such as Peretz Wiernik and Gedaliah Bublick in the orthodox press; Abraham Cahan, M. Baranoff, and Dr. A. Ginzberg in the radical press; and Louis Miller and Jacob Fishman in the middle-class nationalist press, were added European figures such as Dr. B. Hoffman (Zivion), Dr. S. Melamed, M. Olgin, Dr. A. Mukdoni, later Hayim Greenberg and a number of others. There appeared, in addition, a number of weekly magazines, Zionist, Labor Zionist, and socialist, apart from the professional magazines; and from time to time purely literary almanacs, journals and weeklies were published. After the October revolution in Russia, the left-wing daily *Freiheit* made its appearance and later a number of other left-wing publications.

In the period between the two world wars, Yiddish underwent the richest and most intensive period of its development, especially in the field of belles lettres. It was a period of great self-awareness. That attitude had also existed among the classicists, especially in the circle gathered around Yitzchok Leibush Peretz. But that earlier generation of writers lived during the blossoming and spreading of the language, whereas the new generation in the United States stood face to face with a powerful wave of assimilation and knew that the only force which it could use to combat linguistic assimilation—at least among some sections of the Jewish population—was the quantitative and, even more, the qualitative nature of its literary output. Thus there began an intensive period of literary productivity which, in form and content, might withstand the threatening storm.

Dozens of writers participated in the work. Books, large and small, poured from the presses, in prose and verse, to add to the national culture. No less energy went into the fashioning of the language. In the hands of these creative artists Yiddish became a purified, colorful, and smoothly flowing instrument, able to express the most elevated soarings of the Jewish spirit as well as the most workaday experience of the modern man in the modern world. Space limitations do not permit listing the names of those who contributed to this new blossoming of the language, but even the most cursory account must make mention of the leading architects of the new literature—H. Leivick, author of the dramatic poems *Der Golem* and the *Guela Comedie* (Comedy of Deliverance), and many plays; Manni Leib, lyricist and author of folk ballads; Moshe Leib Halpern, romanticist and satirist; Yosef Rolnick, quiet lyricist of melancholy old-world life; A. Leieles, founder of the introspectionist school; Jacob Gladstein, poet, novelist, and essayist; and the poet steeped in the mood of the psalmists, J. J. Segal. Among novelists must be mentioned J. Opatoshu, author of *Die Polische Velder* and a number of historical and modern novels; Dovid Ignatov, novelist; A. Raboy, author of stories of Jewish life in the Old and New Worlds; and Baruch Glassman, author of realistic novels of American life. American life as a whole, as well as Jewish life, were mirrored in poetry and prose by the new generation of writers and by the older ones, such as Sholom Asch, Avram Raisin, Dovid Pinski, L. Shapiro and many others. During this period the number of creative writers in the United States was also increased by such new European arrivals as the novelist Jonah Rosenfeld, I. J. Singer of *Brothers Ashkenazi* fame, the poetess Kadia Molodowski, the essayist Dr. S. Bickel and others.

The great—probably the greatest linguistic accomplishment of the period was the complete translation of the Bible to which the poet, Yehoash, (S. Bloomgarden) devoted practically all his mature life. The same period also saw the appearance of many other important translations. Earlier Yehoash had translated into Yiddish Longfellow's *Hiawatha.* J. J. Schwartz, author of the heroic American-Jewish epic, *Kentucky,* had translated a number of Shakespeare's dramas and later large sections of ancient and modern Hebrew poetry. The poet, B. Lapin, translated a good deal of Russian poetry as well as the Shakespeare sonnets. H. Rosenfeld translated *Kalevala.*

VI

The rise of Hitlerism and the annihilation of more than two-thirds of European Jewry moved the center of world Jewry to the American continent. The greatest center of Jewish culture in Europe—Poland—had been obliterated. Whatever the number of Jews that adapted themselves to the new conditions there, that country will for many years be a consumer rather than a producer of new cultural values. In the Soviet Union the Jewish population has all facilities for developing a rich Jewish cultural life, but the future of that life is questionable. In the years following the October revolution, Yiddish, recognized as the official Jewish language, experienced a real renascence. A new literature blossomed forth in the Ukraine, White Russia, as well as in Moscow. There were a number of Yiddish dailies and periodicals, a large network of Yiddish schools, Yiddish theatres that were regarded among the best in the country, scientific and cultural institutions, and courts conducted in Yiddish. In the autonomous regions of Jewish

colonization in the Ukraine and in the Crimea, and later in
the autonomous territory of Biro-Bidjan, Yiddish as the language of instruction was mandatory for the non-Jews attending
the Jewish schools. The years preceding the war marked a strong
decline both in the field of Yiddish press and instruction. But
Yiddish literature and the theatre in Soviet Russia prided themselves on a number of outstanding novelists, poets, playwrights,
and actors. And there is still room under the Soviet constitution
for the restoration of a school system and other cultural institutions as powerful as they were a decade or two ago. Outside
of the Soviet Union* and Poland, there is also Romania with its
350,000 Jews, in certain parts of which Yiddish flourished before the war. There is an attempt at a revival of Yiddish institutions in France.

Today the American continent is the greatest producer and
consumer of the printed Yiddish word. The war brought to
the United States a great number of new creative talents and
also transplanted onto American soil the most important cultural
institution which Polish Jewry had created between the two
world wars—the Yiddisher Vissenshalftlicher Institut—Yiddish
Scientific Institute. The Institute had won a great deal of recognition in scientific circles, Jewish as well as non-Jewish. In
recent years there has also come about a change in the attitude
towards Yiddish on the part of those sections of the Jewish community in America who do not use the Yiddish speech. Local
welfare funds give support to Yiddish schools as well as to
the Hebrew and English schools. The same is true of the Jewish
Educational Association. An annual Jewish Book Month has
been instituted to call attention to Jewish books in all three
languages, and a trilingual annual literary almanac is issued
to mark the occasion. The circulation of the Yiddish press declined from 605,000 in 1915 to 403,000 in 1940 and the daily
papers in cities outside New York disappeared—an indication of
the gradual disappearance of the generation of immigrants for

* See the essay Jews in the Soviet Union, Part II, for the plight of
Yiddish after World War II. On August 22, 1961, the first Yiddish-language
periodical published in the Soviet Union since 1948—a bi-monthly literary
review, Sovietish Heimland—made its debut.

whom the Yiddish press was a necessity.** The new immigration into America from World War I to the present could not serve to strengthen the Yiddish press because for the most part it consisted of those who had already been linguistically assimilated in the countries of their origin. But the drive toward Jewishness among the second and third generations became stronger, and a large number of children in the Yiddish schools were now the children of native-born Jews whose own language was English.

The development that has taken place since 1880 in the United States was paralleled on a smaller scale in a number of other countries in the Western Hemisphere, chiefly in Canada, Argentina and Mexico. The Dominion of Canada has a number of Yiddish dailies, periodicals and a large group of Yiddish writers. The Yiddish day schools in Montreal, Winnipeg, Toronto, and a number of other communities are regarded as the best on the continent. The Argentine Jewish community with its two great dailies—*Die Presse* and *Die Yiddishe Zeitung*—its periodicals, its schools, its section of the Yiddish Scientific Institute, its novelists, poets and journalists, actively combat assimilation to a far greater degree than the Jewish community of this country. This is partly due to the thorough integration of communal Jewish life there. The same is true of the young Jewish community of Mexico with its press and excellent school system. Other countries such as Brazil and Chile still supply a large number of consumers of Jewish books and periodicals.

There can be no doubt that Yiddish will remain alive in the printed page as a historical speech of the Jewish people. It will be utterly impossible to understand Jewish life of the past several hundred years without recourse to Yiddish works. East and West, religious and secular life, Jewishness and universal ideas, have become so completely integrated into the language that it has become the mirror of entire generations of Jewish life.

Moreover, the survival of the Jewish people throughout the

** In mid-1961 the circulation of *The Jewish Daily Forward* had decreased to about 60,000, and *The Jewish Day-Morning Journal* was about 40,000.

world will depend in great measure on the degree to which Jews develop a sense of their own dignity, on the extent to which thy learn to cherish the cultural values their own people have created. The national treasures of the Jewish people expressed in the Yiddish language will occupy a significant place in that cultural development.

If the future of the written word seems assured, what of Yiddish as a spoken language? Prospects for the Yiddish language in the American Jewish community are difficult to assess. Much of the strength of Yiddish in the past derived from the fact that it was a world speech. Jews from all lands were able to establish contact with each other through its medium. The language may continue to serve that role in the future. Much, however, will depend on whether or not any Jewish folk life will remain in eastern Europe.

Much more, however, will depend on what happens to the Jewish community in the United States. During the past several years there has been an increasing consciousness on the part of American Jews of their heritage and problems as Jews. That tendency may find expression in purely religious forms. But it may also cause the American Jew to look more closely at the historic cultural forms of Jewish life.

If we were to take external circumstances alone into consideration, we might predict, with some degree of certainty, that Yiddish would cease to be a living force in one or two generations. But Jewish history throughout the centuries has always been a history of struggle with so-called "objective conditions"; and the survival of the Jewish people is the record of triumph over these conditions. Always, the people have discovered new energies and powers within themselves. Despite the fact, therefore, that the Yiddish language has lost some of its most important strongholds, qualitatively it has become a more powerful and decisive instrument of Jewish survival and spiritual regeneration.

CHAPTER EIGHTEEN

THE STORY OF HEBREW

by MEYER WAXMAN

The renaissance of the Hebrew language, like the creation of the Jewish state itself, has been one of the miracles of our age. The movement for the recognition of Hebrew as the language of the Jewish people has grown and taken root in the perception of conscious Jews everywhere.

Checkered and varied as the destiny of the Jewish people has been throughout its long history, neither Jews nor Judaism ever separated themselves from Hebrew, their cherished language. To Jews, Hebrew has been the "sacred tongue." According to the view of the sages of the Talmud and Midrash, it was the language used by God in the creation of the world and spoken by the first generation of mankind. Jews continued to develop the language, using it as a bond to unite the scattered Jewish settlements the world over. Hebrew was never a dead language in any part of Diaspora Jewry, so long as that part was itself alive and Jewishly active.

The oldest of all living languages, Hebrew, was spoken in Canaan before the conquest of the land by the first Israelites or *Ivrim*,[1] and their language was called *Ivrit*, or Hebrew. Linguistically, Hebrew is a branch of the North Semitic group of languages, spoken with variations of dialect by the Israelites who lived in Palestine and adjoining lands, as well as by the Phoenicians or Canaanites, and the people of Moab, Ammon, and Edom who inhabited the territory in and around what is today Jordan. Through the Jewish people, Hebrew became

[1] *Ivrim* means "those who crossed over," in this case either the Jordan or Euphrates rivers.

377

the medium of expression of a great literature which begins
with the Bible and extends for more than 3,500 years to our
own day.

Despite Hebrew's long and varied history, its evolutionary
development and change, the basic core of the language has
survived to such an extent that the text of those ancient Hebrew
inscriptions is intelligible to an Israeli schoolboy. Similarly, the
host of modern Hebrew newspapers, periodicals, and books
would be understood by the boy's historic ancestors should they
arise today, despite the many new ideas and modes of thought
strange to them which have enriched the language over the
centuries.

Hebrew Through the Ages: The Script

Until the downfall of the First Commonwealth (586 B.C.E.),
Hebrew was the main language spoken by the Jews. The range
of its vocabulary at that time cannot be gauged because the
biblical books of the period reflect primarily the spiritual phases
of life; but it was apparently adequate enough to give expression to all aspects of daily life.

More than a century later, from the time of Ezra's arrival in
Jerusalem (458 B.C.E.) from Babylon, the Scribes (sofrim)
under his leadership as priest and religious organizer, were
active in reviving the use of Hebrew which had been largely
forgotten during the Babylonian exile, and in giving it a more
graceful and suitable script.

Hebrew was written in the common Semitic alphabet, used
alike by Moabites, Hebrews, Phoenicians—who transmitted it
to the Greeks—and Arameans. The transition to the "square
script" was effected first in Aramaic and later in Hebrew,
undoubtedly as a consequence of the growing influence of
Aramaic during the Second Commonwealth. It was called the
"Assyrian script" on the assumption that it was in the land of
the Eastern Arameans that the Jews adopted it for their own
during the fifth century B.C.E.

There have been several editions of the Hebrew alphabet.
What are called the Samaritan characters were in use from the
earliest times up to the period of Babylonian captivity and

after that gradually passed into disuse. The square Aramean characters which are now invariably used came into vogue in the fifth or fourth century B.C.E. Tradition ascribed this change to Ezra; but inscriptions, or fragments of pottery and manuscripts, prove that it was a gradual process which was not completed in Hebrew by 400 B.C.E.[2] From these were developed the "square characters" used in biblical manuscripts, important texts, and most printed books; the "rabbinic" scripts, used in every kind of treatise, and the "cursive" writing of letters and informal documents which were not generally printed.

Throughout the subsequent centuries the Jew preserved all his intellectual treasures in Hebrew and in this language he corresponded. He even Hebraized foreign languages, by employing them in a Hebraic script—alike in Persia and India, in Greece and in Spain, on the Seine, on the Tiber, and on the Rhine.

The Mishnah and Rabbinic Hebrew

When the Jews returned from the Babylonian exile, they seem to have brought with them the Aramaic language they had used there. It took deep root among the people, and during the subsequent centuries of the Second Commonwealth period—until the destruction of the Temple in 70 C.E.—Aramaic, with an admixture of Hebrew became the everyday vernacular of the people. Hebrew, however, continued in use in the schools and in literature, was also spoken by the educated sections of the population, and in all likelihood was not unintelligible to most of the Jewish people.[3]

The language of the Mishnah, the collection of laws and lore

[2] Before the return from exile, it has been stated that the Torah had first been written in ancient Samaritan or Hebrew characters. But in the time of Ezra the scribes desired to give the Torah a distinctive character that would distinguish it from the Samaritan Pentateuch with its earlier script. The new square characters were called *ketab ashuri*—Syrian or Aramean script—as contrasted with the forms of the ancient Samaritan or Hebrew characters.

[3] That Hebrew was widely used and was considered the official language, at least until after the Wars of Bar Kochba, can be inferred from the fact that all the coins struck both by the Maccabean princes and by the government of Bar Kochba—of the latter we have fourteen different coins—bear Hebrew inscriptions. Since the coins were used by everybody, it may be assumed that all Jews understood Hebrew.

made at the beginning of the third century, clearly indicates that, during this period, a new form of Hebrew was developing with an increased range of vocabulary and a more pliant construction and style.

Compiled about 210 C.E., the Mishnah is a landmark in the development of Hebrew. This work, second in importance only to the Bible, written in Hebrew with a slight admixture of Aramaic together with some Greek and Latin, reflects the great development which Hebrew had undergone since the Bible. The Mishnah became the standard text for study and comment in all the academies of Palestine and Babylonia. It reveals an enriched and greatly enlarged Hebrew vocabulary which deals with every facet of living: agriculture, economics, civil and criminal law, theology and ethics, in addition to legal terms and abstract concepts. There were, as well, extensive changes in the usage and construction of verbal forms, which made the language more flexible and elegant in style, and a more expressive medium.

The use of Hebrew apparently declined after the compilation of the Mishnah, while Aramaic became more prevalent and even made inroads in literature. In fact, the language of the bulk of talmudic and haggadic literature, produced both in Palestine and Babylonia during the five hundred years from the end of the second century to the middle of the seventh century, is Aramaic with an admixture of Hebrew. The rabbis of the medieval period, in using the language of the Mishnah in their "responsa" (questions and answers) and letters, created a convenient rabbinic literary medium, though this Hebrew was never spoken among the people.

Hebrew Revival: 600-1100 C.E.

The following five centuries, from the seventh to the twelfth, were a period of Hebrew revival. Hebrew was extensively used during these centuries for literary production. Its linguistic development was considerable, as it added to its vocabulary and stabilized its pronunciation and grammatical construction, and gained in flexibility of expression and variety of style. This revival is first evident in a number of later Midrashim or haggadic works which, unlike earlier works of this type, are written in almost pure Hebrew. This was followed by extensive activity in the field of religious poetry, commonly known as Piyutim, a form of literary activity which continued for centuries.

It is difficult to determine the cause of this sudden revival and the greater interest in the language on the part of a large section of the people for whom the literature and poetry were written. It is likely, however, that the spread of Islam and the Arabic language in the East, where the two great Palestinian and Babylonian Jewish centers were located, was a significant factor. Although Arabic had for a time already supplanted Aramaic in popular use, it had not yet become a literary medium. Jewish scholars and writers, therefore, once again turned to Hebrew. The Arabs always displayed great love and devotion toward their language: poetry flourished among them, treatises on grammar were numerous and such activity undoubtedly influenced the Jews. It was during the eighth and ninth centuries that the Masorites, scholars who busied themselves with the preservation and stabilization of the text of the Bible, completed their work, and invented and introduced both the Hebrew vowels and the accents.

Vowels and Accents

Before the Masorites, only a few marks indicating vowel sounds were actually written in the ancient Hebrew manuscripts. Any other kind was omitted. In a language of consonants whose vocalization depends almost entirely on its indicated vowels, this presented a serious handicap to complete accuracy in prayer. With the exception of the four letters Aleph, Yod, Vav, and Hey, called "helps to reading" by old grammarians, there was not a single vowel in the written text of the Bible from beginning to end.

Thus, as the first verse of Genesis illustrates, the Bible then appeared as if we had taken away the English vowels and left only the consonants:

N TH BGNNG GD CRTD TH HVN ND TH RTH. (In the Beginning, God created the Heaven and the Earth.)

By degrees a system of vowel points to help the reader was invented and completed by the seventh century C.E.[4]

In the Bible, Hebrew words also carry accent marks. This accentual system helps to perpetuate the synagogal recital which was the traditional utterance of the reader during prayer. These accents were called *Taamim*, which means taste or flavor, since they were the "salt and pepper" of recited Hebrew. Give the accents of the Masorites their force, and the plain statement in the Torah is changed into the living voice of a prophet filled with emotion and dismay as he gives vent to his indignation.[5]

These vowels and accents helped make the pronunciation of Hebrew uniform and eased the study of the Bible as well as of later works, which henceforth employed the vowels, and lent impetus to the mass diffusion of the knowledge of Hebrew. This was the first attempt to study Hebrew scientifically. The primary labor of these students of the Bible was to establish a correct text, to count every letter and preserve the proper spelling of every word. Thus the Masorites made significant contributions to both written and spoken Hebrew.

This furnished the background for the study of Hebrew grammar as such, which was first made a separate branch of scientific study by Saadia Gaon (d. 942) who wrote his *Kitab Al Lugah* (Book of Language) in Arabic, as a guide to the knowledge of the Bible language.

The "Golden Age" in Spain

The tenth century C.E. saw the rise of the science of Hebrew grammar and lexicography. The work begun by Saadia Gaon

[4] The Hebrew script writes the consonants only and suggests some vowels. If it is desired to indicate vowels it is done by signs above and below the preceding consonants in the form of small points and dashes known as vowel points. This is called *Nikkud*, or pointing. According to this system of Hebrew pointing there are five long vowels, five short and three very short, like the catch of breath in the letter "A" in geography.

The vowels are indicated only in the Bible, prayer books, children's books, and poetry. All normal Hebrew print is unpointed.

[5] Hosea; vi, 10—"In the house of Israel I have seen an horrible thing," thus became "In the house of Israel!

"I have seen—an horrible thing."

Hebrew stops correspond roughly with our period, colon, semi-colon, comma and dash.

was continued in the new Jewish center of Spain, by Menahem ben Saruk (910-970) and Dunash Ibn Labrat (920-970). Their grammatical and lexicographical works, written in Hebrew, developed the language and exerted great influence beyond the borders of Spain. During the following two centuries that marked the Spanish "Golden Age," the Hebrew revival reached a pinnacle of literary expression and linguistic development. It was during this brilliant period that the grammarians and lexicographers, Judah Ibn Hayyuj (first half of the eleventh century), Jonah Ibn Jannah (990-1050), Abraham Ibn Ezra (1093-1167) in Spain, and Joseph and David Kimhi (twelfth century) in Provence (France), as well as a host of other scholars perfected the structure of the grammar, and through their dictionaries made a comprehensive knowledge of the language possible. The vibrant literary activity of this period in Spain which expressed itself primarily in religious and secular poetic productions, contributed to elegance of style and enrichment of vocabulary both with new words, and fresh nuances of meaning for old words and phrases. The Hebrew language could thus serve as the vehicle of emotional and intellectual experiences and ideas heretofore unexpressed.

At the same time, more intense and extensive, if less brilliant literary activity in Hebrew went on in the second Jewish center of France and Germany. There, unlike Spain, where Arabic was used by the Jews as a literary medium for scientific and intellectual works, Hebrew was the only language of Jewish literature. Works were produced mainly in prose: legal treatises; religious responsa; commentaries on the Bible and Talmud, of which Solomon ben Isaac's (Rashi—1041-1105) are the outstanding; works on grammar; and numerous religious poems.

It was also in this Ashkenazi-French center during this time that a greater impetus was given to the translation into Hebrew of scientific and philosophic works, written in Arabic both by Jews and non-Jews. The movement, initiated in the Provence by Judah Ibn Tibbon and his son, Samuel (1160-1239), was followed by many others for several centuries. It resulted in the translation of hundreds of works among which were the philosophic studies, *Emunot we-Deot* (Doctrines and Beliefs) by Saadia Gaon; *Hovot ha-Levavot* (Duties of the Heart) by Bahya (c. 1250-1390); the *Kuzari* by Judah ha-Levi; the *Moreh Nebukhim* (Guide for the Perplexed) by Maimonides (Rambam—1135-1204), and works of Aristotle. Again the Hebrew language was enriched with scientific and philosophic expressions, either newly-coined or adopted. The great Code of Maimonides, the *Mishne Torah*, written originally in Hebrew, through its masterful use of the language and precision and variety of expression, also served as a factor in this further development of Hebrew.

The Hebrew language, however, was not solely the literary medium of the Ashkenazi-French center. It was both widely spoken and the instrument of discussion and instruction in the scholarly higher academies.

Marking Time: 1100-1700 C.E.

The subsequent five centuries, from the twelfth to the eighteenth, can be properly termed a period during which the development of Hebrew marked time. It was still the literary language of all the Jewish centers of Europe, especially of Poland and the Turkish empire, including Palestine. Books in Hebrew appeared by the thousands, but because their content was limited primarily to scholarly rabbinic and religious subjects, their influence upon style and usage resulted in a marked reversion to the use of the rabbinic, mixed Hebrew and Aramaic form of writing. The Renaissance, however, was not entirely without influence on Hebrew. In central and north European countries, the Renaissance and the Protestant Reformation combined to arouse interest in the study of Hebrew on the part of non-Jews. The language was introduced to the outside world and became part of the curriculum of great universities. Christian grammarians and lexicographers wrote numerous works on Hebrew letters. Prominent among these scholars were Johann Reuchlin (1455-1522), defender of the Talmud, and the Buxtorfs, father and son (1564-1629; 1599-1644), who translated Hebrew masterpieces such as Maimonides' *Guide* into Latin. With William Gesenius (1786-1842), Hebrew grammar began to use modern forms of explanation and interpretation, and by the twentieth century the study of Hebrew had been placed upon as solid a foundation as that of any other language.

The Role of Prayer Books

This was the history of Hebrew before the period of the Haskalah (Enlightenment). Today, Hebrew, the oldest of all contemporary tongues, is a virile, living language—the language of a nation and its people. The fact is that although spoken Hebrew is the youngest of all national tongues it was never at any time a dead language. Unlike Latin, which became merely an item in academic curricula and restricted to an élite of scholars and scholarship, Hebrew was the "sacred language," the *leshon hakodesh* of the people in the ghettos of Europe, most of whom understood the Hebrew prayers.

In this regard the role of the prayerbook, the Siddur, is central to the language whose life-giving roots were in books and which throughout its history drew for sustenance upon the Holy Book.

It is true that biblical Hebrew, which remained the language of the people down to about 250 B.C.E., was then replaced in Palestine by the western dialect of Aramaic, and in Babylonia was gradually superseded by the eastern dialect of Aramaic, and in Egypt, by Greek, which served as the vernacular. But even in these ancient times the knowledge of Hebrew was kept alive by Bible translations and by the necessity of studying the Law and the teachings of the Prophets on the one hand, and on the other by the development of prayer in the synagogue.[6] And although it was more extensively used as a written than a spoken tongue, it remained the language of the Torah, cherished in dispersion by the Jew who, through the generations, and in whatever land he sojourned, never ceased his devotion to three pos-

---

[6] According to Maimonides the use of foreign languages by the Jews who were exiled in Persia, Greece and elsewhere from the time of Nebuchadnezzar motivated Ezra and his synod to formulate the prayers in pure Hebrew so that all Israelites might pray in unison. However, private prayers in Aramaic were later inserted in the prayerbook and Saadia Gaon, principal of the Yeshivah of Sura (928-942), included some in Arabic. Since the sixteenth century, the prayerbook has been translated into most European languages.

sessions which he counted holy: the Holy Book, the Holy Language, the Holy Land.

In the years and lands of exile the thought of the ancient homeland awoke of itself the thought of the ancient language, as in the words of the learned teacher of the second century C.E., Rabbi Meir: "Whoever lives in *Eretz Israel,* speaks the holy language, and reads the *Shema* morning and evening is sure of partaking in the future world." But though the Jew continued to live in the countries of the Diaspora, the love of Zion remained in his heart and the language of Torah remained on his tongue, as daily he expressed his aspirations and emotions, his devotion to God, only in Hebrew. These prayers for the year's weekdays, Sabbaths, holy days and fast days were collected into the book generally known as the "Seder Tefillot," or as it is simply called, the Siddur. Thus, through the centuries of constant use of the Siddur, despite the vagaries of time and place, the sacred language continued upon Jewish tongues speaking their holy prayers.

Hebrew in the Life of the Jews

Did Hebrew live only in the synagogue, in intellectual discussion, in learned correspondence, in scholarly books during medieval and pre-modern times? Was it only through this medium of books and especially *the* Book that Jews tenuously clung to their own language?

It is true that often the same Jew who corresponded with his fellow-Jew abroad in Hebrew, spoke to him at home in another language—that the spoken language of the land of his abode often displaced Hebrew in his own house.

But although Jews generally no longer conversed in Hebrew, evidence also reveals that throughout these long years of living in foreign lands there was considerable Hebrew intercommunication in the Jewish world. Indeed, the knowledge of Hebrew spread universally and it was used—unlike Latin—for both ordinary and secular activities as well as for learning.

Education was universal among the Jews in former generations. They had extraordinarily advanced educational systems based upon the study of the Hebrew language and literature.

Indeed, Jewish children were introduced to the study of Hebrew at an extremely early and impressionable age. To persons who were introduced to their studies so early, Hebrew must have become second nature—possibly more intimate than the language in everyday use. Indeed, Jews were so thoroughly at home with the Hebrew alphabet that in almost every country the vernacular was written, and even printed in Hebrew characters.

But the Jews did not confine the use of their ancestral tongue to the synagogue and the house of study. It was not only that the ancient language carried within it their sacred heritage and destiny, and placed its indelible imprint upon their thought and their way of life; it also became an important medium in those secular pursuits which required Jews to use the native language.

Throughout the Middle Ages and after, it was customary for Jews to keep their accounts in Hebrew. Important betrothals and marriages were the occasion, even in the smallest ghetto, for a flood of Hebrew verses by the local poet-laureates, who could count upon a wide and appreciative audience. The notaries in every community drew up business documents in Hebrew. And, of course, Hebrew was the language for transacting synagogal business and rabbinical correspondence. Cecil Roth, the Jewish historian, has a whole series of private letters written in Hebrew to Nottingham, England, dating back to the thirteenth century; while Jews who had been in Winchester Castle carved their names and personal notes on its wall, in Hebrew. In northern Europe during this period, whatever language Jews spoke among themselves, it appeared natural for them to slip into Hebrew as soon as they took pen in hand. The laws for communal taxation throughout the seventeenth and eighteenth centuries, which in Mantua and elsewhere were drawn up and circulated in pure Hebrew, meant that it was a language which every member of the community understood.

Solomon ben Abraham Ibn Parhon, a twelfth-century Spanish philologist, points out that in the Moslem world the fluency of Italian and Ashkenazi Jews in spoken Hebrew was a common fact. "In countries like Italy, above all, Hebrew speaking was recognized as one of the necessary accomplishments of the Jewish scholar and gentleman"; and as Azariah di Rossi, the Jewish humanist, wrote in the mid-sixteenth century, "Though we all speak Italian here, the numerous members of the intellectual class among us meditate, speak and write in the Holy Tongue."

Moreover, Hebrew was considered the natural language in which Jews conversed with foreigners, and in the famous Etz Hayim Academy at Amsterdam the language was taught by the modern direct "Ivrit B'Ivrit"—Hebrew in Hebrew—method.

Influence on Yiddish

Jewish vernaculars were as varied as the lands of dispersion. Rashi in France, spoke Old French; an Italian Jew, Obadiah of Bartanura wrote on the Mishnah; Don Isaac Abarbanel was a high functionary at the Spanish Court until 1492 and a poor exile in Italy afterwards; there were Hebrew writers in Amsterdam, in Berlin, in Vilna and Warsaw.

Like every living tongue Hebrew has various dialects or manners of pronunciation. The foremost are Ashkenazic (German) and Sephardic (Spanish). The former is generally heard in the Diaspora, the latter in Israel.

Despite the fact that eventually Hebrew had been largely displaced as a popular medium by Yiddish in northern Europe, and by Ladino in the Levant, yet these two principal Jewish folk tongues themselves bore eloquent testimony to the vitality of the Hebrew inheritance. Not only were they written in cursive Hebrew script and printed in the square Hebrew characters, but they are replete with Hebrew and talmudic (Aramaic) words and expressions transmitted from generation to generation.

Modern Hebrew: 1750—

The last two centuries, from the middle of the eighteenth to our own day, embracing the period of modern Jewish history, saw a resumption of the process of development of the Hebrew language. It culminated in its present status as a spoken language in a Jewish land once again, fully equipped to express the manifold shades and colors of thought and feeling over the entire range of human knowledge and experience.

The initial phase of this revival is revealed in a rather elementary form in the first Haskalah, or Enlightenment movement in Germany. This movement, the result of the early impact of the modern spirit on Jewish life in the ghetto, strove to effect a renaissance in that life to bring it closer to the modern world.

The life of German Jews in the eighteenth century was self-centered and cloistered. Dealings with the outside world were limited to business and trade and did not extend to the world of intellect and culture. Their children were educated on sacred Hebrew books. Like the Jews in the ghettos of eastern Europe, their own learning was circumscribed within the scholarly realm of talmudic study. In this sequestered world, concern with foreign languages or general scientific studies was forbidden. Besides their German-Jewish vernacular, Hebrew was the only tongue permitted, and even that was merely the "holy language."

It was into this tight Jewish world that the Enlightenment began to penetrate. And as the intellectual movement gradually took root among the Jews of Germany, it became obvious that Hebrew was the only medium for spreading the new movement and its ideas in the community.

To accomplish this purpose, an attempt was made to broaden the field of Jewish education, hitherto limited to rabbinic and religious subjects, so as to include new values, such as an appreciation of beauty, nature, and the cultivation of the sciences and of literature. Just as the leaders of the European Renaissance turned to the classic works of Greek and Latin for inspiration and guidance in their plan to change the pattern of life, so did the leaders of the Haskalah turn to Hebrew and its classic expression, the Bible, as the instrument of their renaissance.

This result was a break from the path of linguistic development that had produced the post-biblical Hebrew of the Mishnah and the Spanish period. The early intellectuals, or *Maskilim*, were drawn by the poetical strain of the Hebrew of the Bible even though its rhapsodical character made it an inadequate instrument for modern literature. They did not relish the style of rabbinic scholasticism. They desired a new style, one with new vigor, and chose as its vehicle of expression the Language of the Prophets.

The result of these activities of the Haskalah movement in which Moses Mendelsohn (1729-1786) was an important figure, was the creation of an extensive literature embracing poetry, popular scientific books, works on grammar, lexicography, biography, ethics and collections of fables. However, its literary value lies more in the modernity of its content than in its quality and style. For in their stylistic revival the Maskilim went to extremes in reverting to "the language of Isaiah and Job." Entire biblical sentences and phrases were used even though they had only vague connection with the author's subject. The consequence was that their literature was ornate and artificial in style, and displayed, with few exceptions, little creativeness. It was an elusive, metaphorical style of unnatural, over-refined writing shown as *melitzah*—the counterpart of euphuism—which paradoxically achieved the utmost artificiality in its sincere search for naturalness.

Its scientific studies were of far greater value and practical use. They spread knowledge and helped the study of Hebrew. An important contribution of the movement was the beginning of Hebrew periodical literature with the pioneer publication of the *Measef* (A Miscellany), founded in Germany in 1784 as a monthly, although irregularly published for fifteen years. By devoting space to contemporary events, it helped to reflect daily life to some degree.

But the attempt to erase twenty centuries of linguistic development did not succeed. This phase of the Haskalah in Germany did not last long. However, the Hebrew revival continued. It was merely transplanted to another Jewish center, the Austro-Hungarian empire, with its provinces such as Galicia, where Jewish life, completely integrated within its own communities, was unaffected by assimilation and where there was an avid desire for scholarship and learning. Nor was the spirit of modernity entirely foreign to the Jews of these provinces, for they were close to the West European countries. In such an atmosphere, the Haskalah movement flourished, though not without some opposition from ultra-orthodox groups. It struck roots and encouraged the study of Hebrew as a language. The movement underwent some change of purpose. It still aimed at enlightenment, but more stress was placed on creating permanent values in Jewish life itself rather than merely transforming it in the image of the general environment.

This change brought about a varied literary activity which saw the production of many able works on Jewish history, literature, the Bible, and kindred subjects. These laid the foundation for a ramified literature and for Hebrew as the vehicle of modern Jewish learning. The study of the past deepened the conception of the Jewish spirit and of the position and destiny of the Jewish people. Indirectly, it served as one of the forces leading to the regeneration and rebirth of Israel through Zionism. Its first echoes were heard in Naphtali Herz Wesseley (1725-1805) who wrote the epic poem about Moses in Exodus, *Shiré Tifereth;* and Meir Letteris' (1804-1871) national lyrics and historical ballads.

When the Haskalah movement was transplanted later in the nineteenth century to the Russian Empire—especially Poland and Lithuania—the revival of Hebrew made important strides. Conditions in that center were not unlike those in Galicia, but they gave a stronger impetus to the activity of the movement. The number of Jews in Russia being far larger, their urban compactness greater, and their response more positive, the activity assumed wider proportions. In Lithuania, a center of Jewish learning and rationalism, and one of the two centers of Haskalah, there was, as well, more forbearance toward the movement from orthodox groups.

Here, too, enlightenment was an important purpose and voices were heard stressing the need for greater emphasis on general culture and a closer approach to secular life. But even more stress was placed on enriching inner Jewish life and creating new Jewish values, leavened by a spirit of modernity reflecting contemporary Jewish life. The reflection is especially evident in the numerous periodicals published during the period —monthlies and several weeklies—such as the *ha-Melitz* (The Advocate, established 1860), a weekly up to 1882, and the *ha-Zefirah* (Daybreak, established 1862).

This century of Haskalah (1781-1881) filled both an intellectual and aesthetic need. It was more than a rebellion against the accepted norms of Jewish life. An unrest, not unlike that experienced during the Renaissance period, seized many Jews. They sought an answer in secularism in literature, and there developed what can best be described as a naïve romanticism found, for example, in the poetic novels of Abraham Mapu, (1808-1867).

Gradually, the intellectual horizons of the Jews expanded, and the Haskalah period was thus a harbinger of the Hebrew revival that was to follow. The spirit of modern nationalism, although not too marked, found expression in the Haskalah movement.

Rise of Nationalism

Beginning in the early 1880's, the vigorous nationalist era made its imprint upon modern Jewish history and launched the third important period in the revival of Hebrew. Raised to the status of the language of Zion by those dedicated to the cause of Zion, the tongue gave expression to the cause; the cause gave importance to the tongue; and both culminated in the modern recreation of the Jewish state, where Hebrew was reborn as a living language spoken not only in Israel but also in the lands of the Diaspora.

There was a mutual, complementary relationship between the Hibbat Zion(Love of Zion) movement, founded by Russian Jews for the purpose of settling on the land in Palestine; its successor, political Zionism; and the revival of Hebrew. Hebrew writers became the heralds of the Return-to-Zion movement, successfully aiding its spread among the Jewish masses. The results were: an expansion of Hebrew literature in many directions, an increase in the study of Hebrew in Jewish schools, and the establishment of daily Hebrew newspapers in Russia: ha-Yom, the Day (1886-1888) was the first Hebrew daily, followed by two weeklies converted into dailies, ha-Melitz (1885-1905), ha-Zefirah (1886-1914), and, at the beginning of the present century also ha-Zman (The Time) and ha-Zofeh (The Observer).

The real expansion of Hebrew, however, into a fully mature and richly endowed spoken language came not from the peripheral lands of the Diaspora but from its birthplace—Palestine. With the founding of a number of colonies by the Hoveve Zion (Lovers of Zion), schools were established with Hebrew as the language of instruction. Vigorous efforts to adapt the language to the needs of life and learning brought hundreds of new terms into use, drawn from the extensive literature of the ages, or coined and invented by scholars. The leading figure in this activity was Eliezer ben Yehudah (1850-1923) who, upon settling in Jerusalem in the early 1880's, pioneered as the first to introduce Hebrew speech in his home as well as in wide social circles. He set himself the task of adapting the language to modern usage in daily life as well as in the schools. His work culminated in the great Ben Yehudah thesaurus, ten volumes of which appeared in his lifetime and another six volumes posthumously as a memorial to his pioneering contribution. A host of followers continued this work, composing popular dictionaries, educational textbooks, and manuals for daily use.

In addition to such individual efforts, there were important organized endeavors which helped turn the Hebrew revival into a successful movement. An organized attempt to make Hebrew culture part and parcel of Zionism was led by the "democratic faction" at the Fifth Zionist Congress in Basle, Switzerland, in 1901. Its leaders were the late Chaim Weizmann, President of Israel, and the late Leo Motzkin. The great Hebrew writer, Ahad ha-Am (Asher Ginzberg) was also instrumental in formulating a theoretical as well as practical program for a Hebrew movement, in his essay, "Tehiath Haruah" (Spiritual Revival). In 1903 the first active Hebrew organization for the dissemination of culture was founded at Basle during the Sixth Zionist Congress. Three years later a group of leading Hebrew writers, philosophers, and Zionists convoked the first World Conference for Hebrew Language and Culture, and thus the Histadrut Lesafa u-le Tarbut was formed in Berlin, to advance the use of Hebrew language, literature and culture. However, it was not until June, 1931, in Berlin, that a permanent Hebrew organization named Brith Ivrith Olamit (World Hebrew Alliance), active to this day, was founded under the guidance of Dr. Simon Ravidowitz.

Finally, with the mass settlement of Palestine by Jews in the wake of the Balfour Declaration, Hebrew became the primary language of a half million people, and Israel has now become a vibrant, creative center of Jewish literature and learning to whose source of inspiration and intellectual ferment and receptive environment hundreds of writers and scholars from all over the countries of Europe gravitate.

The result is a literary production unparalleled in quantity and variety not only in Israel, but in the most cultured countries. At least two and a half to three books a day are published in Israel. The total number of periodicals devoted to education, literature, labor, art, science, medicine, aviation, sports, etc., exceeds one hundred, including fourteen dailies. Among the foremost literary journals are *Gilyonoth* (Scrolls), *Moznayim* (Scales),[7] *Molad* (Crescent), *Gazith,* an art and literary monthly, and collections such as the annual *Kenesset* (Gathering). To meet the language needs of life and culture, Vaad Halashon, a committee of philologists and writers, was established to formulate new terms for science, agriculture, the theatre, and a host of arts and crafts, including the culinary.

How Words Are Added

The facility with which new Hebrew words are brought into the language illustrates its pliancy as a living tongue.

All Hebrew words are based on certain roots, each with a special meaning of its own. And all the words from a common root, including the modern additions, have a certain common element of meaning. Thus the root L-M-D, for example, conveys the general idea of learning, and from it are derived *lamād,* "to learn," *lamed,* "to teach," *talmud,* "study," *melammed,* "a teacher," *talmid,* "a student," and *lamdan,* "a learned man." By such methods Hebrew is capable of an infinite extension of vocabulary and yet avoids the many syllables which characterize the Indo-European languages.

In this manner, modern terms for new machines, inventions, scientific discoveries and technological achievements are easily

[7] *Moznayim* has suspended publication for the present.

incorporated within Hebrew as, e.g., typewriter and correspondent.

Just as with all other living languages so the origins of
Hebrew words are the concern of the research study, not the
marketplace where they are on all lips. The new acquisitions
are soon integrated into the language as the everyday vernacular of the people, and even the old language forms become
known in their new incarnations; for people create words which
scholars accept and often reject words proposed by scholars.

The language spoken and written in the State of Israel is
thus marked by fertility of thought and picturesque idiom, and
the ideas in the Hebrew language which are found to shelter
under a common root are both numerous and varied. To the
old virtues of the Hebrew language which continue today—its
pithiness, its associations possessed only by a language rich
in ancient memories—have been added the resiliency, adaptive-
ness, vigor, thought and feeling of the nation-builders of Palestine who have forged a new state and given it a Hebrew name
with a wealth of meaning—Israel.

This is a short history of the principal trends of the Hebrew
language. But what of the great figures who wrote its finest
literature, sang its loveliest songs and contributed to its most profound thoughts and ideas?

Great Literary Figures

With the exception of the prophets, ancient literature is
primarily a collective product. In medieval literature the individual writer is the central figure. The most important figures
in medieval Hebrew poetry were Solomon Ibn Gabirol (1021-
1052) and Judah ha-Levi (1081-1142). The immortal Heinrich
Heine has described both. Of the first, Heine said: "Gabirol,
the nightingale of piety whose rose was God." Ibn Gabirol is
the religious poet nonpareil, though also a writer of brilliant
secular poems. In his poems, Jewish religious fervor, exquisitely
phrased, reaches its peak. His religious philosophical poem,
Keter Malkhut (Royal Crown), is a gem of world as well as
Hebrew literature, because of its brilliant style, depth of feeling, and its philosophical conception of the world, life, and man.

Of the second, Heine said: "When God created the soul of ha-Levi, He was so enraptured by its beauty and exquisiteness that he could not restrain Himself and kissed it." Ha-Levi is the national Jewish poet of the Middle Ages, whose songs expressed a love for Eretz Yisrael, even in its desolation. His poems are recited to this day as prayers on the ninth day of Ab, when Jews mourn the destruction of the sacred Temple.

Moses Ibn Ezra (c. 1100-1138), and Judah Ben Solomon (c. 1200), also wrote in Spain. The former, "the poet of penitential prayers," whose poems were in the liturgies of the Jews of Provence and North Africa, is best known for his work *Tarshish*. The latter wrote *Tahkemoni,* a collection of rhyming prose.

In Italy, Immanuel ha'Romi (Al-Harizi, 1268-1330), introduced the sonnet into Hebrew. He was a friend of Dante, and a chapter in *Mahbarot,* his most famous work, "ha-Tophteh ve-ha-Eden," is modeled on the Italian poet's *Divine Comedy.*

The foremost philosophers whose works were originally written in Hebrew were Levi ben Gershon (1288-1340), Hasdai Crescas (1340-1410), and Isaac Abarbanel (1437-1509). Ben Gershon's *Milhamot Adonai* (Wars of the Lord), occupies an important place in the Aristotelian phase of Jewish philosophy next to Maimonides' *Guide for the Perplexed.* The work of Crescas, *Or Adonai* (The Light of God), besides developing an interesting original philosophy, also presented the first criticism of Aristotelianism which held sway in Arabic and European thought for a thousand years. It influenced both Spinoza and non-Jewish circles. Abarbanel's literary activity was particularly devoted to Bible exegesis and philosophy.

At the opening of the modern period stands Moses Hayim Luzzatto (1707-1747), the Italian mystic and poet. Steeped though he was in mystic lore, his lyric poems and especially his three dramas: *Maase Shimshon* (Samson's Deed), *Migdal Oz* (A Tower of Strength), and *La'Yeshorim Tehillah* (Praise to the Just), are permeated with the modern spirit. His work exerted an influence upon generations of poets and writers during a large part of the Haskalah period. J. L. Gordon (1831-1895) is the most voluminous and versatile poet of the Russian

Haskalah. He wrote lyrics, narrative poems, historical ballads, polemics, and fables, but is primarily a social poet and trenchant satirist. He also distinguished himself in his prose writings, especially the feuilleton, the European equivalent of the American "column."

Peretz Smolenskin (1842-1885) is the foremost author of the Haskalah period. Most of his stories are dominated by the militant spirit of the Enlightenment, dissecting what he regarded as its orthodox bigotry and what seemed to him the less appealing, confining aspects of the religious life of the day, especially in the practice of Hassidism, while retaining reverence for certain aspects of Jewish tradition, especially its passion for learning. In some of his later novels he echoes the spirit of nationalism then beginning to assert itself. Smolenskin's important works are: *Hatoeh be'Darkai ha'Hayim* (Adrift on the Highways of Life), *Even Negeff* (Stumbling Rock) and *Simchat Choneff* (Sycophant Joy).

On the periphery of the Haskalah period and well entrenched in the subsequent history involving the emergence of political Zionism is Nahum Sokolow (1859-1936), one of the first editors of the Hebrew daily press, a scholar, publicist, orator, and diplomat, with Dr. Theodor Herzl and Dr. Chaim Weizmann, one of the major figures of modern political Zionism.

To the same peripheral epoch belongs Mendele Mocher Sforim (Shalom Yakov Abramowitz, 1836-1918), the first truly modern and impeccable Hebrew novelist whose style is a mosaic of biblical, talmudic and midrashic elements. Mendele, as he is called, was the "grandfather" of modern Yiddish literature and subsequently recast his novels into Hebrew. In delineating the East European ghetto of the nineteenth century, his novels covered a large canvas ranging over the entire gamut of Jewish life. Even his images and metaphors of landscape were thoroughly Jewish, thus he depicts the "forest praying," the earth covered by snow like an immaculate prayer shawl, the horse engaged with the driver in folksy dialogue.

The leading poets of the post-Haskalah period who emerged simultaneously with the Zionist renaissance, and are probably still the foremost figures in contemporary Hebrew literature are:

Hayim Nachman Bialik (1973-1934), Saul Tchernichovski (1873-1944), and Zalman Shneour (1887-1959). Bialik was the acknowledged national poet. He was the medium through which the manifold life of the Jews spoke. The Jewish tragedy of the day, the pogroms, massacres, and persecution are depicted in soul-searing stanzas in the famous poem, *be-Ir ha-Harega* (In the City of Slaughter). Bialik's Jewish love of learning and his concern with the contemporary decline of spirituality are epitomized by his *ha-Mathmid* (The Yeshiva Student). He is the author of splendid folk songs. His allegorical poem *Methéi Midbar* (The Dead of the Wilderness) is a major achievement in modern Hebrew literature. Then there are his playful yet meaningful legends collected in the volume *Va'Yehi Hayom* (Once Upon a Time). Bialik's work on the Mishnah, his incisive essays on writers and literary problems as well as his compiling of the *Sefer ha-Agada* and collections of medieval poetry with notes, contributed to the development of the language, its style and vocabulary.

In Tchernichovski, the universal human element predominates in elegant poetic description of the cosmic beauty of nature, and in exquisite love songs. For a time he evinced a rebellious spirit against ghetto life and the dominating tradition, but he later wrote a remarkable series of idylls on Jewish folk-life. Among these were *Chatunatah Shel Elka* (Elka's Wedding), and *Levivot Mevushalot* (Pancakes). Hope of rebirth of Israel echoes strongly in numerous poems, especially in those written after he settled in Palestine. He did numerous translations among them, Homer's *Iliad,* some of Plato's works, and Longfellow's *Hiawatha.*

In Shneour's poems, as in Tchernichovski's, universal themes prevail over the specifically Jewish. He especially excels in reflective, descriptive nature poems and passionate love poems, as in his cycle, *Beharim* (In the Mountains), *Mishire ha-Goral* (Songs of Destiny), and *Pirke Yaar* (Forest Chapters). In *Manginoth Yisroel* (Melodies of Israel), in the sonnet cycle *Mishire Ukraina* (From Songs of the Ukraine), and in shorter lyrics he deals with a renascent Israel.

Among the foremost critical writers of the immediate post-

Haskalah and early Zionist period was David Frishman, whose critical essays, poems and short stories and his yeoman work as editor have helped to stamp the continental image on contemporary Hebrew letters at the period which saw a departure from the purely propagandistic and flowery Haskalah style. A powerful ideological influence was Asher Ginzberg, known under his pseudonym Ahad ha-Am (1856-1927). His collected essays in four volumes entitled *Al Parashat Derachim* (At the Crossroads) developed the philosophy of "spiritual Zionism," which urged that the major importance of Palestine to the Jewish people should be its role as spiritual and cultural center. He was a rationalist and yet a traditionalist, who advocated the adaptation of the Jewish ethics of the past to the needs of contemporary Jewry whom he believed only Zionism could save from assimilation.

These major figures at the crossroads of Haskalah and the early renaissance of Zionism and contemporary Hebrew letters were the illustrious predecessors of the poets, novelists and scholars of contemporary Hebrew letters. Some of the moderns have spanned several periods of early Zionism and Israel in their careers. As cases in point, Yaakov Cahan (1881), Jacob Fichman (1881-1958), David Shimonowitz (1886), and Jacob Steinberg (1886-1948), are four poets who began their careers in Russia and perfected their genius in Palestine—each contributing to Hebrew poetry their own strong and sweet notes in various degrees. Cahan translated Goethe's *Faust* into Hebrew, while Fichman, like Steinberg, is also a distinguished essayist.

The rebirth of Israel inspired a host of new Hebrew poets. Prominent among these are Yehuda Karni (1884-1948) preoccupied with the grandeur of Jerusalem; the fiery Avigdor Hameiri (1886), author also of the great Hebrew war novels *Ha-Shigaon Ha-Gadol* (The Great Madness) and *Be-Gehinom Shel Matta* (The Hell Below); the ultra-nationalistic Uri Zvi Greenberg (1894) whose imagery, though lost occasionally in a sea of rhetoric, is pseudo-cabalistic and biblical in rhythm; Yitzhak Lamdan (1900) the author of the epic classic of Halutziut, *Massada;* Abraham Schlonski (1900) expressionist harbinger of the "new" poetry influenced in form by the Russian early revolutionary school; Sh. Shalom (1905) Galuth and Yishuv poet who sings of the travail of the Jew in the modern world now trying to find himself in the new homeland, whose abstractions have warmth; Nathan Alterman (1910), a subtly polyphonic and satirical, anti-British poet.

Novelists and short story writers who, like the poetic triumvirate Bialik, Tchernichovski and Schneour belong to the periphery of the post-Haskalah and early Zionist period, are David Frishman (1860-1908), Micha Joseph Berdichevsky (M. J. Ben-Gurion) (1865-1921), and Mordecai Zeev Feierberg (1872-1899), Judah Steinberg (1863-1908), S. Ben Zion (1870-1930), Isaiah Bershadski (1870-1910). Each of these was a powerful influence both ideologically and as a creator of the modern Hebrew novel.

Joseph Hayim Brenner (1881-1921) marks a new period in Hebrew fiction. Although in a sense a primitive, Brenner had the gloom of a Dostoievski. He depicted the bankruptcy of the emancipated Jew and advocated self-redemption through *Halutziut*—pioneering in Palestine. Brenner represented in his person and fiction the early Zionist socialist pioneer. He settled in Palestine and died in the Arab riots of 1921.

Prominent writers of the same period, although of a different genre, are Uri Nissan Gnessin (1880-1913), A. A. Kabak (1883-1945), Gershon Shoffman (1880), J. D. Berkowitz (1884).

Gnessin was a prose poet, a lyrical short story writer whose pithy stories of Russian Jewish intellectuals are in the melancholy, contemplative Scandinavian mood.

Kabak, who settled in Israel, turned in his maturity to historical novels which have made his reputation. His trilogy *Shlomo Molkho* is the best known of these. His important works include *Bamishol Hazar* (Along the Narrow Path), a novel on the life of Jesus, and his tetralogy on Zionism, *Toledoth Mishpahah* (The Story of a Family), depicting its conflicts with the old Russian revolutionary movement which had made great inroads among the Jews.

Shoffman is the creator of a unique genre, a combination of the short story and the feuilleton; a few deft strokes and a mood come to life, at times ironical, at times excessively lyrical. He, too, resides in Israel.

Berkowitz helped further the realistic school in modern Hebrew fiction, and having lived in America, he was of the first important Hebrew writers to depict the American scene. He now resides in Israel. He will probably remain best known in Hebrew letters for his masterly translation into Hebrew of the works of his father-in-law Sholem Aleichem in which he bridged the idiomatic gulf between Yiddish and Hebrew, which had been attempted in Hebrew poetry by Bialik in the early Zionist renaissance, and by Schlonski in more contemporary Hebrew poetry.

Samuel Joseph Agnon (1888) belongs to the generation that started its career outside Israel, and whose work reflects the two cultures of eastern Europe and Israel. Agnon fused Midrashic and folk elements into a unique mosaic. His *Hachnassat Kallah* (Bridal Canopy) has been translated into English, while other important works are *Oreakh Natta Laloon* (A Guest Tarries for the Night), an epic of eastern European life, and *Etmol Shilshom* (Yesterday and the Day Before), a novel of the Second Aliyah, to whose pioneering generation the members of the present Israeli cabinet belong.

Contemporaries of his, Asher Barash (1889-1952) and Hayim Hazaz, next to Agnon probably the foremost writers of Hebrew fiction in Israel, are also members of the same generation as Agnon which later became rooted in what is today the new State of Israel, and whose work expresses both continental and Israeli life. Judah Burlo (1886), a Sephardic Jew, depicts the life of Arab-Jewish communities in Arabia and Israel. Thus Israel today is a vibrant center of Hebrew literary creativity.

Foremost among the scholars and literary historians of contemporary Hebrew literature are: Zeev Yaavetz (1848-1928), a historian whose approach was orthodox religion and a departure from and challenge to the pioneer historian Graetz. Joseph Klausner (1874-1958), editor of the former magazine *ha-Shiloah*, is the exponent of a synthesis between Judaism and humanism, whose numerous monographs on writers constituted the first attempt at writing the history of contemporary Hebrew letters. These were collected into a series titled *Yozrim U-Bonim* (Creators and Builders). Klausner and Fischel Lachower (1884-1947), each wrote extensive histories of modern Hebrew literature.

Others of note are A. S. Horodetzky (1871-1957), author of a history of Hasidism; Simon Bernfeld (1860-1940), author of *Sefer Ha-Demaoth* (The Book of Tears), a lasting chronicle of Jewish martyrdom; Jacob Klatzkin (1882-1948) and Ezekiel Kaufman (1889). Klatzkin and Kaufman are probably the greatest Hebrew thinkers since Ahad ha-Am. Klatzkin's works, showing profound erudition and couched in a nineteenth-century continental style, include *Shekiat ha-Hayim* (The Sunset of Life), *Zutot* (Miniatures), and a voluminous *Ozar Le'Munahim Philosophiim* (A Dictionary of Philosophical Terminology). Ezekiel Kaufman's monumental work is *Toledoth ha'Emunah ha'Yisraelit* (A History of Jewish Religion), which expounds fresh concepts both broadly and meticulously, and *Golah ve-Nechar* (The Diaspora and the Alien World). A. D. Gordon, the propounder of the "religion of labor," was another thinker as well as a publicist and essayist. The late Vladimir Jabotinski (1880-1940), founder of the Zionist Revisionist movement and the Irgun, a great, controversial Zionist ideologist, a political publicist, and novelist, did the best Russian translation of Bialik and translated leading Russian poets into Hebrew, which he mastered as an adult after attaining a reputation as a liberal political writer.

And in America also the Hebrew cultural movement has become an integral part of positive Jewish life and Zionism.

Hebrew in America

Hebrew is a subject with a history in American life as old as the landing of the pilgrims. During the colonial period and until about a century ago, Hebrew was a required course in most American universities. The Old Testament and the Hebrew language were revered by the pilgrims and Quakers, and the great debt English literature owed them was readily acknowledged.

However, the earlier Jewish settlers in this country, both the Sephardim and the German Jews had, on the whole, little interest in Hebrew and its literature. Then, Hebrew interest was limited almost entirely to the prayerbook. In the case of the German Jews who were inclined toward Reform Judaism, Hebrew was eliminated to a large extent even from that book. Yet even among them there were a few scholars who mastered the language and wrote Hebrew works. As early as 1834, Joseph Aaron published in New York his *Mafteah El Lashon Ivri ve-Hokhmat ha-Dikduk* (A Key to the Hebrew Language and the Science of Grammar), which contained a Hebrew text and an English translation. The year 1838 saw two books, a Hebrew grammar by Isaac Nordheim and the *Imre Sheffer* (Beautiful Speech), a dictionary of biblical Hebrew and Aramaic by M. Henry. Among the German Jewish immigrants of the later period, there were a considerable number of Hebrew scholars, especially among the rabbis who came from Germany with a good background of Jewish education, such as the able Isaac Leeser (1806-1869), and Benjamin Szold (1827-1902), the author of a commentary on Job.

The expanded and intensified cultivation of the Hebrew language and literature began in the 1880's when the migration of masses of East European Jews increased to a flood. It was at the stage of Zionist development, when the clear affirmation was made that Jewish nationalism could find its true expression only through the medium of the ancestral tongue, that this coincidental mass exodus to the United States brought with it a number of Maskilim and Hebrew writers as a New World segment of the Old World Hebrew cultural movement. At first the faith and idealism of initial efforts to organize the Hebrew-speaking societies and to inaugurate a Hebrew press in America could not overcome the practical obstacles to a Hebrew cultural renaissance presented by the hard, energy-exhausting immigrant life. Yet, as early as 1870, Zevi Hirsch Berenstein (1845-1907) began to publish a Hebrew weekly, *ha-Zofeh be-Eretz ha-Hadashah* (The Observer in the New Land).

Nonetheless, within a few decades Hebrew writers appeared. Among them were Gershon Rosenzweig (1861-1914), epigrammist and versifier. Israel Davidson (1870-1939), well known by important work in medieval Hebrew literature in Hebrew and in

English, whose *Ozar ha'Shirah ve'hapiyut* (Treasury of Poetry and Poetics) is a landmark of research in ancient Hebrew poetry; and J. D. Eisenstein (1854) editor of the Hebrew Encyclopaedia, *Ozar Yisrael* (Treasury of Israel).

By the end of the first decade of the present century, the struggle for adjustment among the Jewish masses who hailed from the lands of eastern Europe abated, and by strength of numbers they began to exert influence for a deeper interest in Judaism and Jewish culture also upon the upper strata of Jewry—the German Jews. A contributing factor was the arrival during the years 1905-1920, of numerous young Hebrew writers and Zionist leaders, the influence of an invigorated Zionist movement and of the revival of Hebrew in Europe and especially in Israel.

Hebrew Publications in America

Hebrew literary weeklies began to appear: In 1914 the short-lived *ha-Deror* (The Swallow) appeared, edited by the distinguished Hebrew essayist, fiction writer and editor, Reuben Brainin (1868-1939). Soon after, in 1915, the *ha-Toren* (The Mast) appeared, edited for two years by J. D. Berkowitz. It later was changed to a monthly under the editorship of Brainin, and appeared until 1925. In 1916 the *ha-Ivri*, edited by Meyer Berlin, was launched and continued for seven years. Berkowitz also edited the monthly *Miklot*, founded in 1919 but no longer extant. Another attempt was made by M. Lipson to issue a daily paper, the *Hadoar* (The Post), which expired after eight months, but was then turned into a weekly, edited from 1922 to 1953 by Menahem Ribalow, who made both the *Hadoar* and the *Histadrut Ivrith* (Organization for Hebrew), his life work. *Hadoar* is now edited by Moshe Yinnon.

Also, in addition, the *Histadrut Ivrith* published under Ribalow's editorship the *Sepher ha-Shanah* (A Year Book), an annual collection of poetry, fiction, essays and scholarly studies. *Ha-Tekufah* (The Era) founded in 1918 in Moscow with David Frishman as its first editor, and published for years in Europe and Palestine, was resumed in this country. Once issued in New

York, under the editorship of Aaron Zeitlin* and E. Zilberschlag, it closed a period of more than thirty years during which time over thirty weighty volumes appeared. It owed a great deal to its late publisher, the Hebrew Maecenas, Abraham Joseph Stybel. First published in 1939, the monthly *Bitzaron* (Stronghold) was edited by the noted scholar Chaim Tchernovitz (Rav Tzair).

Talpioth, a quarterly, is edited by S. K. Mirsky; *Horeb*, devoted to Judaica, was edited by P. Churgin, and *Harofeh Haivri*, the first medical journal, is published by Dr. M. Einhorn.

All these weeklies, monthlies, and annuals served as the seminary for a generation of American Hebrew writers, who during the years collected their scattered productions in many volumes or published separate works.

Language Study

Early in the century, the *Mefitzeh Sfat Ever*, (The Disseminators of the Hebrew Language), a Hebrew-speaking society, was founded in New York to be later followed by the *Ahiever* (Hebrew Brotherhood) and a number of such groups in various parts of New York as well as in other large cities. Many of their members later distinguished themselves as poets, novelists, and essayists, rabbis and educators. As early as 1913 an attempt was made by M. Goldman to establish a Hebrew daily, *Ha-Yom*, which was published for eight months. New schools were established and the curriculum was extended to make Hebrew the language of instruction. Hebrew high schools and teachers' institutes were founded. In the 1930's and 1940's the movement for parochial schools and *Yeshivot Ketanot* began to spread and many of these use Hebrew as the language of instruction. An additional impetus was given too by the introduction of the study of Hebrew in the New York public high schools and its more intensive study in the Jewish theological seminaries, religious institutes and *Yeshivoth*.

Today, thousands of American Jews speak Hebrew fluently. Conversational Hebrew is not only taught in hundreds of He-

* Chaim Leif succeeded Zeitlin.

brew schools, but also in many public high schools and many colleges and universities throughout the United States.

In New York after a thirty-year experience as an approved modern language in the city's high schools, Hebrew's popularity still grows steadily. Today Hebrew is taught to several thousand students in secondary schools as a living language just as it is spoken in Israel. Modern textbooks are used and Hebrew civilization and culture, the history of the Jewish people, the geography of Israel, its literature, as well as its songs and folk dances are also learned.

Hebrew is also taught to New York children in weekly afternoon, parochial and Sunday schools, and outside of New York City to children throughout the country.[8]

In addition, there has been a growth of Hebrew-speaking camps, campus Hebrew study groups, adult language courses, and small home classes—all testifying to a definite trend toward a Hebrew renaissance in this country which is expected to thrive under the stimulus of the creation of the State of Israel and the vital interest it and its living, creating culture hold for American Jewry.

As a result of this constantly increasing interest, the American Jewish community is beginning to reap the harvest in the contribution which the knowledge of Hebrew and Hebrew culture is making toward the enrichment of American and Jewish life.

Thus Hebrew culture clubs in the high schools stimulate student interest in the cultural heritage of the Jewish past and creative expression in the present. In a variety of ways, including special cultural programs for school assemblies, these clubs make all students and teachers aware of the beauty and importance of Jewish cultural values, and serve to influence many of them (even teachers) to enroll for courses in Hebrew language and literature. The courses in Hebrew, as well as the work of the Hebrew culture clubs, have had a tonic effect on the morale of Jewish students in the New York high schools. Jewish prestige has gone up not only with the Jewish students, but with their non-Jewish schoolmates as well. Both have be-

[8] See "Educating the Jewish Child" by Uriah Zvi Engelman.

come aware of the fact that Hebrew is not something that is associated only with the ancient and original Bible, but is a rich, living language through which a new life and literature are being created in our own day.

The Jewish students who are enrolled in these courses become aware, many of them for the first time in their lives, that their people possess a modern language and culture that can take their place without apology beside other languages and cultures. The non-Jewish students, too, invariably acquire a greater appreciation of Jewish life and culture through contact with the students of Hebrew at the special assemblies where Hebrew pageantry and folk dances are featured, and through other cultural activities of the Hebrew classes and Hebrew culture clubs.

Today, with the State of Israel a reality, Hebrew literature stands on the threshold of a new Golden Age. Not only is there an epic theme in the establishment of a homeland and democratic government after 2,000 years, the new exodus from Europe and the future upbuilding of Israel—but the voices and pens to give it Hebrew expression are also at hand. And in the United States also, the accelerated growth of Hebrew study gives promise that the opportunity to build a bridge between the dominant Hebrew culture and American Jewry will not be lost, but that the Hebrew Renaissance has also reached these shores where more and more Jewish youths are joining in developing a literate, receptive audience for future creative Hebrew expression.

SUPPLEMENTARY LIST[1]

Israel

Some outstanding Israeli writers:

Rachel Bluvstein (1890-1931); Anda Pinkerfeld (1902); Bat Miryam (1901); Leah Goldberg (1911), poetess; Deborah

---

[1] The author regrets that space limitations have made it necessary to omit the detailed descriptions which so many of the eminent figures among those listed here deserve.

Baron (1887-1957), novelist, short story writer; Eliezer Steinman (1892), novelist, essayist; Joseph Lichtenbaum (1895), poet; Joshua Rabinow (1905), poet; Yitzhak Sheinberg (1905), novelist; Mattathias Shoam (1898-1938), dramatist, poet; Abraham Braudes (1907), poet; Shimson Meltzer (1912), poet; Shalom Streit (1889-1947), critic; R. Eliaz, poet; Noah Stern, poet; Sh. Kadari, novelist; D. Kimchi (1889), novelist; Jacob Rabinowitz (1876-1948), editor, essayist, versatile in many literary forms; Joseph Aricha, novelist; Menashe Levine, novelist; Yigal Moseson; Mishamir; Aaron Meged; Yacov Koplowitz (1893), poet; *Novelists:* Naomi Frankel; Yacov Churgin; Z. I. Anochi (1887-1947); Ever Hadani (1899); Yizhar Smilansky (1918). *Critics, essayists and editors:* Zvi Vislavski; Sh. Zemach (1886); essayist Ephraim Shmueli; Berl Katzenelson, also political writer and labor Zionist ideologist; Shazar (Shmul Zalman Rubashov) (1889), Israel Minister of Culture, historical researcher; Isaac ben Zvi (1884), President of the State of Israel, author of books on scattered Jewries in Asiatic countries; Dov Shtok (1902); S. J. Penueli; Rabbi Binyamin (d. 1957); A. Druyanov (1880-1938); A. Karil. *Scholars:* Ezekiel Kaufman; M. D. Cassutto (d. 1952); N. H. Tursenai; A. Aurbach. *Historians:* J. L. Maimon; F. I. Baer; Avigon Zerikawei; Gedaleya Alon; S. Klein; A. Yaari. *Historians and Archaeologists:* M. Abiyona; S. Yevin; Hayyim Sherman.

Europe

Some European Hebrew writers:

Isaac Baer Levinsohn (1788-1860), essayist; Rachel Marpurgo (1790-1871), poetess; Isaac Erter (1792-1851), satirist; Abraham Lebenson (1794-1879), poet; Yacov Lerner (1880-1918), poet; Moses Leib Lilienblum (1843-1910), essayist; Micah Joseph Lebenson (1822-1852), son of Abraham Lebenson and Mordecai Zvi Manne (1859-1886), first modern Hebrew lyrical poets; Yitzhak Katzenelson (1886-1944), poet; Zvi Diesendruck (1891-1940), essayist; David Vogel (1891), poet; B. Pomerantz (1902), poet; Hayim Lenski (1905-?), banished to Siberia in 1930's for alleged Hebrew Zionist activities, has not been heard of since.

United States

Poets: Naphthali H. Imber (1857-1910), author of "Hatikvah"; Benjamin Nahum Silkiner (1883-1934); Ephraim Lisitzky (1885); A. S. Schwartz (1876-1957); Hayim Abram Friedland (1891-1939); M. Feinstein (1897); Baruch Katzenelson, now residing in Israel; Reuben Grossman (1905), also anthologist, an American born, residing in Israel; Israel Efros (1891); Hillel Bavli (1893-1961); S. Halkin (1899), also critic, essayist, novelist, appointed to the Chair of Hebrew Literature at the Hebrew University, Jerusalem; A. Regeson (1896); Gabriel Preil (1911); El. Endelman. *Novelists and short story writers:* Abraham Soyer (1869-1939); S. L. Blank (1892); Yochanan Twersky (1904); Harry Sackler (1884); Reuben Walenrod (1901), one of the first to discuss the American scene; Abraham Shner; L. A. Anili; B. Isaacs; S. L. Blank; J. Ovsay. *Essayists, Scholars:* David Neumark (1866-1924); Abraham Goldberg (1883-1942); Nissan Tourof (1877); Abraham Epstein (1880); Daniel Persky, satirist; A. R. Malachi (1894); Samuel Feigin (1893); Zevi Sharfstein (1884); A. S. Yahuda (1877); Samuel Zevi Setzer (1880); Simon Bernstein; B. H. Amishi (Moshe Maisels, 1903); Isaiah Rabinovitz; I. Ovsay; Jekuthiel Ginzburg (1889); Isaac Rivkind; S. B. Maximon; M. Maisels, editor *Hadoar*; Menachem Ribalow, founder of *Hadoar*, (d. 1953); M. Waxman (1877) author of essays and books on literary, historical and philosophical subjects.

CHAPTER NINETEEN

AMERICAN JEWISH WRITERS AND THEIR JUDAISM

by HAROLD U. RIBALOW

The Judaism of creative American Jewish writers has undergone a startling metamorphosis during the past few decades. It is a phenomenon too seldom reported, or too infrequently realized. Its truth is reflected, as it should be, in the published works of the writers themselves. Between Ben Hecht's notorious *A Jew in Love*, written some thirty years ago, and Charles Angoff's continuing series of novels on Jewish life in America (including *Journey to the Dawn, In the Morning Light, The Sun at Noon* and *Between Day and Dark*), there is, literally, an entire world of difference. Hecht wrote out of gnawing self-hate as a Jew; Angoff creates out of an overwhelming love for Jews and Judaism. The difference between the two is vast and perhaps not an entirely accurate gauge of the change in attitude during the last twenty-five years. But the venomous Hechts, the indifferent Jewish proletarian novelists and the superficial popular yarn spinners who sought out the exotic in Judaism for their ignorant readers, have yielded to a group of novelists who approach their Jews—and Judaism—with admiration, honest understanding and, at times, veneration.

As a result, the Jewish fiction now being produced deserves the serious perusal of Jews who would understand themselves. Those Jews who believe that fiction is "frothy" or "trivial" are missing some of the most important Jewish writings being produced in this country.

Nearly two decades ago, in the February 1944 issue of the *Contemporary Jewish Record,* the precursor of *Commentary,* the editors polled eleven novelists, poets and critics of Jewish birth and queried them on their attitudes toward being Jewish. The symposium, titled "Under Forty," provoked considerable controversy for years. Only three of the eleven writers—ironically, Howard Fast, later better known for his extreme left-wing leanings and activities, was one of them—seemed to discover values in Judaism as well as in Americanism. The contributors to the now-famous symposium were Muriel Rukeyser, Alfred Kazin, Delmore Schwartz, Lionel Trilling, Ben Field, Louis Kronenberger, Albert Halper, Howard Fast, David Daiches, Clement Greenberg and Isaac Rosenfeld.

Curiously, all of these literary personalities, with the exception of the novelist Ben Field, became far more prominent later than they were in 1944. Since then, Howard Fast produced many novels (including *My Glorious Brothers,* a historical work of fiction based on the revolt of the Macabees, which is celebrated at Hanukkah), broke with the Communist party (and wrote a book about it), and is back as a popular American novelist. Alfred Kazin, in an autobiographical memoir, has discussed his Judaism in greater detail. Delmore Schwartz has enhanced his reputation as a poet and, following the "Under Forty" symposium, published a collection of Jewish short stories. Isaac Rosenfeld, who died prematurely a few years ago, wrote a novel about a Jewish adolescent, and some of his Jewish short stories appeared posthumously. Clement Greenberg became an editor of *Commentary* and after he left that magazine, strengthened his reputation as one of the nation's leading art critics. The remaining contributors were prolific as writers but, except for Albert Halper, who also published a Jewish novel, did not produce anything of specific Jewish interest or content.

Muriel Rukeyser, a well-known poet who has continued to write poetry as well as sensitive prose works, responded to the editors of the *Contemporary Jewish Record* by saying, "There was no mark of Judaism in my childhood home except for a silver ceremonial goblet. . . . There was not a trace of

Jewish culture that I could feel—no stories, no songs, no special food—but then there was not any cultural background that could make itself felt. . . . I grew up among a group of Jews who wished, more than anything else, I think, to be invisible. . . . I was brought up without any reason to be proud of being Jewish and then was told to be proud; without any reason for shame, and then saw that people were ashamed."

The teacher, critic, novelist and short story writer Lionel Trilling, declared that "the Jewish social group on its middle and wealthy levels . . . is now one of the most self-indulgent and self-admiring groups it is possible to imagine." He insisted that "as the Jewish community now exists, it can give no sustenance to the American artist or intellectual who is born a Jew."

Alfred Kazin, in his *A Walker in the City*, expanded on his "Under Forty" thoughts. In the 1944 symposium, he said, "I have never seen much of what I admire in American Jewish culture, or among Jewish writers in America generally." He added that "I think it is about time we stopped confusing the experience of being an immigrant, or an immigrant's son, with the experience of being Jewish." And, as a final remark, he stated, "I learned long ago to accept the fact that I was Jewish without being a part of any meaningful Jewish life or culture." Yet in his book, a tender, penetrating, nostalgic and yet bitter memoir, Kazin has revealed, perhaps unwittingly, that in his alienation from his people he discovered a curious attachment as well. "We had," he wrote, "all of us lived together so long that we would not have known how to separate even if we had wanted to. The most terrible word was *aleyn*, alone." He was writing here of himself and his family, but he might just as well have been thinking of himself, his family, and the Jewish people.

The theme of rejection and nostalgia was reiterated by another intellectual, Leslie A. Fiedler, who said, "When anybody asks me, you understand, I am a Jew; when I question myself, I am not so sure." This remark is frighteningly close in spirit to Franz Kafka's diary notation: "What have I in common with Jews? I have hardly anything in common with myself and should stand very quietly in a corner, content that I can breathe."

But these convolutions were, in reality, indicative of a revolutionary change in the American Jewish writer. From Ben Hecht's hatred, to the neurotic fence-sitting of the intellectual, the road led, without too many windings, to a more level terrain. Yet even in attempting the approach, there were obstacles. Arthur Miller, the noted playwright, who later wrote a profound short story of Jewish self-discovery in "Monte Saint Angelo," said in a 1947 speech:

> I think I gave up the Jews as literary material because I was afraid that even an innocent literary allusion to the individual wrong-doing of an individual Jew would be inflamed by the atmosphere, ignited by the hatred I suddenly was aware of, and my love would be twisted into a weapon of persecution against Jews. No good writer can approach material in that atmosphere. I cannot censor myself without thwarting my passion for writing itself. I turned away from the Jews as material for my work. . . . I have been insulted, I have been scorned, I have been threatened. I have heard of violence against Jews, and I have seen it. I have seen insanity in the streets and I have heard it dropping from the mouths of people I had thought were decent people. . . . Instantly, therefore, and inevitably, when I confront the prospect of writing about Jewish life my mood is defensive, and combative. There is hardly a story or play I could write about which would not have to contain justifications for behavior that in any other people need not be justified.

Nevertheless, in spite of his reluctance to do so, Mr. Miller wrote a brilliant Jewish short story five years later!

In 1951, there was a spate of Jewish fiction and this writer, impressed both by the quantity and the quality of the writing, composed a letter to nine Jewish novelists, asking them why they chose to do a novel or a short story collection on Jews or Jewish themes. The replies, penned less than ten years after the "Under Forty" symposium, and published in the November 26, 1951 *Congress Weekly*, reflected the change that was already taking place. Instead of the intellectual twistings and turnings of the earlier discussion, and in spite of the publicly stated doubts of so fine a writer as Arthur Miller, these nine spoke out as sharply aware Jews.

Zelda Popkin, who used to write detective stories, produced *Small Victory* and *Quiet Street*, the first, a novel about DP camp survivors and the anti-Semitism of American Military Government in Germany, the second, an account of the siege of Jerusalem. As Mrs. Popkin phrased it, "*Small Victory* was a product of anger and pain; *Quiet Street* is a gift of love. I am not," she added, "a Johnny-come-lately in discovering my Jewishness and it has never been a source of conflict, self-hatred or even minor trouble to me. I was reared in Orthodoxy and I liked it. The festive spirit of the Holydays and the Shabbat are part of the richness of my childhood. I went to Cheder; I wrote Purim and Chanukah plays and childish poems of religious content. Perhaps because my Jewishness was affirmative, or perhaps because I grew up in American small towns, or perhaps, too, because I have long been a writer, no door has ever been closed to me and I have personally never known the frustrations and cruelties of anti-Semitism." She explained that she wrote *Quiet Street* "because it was one of the great stories of all time and it moved me deeply."

Ethel Rosenberg, whose humorous books *Go Fight City Hall* and *Uncle Julius and the Angel with Heartburn,* are so much superior to and different from the Montague Glass "Potash and Perlmutter" stories of an earlier era, said, significantly, "It seemed to me there was room for a book to present the Jews without problems, other than the everyday garden variety, and with their capacity for joy and humor and warmth shown—in other words, one more side of the picture that we don't get to see often enough."

Yuri Suhl, who introduced himself to the American Jewish audience with his pleasant *One Foot in America* and followed it up with *Cowboy on a Wooden Horse,* said that "for me the selection of a Jewish theme for my first novel is a natural one." A Yiddish poet and an immigrant, Mr. Suhl pointed out that "the process of my Americanization was not accompanied (as so frequently happens) by a process of alienation from my cultural heritage of the past and the American Jewish community.

Quite the contrary. It was here, in America, that I came to know the secular face of this heritage. . . . This dual process is still going on with me and I do not find it in any way contradictory or conflicting. . . . I believe . . . that the choice of the Jewish theme does not constitute a limitation of the writer's literary range. I consider a work of fiction on the Jewish theme as integral a part of the broad stream of American literature as the American Jewish community is of the American scene generally."

David Miller, whose historical novel *The Chain and the Link*, received wide critical acclaim, stressed that if Jewish books receive poor notices and they are not bought, it becomes difficult for the Jewish writer to continue stressing Jewish themes. "The table cannot be set," he wrote, "if too few come to dine." But like Mr. Suhl and others who went somewhat afield to comment on the difficulty in getting a Jewish novel published, Mr. Miller insisted that "I wish to continue writing on Jewish themes and to develop Jewish characters," and he exhibited none of that pessimism or defeatism common to the group of writers who contributed to "Under Forty."

In explaining the reasons for dipping so generously into his Jewish past for his long narratives, Charles Angoff said that his fiction, to use a phrase of Willa Cather's, was his "cremated youth." The people and the themes of *Journey to the Dawn* and *In the Morning Light* selected the writer far more readily than he selected them. The people in these books captured and held him and he was unable to escape from them. "My distant past," Mr. Angoff confessed, "is becoming more 'real' to me than my immediate past or the present"—and it was a past "steeped in Jewishness."

Herman Wouk, who had then written *The Caine Mutiny* and had not yet created his controversial *Marjorie Morningstar*, when asked about Barney Greenwald, the Jewish lawyer in *The Caine Mutiny*, said that "as Jewish characters and themes occur to me I will certainly use them. I know of no reason to avoid them."

Mr. Wouk was a man of his word. His *Majorie Morningstar*, which depicts the "ideal" girl of the Jewish middle class in the United States, was his most ambitious fictional reworking of the patterns of Jewish life in this country. A book written with a heavy hand, *Marjorie Morningstar* nevertheless projected Mr. Wouk's viewpoint that middle-class Jews in America are far from admirable and that the only hope they have for happiness as Jews as well as Americans, is to conform to the behavior patterns set and approved by our society as a whole. That nearly all the Jews in the novel are shallow, superficial and unappetizing human beings and that Jewish customs and religious rituals are mocked by Mr. Wouk, was observed by the critics; a large reading public loved the novel.

Stephen Longstreet, a Hollywood script writer and prolific novelist who wrote *The Pedlocks*, a chronicle of a Jewish family in American life, was so intrigued by the queries directed at him, that he wrote an extraordinarily long letter in which he unburdened himself of varied and fascinating thoughts on Jews and Judaism. If there was a time when popular Jewish novelists studiously avoided writing on Jewish subjects, that time seems to have vanished. Mr. Longstreet, after describing his book, said, "I hate self pity and most Jewish writers roll in it. I dislike black and white in anything and the relationship of Jews and Gentiles is almost always presented in black and white. My Jews are human beings first. . . ." and the rest of his letter disclosed his enormous interest in Judaism and Jews.

The others, novelist and short story writer James Yaffe, and Miriam Bruce, insisted that they would continue to write about their fellow Jews. Mr. Yaffe said, "I don't suppose I'll ever stop writing about Jews completely—you don't get away from your childhood that easily. Besides, Jews are fun to write about."

Mr. Yaffe proved this in his novels published after the issuance of his short story collection *Poor Cousin Evelyn.* In both *The Good-for-Nothing* and in *What's the Big Hurry?* Mr. Yaffe wrote of Jews with humor, insight and occasional brilliance.

The very concept of Jews being "fun to write about" would have struck the novelists of the last two decades as preposterous. Yet practically all of the novelists participating in the *Congress Weekly* symposium said the same thing in their own fashion. Yuri Suhl, Charles Angoff, Ethel Rosenberg, Zelda

Popkin and David Miller accomplished what none of the novelists of the past were able to do—that is, to show their readers that they were completely in control of the material they had in hand. They did not grope for the raw material of Jewish life. It lived within them; they had only to project it, not to find it.

Yet even the novelists who, in a sense, "returned," managed to write movingly of contemporary events in Jewish life. In particular, Michael Blankfort, like Longstreet a Hollywood writer, and once a Marxist, visited Israel and wrote a novel about the new state. His book, *The Juggler,* is a "chase" story, but it utilizes with great effect the terrain of Israel and probes the psyche of a maladjusted DP, who finds peace and a home in Israel.

This was Mr. Blankfort's first "Jewish" book. His second, *The Strong Hand,* a novel about a modern American Orthodox rabbi and his ill-starred love affair with a woman he cannot marry, contains illuminating insights into Jewish religious patterns of thought and is one of the most persuasive books on a rabbi produced by an American in the United States.

The Juggler created controversy in Jewish circles (as did *The Strong Hand*), and was made into a motion picture. But more significantly, it led the author to reflect upon his past life, and that he was one of the most articulate of those who returned by a brief fragment called "The Education of a Jew," which appeared in a national magazine soon after the publication of his novel.

In it, Mr. Blankfort revealed that he had been brought up in an Orthodox Jewish home of American-born parents. He was sent to Heder up to the time he was fourteen; in other words, he received a Bar Mitzvah education. "During that time," he wrote, "I learned how to read the Hebrew prayer book and Torah Hebrew, chanted without the vowel signs, and with a speed and accuracy which were miracles of learning by rote. I understood, however, no more than one one-thousandth of what I read. . . ."

In adding detail upon detail of his past life, Mr. Blankfort concluded, "To be blunt, I was an Orthodox illiterate."

In his twenties, he became a teacher of psychology and his

"views and values were a compound of behaviorism, pragmatism, Freudianism." For him, "God was superstition and Judaism was a backward religion." Marxism seemed to him to be the true faith. And then came disillusion with Marxism. Yet, "it seems to me now that even during those years I had never entirely lost what was pervasive and lasting in my Jewish experience. There were strains of remembrance even with this Orthodox illiterate whose childhood was immersed in prayers ('How can God's judgment on our sins be averted? By Penitence, Prayer and Charity,' and a charity which meant Justice). The borders of my consciousness were marked by the weekly repetition of the Pirke Aboth ('The Ethics of the Fathers'), the gentle homilies of my grandfather at the Sabbath table, each an anecdote of Talmud, of charity and genuine saintliness. There was more to it than sentiment; there had been deep and unconscious learning which had ingrained a yearning for a charity which was justice, and a justice which did not demand blood sacrifices and the acceptance of an absolutism in order to pursue it."

In pronouncing his credo, Mr. Blankfort declared that "in the communion of Judaism, the identification with my people, my active affection for the Land of Israel, my faltering efforts to live by the precepts of the prophets, I have found a peace of the spirit."

This peace of the spirit seems to have enveloped many other writers of the 1950's. It is in the existence of their works, apart from their personal statements of their beliefs, that one finds the metamorphosis referred to at the outset of this essay.

The novels of Mr. Angoff, Mr. Suhl, Sam Ross and Albert Halper discuss the adjustment of the Jew to America and the gradual but pleasant Americanization of the European Jew without the raw and realistic aspects of the earlier novels on the same theme. Hyman and Lester Cohen's *Aaron Traum* and even Abraham Cahan's minor classic, *The Rise of David Levinsky*, emphasize the difficult life in the New York sweat shops. Mr. Suhl and Mr. Angoff comment on the importance and influence of unionism; Mr. Ross and Mr. Halper, in their narratives (*The Sidewalks Are Free* and *The Golden Watch*) project their characters on the stage with loving kindness. Once upon a time, in *I Can Get It for You Wholesale* and in *What's In It for Me?* Jerome Weidman wrote acidly about the garment industry. Mr. Angoff manages to infuse it with warmth. His account of the rise of a Jew to eminence in this field lacks the bitterness and unscrupulous shadings of Mr. Weidman, but his tale is no less authentic. Mr. Ross' novel deals with the jungle of the city and its impact on a sensitive little Jewish lad. Henry Roth's *Call It Sleep* of a previous era was a more powerful work of art; it, however, was suffused with fear. The hero —and, it appeared the writer—were frightened of New York and America. Mr. Ross writes less ambitiously, but he also writes more realistically. The world no longer seems to be a nightmare universe for the Jewish youngster. There is a normality in Mr. Ross' book which is missing in the brilliant 1934 novel of Henry Roth, recently reissued after twenty-five years of neglect.

Mr. Halper's *The Golden Watch* is far more Jewish in content and in approach than the books he published in the 1930's which gained his reputation for him. *Union Square, The Foundry* and *The Chute* were products of the proletarian era, and it was no wonder that in the "Under Forty" symposium Mr. Halper said that at the outset of his career he would have said, "Hell, I want to become a good American writer, what has being a Jew got to do with it?" But the Hitler catastrophe made him feel that the Jew was different, and in his latest novel he revealed a tenderness toward the Jew lacking in his earlier, more ambitious works.

Louis Falstein wrote *Face of a Hero,* which was a fine book about the last war. It was also one of the few war novels in which a believable Jew appears: not a symbol of a Jew (typical of the Irwin Shaw, Ira Wolfert, Norman Mailer, James Jones war novels) but a Jew who remembered pogroms in Russia, who knew what a Hitler victory would have meant to American Jews. Falstein wrote a second novel and it was inevitable that it deal with Jewish families in Europe emigrating to the United States. It was not as inevitable, but welcome, that Falstein's next serious novel, *Sole Survivor,* was concerned with a DP in

America and how he illuminates the death of six million Jews to an indifferent America. Equally significant is the fact that this novel appeared in a twenty-five-cent paperback original and was aimed at the mass book buyer, not the selective purchaser who obtains his books in one of the handful of bookstores throughout the nation. Mr. Falstein produced a meaningful war narrative and then developed into a completely Jewish novelist. It would have been a miracle for a Falstein to have emerged thirty years ago (there were one or two in those days; Ludwig Lewisohn and Meyer Levin), but it has become far more common today.

Other writers of stature and significance have made their impression within the last ten years, all of them talented and the authors of useful books, good as fiction, as commentary on Jewish life in America, and as works of art.

Sam Astrachan, who wrote *An End to Dying*, is typical of the young American Jewish novelist who has been able to draw upon the materials of European Jewish life, based on his keen remembrance of what he heard about the experiences of his grandparents in Europe. In this novel, Mr. Astrachan recreated the milieu of the *shtetl* with vigor and with artistry. Oddly, when he reverts to modern Jewish life, he is less convincing than when he depicts an earlier age. He is, however, one of the vanguard of youthful writers from whom more will be heard in the future.

Ernest Pawel, who produced *From the Dark Tower*, has taken as his material the life of Jewish suburbia, a theme seldom treated in American fiction, and he handles it with intelligence and skill. For that matter, a host of young men have given us novels well worth reading, even if they repeat the plots and background of the works of fiction written by Abraham Cahan, Charles Angoff and Yuri Suhl. Arthur Granit, in *The Time of the Peaches*, has written a finely-phrased series of vignettes about Jewish life in Brownsville, Brooklyn; Jerome Weidman, returning to Jewish characters and situations, wrote a controversial and provocative book entitled *The Enemy Camp*, in which Jewish suspicion of Gentiles is the recurrent and dominating theme. It is significant of the acceptance of the "Jewish novel" that it was a Book-of-the-Month-Club selection. Gerald Green, in *The Last Angry Man,* also chose to describe Jewish life in a highly-populated Jewish neighborhood, selecting as his hero an idealistic Jewish doctor, not unlike the Dr. Gottlieb in Sinclair Lewis' *Arrowsmith.* Harvey Swados, one of the best of the younger novelists, in *Out Went the Candle,* wrote a novel about a Jewish businessman and his relationship with his daughter. And Meyer Levin managed, in *Compulsion,* to retell the Leopold-Loeb murder case without distaste and with some telling remarks about the "Jewish angle" on the senseless and violent murder of an innocent child.

Israel, once an orphan of the Jewish novel, has now found a small home in American fiction. Mr. Lewisohn and Mr. Levin had written fiction on Israel in the past, but the Halpers, the Hechts, the Schulbergs and other popular Jewish novelists considered Israel an alien island. They were completely indifferent to it. It would not even be true to say that they were opposed to the Zionist idea. They were not. They merely were unaware of its existence. Except for Meyer Levin's *Yehuda,* no novels were written by American Jews on the experiment which blossomed into an independent nation. When Mr. Levin wrote *My Father's House;* Zelda Popkin came through with *Quiet Street;* Michael Blankfort offered *The Juggler* and A. M. Klein created his complex, intricate *The Second Scroll.* Mr. Levin wrote out of twenty-five years of knowledge; Mrs. Popkin, after an extended trip to the land; Blankfort, following an intensive tour of the country; and Mr. Klein out of his knowledge of the land and the language. These were not people jumping on a bandwagon. They created out of a need and a desire. It was apparent in their novels.

Then there came the most remarkable book of them all on Israel. It is, of course, Leon Uris' *Exodus.* A huge novel, full of undigested bits and pieces of Jewish history of the past fifty years, *Exodus* became one of the most widely read books in American history. Its sales have been astronomical; in paperbacks more than two million were sold. The plot is unoriginal and unimportant. What is significant is that Mr. Uris recognized the miracle of Israel's rebirth and wrote of it with bursting pride. The raw material is dramatic and unforgettable, so that even if many critics carped at the lack of literary quality to the book, the narrative incorporated the Israeli war for independence, the ghastly murders in the Hitler extermination camps, the annals of Zionism over the last five decades, the transit camps from which thousands of refugees came to Palestine—the entire shocking and thrilling history of fifty years. The result was that millions of readers were stirred and emotionally excited by Mr. Uris' novel. And if it is not literature, well, neither was *Uncle Tom's Cabin*. Uris has followed up with *Mila 18*, a story of the Warsaw Ghetto and another best seller.

Even in the field of the short story, Israel, formerly completely overlooked, began to play a minor role. When this writer edited an anthology of Jewish short stories (*This Land, These People*), he apologized for the lack of Zionist fiction, and tried to explain that Israel, or the yearning for the Holy Land, had not attracted more than a few Jewish writers in America. Two years later, when a sequel was published (*These Your Children*), there were a handful of tales about the war in Palestine and the importance of the conflict to the American Jew. In the first omnibus, there was one story by Meyer Levin which dealt with a maladjusted Jew who found peace in Palestine by drawing mediocre paintings. In the second anthology, there were passionate stories about fighting and dying for the idea of a state. In a third collection, *The Chosen*, there were more tales on Israel. The progress is evident.

The Judaism of the American Jewish writer may be measured in another way as well. The ivory tower artist vanished with the end of the Hitler era, or perhaps it is more accurate to say, with the beginning of that era. Thus, the Jewish writers who did begin to write about their own people, became active in organized Jewish communal life in America. It did not start with, but it found its most dramatic illustration in Ben Hecht, who became an active propaganda writer for the extremist Zionists during the Jewish fight for independence in Palestine. Mr. Hecht, formerly the author of diatribes against Jews, now saw the Jew as a holy warrior and utilized his typewriter to stress this concept to Americans and Englishmen. After the establishment of the State, Mr. Hecht returned to luxurious Hollywood life and to the writing of Broadway and TV scripts. More recently, he published his autobiography and in it his activities on behalf of the Irgun Zvai Leumi received a good deal of space.

Charles Angoff, following the publication of his Jewish novels, became a prolific contributor to English-Jewish magazines and lectured before Jewish audiences.* Michael Blankfort, now deeply involved in Jewish cultural and communal affairs, participated in forums on Jewish writing and wrote movingly on the responsibility of the Jewish novelist to the Jewish people. Louis Falstein, too, appeared on the lecture circuit briefly and began to write for Jewish periodicals about which he had previously never heard. A poet of the stature of Karl Shapiro, who once said that he wrote one day as a Jew and the next as a Christian, composed a stirring poem on the birth of Israel and more or less stopped writing his Catholic-tinged verses. When he was approached by Jewish editors he no longer brusquely rejected their invitations to contribute to their journals. He said that if he could find the time, he would be happy to write for them. In a subtle way, this, too, reflects a change. Just as it is a change for Budd Schulberg, author of *What Makes Sammy Run?* to write a long apologia for the Modern Library edition of his book, explaining why it is not a work of anti-Semitism, but a deeply-felt pro-Jewish book. The persuasiveness of his argument is less significant than the fact that he went to the trouble of composing the argument at all. And Mr. Schulberg, in a letter to this writer, wondered why someone did not do a critical volume on Jewish fiction in America. This attitude, too, is typical of a Jewish awareness, not necessarily a communal one, but a spiritual one, of Jews long on the outside of organized Jewish life, either trying to come within, or at least wanting to visit.

* EDITOR'S NOTE: Concerning the April 1961 *Commentary* symposium and its particular selection of "Jewish intellectuals," Angoff said: "These 'intellectuals' . . . really are not at home in the Jewish world and yearn for a time when their Jewishness, such as it is, will no longer be a burden to them."

Of course, the picture is not entirely a rosy one. Writers like Norman Katkov, when they produce novels, harp on the rigidity they find in Jewish life, and when they discuss intermarriage, their attitude generally favors the Gentile over the Jew. New novelists like Leonard Bishop discover Jewish dope addicts and racketeers. Irving Shulman has made the Jewish gangster the "hero" of three of his novels. Harold Robbins never overlooks the Jew in his books and they are, invariably, a rather poor and revolting lot. Myron S. Kaufmann, in *Remember Me to God*, drew a bitter and unbalanced portrait of a Harvard student who tries desperately to "pass" as a Christian. In contemporary Jewish fiction there are very few books on Jewish religious life in America: the rabbi is a character seldom treated understandingly, if at all. The synagogue hardly ever plays a role in a Jewish novel. Jewish Center life is non-existent, although Hadassah, B'nai B'rith and the Zionist Organization of America have appeared from time to time. Jewish publishers still do not encourage Jewish fiction simply because they do not accept and publish novels. The Jewish writer never knows, while he is working on a book, who will publish it, but he does know that the eventual publisher will not be a Jewish firm. Bloch, Behrman, the Jewish Publication Society, the major Jewish houses, seldom accept fiction. When Schocken published in this country, the firm did issue fiction, but not by American writers. This is another discouraging factor to the Jewish writer, who likes to believe that he has a ready, even though small, audience.

At this point, mention must be made of two novelists who have transcended the "Jewish field," with due respect to many of the others whose works have been widely read and reviewed and who certainly deserve, on the basis of talent and performance, to rank with them. The two are Saul Bellow and Bernard Malamud.

Mr. Bellow's *The Victim* is a tightly-written, Dostoievski-like novel concerning the relationship of an anti-Semite and a Jew. An acute statement of Jew-hating, *The Victim* is, at the same time, a story with a twist, for it appears that it is the Jew, not the Jew-hater, who is the persecutor. Mr. Bellow's novel stands as an imaginative and compelling study of the impact of anti-

Semitism on a Jew and the influence of a sensitive Jew on a complex and disturbing Christian. In *The Adventures of Augie March,* Mr. Bellow has produced a book which critics like Leslie A. Fiedler call the best Jewish novel ever written in America. Mr. Fiedler is ecstatic about Henry Roth's *Call It Sleep* and also has considered Mr. Roth's novel to have been the most brilliant evocation of Jewish life in this country. I am more inclined to agree with him on Mr. Roth's novel than Mr. Bellow's, for Augie March is a peripheral Jew. Nevertheless, Mr. Bellow, in the picaresque *Adventures of Augie March* has shown that a Jewish writer can create a book dealing with an American Jewish family which can be placed most naturally on the American literary canvas.

Bernard Malamud is one of the most extraordinary novelists and short story writers in this country. His novel, *The Assistant,* is a brief, highly disciplined work of art about a Jewish grocer, his wife and daughter and their relationship with an Italian who, in the end, converts to Judaism. The poverty of the Jews in the throes of the great depression of the 1930's, the agonizing awareness of the Italian that he has betrayed the Jews, the side remarks on the meaning of being a Jew—all these elements are blended by Mr. Malamud in a tremendously moving and richly conceived novel.

In *The Magic Barrel and Other Stories,* Mr. Malamud continued to display his sensitive approach to the American Jew. More than half of the tales in his book are about Jews and they are curiously old-fashioned. The dialogue seems to be directly translated from the Yiddish. The moods are gentle and caught on the printed page by a master of atmosphere. There is a story about a rabbinical student who tries to find a wife through a matchmaker and finally accepts a girl without morals; there is another about a Jew in Italy who finds in a refugee a man who is a symbol of his own conscience; there is a story about a baker who cannot lend money to an old friend because the baker's second wife doesn't understand the friendship between the two men. Each narrative is brief, incisive and gemlike. Mr. Malamud won the National Book Award for this collection and on the basis of his novel and short story collection is ranked as one of the most imaginative and gifted of American writers. That his material, his approach and spirit are Jewish, has done nothing to lessen the power of his work. That he has gained a national reputation is only further evidence that the Jewish writer, when he attains a peak of creativity, can be recognized as a major *American* writer.

It is remarkable, in view of the obstacles, that so much has been produced by so many and, in comparison with other American fiction, on so satisfactory a level. This writer once complained to the editor of a leading Jewish monthly that his magagine reviewed few Jewish novels in the course of a year. "Naturally," he replied. "Jewish fiction is so bad, why bother with it?" I remonstrated that the magazine reviewed Hemingway and Faulkner, when, as a Jewish magazine, its function was to give space to Jewish works, "Why," I asked, "do you expend space on Hemingway?" "Oh," he replied airily, "Because he interests me; the Jewish writers don't."

Listening to such views, it was no wonder that this writer at least has come to the conclusion that the Jewish writers in America often exhibit far deeper interest in Jews and Judaism than the editors who are theoretically duty-bound to seek them out and to encourage them to write on Jewish themes for American Jews.

In forty years, hundreds of Jewish novels have been published, more than two score of them outstanding works of fiction. On the basis of past performances, it is safe to predict that during the next two decades, American Jewish literary creativity will far excel and exceed the products of the past, for in the last ten years alone the caliber and the quantity of Jewish works of fiction have overshadowed the three previous decades. In spite of the plaints of the pessimists, we are in the midst of a rich period of creativity. Perhaps we need the perspective of time to judge it as it deserves to be judged.

PART IV

FAITH AND FUTURE–THE
DIASPORA-ISRAEL DIALOGUE

The observer of Jewish life can easily find plenty of arguments for or against the possibilities of Jewish survival in America. On the one hand there is ample evidence of desire for continuity. It can be seen in affiliation, preference for marriage with Jews, and loyalty to the Jewish people. . . . Some of these manifestations have been widely criticized, as for example, the substitution of philanthropy for learning and cultural or religious expressions, or the preoccupation with good will and non-sectarian activities. However, the desire to enhance the position of the Jewish group is also in part a result of loyalty to it, even when evinced in attempts to emphasize the worthwhileness of the Jewish people through contributions to non-sectarian institutions, to the general community that comprises both Jews and non-Jews, as well as through the support of Christian institutions. . . .

On the other hand, the case can also be made for the application to American Jewry of Ruppin's classical diagnosis that emancipated communities are headed for assimilation, in this particular case, because of the impact of emancipation and acculturation in the general American culture. . . . The integration of Jews into general American culture has been far-reaching in contrast to the diminution of integration of the individual in Jewish culture and the steady reduction of Jewish cultural expression with its own languages, literature, theatre and rich culture patterns in the home and community. . . .

While there has been a marked return to Jewish affiliation and identification among the "third generation"—the grandchildren of the immigrants—the position of the fourth generation remains a puzzle, particularly in view of its limited Jewish education and narrow Jewish contacts within a particular synagogue, class or association.

Indeed, it is possible to note both positive and negative trends, signs of hope and despair, in a community estimated to be to six million strong and in various stages of acculturation to American life and of readjustment to Jewishness.

ABRAHAM G. DUKER,
"Some Trends Affecting American Jewish Life"

INTRODUCTION

by JACOB FREID

JEWS UNDER DEMOCRACY AND DICTATORSHIP

Moshe Sharett in his essay "Jewry between East and West" argues that "the democratic climate of general liberty affords Jews the chance of exerting themselves for the preservation of their identity." This democratic opportunity is in virtual life-and-death contrast to the conditions of Jewish being and expression in certain totalitarian regimes, which even if not intrinsically or deliberately anti-Jewish, nevertheless "strike at the very roots of Jewish existence." Mr. Sharett's views have poignant import today when, despite Mr. Khrushchev's protest at the National Press Club during his visit to the United States in late Summer 1959, the curtain has descended on some three million Jews in the Soviet Union, and no Jewish voice is permitted in competition with the clank of their jailer's chains.

In Juan Peron's Argentina, totalitarianism was not especially anti-Semitic, and Jews were able to walk the tightrope required by life in the Peronist dictatorship until the overthrow of the government. In Joseph Stalin's and Nikita Khrushchev's Russia, beginning in 1938 when the Hitler-Stalin pact became a possibility, and particularly since 1948, this opportunity has not been vouchsafed the Jewish people. In Cuba in 1961, under Castro, the 12,000 Jews who are primarily middle class, were under economic duress. In 1962 their numbers are diminishing heavily.

A contrast in point between Franklin Roosevelt's America and Adolf Hitler's Germany illustrates the different experiences of Jews who lived in the United States democracy and the Nazi-Reich dictatorship during the years beginning with 1933.

Franklin Delano Roosevelt and Adolf Hitler both assumed the chief executive power in early 1933 at a time of profound

429

economic and political crisis for both the United States of America and Germany. The polarity of the opposite use each made of his power as the ultimate "yes" of a polity and people *in extremis,* will serve future historians, political scientists, and social psychologists as a classical demonstration of the different methods and ends of democracy and totalitarianism in a period of acute national distress. To the Jews the stark contrast was, and is, more than academic. It is imbued with life and death, with the mute testimony of six million witnesses. For Diaspora Jewry today, and for Israel and their future interrelationship and destiny, the debate on the reliability and validity of the difference for Jews and Judaism has fateful significance. It is at the heart of the question raised by the *sholele hatefuzah* (negators of the Diaspora) and the replies by American Jewry which follow.

The economic depression had started in 1929 and by 1933 had wrought havoc in both America and Germany. In the United States it had punctured the bubble of the post-World War I era of transient prosperity. Conditions were at their worst when Mr. Roosevelt entered the White House, March 4, 1933. Banks in thirty-eight states had been closed; 12,000,000 persons were unemployed, and bread lines formed in virtually every city. Farmers showed their contempt for law and order by carrying shotguns to farm foreclosure sales. In 1932 the American's quadrennial catharsis by ballot, not bullet, had elected a new leader.

"That man," as he was called by his foes, in his first inaugural address dissipated much of the gloom that enshrouded the nation with the inspiriting declaration that "the only thing we have to fear is fear itself." Evincing an abiding faith in America, Roosevelt's first great address was a prescription of social psychiatry by an intrepid democratic leader and consummate politician, infusing hope and courage into a country seeking a way to crawl out of the slough of economic despondency. His handling of the bank situation was prompt and courageous, and within a hundred days the government, at his behest, set up thirty emergency agencies—from AAA to TVA—to cope with the Depression by means of a New Deal in American presidential administration and exertion of executive power.

In demonic contrast, Adolf Hitler effected a collective paranoia clamorous to discover more enemies of the fatherland than the world had to hide. The same crisis which had projected Franklin Roosevelt out of the governor's mansion in Albany, New York, into the White House, after 1929, enabled the Hitler movement to become almost at once the dominant dynamic force in German public life. Hitler's movement was Nazism. Its leader was "Der Führer" whose semantic equivalent is unknown in the lexicon of American democracy and political history. Hitler's party was built on a military leadership principle with brownshirt stormtroopers (SA), and blackshirt élite guards (SS), prepared for civil war. Hitler showed his ability to play German intramural *machpolitik* by ear by his correct appraisal of the masses whose passions and fears he raised to a pathological fever pitch by his oratory against democracy, the Jews, and foreign powers as insidious foes responsible for the fatherland's plight.

On January 30, 1933, less than five weeks before the inauguration of Franklin Roosevelt, President Paul von Hindenburg made Adolf Hitler chancellor of Germany.

In the United States, Franklin Roosevelt was calming and encouraging the American people. In Nazi Germany, Adolf Hitler was enflaming the German people into the pathic mold of Nazism. Hitler's doctrine of the abomination of the Jews as the authors of all evil had its predictable results, as detailed by Jacob Lestchinsky's "Balance Sheets of Extermination." To the psychiatric quackery and cunningly ruthless Machiavellianism of the totalitarian society's chief demagogue, the public neurosis was an opportunity for seizure and exploitation. Its three greatest practitioners until their deaths, Benito Mussolini, Joseph Stalin and Adolf Hitler knew this then, just as Nikita Khrushchev, Mao Tse-Tung, Fidel Castro and other successors know it today. As masters of all media of communication in state-controlled, monolithic propaganda systems where the people were a captive audience, each was aided by the fact that in politics and propaganda there is no formal curb on charlatanry.

The very soberness of the post-World War II autopsy of Hitlerism with "churban" (catastrophe) literature's detailed description of Nazism's mammoth "Operation Murder," had a searing effect on world Jewry. Factual reports related the story of genocide perpetrated and successfully executed by the *Einsatzgruppen,* special Nazi task-forces created for the efficient, calculated extermination of men, women and children. Its readers were numbed into admission that in death, as in life, the Hitler story, including its chapter by Adolf Eichmann now being retold, still remains the greatest symbol of the malaise of Western culture and national racism, of the seductive lorelei call of the Emancipation in Germany summoning the Jews as lemmings to their doom.

The toll, in the case of the Einsatzgruppen, breaks down into statistics adding up to one million persons—one-sixth of the total Jewish victims. The human mind cannot visualize that figure of death in the living shape of myriads of individual human beings, innocent and defenseless men, women, and children falling before executioner's guns in massed graves; asphyxiated in ingeniously disguised gas-vans, scientifically exterminated in concentration camps. Nor was this a crime of passion, but deliberate, planned, premeditated murder, carried out as part of a systematic program of genocide, aimed at the destruction of foreign nations and ethnic groups by murderous extermination. The head exterminators were not underworld characters or *lumpenproletariat.* They were lawyers, sociologists, economists, college professors, intellectuals, artists, and even a clergyman, who performed their assigned tasks of liquidating Jews, gypsies and other racially "inferior" or "politically undesirable" people in the Nazi-occupied eastern territories. Odd Nansen, son of the Norwegian statesman Fridtjof Nansen of World War I refugee fame, said: "What happened is worse than you have any idea of. And it was the indifference of mankind that let it take place." The whole macabre story of this assembly-line death factory is summed up in the opening statement of Justice Robert H. Jackson, American Chief Prosecutor at Nuremberg: "If I should write these horrors in words of my own, you would think me intemperate and unreliable."

It is no wonder then that the death trauma of Jewry in Nazi-occupied Europe should have emotionally conditioned and affected the survivors who are now in Israel, and the people of

Israel, so many of whom had intimate kinship with one or more of the living or dead victims. To the negators of the Galuth the Nazi's toll was overwhelming evidence of the tragic history of exile. The East European Shtetl world of Sholom Aleichem had been destroyed—its only self-contained Jewish communities were cemeteries. German Jewry—the Germans of Jewish persuasion—mocked the handsome prints which had decorated Jewish homes of Prince Bismarck's victorious, proud, loyal Jewish soldiers of the fatherland at prayer before the fallen French city of Metz in 1870. The fate of their grandchildren and their great grandchildren was an unanswerable argument.

But to American Jewry the analogy was not appropriate. For them, fate and environment were as different as America and the Nazi Reich, and as Roosevelt and Hitler during the same fateful twelve years-plus of leadership which began in the same year 1933, and ended with their deaths in the same year, 1945.

The American-Israel dialogue which follows is conditioned by these differing experiences. To the extent that the reader, in addition to affirming the contentions of his own spokesmen in this exchange, can also be objective, as it were—appreciate intellectually (if not emotionally), and comprehend the vital arguments of the side he disagrees with—to that degree will he be able to bridge the psychological, educational and historical gap of understanding between Diaspora and Israel.

Weighing the arguments debated in the dialogue between the Diaspora and Israel in the balance with the pluses and minuses of Jewish life, it is legitimate for the American Jew to conclude with Robert Gordis, that it is not a case of Palestine *or* the Diaspora, but of Palestine *and* the Diaspora. That assimilation and deculturation are vital processes—are negative facts of Jewish life that must be admitted, recognized, lived with and contained. That regeneration, renascence, creativity, and growth are positive facts of Jewish life is also true. That the totals indicate there is significant actual and potential expression for creative American Jewish life cannot be denied.

The level of Jewish life will determine the degree to which its institutions and organizations sponsor activities infused with meaningful Jewish content and religious and cultural values.

There is already evidence of such a positive, incipient trend. It is sufficient to hope that gregariousness will become less and less the motivation for a maturing, self-educating and participating community, appreciative and attentive to past and present Jewish scholarship, religious commitment and secular morality and idealism.

American Jewry is in ferment. Allegiances, practices and forms are changing. The next generation should disclose whether this unique Jewish communal experience in the history of Diaspora will result in a mutation of distinct American Jewish forms, concepts and expression as the result of the amalgam of new social, economic, political, religious, and intellectual pressures.

AN UNORGANIZED COMMUNITY

As the catalytic reactions set in motion by Israel's statehood, the East-West conflict, and American Jewry's search for its *raison d'être* exert their influence in the new decade of the sixties, new relationships between the Diaspora, Zionism and Israel will emerge.

Mordecai Kaplan's vision of the possibility of American Jewish bodies joining the World Zionist Organization to make it the concrete symbol of the entire Jewish people—to give reality, direction and purpose to Jewish life—at present remains hope deferred. At the 1959 convention of the United Synagogue of America the proposal to have it join the WZO was not approved.

In the United States, Bernard Richards relates the story of "Organizing American Jewry" in his essay. Today the parts are still greater than the whole of American Jewry. B'nai B'rith and the American Jewish Committee remain as defections from the overall community relations body of American Jewry, the National Community Relations Advisory Council (NCRAC). A hopeful glimmer was the pro tem unity through the President's Conference made up of the leaders of eighteen national Jewish organizations, plus the American Jewish Committee's agreement to meet with Premier Khrushchev during his visit to the United States in 1959, although the meeting itself did not take place.

That the various important agencies are performing vital functions is not to be denied. That they believe these functions will be impaired by their affiliation with an organized, unified, representative Jewish community is a reflection of American Jewry's anarchic, still unachieved struggle for maturity and cohesion under an overall democratic discipline which permits diversity within unity. The President's Conference, the Synagogue Council of America, the Council of Jewish Federations and Welfare Funds, the American Zionist Council, and NCRAC are the current links in the chain of organization of the American Jewish Community. The needs of the early twentieth century spawned the American Jewish Committee, as the demands of World War I did the American Jewish Congress; those of World War II brought forth the American Jewish Conference. Whether, like the lost years from Hohenzollern to Hitler, from the Treaty of Paris in 1919 to the Fall of Paris in 1940, nothing will be done until the next cataclysm, is for the future to disclose. Perhaps some quasi-Federalist arrangement will evolve with autonomy for its constituent members, but with an overall representative organization entitled to speak on behalf of the entire community. Certain short-lived unity will occur in response to opportunity or crisis, if only for pro tem conferences as occurred in the case of the hoped-for meeting with Premier Khrushchev which did not materialize. With the end of the opportunity or crisis such marriage-of-convenience ententes splinter apart like weak confederacies into a pattern of self-contained, individual independencies.

CHAPTER TWENTY

EDUCATING THE JEWISH CHILD

by URIAH ZEVI ENGELMAN

Most of the Jewish institutions, traditions and ideals which were brought over from Europe and transplanted in American soil have undergone marked changes. They have taken on the color and quality of American civilization; they have become at once more vigorous and more efficient. This is exemplified by the transformation, for instance, of the Old European *Beth Keneseth* into the modern American Jewish Community Center; by the integration of the numerous tiny, well-meaning, but wasteful, charity societies into efficiently administered and expertly guided American Jewish social services; by the remarkable metamorphosis of the old tradition of *shtadlonut* into national democratic organizations. Even the old European *shul*, turned Temple, has become a socio-religious institution, irrespective of our attitude to the pietistic phase of its adjustment to American life and a strong factor for Jewish cohesiveness and greater social usefulness.

Yet it could still be said at the end of World War II* that Jewish education alone remained unadjusted to the general efficient tenor of American life. It remained almost exclusively old-world in organization and outlook; it remained, so to speak, un-Americanized, retaining both in content and in structure, with a few exceptions, the old-world *Heder pattern*—a multiplicity of small, independent schools, most of them poorly housed, conducted on a shoestring, with inadequate staffing, casual lay leadership, and archaic curricula.

* The 1958 findings of the first National Study of Jewish Education reported here, compared to those of 1946 will indicate recent trends—ED.

During the last decades, however, and particularly in the decade and a half since VE Day, new forces and trends have come into play in Jewish life, whose cumulative influence on Jewish education has yet to be appraised. Their immediate effects, however, can be seen in an acceleration of efforts to bring Jewish education at least organizationally to the level of efficiency of the other major institutions in the land, and culturally to bring it more closely within the general context of American life. The 1959 national report of the Commission for the Study of Jewish Education in the United States, sponsored by the American Association for Jewish Education, was a major step in this direction.

Almost invariably studies of Jewish education in America charge that Jewish parents have become progressively less interested in the Jewish education of their children. The over-sophisticated modern Jewish parents, the usual charge runs, unlike their old-fashioned parents of a generation or two ago, feel no loyalty to the religio-cultural tradition of their fathers and hence do not care to send their children to Jewish schools.

This charge, and this should be recorded at the very beginning, proves unfounded when tested in the light of facts. As a matter of statistical record, the number of children attending Jewish schools today is proportionately much larger than it was thirty or forty years ago.

While complete enrollment statistics for Jewish schools are not available for the entire country, estimates of such enrollment based on actual registration reports from many cities were made from time to time. The earliest such estimate was made by Dr. Charles S. Bernheimer in 1900. Another was made by this writer for 1946. The latest was made in 1958. In 1900, according to Dr. Bernheimer, 36,000 children were attending congregational and non-congregational Jewish schools. In 1945-46 the number grew to 231,028, an increase of 542 percent. (These figures do not include those for children taught privately.) In 1958, there were 553,600 Jewish children and youth (age seven to seventeen) enrolled, an additional gain of 240 percent. During this period the Jewish population increased from 1,058,135 in 1900 to close to 5,000,000 in 1945, an increase of 373 percent. Since

1945 the gain has been small, *The American Jewish Yearbook* for 1958 estimated it to be 5,255,000.

Jewish school enrollment during the six climactic decades of this century has thus more than kept pace with the increase in Jewish population. But what is even more significant, the number of families today giving their children some kind of Jewish education is relatively much larger than is indicated by the above percentages. For one thing, the size of the Jewish family in 1961 was much smaller than it was at the beginning of the century. In 1890, the Surgeon General of the United States in a special inquiry to determine "the birth, death and marriage rate of the members of the Jewish race . . ." had found that the average number of children per Jewish family was 4.66. Studies made by the author and other investigators showed that the American Jewish family was about 40 percent smaller (from about one to two children less per family). It was thus evident that in 1961 a larger number of families was required to make up a given school enrollment than in 1900. However, the average child in 1946 and today spends less time in the Jewish school than his schoolmate did several decades ago with the result that while there is a larger turnover there is also a smaller enrollment at any one time.

Enrollment

What proportion of Jewish children of school age is enrolled in Jewish schools is difficult to tell, since we do not know exactly how many Jewish children of school age there are in the country. Jewish population statistics published in the *American Jewish Yearbook* are very inadequate; for the most part they consist of rough estimates of the total population without subdivisions by sex or age. However, figures for the proportion of Jewish children of school age enrolled in Jewish schools are given in a number of community educational surveys made in recent years by the American Association for Jewish Education. This information, though not complete, does offer a useful basis for estimating conditions throughout the country as a whole.

In 1946 the proportion of children of school age attending Jewish schools, was 30 percent or below in the large metropolitan

centers, and varied between 30 and 56.2 percent in the smaller
towns. This statement requires some qualifications. The proportions related to the number of children attending Jewish schools
at any one time. The number of children who already had or
would attend Jewish elementary schools before they will have
reached adolescence, is much larger.

In New York City in 1958 the proportion of elementary school
children receiving Jewish schooling was 36.5 percent. For the
entire country the proportion was approximately 40 to 45 percent.

Dr. Israel S. Chipkin in his study *Twenty-Five Years of Jewish Education in the United States* called attention to this fact.
"It is wrong to conclude," he wrote, "that the number of children who receive a Jewish education in any community is limited to those who are counted in school at any particular time."
Thus he stated, "it would be more correct to say that not 23
percent but probably 70 percent of the Jewish children of New
York City in 1935 have received or will receive a Jewish education during their school age." Jewish educators estimate that
between 70 and 85 percent of the Jewish children in the United
States have received or will receive some Jewish education.

The Jewish School System

The Jewish schools fall into three categories: (a) the Sunday
school, (b) the weekday afternoon school and (c) the all-day
(parochial) school. The Sunday schools had slightly more than
half of the total Jewish school enrollment, 120,365 or 52.1 percent in the school year of 1945-46. The afternoon weekday
schools had a registration of 101,384, or 43.8 percent (included
in this number were about 13,000 children who attended the
Yiddish schools), and the day schools claimed 9,279 pupils, or
4.1 percent.

In 1958 the Sunday schools had 249,662, or 45.1 percent; the
the afternoon weekday schools had 261,287, or 47.1 percent (including the Yiddish schools enrollment of only 1.0 percent);
the day schools had 42,651, or 7.8 percent.

Since 1948 the proportion of Sunday school pupils *decreased,*
and that of the weekday afternoon schools *increased;* whereas
the day schools *kept pace* with the general enrollment increase

in all types of Jewish schooling. The increase was largest for weekday afternoon schools (161.2 percent), next largest for day schools (131.2 percent), and least for Sunday schools (106.7 percent).

The general direction appears to be toward more intensive Jewish education for a larger number of children.

The economic depression of the thirties adversely affected the Jewish schools. Cuts in budgets led to a general deterioration of the Jewish school system which was reflected in curtailed number and length of school sessions, reductions in teachers' salaries, smaller enrollments and lowered scholastic standards. The war sharpened these trends still more. But as the war continued there developed in the country, as a reaction to the irreligious and inhuman doctrines of Nazism, a reawakening of interest in religious education, coupled with a re-emphasis on the religious basis of our civilization. Jews shared in this general reawakening. They were also moved to greater affirmation of their Jewishness under the cumulative effect of the assault of European anti-Semitism on Jewish life and culture. Under these influences, active Jewish interest in Jewish education in America became increasingly stronger as the war lasted. Jewish school enrollment increased in many cities, both small and large. Programs were intensified and greater appropriations for Jewish education were made in most communities.

In the first school year after the war, Jewish Sunday school enrollment in the entire country—on the basis of a polled sample of ninety cities—increased 5.2 percent. In New York City the registration in the Reform Sunday schools, according to the report of the New York Federation of Reform Synagogues, which comprise thirty-four synagogues conducting schools, increased from 7,245 to 7,822, or 7.3 percent. In the afternoon weekday schools the enrollment in the country was 7 percent greater. The elementary afternoon schools of all types shared in the general increase. The two-day-a-week schools, however, claimed the largest proportionate increase with 23.7 percent, followed by the three-day-a-week school with an 8 percent increase, the four-day-a-week school with 7.8 percent and the five-day-a-week school with approximately 2.1 percent.

There was a marked postwar increase in the enrollment of pupils in the Hebrew high schools. The *Herzliah* Hebrew Academy of New York opened a junior Hebrew high school in 1945. The enrollment of the entire school rose from 333 in 1942, to 437 in 1945, and to over 500 in 1946. The Hebrew high school *Marshalliah*, conducted by the Jewish Education Committee of New York, reported a yearly increase in registration of 12 to 15 percent from 1943 to 1946. Its present enrollment is over 600. Increased Hebrew high school registrations were also reported from Philadelphia, Buffalo, Boston, Los Angeles, Cincinnati, Minneapolis, and many other Jewish centers.

Hebrew classes in the public high schools of New York recorded an increase in registration of close to 6 percent. During the academic year 1945-46 Hebrew was taught in New York City in sixteen senior, two junior, and two evening high schools.

The teaching of Hebrew in New York colleges also expanded considerably during the past few years. The New York School for Social Research introduced Hebrew in its curricula for the 1945-46 sessions. New York University established a chair in Hebrew culture and education in 1944. Hunter College in 1945 incorporated Hebrew and cognate courses into the college's regular program and their maintenance will be covered by the college budget. Hebrew is also taught at Columbia University and Brooklyn College. Outside of New York, according to a report made in 1946 by Dr. Abraham I. Katch, assistant professor of education at New York University, at least 261 American colleges and universities accepted Hebrew as meeting the school's language requirements, while at least 95 other colleges and universities (exclusive of theological schools and seminaries) teach Hebrew.

The Sunday School

The earliest Jewish Sunday schools in the United States appeared, according to Dr. Julius H. Greenstone, a historian of Jewish community life in America, in response to the need for free Jewish communal educational institutions, unattached to any congregation. The first such schools were organized in Philadelphia and in Charleston, S. C., in 1838. In the following years free Sunday schools were established in Richmond, Va., Cincinnati, New York and other communities. In the course of time, many of them came to be conducted under congregational auspices. The schools met on Sunday mornings for sessions lasting from one to three hours. Originally, the course of instruction in a Sunday school consisted of Bible history and catechism.

A modern Sunday school curriculum embraces a variety of subjects: Jewish history, ancient, medieval and modern, customs and ceremonies, readings from the Bible, Zionism, Jewish problems, current events, Jewish community organization, the Hebrew language, Jewish literature, singing and artcraft. Many Sunday schools, however, teach only Jewish history, customs, and ceremonies. The addition of any of the other subjects of the curriculum usually depends on initiative of the faculty and the school's available resources.

The major difficulty which besets the Sunday school is that the time allotted for instruction is entirely incommensurate with the program it is called upon to cover. Realization of this deficiency has, in recent years, caused many Sunday schools to increase the time of instruction, first by lengthening the Sunday session and then by adding one, two or more sessions during the week.

In 1924, Dr. Emanuel Gamoran, in a study of 125 schools, found the average length of a Sunday school session was 1.9 hours. A study made in 1946 of 317 Sunday schools distributed over 37 states revealed that the majority of schools, 211, or 63.4 percent, meet for two-hour sessions; 72 schools, or 22.7 percent, for two and a half hours; 10 schools, or 3.1 percent have three-hour sessions; while 24 schools, or 7.5 percent, reported one and a half-hour sessions.

No data is available as to how many Sunday schools have weekday sessions. Their number has increased greatly during the past few years.

In most Sunday schools the program of the weekday session is devoted to the study of the Hebrew language and allied subjects. It is conducted as a separate school. In all cases, however, the weekday school registration is smaller than on Sunday.

Another difficulty that faces the Sunday school is the lack of trained teachers. The short period the school is open during the week and the small budget it ordinarily operates on has deterred capable young men and women from adopting Sunday school teaching as their profession. In consequence, the majority of the Sunday schools operate with volunteer untrained teachers whose knowledge of Jewish subjects is meager. In recent years this defect has been partly remedied by the establishment of in-service training institutes for Sunday school teachers, especially in those cities where central (communal) agencies of Jewish education have been organized. Another favorable development in Sunday school education is the great improvement in the Sunday school text books developed in the last twelve to twenty-five years. The modern Sunday school texts are well graded, well written, attractively printed and bound. A major contribution in this field was made by the Union of American Hebrew Congregations, which, under the leadership of Dr. Emanuel Gamoran, pioneered in the publication of Sunday school text books.

The Afternoon Weekday School

Originally, the congregation and the private *melamed* were the purveyors of Hebrew education to American Jewish children. In the '80's of the last century, when eastern European Jewish immigration grew in volume, communal Talmud Torahs were established which derived their support and leadership mainly from the local neighborhoods. The Talmud Torahs held their classes on weekdays after public school hours. They were, and in a very real sense still are, replicas on a much smaller scale of the East European *Heder*. The curriculum included the study of the *Siddur* and the entire synagogue liturgy, the Pentateuch with the commentary of Rashi, the Former Prophets and the *Shulhan Aruk*. While Jewish life in America has become spiritually and physically markedly different from what it was in Europe, the Talmud Torah curriculum has changed but little from that of the old *Heder*. The same subjects are taught, even in the same sequence, with the same emphasis on orthodoxy and conformity to traditional practices. Only with this difference:

In the East European *Heder* the child attended a whole day from early morning till late in the evening; in the American Talmud Torah the child attends only between one and two-and-a-half hours a day. When the shorter period made it impossible for the child to cover the old curriculum, the latter was simply abridged. There is no time for the study of the entire Pentateuch in the original, so frequently an abbreviated text is used; there is no time for the teaching of the *Shulhan Aruk* in the original so *broches* and customs are taught instead.

The idea of adjusting the curriculum to the new American environment either through the introduction of new subjects, or through a new emphasis in the teaching of the older and basic subjects, did not even occur to the early Jewish educational workers. Nevertheless, in the immigrant milieu of early twentieth-century America, the Talmud Torah, despite all its defects, was a relatively efficient institution. It taught a body of knowledge and a system of *mores* in an environment which was still predominantly East European and one in which these *mores* were still vital.

During the second decade of this century, many Talmud Torahs were large educational institutions, well staffed and supervised. They enjoyed the support of people outside their immediate vicinity, were in a sense communal institutions, and free to children of parents unable to pay the required tuition fees.

But following World War I, the development of the Talmud Torahs was greatly influenced by two factors, both stemming out of important trends in American life.

The period of postwar prosperity accelerated the process of movement away from the original and dense areas of Jewish settlement. The old Jewish neighborhoods in the Talmud Torahs dwindled. More important, the experience of living in America, in a country of political democracy, religious pluralism, and social and economic fluidity, was beginning to change the religious landscape of the Jewish community. The major component in the new religious landscape was the rise of the modern, orthodox and conservative congregations, which were springing up all over the country, especially in the newer sections. These congregations, under the leadership of young American rabbis, soon became the hub around which the social, cultural and religious life of the members revolved. The program of social and cultural activity as well as of religious ritualism developed by the congregations included the late Friday evening service, the social hour, the Bar Mitzvah Brotherhood with its Sunday morning service and breakfast, the greater use of English in prayers, the modified prayer book for the Sabbath and the holidays, the Men's Clubs, the Sisterhoods, the adult classes and book review groups. All these represented a serious attempt on the part of a large segment of American orthodoxy to adjust itself through the synagogue to the American environment. This adjustment, whatever the reaction to it on a religious basis might be, unmistakably constituted an enlargement of Jewish social and cultural life in terms and in accents of the new American milieu.

Regretfully, this cannot be said about the schools which the new congregations opened for the members' children. If the early American Talmud Torah was a diminutive replica of the old East European *heder,* the congregational school in the new neighborhood became a shrunken edition of the former. In theory, the congregational school retained the old curriculum in its entirety. Unfortunately the time allotted for covering the subjects included in the curriculum was greatly curtailed, from about ten to four hours a week. The child's life in the new neighborhood was filled with many new academic and social interests, while the parents' loyalties for the legalistic piety the old curriculum was to inculcate was also greatly weakened. As a consequence less and less was now taught of each of the classical Talmud Torah subjects.

The new congregational schools being both "denominational" and neighborhood in character, lack the broad human and financial base of the community school. They have small enrollments —are one- or two-teacher institutions—while the older Talmud Torahs they are replacing have been reduced to a shadow of their former size.

In 1918 there were forty schools in New York City with an average enrollment of sixty-five pupils, accounting for 6.3 percent of the total enrollment in all afternoon schools; in 1944

the number of such schools, only with smaller average enrollment, was 238, together comprising a third of all children enrolled in the afternoon weekday schools of the city. In other
words, the number of small schools, having each on an average
of fifty children, increased sixfold during the years 1918-1944.
In 1918 there were eleven schools in New York City each having
over 600 students, making up 21.6 percent of the total registration in the city. In 1945 there was not a single school in the
city with 600 or more pupils.

Small schools well organized, supervised and staffed, allow for
careful grading, and are very desirable. They usually make for
the good scholastic progress and cultural development of their
students. The per capita cost of maintaining such schools is
naturally very high. It is beyond the means of the average congregation even in prosperous times. Because of this, and other
factors, such as frequent changes in lay and rabbinical congregational leadership, lack of sustained educational policy, and
in very many cases poor housing facilities, the small congregational schools, both orthodox and conservative, as well as the
small community Talmud Torahs, are for the most part badly
administered, poorly financed, staffed and graded.

Decline in Study Hours

Two or three decades ago, children attended the afternoon
week-day schools five days a week, Sunday through Thursday.
However, by 1946 the five-day-a-week school was no longer the
predominant type. Of 303 week-day schools canvassed in 96
communities, 29.7 percent met five days a week, 26.6 percent
had four sessions per week; 23.9 percent, three sessions; and
19.6 percent met twice a week. These figures tell only half the
tale. In most Talmud Torahs of a generation ago, the daily
session lasted two hours, in some even two and a half. A child
thus received a total of ten and more hours of instruction a
week. In 1945-46, the number of such schools accounted for
only 9.6 percent of all afternoon weekday schools. Three quarters of all afternoon schools in the country in 1946 reported a
time schedule of four or five hours of instruction per week.
This was half, or less, of that which prevailed in the old Talmud

Torahs, while in 16.4 percent of the schools the children met
for totals of from one to three hours each week.

Parochial Schools

Prior to the development of the free public school system,
almost all non-Jewish schools were denominational. Jews, who
were reluctant to have their children study general subjects
in schools conducted by Christian churches, opened their own
all-day schools in which both secular and Jewish studies were
taught. By the middle of the nineteenth century the leading
synagogues of the city conducted all-day schools. In 1854, the
Catholics had seventeen parochial schools in New York; the Jews
seven, with 857 pupils; and the Protestants, six. But in the following years the trend was reversed. By 1860 most of the Jewish
parochial schools disappeared. The reason for this sharp change
was the new attitude of the state to religious education in the
schools which allowed for their secularization.

In the last quarter of the nineteenth century, an immigrant
element bred on Talmud learning came to the United States.
They established *yeshivoth*, under which name the all-day parochial schools have become known. The first such *yeshivah*,
Etz Hayim, was established in 1886. Jewish subjects were taught
in the morning and secular subjects in the afternoon. Growth of
the *yeshivoth* was very slow. By 1918, there were only four
yeshivoth in New York City. During the following years the
yeshivah movement gained a new type of adherent: Jewish
parents who were not so much interested in fostering talmudic
learning as in giving their children a sounder Hebraic education
than was offered in the afternoon weekday school. By 1929,
there were in New York City sixteen all-day Jewish schools with
a total enrollment of 4,290 pupils. During the last decade and
a half, the all-day Jewish school was given an added impetus
by American Jewish orthodoxy. The latter, energized by the
infusion of militant religious elements who came to America in
the wake of Nazi persecution and the war, became very active
in organizing *yeshivoth*, both in New York City and throughout
the country. There were in 1946 all-day Jewish schools in at least
thirty-five cities with a total registration of close to 10,000 pupils.

Many of the new all-day schools were established on a shoestring and were poorly staffed and inadequately housed. Their enduring quality was yet to be tested. "Whether or not the movement will spread or suffer the fate of the Jewish parochial schools that existed in the first half of the last century, time alone will permit us to judge," was the comment made by the writer at that time. By 1958 the evidence was strongly positive that the movement was spreading.[*] This remains true in 1962.

Despite the recent upsurge in the organization of *yeshivoth*, the overwhelming majority of American Jews, according to all indications, will look to the afternoon weekday schools and to the newly developing summer camp-schools as the major educational institutions for giving a Jewish education to their children. But the average man and woman tend to feel that the parochial schools, like the rich private academies and institutions, function somehow outside or beside, but not completely integrated with, the American system of public education. These Jews, at the same time, fully affirm their democratic right to such schools if they want them. What they frequently question, however, is the wisdom of using these rights.

The American Jew values the American public school. It symbolizes to him the best there is in the American democratic tradition. Instinctively, he feels that the public school is America's crucible. Within it children of all ethnic groups, heritages, social backgrounds and religions, meet and mix, and learn to act and live cooperatively as Americans. The average American Jew, though wary about the parochial schools, is not unaware that the present afternoon weekday and Sunday schools have to a large extent failed to teach Israel's heritage to his children, have failed to implant in them a desire to till the gardens of Jewish learning. And what is infinitely worse, he feels that the present afternoon weekday Jewish schools do not give his child the moral wisdom which was always the core and the outcome of all Jewish learning. Great and deep as this failure is, he refuses to despair or rush headlong into parochialism. The failure, he believes, is due to a number of objective conditions, which made the afternoon weekday school ineffective.

[*] See points 5, 9, 18 in this essay on Day Schools.

But these conditions can be corrected. One needs but mention the efforts being made in a number of cities to lengthen the total period the child spends in the afternoon weekday school through the organization of Hebrew pre-school classes, kindergartens, summer city day-camps and rural camp-schools.

The Yiddish Schools

The Yiddish afternoon weekday schools were first established in 1910. In the last decade of the nineteenth and the first decades of the twentieth centuries, radical social and economic philosophies flourished among Jewish and non-Jewish immigrant circles in America. These philosophies were militantly anti-religious. The Yiddish radical press of the period campaigned vigorously against every expression of Jewish nationalism as well as against all Jewish religious and folk customs. Yom Kippur atheistic balls, staged in the very heart of Jewish neighborhoods close to synagogues filled with worshippers, were ungraceful but frequent spectacles in those years. It was a reaction and a corrective to these radical assimilationist philosophies that the Yiddish school movement originated.

From the very beginning the Yiddish schools emphasized the nationalistic and the cultural elements of the Jewish heritage.

With the advent of the Bolshevik Revolution in Russia, there occurred a temporary resurgence of radical assimilationist moods among the Yiddish-speaking working groups. The effect of this resurgence was reflected in the Yiddish schools. The latter attenuated the Jewish phase of their curricula and emphasized the proletarian and international elements. With the rise of Nazism in Europe and the worsening of the Jewish situation in Poland, these trends all but disappeared.

Reflecting a new orientation of the Yiddish-speaking groups, as well as a growing feeling of rootedness in the American soil, the Yiddish schools began to cultivate in the child an appreciation of Jewish values through greater emphasis on the study of the Bible, the Hebrew tongue, customs and ceremonies, and Jewish community life.

Yiddish schools, unlike the afternoon weekday schools, are affiliated with central organizations. There are three such organizations: the Central Committee of the Jewish Folk Schools conducted under the auspices of the Jewish National Workers Alliance and the Poale Zion; The Education Department of the Workmen's Circle; the Sholom Aleichem Folk Institute. In 1946 the total enrollment of all the Yiddish schools was over 13,000. The Jewish Folk Schools of the Jewish National Workers Alliance (Farband) claimed 6,000 pupils. These were distributed in forty-four afternoon schools (fourteen in New York City, twenty in other cities in the United States, and ten in Canada); twelve high schools (one in New York City, six in other cities in the United States and five in Canada); eight kindergartens, and three schools for higher studies. The Farband school system is headed by a Teachers Seminary and People's University.

In 1946, the schools of the Workmen's Circle had a total enrollment of 5,648 pupils. These were distributed among ninety-one schools (thirty-six in New York City and fifty-five outside New York). The enrollment in the elementary schools was 5,030 (1,780 in New York City and 3,250 outside). Eight kindergartens had an enrollment of 195 and the high schools a registration of 385 (270 in New York City and 115 in Chicago, Philadelphia and Toronto). The Workmen's Circle School system also included pedagogic courses for the training of teachers. In 1945 the courses were attended by thirty-eight students.

In 1946, the Sholom Aleichem Folk Institute consisted of twenty-three affiliated schools (sixteen of these in New York City and seven outside), four kindergartens, one high school. The elementary schools had an enrollment of 1,200 pupils (940 in New York City and 260 outside of New York); the kindergartens 105 pupils and the high schools 40.

In 1958, the estimated Yiddish school enrollment for the entire country had fallen to 6,000, a decrease of 54 percent There were 3,367 Jewish schools in the United States. There were 1,760 weekday afternoon schools, 1,393 Sunday schools, and 214 day schools.

Cost of Jewish Education

The cost of Jewish education has risen much during the past generation. In 1935, Dr. Samson Benderly estimated the cost of maintaining the Sunday, afternoon weekday and parochial schools, at $4,900,000. This writer finds that American Jewry spent the sum of $14,800,000 in 1946 on its Jewish schools (Sunday, weekday and parochial), an increase in eleven years of 200 percent. This increase was brought about by the larger school enrollment in 1946 and the general increase in the cost of living, but chiefly because of the greater readiness on the part of communities to allot more money for Jewish education. Thus in 1942, federations and welfare funds in forty-five cities allocated $795,098 for Jewish education out of the total sum budgeted for local needs. In 1944, the aggregate amount allowed for Jewish education in 56 cities by federations and welfare funds was $1,130,931, an increase of 42.2 percent. During this period the total amount allotted in these same cities for local needs by federations and welfare funds rose from $12,470,648 to $14,724,622, an increase of 18.1 percent. The increase in education allotments was thus relatively more than twice as large as those made by federations and welfare funds for local needs.

In 1947, $2,215,911 was allocated for Jewish education out of a total budget of $24,901,458 by fifty-five cities. In 1957, the amounts were $3,902,299 and $38,426,202 respectively.

The total cost of Jewish education in 1946 was actually even larger than the sum of $14,800,000, given above. The latter does not include the cost of maintaining the seminaries for training teachers, nor the cost of private instruction, nor the expenditures of the local central agencies of Jewish education, which in 1945-46 had an aggregate budget of $1,673,183.60. (Between 25-50 percent of a central agency's budget, depending upon the community, is spent on school subventions, and is included in the $14,800,000.)

By 1958 it was estimated that the Jews of America were spending over $60,000,000 annually for the Jewish schooling of their children, elementary and secondary—about $110 per pupil per annum. In 1958 dollars, adjusted for the rise in the cost of living, the sum spent on American Jewish education is estimated to have increased by about 230 percent since 1947.

The per capita cost of educating a Jewish child either in

Sunday, weekday or parochial schools increased greatly during the 1936-1946 decade. In 1936, the per capita cost of educating a child in a Sunday school was $10; in 1946, about $25. Likewise, the cost of educating a child in an afternoon weekday school had risen from $35 a year in 1936 to almost $85 in 1946; the annual per capita cost of parochial education had grown from $100 to over $300. In 1958, as noted, the per capita cost for all pupils was $110 a year.

Problems

Many of the defects of the Jewish school of today derive from the looseness of its organization. This observation applies to all schools whether under reform, conservative, orthodox, or ultra-orthodox management. Each school is a law unto itself and functions outside of a school system. This shows up in the total absence of general standards of admission, achievement and promotion. Thus, for instance, no definite age norm is set for the child's admission either to the weekday or the Sunday elementary school. Hence, at each registration period, in almost all schools, children from seven to twelve years of age and over are admitted. This practice usually results in children of various ages studying in the same classes.

The difference between the ages of the children in the first-year classes is six and seven years. In a normal elementary school these children would be separated from one another by six and seven classes. In other words, some of these children would be in the graduating class. In the case of the Hebrew school, however, they are all together in the beginners' class. The same age spread exists also in the second-year classes. The abnormality of the age composition of the children in each class is also shown by the fact that children over ten and eleven years of age are found in all classes, from the first to the last.

It is obvious, even to the uninitiated, that such an age composition precludes normal scholastic progress and cultural development of the pupils, since children of six, nine, ten, eleven and twelve years of age cannot learn at the same pace and must not be in the same class. And what is equally as bad, such classes are a source of grievous irritation and frustration to the teachers whom it robs of any possible pride or satisfaction in their work.

This absence of admission standards is only equalled by lack of standards in promotion and graduation. But educational sins, like social sins, carry their own penalties. In this case the penalty is the very low retentive power of the Jewish school, especially the afternoon weekday school. According to Dr. Israel S. Chipkin, who made educational surveys in many cities, more than four-fifths of the enrolled children in the afternoon weekday schools stay less than two years. This conclusion has been corroborated by Dr. Leo L. Honor, Dr. Alexander M. Dushkin, Dr. Ben Edidin, Dr. Aharon Kessler, Dr. David Rudavsky, Mr. Judah Pilch, Mr. Louis Ruffman, and a host of other investigators, who have made community educational surveys.

The relatively short period Jewish children stay in Jewish schools—about two years—is the cause of one of the major problems in American Jewish education. Jewish educators have been long aware of the fact that during the short period the child stays in the elementary Jewish schools, the most that can be expected of him, in addition to his acquiring some knowledge of Jewish subjects, is favorable conditioning toward an emotional and aesthetic appreciation of Jewish life and values. But this conditioning fades out and the little knowledge he acquires is soon forgotten unless the child continues his Jewish studies as an adolescent and reinforces his understanding of Judaism on a more mature level. But this is exactly what the Jewish child can rarely achieve because in most cases the Talmud Torah or the congregational school does not prepare him for continuing his studies on a secondary level. And in those cases where the school succeeds in carrying some of its pupils past graduation, the school finds it is unable to maintain high school classes for its graduates. To maintain well-graded high school departments involves considerable expenditure of money and the employment of special personnel, while the yearly number of graduates of an individual school is very small. As a consequence, the per capita cost of Hebrew high school education is prohibitive for most schools. In many cities, of late, in order to meet this difficulty, central Hebrew high schools were organized. But the establishment of such schools involved a degree of community cooperation which not many cities have been able to achieve.

Teacher Shortage

A major problem that faces Jewish education today is lack of trained teachers and executive personnel. The extent of this shortage was disclosed in a community teacher survey. According to it, at least 620 principal Jewish communities, each having one or more congregations, are in need of teachers and principals for their weekday schools, or executive directors for conducting community educational programs. The available supply of such personnel falls far short of the actual need. A canvass of the eight major Jewish institutes in the United States (Baltimore, Pittsburgh, Boston and Chicago Teachers Institutes, Teachers Institute of the Jewish Theological Seminary of New York, Teachers Institute of Rabbi Isaac Elchanan Theological Seminary of New York, Herzliah Teachers Institute of New York, Gratz College, Philadelphia) has shown that during 1946 they graduated altogether only fifty-two teachers.

In the 3,367 Jewish schools of the United States in 1958, there were 17,483 teachers. The average number of teachers per school was 5.2 (4.0 in the weekday and day schools and 6.8 in the Sunday schools). The average size per class was 15.7 in the weekday and day schools and 21.2 in the Sunday schools.

The Community Enters the Field

Jewish education is today historically in the same position in which Jewish social service was a generation or so ago, when Jewish communities were dotted with innumerable charity societies. But as Jews grew in number, in diversity of interests, and became more urbanized and industrialized, the small charity societies coalesced and in time gave place in each city to central agencies of Jewish social service. But this process of coalescence was gradual and was preceded by a reorientation of American Jewry regarding the function of charity in an industrial society and the community's responsibility for it. This reorientation involved the acceptance of the principle that in an industrial society the basis for philanthropy is not pity felt by the individual, but a sense of civic responsibility of the entire community.

A similar process is now taking place in the field of Jewish education. The American Jewish community is coming to realize that the Jewish education of a child, in addition to being a parental and a congregational responsibility, is also a major community obligation.

Bitter experience has taught American Jews that the consequences of a child's failure to acquire a Jewish education is not mere ignorance of things Jewish, but a spiritual void in the child which is only too quickly filled by the non-Jewish environment with a thousand and one subtle insinuations, half-truths, distorted evaluations and downright innuendos about any and all phases of Jewish life which the child, devoid of Jewish learning, accepts as "Jewish knowledge." The hurt such "knowledge" does to his personality, modern psychology tells us, is very great indeed. Belatedly, it has dawned on Jewish community leadership in many cities that it is as much a community obligation to forestall the inflicting of this type of hurt on its members, as to prevent or mitigate hurts caused by economic or other hazards over which the individual has no control.

The prophylactic against this type of personality hurt is effective Jewish knowledge, the ability of the child to take his stand behind the positive values of the Jewish religion, the millenia-old, rich experience of Jewish history and the great aspirations of his people for a national and religio-cultural renaissance. But the Jewish school of the past, the Jewish community has learned to its distress, failed as an educational medium, its failure being mainly due to the fact that it functioned in isolation, being thrown on its own limited resources. The Jewish school, in order to be successful, must become part of a well-organized school system, which would comprise kindergartens, graded elementary schools, junior and senior high school classes, summer school camps, where in the atmosphere of outdoor camp life, the pupils would devote themselves to the study of Hebrew and related subjects, and lastly, it must be supplemented with a year-round program of supervised recreation, integrated with the schools' courses of study.

But such a program is beyond the means of any one single congregation or organization. Only an organized community, which could draw on all strata of the population, could marshall the financial and human resources needed for the task.

Central Education Agencies

This new awareness of the community's part in the development of Jewish education has found concrete expression in the establishment of community central agencies of Jewish education. There were in 1946 twenty-nine such local agencies; twenty-two were organized since 1930. These agencies are usually known as boards, bureaus or councils of Jewish education. Among central agencies of Jewish education are those in the following cities: Akron, Atlanta, Baltimore, Boston, Bridgeport, Buffalo, Canton, Chicago, Cincinnati, Cleveland, Columbus, Dayton, Detroit, Indianapolis, Los Angeles, Miami, Milwaukee, Minneapolis, Newark, New Haven, Omaha, Paterson, Philadelphia, Pittsburgh, Rochester, St. Louis, St. Paul, Syracuse, Schenectady, Toledo. At present, the scope of the Bureau's activities varies in different cities. In some, it may be confined only to the promotion, coordination and servicing of existing Jewish educational programs; in others, it may involve initiation of new programs on a community-wide basis, such as the establishment of central Hebrew high schools or high schools for Sunday school graduates, community kindergartens or summer-school camps. While in still others it may, in addition, develop training classes for in-service teachers, classes for adults, Jewish libraries.

A demonstration of the possibilities of extending opportunities for Jewish education to areas hitherto unreached through community organization and planning was given in 1924, when a program of rural Jewish education was initiated by the regional Bureau of Jewish Education of Southern Illinois. During the first two years, thirty-seven of the sixty-seven scattered Jewish communities in the areas, covering 18,000 square miles, were serviced by the regional Bureau through nine centrally located Sunday schools. Children were transported distances of ten to sixty miles to attend classes.

A similar program was organized in 1945 for the rural communities of Maine, with the addition of the summer school-camp which offered an integrated Jewish educational and recreational program for the Jewish children of the state. The regional bureaus also developed programs of religious and cultural activities for adults.

The central agency of Jewish education is a new phenomenon on the American Jewish scene. But it is a significant development. It carries the promise of a public system of Jewish education, community financed, planned and supervised.

HOW CAN WE IMPROVE THE WORK
OF JEWISH SCHOOLS?

Ever since the earliest beginnings of Jewish educational activity in America, there have been inevitable gaps between ideals and achievements. Many voices were raised in the past calling for the improvement of Jewish education in organization and in results. To this end numerous local studies and surveys were made by communities with a view to increasing the adequacy and effectiveness of Jewish education.

During the past forty years, since World War I ended in 1918, the American Jewish conception of community has grown. The needs of world Jewry and of Israel demanded national action and required a change of emphasis in attention from local communities of neighbors to the trans-local community of historic interests and needs. This, the Jewish traditional meaning of community, is becoming dominant again in 1962, insofar as American Jewry is learning to act as one national community, not only in overseas programs but also in meeting its inner needs, which are becoming increasingly identified with needs of Jewish culture. The first National Study of Jewish Education in the United States is another indication of that growing process of planning and action on a national scale. Its purpose was to outline "the national image" of American Jewish education.

This study of Jewish education in the United States concentrated on elementary Jewish schooling and left other important areas for future studies. In this basic area, the study may prove a valuable frame of reference for local community evaluation and programming. Because there is still the inevitable gap between the ideal and the achievement in all educational effort, it is important that we consider which of the difficulties are inherent in the general situation and which in the conduct of the schools; which educational shortcomings can be solved by the efforts of individual institutions and which must inevitably call for common efforts and the joint commitment of the entire local or national community.

The study was organized to answer these five questions: What is Jewish education? Is Jewish education wanted—how much and what kind? How is the community organized for Jewish education? What do we teach our children? How can we improve the Jewish schools? The résumé of the study's findings, implications, and suggestions is incorporated in the following seventy-eight points:

1. Much progress has been made during the past decades (a) toward interesting parents and community leaders in the Jewish education of their children, (b) toward increasing enrollment in the Jewish schools, and (c) toward promoting in the children the sense of Jewish identification and of satisfying fellowship; but (d) little has been accomplished toward teaching our children the literary historic culture of their people. Consequently, American Jewish schooling is like a shallow river, "a mile wide and an inch deep."

During the coming decades, combined cooperative efforts will need to be made to deepen the stream of Jewish education.

2. Twelve community studies* bearing on local Jewish edu-

---

* Community reports were submitted to Akron, Ohio; Atlanta, Ga.; Buffalo, N. Y.; Camden, N. J.; Cleveland, Ohio; Detroit, Mich.; Miami, Fla.; Omaha, Neb.; Savannah, Ga.; Rochester, N. Y.; Los Angeles, Calif.; Washington, D. C. All reports were prepared by Dr. Uriah Z. Engelman, with the exception of Cleveland and Savannah, which were prepared by Prof. Oscar I. Janowsky and Dr. Engelman.

cational needs and problems require current organization for follow-up, leading to periodic self-study and evaluation on the basis of these reports and such additional investigations as may be found necessary.

What is American Jewish Education?

3. Eight thousand persons were questioned, including parents, community leaders, teachers, school principals, and high-school pupils, to learn what is in the minds of people when they think of the purposes of Jewish education. This type of investigation is important toward clarifying and emphasizing objectives, and toward increasing understanding among teachers, parents and all others involved in the education of our children.

4. Four categories are inherent in every complete statement of aims of Jewish education: (1) fostering the sense of belonging and identification; (2) imparting knowledge, specific and general; (3) engendering beliefs and values, attitudes and appreciations; and (4) inculcating practices and participation, ritual and communal. The prime though vague desideratum stressed by all groups interviewed or questioned was the imparting of knowledge in its various forms. However, most respondents are hazy as to the *nature* of that knowledge, though they feel that somehow "Hebrew, history, customs and ceremonies, and Bible" are parts of that knowledge.

This study of opinion has definite implications for Jewish education:

(*a*) The teaching of desired beliefs, attitudes, values, practices should be taught not abstractly as verbalized ideas or as imperatives, but as growing out of Jewish knowledge acquired in the study of literature, history, language and current life.

(*b*) If knowledge is to be a prime desideratum, then the time usually devoted to Jewish schooling and the conditions of its teaching and learning are quite inadequate. One or two school sessions per week, totaling two or three hours of study, may be of value in arousing in the child a sense of belonging and identification; it may even have value in attempting to inculcate certain ritual practices or doctrinal beliefs. It is not the way to acquire knowedge through study; especially if that knowledge is to be in the Hebraic sources and forms of our culture.

(c) Parents and community leaders must come to understand that they cannot project an "image" of Jewish education and yet accept conditions which make the realization of that image impossible. If they really desire their children to be Jews who have Jewish knowledge, then they must provide at least four basic conditions to make possible the achievement of that desire:

1. arrange for their children to give more time to Jewish study;

2. help them continue in Jewish school beyond Bar Mitzvah or Confirmation during the crucial years of adolescence;

3. insist that their children be taught by full-time, well-trained, knowledgeable Jewish teachers;

4. provide in the homes and in the community an atmosphere of respect and desire for Jewish culture and learning.

5. Of 1,560 community leaders queried, three-fourths were opposed to Jewish day schools, one-fourth approved. Jewish day schools are not viewed as "parochial"; the great majority (77 percent) are in fact, "noncongregational" schools. Besides the Orthodox elements, Conservative congregations and other groups are becoming interested in complete day schools or in foundation schools for young children.

6. There is a striking similarity in the official Orthodox, Conservative and Reform groups regarding fundamental or guiding principles, although they are implemented differently in educational practice. All three official curricula stress the teaching of Jewish knowledge. There is thus a community of basic ideas and principles on which the community and the different ideological and "denominational" groups can and should work together.

A National Curriculum Institute should be set up to concern itself continuously with the tasks involved in translating the general objectives of Jewish education into the realities of curriculum and teaching.

Is Jewish Education Wanted—How Much and What Kind?

7. In 1958 there were 553,600 Jewish children and youth (ages five through seventeen) enrolled in Jewish schools. The proportion of pupils to the total population was 10.5 percent for Jewish schools as compared to 22.4 percent in the general public and non-public schools. The great majority of parents want and provide some sort of Jewish schooling for their children. Jewish educators are therefore right in insisting that our problem is no longer that of getting our children to Jewish school, but of having them stay in the schools long enough to make that education valuable.

8. During the past decade (1948-1958) the total school enrollment increased by 131.2 percent; very much more than any assumed increase in the total Jewish population. Sociological and historic developments influenced groups and strata of Jewish parents who had hitherto not been enough concerned with Jewish education to send their children for Jewish schooling.

9. The enrollment in 1958 was distributed: 47.1 percent in weekday afternoon schools; 45.1 percent one-day Sunday schools; 7.8 percent day schools. The distribution in New York City where there were 154,000 pupils, was different from the rest of the country; fewer in the one-day schools (35.0 percent) and more in the day schools (21.4 percent). During the past decade, the largest enrollment increase was in weekday afternoon schools (161.2 percent), then in day schools (131.2 percent), and least in the one-day schools (106.7 percent).

There seems to be a rather constant general trend toward more intensive Jewish education for an increasing number of children.

10. There has been a steady growth of congregational schools as the prevailing type of Jewish schooling. In 1918 only 23.6 percent of Jewish pupils in New York were taught in congregational schools. In 1948, 82.7 percent of all pupils in the United States were in such schools, and in 1958 this proportion stood at 88.5 percent. It is therefore incumbent on leaders of the congregational organizations to reconsider the relation of these schools to the community with a view to clarifying their functions and increasing their effectiveness.

11. The *Hedarim* and *Melamdim* of a half-century ago, who then taught 36-38 percent of Jewish children, have virtually disappeared. In their place is an increase in the proportion attending one-day school at one end, and day school at the other. Despite shortcomings and basic difficulties, the overall pattern of American Jewish education has changed for the better during the past forty years.

12. During the past decade the enrollment increase was twice as large in the Jewish schools (131.2 percent) as in the non-Jewish religious schools (57-61 percent). The general "upsurge of religious sentiment" can thus account for only a minor part of the increase in Jewish schooling, which apparently resulted from a maturation of Jewish attitudes from within.

13. Jewish education is still wanted more for boys than for girls. Proportions are about equal in the one-day schools, but there are sixty-two boys to thirty-eight girls in the day schools, and seventy-one boys to only twenty-nine girls in the weekday afternoon schools. Tradition seems to be but one factor, and investigation of the causes of this inequality is necessary.

14. There is too great a concentration of enrollment (82 percent) of children eight through thirteen years old as compared to public school enrollment for those ages (47 percent); and consequently, insufficient enrollment (10.3 percent) at the primary level (ages four to seven) and at the high school level (7.7 percent).

Our children begin their schooling too late and leave it too early. In the weekday schools there is a marked and sudden drop in the enrollment of boys twelve to thirteen years old (17.7 percent) and those over thirteen years (3.8 percent). This verifies the well-known fact that for many boys Bar Mitzvah is the terminal point of their education. Efforts must be made to counteract the terminal character of the Bar Mitzvah ceremony. Also, greater efforts should be made to provide the proper educational setting for young children below the age of eight.

15. School enrollment is proportionately higher in the smaller communities than in the larger, in the less populous than in the more populous, in towns than in big cities.

16. Conservative orientation predominates in the weekday schools, the Orthodox in the day schools and the Reform in the one-day Sunday schools. The combined enrollment is 21 percent Orthodox, 38.6 percent Conservative, 28 percent Reform, 1.3 percent Yiddish, and 11 percent in other or multiple orientations.

17. Excluding the pupils in day schools, the average child outside New York devotes 1.8 sessions per week to Jewish education, and in New York City 2.7 sessions per week. There has been a marked trend during the past twenty years toward reducing the number of sessions for weekday pupils.

The best teacher in the best schools can achieve little in less than three sessions of one to two hours instruction per week. No far-reaching changes can be made toward more serious study and teaching until instruction time is extended. This is the challenge for the majority who wish their children to attend public schools and to receive supplementary Jewish education.

18. During the past fifteen years, Jewish day schools increased from 33 schools—26 in New York—to 214 schools—136 in New York. In 1958, there were 78 day schools outside of New York. The great majority of the day schools (77 percent) are non-congregational. Of all American children attending non-public schools in which both general and religious studies are taught, 91 percent are Catholic, 8 percent Protestant, 1 percent Jewish. The Jewish day schools resemble in auspices the "parent-society" type of school rather than the "parochial."

The dramatic increase of Jewish day schools indicates that they have met a deeply felt need for more intensive Jewish education. This increase, as of 1962, is continuing.

19. The daily attendance in the Jewish schools is good; somewhat better in the weekday schools (85-90 percent) than in the Sunday schools (80-85 percent). This better attendance in the weekday schools despite the greater demands on the child's time, may be an indication of a more serious attitude to the school by the children and parents.

20. However, the holding power of the schools through the years of schooling is not good. The average child attends about three years in a weekday afternoon school, or about four years in a Sunday school.

21. The reasons why children leave school, besides Bar Mitzvah, appear to be loss of interest by children, indifference of parents, and the lack of a transfer system to permit continued schooling in a new area.

Attitudes and Opinions

Some 11,000 pupils were questioned on their attitudes to Jewish education. The summary of their responses follows:

22. More than nine out of ten accept Jewish education as natural and desirable in the American environment, where, they say, all children should receive some form of religious education.

23. Most of the children—six out of ten—like their Jewish school and would attend it if given free choice. While this should be a source of encouragement, the fact that so large a minority of our children feel negatively about the Jewish school is a continuous challenge to teachers and community leaders.

24. The Jewish school interferes with free-time activities of almost three out of four children (72.9 percent), but only one out of four minds this interference "very much." Most of the children accept the interferences and limitations as rather natural in the American Jewish setting.

25. More pupils in Hebrew weekday schools like their schools than do pupils in one-day schools (65.8-62.9 percent), and more would attend that type of school if given free choice (61.5-56.9 percent). This is interesting in view of responses to other questions that would imply the contrary: the sense of greater interference of the weekday school with free-time activities (78.5-68.2 percent), the feeling that Hebrew school is "harder" than public school (53.8-25.1 percent), and that Hebrew teachers are less liked (72.7-79.3 percent). The data may imply that these children express an earnestness of attitude in "wanting to learn," despite difficulties.

26. More Jewish children like their public school than they do the Jewish school (91.6-64.2 percent). The fact that they like the public school teachers more than the Jewish teachers (84.4-76.1 percent), is one factor, with all it implies in teaching personality, training, methods and relationships. Children also make "many" more friends in the public school (85.7-63.9 per-

cent), due possibly to its larger number of pupils, its longer retention power, its more varied learning and social opportunities. Interference with free-time activities is doubtless also a factor, though not so determining as hitherto supposed. The atmosphere in the Jewish schools where 24.6 percent of the children report they "rarely or never have fun," the content of studies, the methods of learning, are other important factors that need further study.

27. The children in Orthodox schools have a more positive attitude toward their schools and studies than do the children in other schools. This is in all likelihood connected more with intensity of schooling and the ensuing sense of achievement than with any other factor.

28. Considerably less than half (41.2 percent) expected to continue their studies after Bar Mitzvah or Confirmation. Communities differed widely in this (26 to 61 percent). This needs further study because of its significance for efforts which must be made to extend Jewish schooling into the adolescent years.

29. The majority of 5000 Jewish high-school students (52 percent) interviewed to determine their attitudes, stated they continued their Jewish education beyond elementary school because they "wanted to learn more—religion, Hebrew and other subjects." If given a choice, 60 percent would continue to attend freely. They pointed to the content of their studies as the chief reason for their liking Jewish high school, and to poor teaching as their chief reason for disliking it.

30. Of parents interviewed, 90 percent stated they have greater interest in Jewish education now than they did fifteen to twenty years ago. Their reasons for choosing the particular school for their children were:

1. Convenience and social considerations (18.5 percent);

2. Family background and synagogue affiliation (27 percent);

3. The school's ideological orientation (9.7 percent);

4. School reputation and program (25 percent);

5. General educational goals (19.8 percent).

Denominational orientation does not seem to be a major factor in the choice of school. This is probably more prevalent in the new and suburban areas of population than in the older settlements.

31. Among Sunday school pupils, 84 percent of the mothers and 79 percent of the fathers were native-born; among weekday school pupils, 72 percent of the mothers and 64 percent of the fathers; among day school pupils, 64 percent of the mothers and 56 percent of the fathers.

The more intensive the type of education the lower the proportion of native-born parents. Whether this is a trend or only a descriptive fact deserves to be studied further.

Evidence from Financial Support

32. We estimate that 60 million dollars are spent annually on Jewish elementary and secondary schooling. This is an increase of 230 percent since 1947, as against an increase in school enrollment of 140 percent during those eleven years. This proportionately large increase was due to greater cost of all units (beyond adjustment to living index), and also due to the large increase in sums spent on the day schools which are the costliest.

33. About half the total educational budget is paid by parents in tuition fees and other forms. Considering that many parents cannot pay the full fees, and some must depend on free scholarships; considering also that no American schools, except the wealthy private schools, meet their expenses from tuition fees, the fact that Jewish parents not only send their children to Jewish school voluntarily, but pay a major part of the school budget, is another indication of the devotion of American Jewish parents to the tradition "thou shalt teach them. . . ."

34. The organized community, through federations and community councils, in 1957-58 contributed 7-8 percent of the sixty million dollar education budget. The rest of the funds needed (35-40 percent) is collected by the schools through wasteful methods from general contributors.

35. In fifty-five communities the total community budget for local needs increased by 54 percent during the past decade,

whereas the community allocations for Jewish education increased by 76 percent. However, the increases were only in the larger communities, and even these have not kept pace with enrollment increase—131 percent—during the decade.

36. Three-fourths of 1,560 community leaders who were asked who should bear the cost of Jewish education, stated that the cost should be shared among parents of the pupils, congregations and federations.

The progress to be made in creating cooperative community efforts for improving Jewish schools will depend in no small measure upon the readiness of federations to enter more actively into the area of Jewish education.

How Is The Community Organized for Jewish Education?

A. The Conditions of Jewish Schooling

37. There are many modern, fine Jewish school buildings. However, from more than a third to more than one-half are in need of repairs, renovations, replacement and construction. Communities should establish loan funds for this purpose to help schools to meet minimal housing requirements and to aid in planning and erecting buildings in new neighborhoods, in accord with the movement of Jewish populations.

38. There are 3,367 Jewish schools in the United States: 1,760 weekday afternoon schools; 1,393 one-day Sunday schools; 214 day schools. The great majority are small schools with enrollments smaller than needed for effective teaching and management. In the weekday schools outside of New York, 60 percent have enrollments of 100 pupils and less; 80 percent enroll 150 pupils or less. In New York City, 53 percent of all schools have enrollments of 100 pupils or less. In the one-day schools, half have enrollments of 100-125 pupils or less; only 30 percent have enrollments of 200 or more pupils.

The attempt to maintain tiny-sized weekday afternoon Jewish schools in cities and towns pays a tragic toll in ineffective part-time teachers, ungraded classes, practical impossibility to continue the educational program beyond the lowest levels, poor teaching (but for rare exceptions), poor educational results, "confused" children, frustrated parents, disheartened teachers and leaders.

For the good of American Jewish education, and particularly for intensive weekday Hebraic education, the number of small schools must be drastically reduced by reorganization and consolidation.

39. Congregations should be encouraged to limit one-day schooling attendance only to the primary grades (ages five to seven) and require all children thereafter to attend weekday afternoon schools.

40. There is no agency at present which is concerned with, or equipped to direct or to initiate experimental efforts in Jewish education on a large national scale. An immediate and vital need in American Jewish education is the establishment of a National Curriculum Institute for stimulating, guiding and aiding experimental undertakings by Jewish school teachers and administrators throughout the country.

41. Classification and grading in the schools are unsatisfactory. It is not economical, administratively or pedagogically, to teach classes of fewer than twenty pupils such as is the case with the great majority of classes in American Jewish schools.

42. Small classes and poor grading are inherent in small, self-isolated schools, and are among the pressing reasons for urging the consolidation of small schools wherever possible.

43. For the convenience of the children and for the better management of the schools, communities should organize common transportation systems, such as developed in Detroit and elsewhere.

44. The cost of schooling per pupil per annum, for all types of schools combined is $110, varying from $28 in the one-day schools, to $160 in the weekday schools and $480 in the day schools. The day schools cost $.23 per hour per year, the weekday schools $.45, and the one-day schools $.39.

45. Generally 70-75 percent of the school budget goes for staff salaries and instructional supplies; about 10-15 percent for building maintenance, and the rest for transportation, debt services, fund raising and other costs.

46. Efforts should be made to introduce more uniform and more reliable school records.

B. School Personnel

47. There are estimated to be 17,483 teachers, of whom 7,924 teach in weekday afternoon and day schools and 9,559 in one-day schools. The average weekday school has a staff of four teachers and the average Sunday school about seven.

48. Jewish teaching is a part-time occupation, not only in the one-day schools but to a large extent also in the weekday schools. Less than one-half of the teachers in the Hebrew weekday schools devote their full professional time and energy to Jewish education. Only 20 percent of the weekday school teachers teach a full-time schedule of twenty or more hours per week.

Few people can be expected to have as serious a commitment to part-time "extra" occupations as to their job in life. Some of the most difficult social-psychological problems in American Jewish education arise from the fact that so many teachers do not consider Jewish teaching seriously enough.

A far-sighted fundamental change of attitude toward teacher employment is necessary, based on commitments by school boards and parents: (a) that Jewish teachers in the weekday schools must be fully occupied in Jewish teaching and compensated according to the scale of salaries in the better elementary public school systems; and (b) the teacher's employed time should be supplemented on the basis of all educational needs and possibilities locally.

This will be more costly, but far less "expensive" than the present wasteful situation.

49. The general education of Jewish teachers is satisfactory. But their Jewish education is very uneven. Of the Sunday school teachers, 58 percent claim only elementary Jewish schooling of some sort, and 9 percent state that they had no Jewish schooling whatever. The perennial inbred weakness of the one-day schools is that they depend on the "ignorant to teach the ignorant."

50. Only 40 percent of the Jewish teachers in all schools received professional pedagogic training.

51. There is a constant and rapid turnover of staff. Twenty percent of the teachers in one-day and weekday schools are in the present post less than one year, and the majority less than three years. The lack of pedagogic training and the large turnover emphasize the need for proper supervision of their work and for their continued in-service training.

52. The school principals are older and more experienced than the teachers, but not much better trained professionally. A large plan of fellowships should be developed for the purpose of providing the special training required for the work of principals and supervisors. The National Board of License of the AAJE (American Association for Jewish Education) should issue and seek to enforce principals' licenses.

53. The teachers find especially satisfying in their work: the teacher-student relationship and helping children to become better Jews. They find especially dissatisfying: professional conditions (low salaries, no fringe benefits), attitudes of parents, and difficulties with curriculum and materials.

C. School Management

54. Over 30,000 men and women serve on Jewish school boards and committees. Common School Councils should be organized as instruments for broadening the educational outlook of schoolboard members, and to bring to them professional ideas and experiences.

55. The management of the congregational school presents special problems and opportunities. The large and adequate congregational weekday schools should be attached as such to the community system of weekday Hebraic schooling, so that responsibility and direction can be shared in the conduct of the schools on a mutually agreeable basis. Small and inadequate schools should be consolidated for weekday class instruction under joint management of the congregations involved and the community agency. The congregations should supplement the weekday class instruction of their children by various forms of religious-cultural teaching and activity.

D.   Schools and Parents

56. The Jewish family today is less intensively "Jewish" than a generation ago but communication between parents and children is better.

57. Parents do not know what their children are learning in the Jewish schools. There is a lack of elementary communication with parents. Parental interest, while general, is too diffused and hazy, without real responsibility. Schools do not seem to be doing enough to deepen that interest.

58. Parent-Teachers Associations exist in only half of the schools. A National Association of Jewish Parents should be organized.

59. In most schools (84 percent) pupil report cards are given to the parents; but they are usually formal and little effort is made to interpret them to the parents through personal contact.

The parent-teacher relation is psychologically a complicated one. For proper work with parents, teachers (a) must receive definite training; and (b) must set aside definite time in their weekly schedule.

E.   Larger Communal Relations

60. There are four problems of larger communal relations in Jewish school work: (a) what should be the relation to Jewish education of the community council or federation; (b) what are and should be the functions of the communal educational agency or bureau; (c) what should be the relations of the communal agency to the national bodies representing the religious-cultural groupings in Jewish education; (d) what should be the respective spheres of responsibility and activity of congregations and community in American Jewish education.

61. Community responsibility for Jewish education was first recognized by the New York Federation of Jewish Philanthropies in 1917. Today there are more than forty community central educational agencies throughout the land and the American Association for Jewish Education, with its multiple functions.

62. The opinion of 1,560 community leaders favor the sharing of responsibility in making educational policy and for financing Jewish schools, among parents, individual schools or congregations, the community educational agency and the local community council.

63. There has been an ever increasing personal concern with Jewish education on the part of the leaders in federation communities. They appear ready to direct themselves to three important questions:

1. The need to strengthen cooperative planning and service;

2. The need to improve the quality of education without interfering with the ideological requirements of different groups in the community;

3. The need to give high priority to fundamental Jewish culture on all levels, including the highest scholarly study, such as research and publications.

Implications and Suggestions:

(a) The federation community should establish and recognize only one central educational agency.

(b) The federation community should undertake more direct and generalized responsibility to plan and to meet educational needs.

(c) The federation community must share in shaping the Jewish education of its children to assure that they learn the deepest meanings of community as one of the perpetual priorities in Jewish life and outlook.

(d) The community and the national congregational bodies should cooperate toward making all weekday Hebrew schools community schools under common auspices.

(e) There is a sufficient minority interest in day schools to warrant community support of these schools for those who want them. Such support should be on the basis of the cost of Jewish studies, but with full scholarships to selected children and youth who could later be trained for the Jewish professions.

(f) Federation community support of Jewish cultural activity on the highest level (scholarship, research, publication), would help create a more favorable cultural community climate for Jewish education of children.

64. The bureaus and other community educational agencies have only partially succeeded in their main task of creating coordinated school systems in their communities.

What Do We Teach Our Children?

A. The Curriculum of Studies

65. The curricula of Orthodox and Conservative weekday schools resemble each other at the elementary levels. Most weekday school programs are planned for four to five years for ages eight to thirteen. The Yiddish elementary program is for four years. The day school elementary program is for a full eight years; likewise that of the one-day school.

B. Subjects of Instruction

66. Hebrew language instruction is considered as basic and the key to other studies. However, its teaching suffers from lack of time and confusion of purpose. The average weekday school teaches Hebrew somewhat less than four years, for 36-38 weeks per year, 1½ hours per week, or an aggregate of about 228 hours. This would be the time equivalent of only 1½ years of foreign language instruction in the public schools.

67. Emphasis on individual mechanical reading of Hebrew prayers is wasteful and ineffective. A good deal more could be achieved in less time through functional socialized-rote methods.

68. Bible: About one-half the afternoon Hebrew schools do not succeed in preparing their pupils for the study of Bible at all. With the exception of the day schools, probably no more than 25 percent of our children learn enough Hebrew to be able to begin the study of the Hebrew Bible, even in simplified texts; and probably less than half of these, 10-15 percent, can read the simplest Hebrew Bible text without considerable assistance. The likelihood is that the vast majority of our children grow up without any knowledge of Bible text, either in Hebrew or in English.

Implications and Suggestions—Heroic efforts must be made:

(*a*) to improve the teaching of Hebrew through scientific laboratory analysis and directed classroom experimentation;

(*b*) to increase the amount of time required weekly;

(*c*) to lengthen the years of study.

Junior Hebrew high schools should be organized for the ages eleven to fifteen, including the Bar-Bat Mitzvah period. This type of school should become the Bar Mitzvah Bible School, with focus on the study of the Hebrew Bible.

(*d*) Hebrew summer camping should be made a necessary and integrated part of the Junior Hebrew High School program. Such "Hebrew-speaking" camps as Massad and Ramah have proven themselves not only to be sources for adding to Hebrew knowledge, but attractive means for enlivening the Hebrew language and making its acquisition pleasurable and "natural" in the encompassing setting of the summer camps.

(*e*) Student pilgrimages to Israel should be begun at the junior high school level as an integral phase of their Hebrew-biblical education.

69. Talmud, Religion and Ethics: Aside from the day schools, very little Talmud is taught. But there is growing awareness of the importance of teaching the values of rabbinic Judaism as relevant to the classic way of Jewish life.

70. Jewish History: There are debatable issues regarding the values to be derived from the teaching of Jewish history, and at what age and how it is to be taught. The values generally stressed are the sense of identification with the Jewish people and its heroes; the cultural security and the sense of continuity derived from knowing the story of one's people; the background for understanding Jewish life and problems today.

71. Customs and ceremonies is a popular study in all schools. It is repetitious unless care is taken to make the holiday projects also occasions for increasing and deepening knowledge.

72. Israel and Current Events: Surprisingly little time is set aside for teaching about modern Israel. Self-study techniques should be developed for stimulating and guiding the reading of children about Israel and current events.

C. Teaching Aids:

73. Teachers use a considerable variety of teaching aids in subjects of instruction. Most schools (70 percent) report having a school library. However, only 34 percent have school library rooms, only 40 percent have librarians, and only 25 percent provide regular budgets for acquiring books. This is another indication of the "thinness" and parsimoniousness of many Jewish schools.

D. Pupil Activities

74. Pupil activities are encouraged in most schools. These may be "extracurricular," additional to classroom instruction, or linked with the studies. Pupil activities in order of frequency are: festival and school assemblies, music, junior synagogue, Keren Ami, trips, arts and crafts, dramatics, dance, student government, and general clubs.

E. Results of Teaching

75. It was not possible to judge the results of teaching on a national scale directly and objectively, because no standardized achievement tests were available. The AAJE has recently begun to develop such tests in Hebrew fundamentals and Jewish history.

76. The results of indefinite data from unstandardized achievement tests indicate that:

(a) in the Fundamentals of Hebrew Language:

1. There is no clear progression of knowledge as the child grows in years; the thirteen-year-olds do not score better than the nine-year-olds.

2. The Hebrew language as such seems to be taught better in the lower grades than in the higher ones.

3. In the weekday schools teaching eight to ten hours per week the total achievement score is better than those teaching less hours, particularly in the noncongregational schools.

4. The pupils in day schools score very much better than those in other types of schooling; but the pupils

in good noncongregational afternoon schools score as well in Hebrew fundamentals as the corresponding pupils in day schools.

5. Girls score better than boys.

(b) in Jewish History:

1. There is general progression of knowledge through the grades.

2. The pupils in the day schools score better than those in their central study.

3. The one-day school pupils score lowest, despite the fact that history is their central study.

(c) in Holidays and Customs:

1. There is more regular progression of achievement score than in the other subjects, possibly because in this subject, children are aided by their experiences outside the school.

2. In this subject, too, the pupils of the day school score best, the nine-year-olds doing better than the thirteen-year-olds in other schools.

3. In the one-day schools there is considerable lowering of achievement scores at the thirteen-year-old level.

4. Girls score better than boys.

77. In attempting to evaluate the "sense of achievement" felt by Jewish school pupils and their parents, it was found that only about 35 percent of the parents are "satisfied" with school achievement. As for the children, the majority "enjoy or like" Bar Mitzvah preparation, holiday celebrations and Jewish history; but only half of the pupils or less express a sense of achievement in any other of the school subjects or activities. In well-conducted schools these proportions of parents and children should be much higher.

National norms for achievement tests would make it possible for lay leaders, rabbis and educators not only to compare and evaluate, but what is more important, to set standards, to discuss specific objectives, and realistically to determine whether the national norms are sufficient and how much knowledge should be expected of children at various levels. This, then, is an essential means for improving Jewish teaching in the country's schools.

F. Levels of Instruction

78. Since most pupils (82 percent) in the Jewish schools are found at the elementary level (ages eight to thirteen), the weekday Hebrew school which is supplementary to the public school should concentrate on extending the years of schooling (a) by developing the primary level for ages five to eight, as the pre-Hebrew school, on more than a one-day basis, and (b) by creating a junior high school level for ages eleven to fifteen, making this the central four-year level of schooling.

During this period the powerful *mystique* of Bar Mitzvah could be converted from the bugbear of a flashy "finish" to the most important experience of personal Jewish "awakening," by drawing the adolescent closer to the Hebrew Bible and its meanings through every possible method and ritual. Beyond the junior high school, efforts should continue toward developing the senior high school level (age fifteen and up) as a comprehensive twofold program: for those who are academically and linguistically capable and interested, and for those who are not. The proposed National Curriculum Institute should make one of its central tasks the experimental study of the many problems involved, on all levels, in attempting to implement such curricular reorganization.

TOWARDS BETTER JEWISH EDUCATION:
WHAT AND HOW

The report of the Commission for the Study of Jewish Education in the United States contains major findings whose inherent implications are the basis for significant recommendations. The value and quality of Jewish education in the next decade will be in large measure a reciprocal of the degree to which these recommendations are successfully implemented. No less than American Jewry itself is involved in this challenge to improve the work of the Jewish schools. For Jewish education is the concern of parents, educators, community leaders, schools, synagogues, community agencies and national bodies such as the Council of Jewish Federations and Welfare Funds, the commissions on education of the national congregational and the noncongregational groups, and most particularly the American Association for Jewish Education.

Admittedly the AAJE which sponsored this report, can only accept the "yoke" of implementing its consequential implications and recommendations as the *Shliah Zibbur*, the agent of the national Jewish community, in cooperation with the CJFWF, the congregational and noncongregational school organizations and others. But its task should be to deal with these seven major areas for improving Jewish education:

1. Curriculum and Teaching: A National Curriculum Institute is proposed under the aegis of the AAJE. It should apply itself to the analytic and constructive tasks involved in translating general aims of Jewish education into specific objectives of study and teaching. The Institute should function as a national cooperative program, flexible and inclusive, in which individual teachers and schools, community bureaus of education, synagogue commissions and noncongregational organizations should pool their efforts. It should deal with research into the educational process as it obtains in the Jewish schools, conduct experimental standardized achievement tests, devise other evaluational instruments, and train selected "fellows" for Jewish educational leadership.

2. Research and Follow-up: Investigations of sociologic and psychologic import which are necessary for understanding the school situation need to be made.

3. Larger Community Relations: Federations should undertake more direct and generalized responsibility for planning and developing Jewish education as they do for other areas of community work, operating locally through *one* central educational community agency which should be enlarged and reconstituted as necessary.

4. Congregations and Consolidation of Schools: Congregational and communal leaders need to agree on what can be done realistically to overcome the smallness, divisiveness and instability of schools which make weekday Hebrew education so full of difficulties. Their aim should be a plan of shared educational responsibility in which the large and adequate congregational schools are to be attached as such to the community system of weekday schooling. The small inadequate schools should be consolidated on an intercongregational basis.

5. The Full-Time Jewish Teacher: Through its National Committee on Teacher Education and Welfare, and its wide community contacts, AAJE should press for the reduction and eventual abolition of part-time Jewish teaching in the weekday schools, and urge the appointment of full-time teachers at adequate salaries; their schedules of work, beyond classroom teaching, to include the many necessary extra-classroom educational services to pupils and parents, supplemented, where indicated, by the teaching of youths and adults in the community.

6. Adolescent Education: The establishment of Jewish Junior High Schools for ages eleven to fifteen should be encouraged. These should become *Bar Mitzvah Bible Schools* in which the study of Hebrew Bible is to be the central subject of the curriculum, together with recurrent public reading of the Bible in synagogue during and after Bar Mitzvah, and culminating in a ritual ceremony such as the *Hatan Torah* and the *Hatan Bereshit* on *Simhat Torah* for the graduates of the Junior High School. Summer camping in Hebrew-speaking camps and student pilgrimages to Israel should be planned as integral parts of the junior high school program.

7. Community and the Day Schools: As partial solution of the need for more intensive Jewish education for some children, AAJE should advise federations and bureaus to accept among the schools which they support or "service," those day schools that are modern in character and which comply with objective standards of school management and of general education.

These recommendations are proposed to AAJE and the other

national organizations concerned with Jewish education, to help them to enable American Jews to rise to a higher *madregah*. In Hassidic literature there is the concept of *madregot*—"steps" or levels of living and being. In that spirit we can say that there are four *madregot* of Jewish living and being. The lowest and the deepest *madregah* is the vital or biologic one—being a member of the Jewish family and accepting identification with it. The second *madregah* is the social—Jewish fellowship, in its many forms of affiliation and participation; synagogal, communal, global. The third *madregah* is the cultural—the study and knowledge of the literary-historic tradition, with its biblical and post-biblical content and its Hebraic forms. The fourth and highest *madregah* is the ethical—integrating the ethos of Jewish culture into personal values, outlook and conduct. The great majority of American Jews in our day have reached the first two *madregot*, the biologic and the social, identification and fellowship. The grand aim of all Jewish educational endeavor is to help them reach the third *madregah*, that of Jewish knowledge and culture; and through it to raise themselves personally to the highest *madregah*, as "witnesses and partners of the Almighty."

In this quest there have been different ways and approaches to the ideal. A generation ago, during the days of the "bootstrap" generation, these differences seemed to represent antagonistic outlooks—culturists and religionists, Zionists and anti-Zionists, Yiddishists and Hebraists, philanthropists and Judaists. That generation found it possible to enable all of these values to "live themselves out" and to arrive at new syntheses for our day; the old antagonisms becoming polarities in a common framework of being. Likewise, and of particular importance for Jewish education, has been the theoretic antagonism in that generation between synagogue and community: Samson Benderly, Judah Magnes and their colleagues stressed common elements and needs, and community responsibility; Solomon Schechter, Bernard Revel, David Philipson, stressed the particular, programmatic, the ideological, the religiously distinctive, as their way to Kelal Yisrael. In this, too, the "bootstrap generation" held on to both approaches as significant and indigenous to Jewish life; and indeed, both approaches proved of great value. In the days ahead, the way to the ideal continues to be the differentiated way, but as in the case of the theoretic antagonisms of the previous generation, there is need to relate congregations and community as polarities in a common integrating framework of Jewish being in which "both these and those are the words of the living God."

Conclusion

Broad community interest in Jewish education has an importance that reaches far beyond the efficiency and quality of the educational system itself. In a very real sense, Jewish education in the United States is the key to Jewish survival.

Just two decades ago Europe contained 56 percent of the Jewish population of the world. It not only held the statistical balance of Jewry; it held the most vital source of Jewish spiritual and cultural achievements. The surrender of Germany found barely one-third of Europe's pre-war population surviving, the overwhelming majority homeless and utterly destitute.

Almost as overwhelming a catastrophe as the loss of six million of our people was the destruction of priceless spiritual and cultural treasures contributed by centuries of Jewish learning and communal endeavor. Great seats of religious learning, scientific institutes, libraries, schools—almost all were reduced to rubble and ashes.

The balance of Jewry has now swung to the United States. The Jews of the world will look increasingly to this country for leadership. We can only meet this historic responsibility if our great material resources are joined with a far richer knowledge of Jewish history, traditions, and problems than is possessed by the average American Jew. In Europe, a comprehensive and thoroughly integrated system of Jewish education provided the basis for an informed public opinion and an enlightened leadership. So far our own system of education has been haphazard and lacking in perspective. The new responsibilities confronting American Jewry make it imperative that the problem of Jewish education be given primary consideration.

CHAPTER TWENTY-ONE

CHAPTER TWENTY-ONE

ORGANIZING AMERICAN JEWRY

by BERNARD G. RICHARDS

From the first days of their exile the Jews have had to adapt the organized forms of their group life to the limitations and requirements of a non-Jewish environment. In certain European countries government law imposed overall organizations upon the Jewish community to represent it as a unified whole. In the United States, in an atmosphere of freedom, organized Jewish life has been voluntary. Organizations have arisen expressing every facet of Jewish life and Jewish interests and their relations to one another determined by a number of complex factors— some with a long historical background, others a product of the fusion in America of the traditional and the new.

One of the common complaints about Jewish communal life in the United States is that it is chaotic and undisciplined. To the average Jew, approached for contributions by scores of organizations annually, there appears to be an appalling amount of duplication and overlapping of effort. Some of the confusion is only apparent. In recent years, particularly in the field of welfare and philanthropy, there has been a marked tendency for local organizations with special functions to merge or cooperate with those performing similar functions either locally or on a national scale. Furthermore, there has been some division of labor in philanthropic, defense and cultural matters.

Despite these trends, large areas of Jewish communal life are plagued by a bewildering multiplicity of organizations competing in the performance of similar functions. The reasons for their failure to merge or cooperate are complex. They may stem from the vested interests of professional and lay leaders. They may be partly due to the apathy of the Jewish public.

But much of the fragmentation of Jewish life stems from sincerely held ideological differences among the different Jewish groups. It has enriched Jewish life almost as much as it has detracted from its orderliness. Indeed there are significant similarities between specifically Jewish and American social and political life. Neither is monolithic. Both have been distinguished by a pluralism of organized interests and multi-party systems.

Throughout American history there has persisted a rough division in political thought, expressed in the different emphasis placed on the role of the masses and the extent to which democratic principles should be extended to all areas of the nation's life. So, too, throughout Jewish history in the United States there has been an analogous division and rivalry between a small group of self-appointed leaders who believed wealth and social position exclusively qualified them to lead the community, and those who believed that organized Jewish life should be democratically directed by the Jewish masses themselves.

The Sephardim

This basic conflict within American Jewry had its origin in the three successive streams of Jewish immigration to this country, especially in the differences between the German and East European Jews who made up the two main streams.

The first of these immigrations, each vastly larger than the one before, was the Sephardic immigration beginning in 1654. By 1840 the Jewish population totalled some 15,000 persons of Spanish and Ashkenazic origin. The Sephardim were chiefly well-to-do merchants, orthodox in religion, and most of their institutions were designed to further their religious life. They considered themselves the aristocracy of American Jewry and tended to remain apart from their more humble brothers from northern and central Europe.

The German Jews

The German Jews who arrived next, differed radically from the Sephardim in several respects. Most of them were quite poor upon their arrival. By industry, courage and ability, they overcame poverty and many developed thriving businesses of one kind or another. With increasing economic success came community prestige and leadership in charity and communal work until the German Jews wrested the controlling interests in Jewish communal life from the Sephardim.

The German Jews were predominantly middle-class and assimilationist in tendency. Their influence in Jewish life, apart from philanthropy, was largely negative in character. They tended to consider themselves as primarily a religious group and their secular expressions, such as lodges and philanthropies, had only the faintest national coloration. With their highly developed skill in organization, particularly in the field of philanthropy, they established many of the great Jewish charitable institutions—orphanages, hospitals, and federations for the relief of the poor. By 1881 some two hundred thousand of the quarter million Jews in America were of German origin.

The East European Jews

From 1881 to 1920 two million Jews entered the United States. This third wave of Jewish immigration was made up almost entirely of East European Jews, for the most part deeply loyal to traditional Judaism, who fled terrible oppression.

The great mass movement of East European Jews to America was a unique migration. It represented the transplanting of entire families and even communities, rich and poor, learned and ignorant together. This new migration also differed from those that had gone before in its vastly greater numbers and the concentration of the bulk of the new arrivals in a few centers. Most settled in New York City. Most were orthodox in their religion; many were Zionists; some were socialists who were not religious at all. They brought Jewish culture in Yiddish and Hebrew with them. Journalists and actors established a Yiddish press and theatre. Zionists developed their own organizations. Yiddish secular schools and Talmud Torahs owe their origin to the Russian Jews, just as the reform synagogues and Sunday schools, the charities and lodges originated with the German Jews, and the first Orthodox synagogues originated with the Spanish Jews.

Conflict between the German and East European Jews was almost inevitable from the beginning. The German Jews regarded Americanization as their aim and communal life as their special preserve. They considered themselves an élite fitted to lead the Jewish community by virtue of wealth or established position. The Russians who had fled from oppression felt that the established leadership was out of sympathy with their national hopes and desires and had little feeling for the positive content in Jewish life as they wanted it to be. As for the Germans, just as the Sephardim had looked down upon them, so in turn they looked down upon their Russian brethren.

Two Jews, Three Opinions

Since 1841, communal leaders have compiled a long roll of efforts to unify American Jewry under a centrally representative organization. And despite a classic quip that "where you have two Jews you have three opinions and four organizations," there is reason for optimism. A measure of coherent structure in American Jewry *has been achieved* since the young Jewish community took its first tentative steps toward unity.

In response to growing religious, welfare and educational needs, the synagogues provided the earliest examples of cooperative action between different American Jewish groups. These took the form of exchanges of religious services by congregations, joint efforts in baking *matzos* and in the support of orphans, the supervision of Kosher meat, and educational activities.

In 1841, Rabbi Isaac Leeser, Philadelphia editor, scholar and Orthodox community leader, set forth an original plan for uniting the country's synagogues. His proposal was designed to meet the primary religious needs of the simple Jewish community of that day. Leeser wanted to set up an ecclesiastical council with headquarters in Philadelphia to take care of the community's religious and educational needs. This synod would meet regularly to consider communal problems. As part of its specific tasks, it would also supervise all spiritual functions, deliver religious decisions, and examine cantors, *shochtim* and teachers. However, even in this comparatively uncomplicated period in the then small community's history, forebodings of vested interests already barred the way.

The Sephardim did not relish their minority position in regard to the Ashkenazim and their leading congregation, Shearith Israel, declined the invitation. The leading Reform congregation, Emanu-El, also declined. Other congregations followed suit. The epitaph that was to write finis to so many efforts for unity made its first appearance:

"Failing wider acceptance the plan was abandoned."

Still, Rabbi Leeser persisted. He made further attempts in 1845 and 1849. This last time he was not alone. Rabbi Isaac M. Wise, the founder of American Reform Judaism, became his ally and brought his influence to bear upon the important body of German Jews. Wise issued a call for a meeting on June 11, 1849, of delegates from various synagogues to consider the original Leeser plan, plus Wise's proposals for a uniform *Minhag Amerika* (a ritual service), and the adoption of a new prayer book with some moderate reforms. Again the Sephardim of Shearith Israel declined because they feared they would be overwhelmed by the Ashkenazic majority. Emanu-El refused to participate because it feared a check to the spread of Reform.

Wise and Leeser separated. The former sought to unite the Reform groups. The latter hewed to his original proposal for a union of all American Jewry. But his idea was deferred, for at the time some congregations were apprehensive lest they lose their preeminent position in the community. Moreover, the 1848 democratic revolutions which gripped Europe caused a minor psychological upheaval among American Jews, particularly the Germans, and interest in a Jewish religious synod was temporarily overshadowed by the promise of emancipation for the Jews in Europe.

However, Leeser continued his unrelenting efforts, and in 1885, with Wise again vigorously pushing the idea, a conference convened in Cleveland. A synod of congregational representatives was to be set up with a platform on which all American Jews could combine.

A familiar pattern repeated itself. The easterners objected to a midwestern meeting place. The rabidly Orthodox suspected a coup by Reform. The rabidly Reform protested against the efforts of the Orthodox to have the Talmud recognized as "the legal and obligatory commentary of the Bible." Another attempt to unify American Jewry into a central organization passed into oblivion. Leeser's goal of an organization that would become the "Sanhedrin of the New World" was not to be.

No Plan, Much Crisis

Apart from the vain efforts of Leeser and Wise, projects for a central, nationwide organization were not to meet vital communal needs. They were instead the forced and chaotic expressions of indignation and outrage at catastrophes visited upon Jews overseas. The records reveal that most plans for a central representative organization have been called into existence by emergencies threatening the Jewish people, rather than by the wish for a more efficient and democratic organization of American Jewry. Attempts at unity bogged down in factionalism, and most alliances were formed under external pressure and tended to dissolve almost immediately the pressure was relieved.

The Damascus Affair

The Damascus Affair of 1840 was the first of these shocks. It involved the imprisonment and torture of a group of Jews on an ancient canard—ritual murder. A committee led by S. I. Joseph of New York was formed to call a protest meeting. The Board of Trustees of Joseph's congregation, Shearith Israel, refused his request to hold a mass meeting in the synagogue, and set a precedent for the timid brethren who were to follow.

The meeting was held at B'nai Jeshurun. Thirteen leading representatives of as many different congregations acted as vice-presidents of the assembly. Mass meetings were also held in Philadelphia, in Cincinnati, and in Richmond where Benjamin Nathan called for unified action with Jewries throughout the Diaspora "to alleviate the suffering of our brethren in the East." These protests, added to those of world Jewry, and to the efforts of Moses Montefiore and Adolph Cremieux, were successful in setting the Jewish prisoners free.

Restricted—Early Swiss Style

In 1857 the American Jewish Community for the first time resorted to political pressure to demand an end to an abuse. For years synagogues and philanthropic societies, etc., had shown concern with the welfare of European Jewry to whom they had been sending food, clothing and relief funds. In no cases had such philanthropy touched on political questions until American Jews became concerned about the denial of the right of domicile and religious freedom to Jews travelling in Switzerland. The American-Swiss treaty then in force did not prevent some Swiss cantons from practicing such restriction.

The struggle against the Swiss treaty is not only a heartening instance of what persistent democratic social action can accomplish, it also offers insight into the nature of the still-existing conflict in Jewish community life. Even in 1855 there was timidity in dealing with important issues. Emanuel Brandeis, who sought to rally resistance to the Swiss treaty, was unable to persuade New York leaders of the desirability of action. He, therefore, approached Dr. Wise of Cincinnati. Wise's newspaper *The American Israelite*, began to urge the Jews of America to protest against the discriminatory Swiss practices.

The year 1857 was marked by meetings in Cincinnati, Chicago and Cleveland demanding action with regard to the Swiss treaty. But the meeting scheduled in New York failed to attract any attendance because the initiative had come from outside of New York! From Baltimore came a call for a national convention to be held in that city, and delegates were actually sent from Charleston, St. Louis, Chicago, Cincinnati and Washington. Opponents of the undertaking, however, questioned the mandate of the delegates. Nevertheless, "the Wise Man of the West" (as Rabbi Isaac M. Wise was sometimes called), disregarded the challenge to his authority and arrived in Baltimore to take charge of the convention. A committee was appointed by the gathering, with Wise as chairman, to lay the grievances of American Jewry before the president of the United States.

Thereupon the Baltimore delegation withdrew from the convention on the grounds that it had gone too far in the claims of its representation. However, Wise and his followers proceeded to Washington and placed the case before President James Buchanan.

New York Jews were outraged by this seemingly hasty action and by the failure to invite their participation. Preference for the quiet, backstage approach caused a committee of New York *shtadlonim* to engage in private efforts to change or modify the existing treaty. Endeavors to assure the full rights of Jews in Switzerland were also carried forward through other efforts and agencies. Finally, in 1874, the new Swiss constitution established religious liberty and made the question of the treatment of aliens a federal matter.

The Mortara Case

In 1858 American Jews were again incensed to a measure of unified action by the "Mortara Case." Catholic clergymen in Italy kidnapped and secretly baptized a Jewish child, Edgar Mortara of Bologna. Because of intense indignation, American Jewry's cry for public action could not be denied. On November 18, 1858, a meeting of delegates from twelve congregations was held in New York. It resulted in the formation of the "Representatives of the United Congregation of Israelites of the City of New York," with S. M. Isaacs as chairman. Two weeks later a mass meeting of two thousand Jews and Christians resolved that the president of the United States be urged to intervene in behalf of the Mortara child by sending an official protest to the Pope.

The Board of Delegates

The Mortara case had repercussions in many Jewish communities. In France it brought into being the Alliance Israelite Universelle in 1860; in England, the Anglo-Jewish Association; and in Austria the Juedisches Allianz. Similarly, in the United States the Mortara case led to the formation of the Board of Delegates of American Israelites as the first national organization of the Jewish community. It was the successor of the local United Congregations of New York which had conducted the Mortara protest.

In 1859, the trustees of the synagogue Shaarey Tefillah formed a committee to summon all other congregations of New York to an election of delegates to a permanent "Board of Representatives of the Jews of America." At the preliminary meeting nine synagogues were represented. A call was issued to all congregations of the country requesting that each synagogue send two delegates to a convention in New York on November 27, 1859.

Again local patriotism manifested itself negatively. Isaac M. Wise offered to join in the movement, but then he withdrew because the call had not originated from Cincinnati. He also feared Orthodox domination over the convention. There were other skeptics and doubters. David Einhorn, speaking for the radical wing of Reform, stated that Jews should act as American citizens, not as Jews. He charged the Board's leaders with plotting a religious hierarchy and a sellout of Reform to Orthodoxy. Another accusation was that the new project was designed to serve political ends.

But opinion was too incensed this time to be turned aside by differences and disputes. The convention was held as scheduled in New York on November 2, 1859, with delegates from fourteen important communities. Congregations of Polish, German and Sephardic Jews were represented and the Board of Delegates of American Israelites was finally established on the model of the British Board of Deputies.

The Board set up headquarters in New York and on the eve of the Civil War functioned through an executive committee of fifteen persons.

The Board's objectives were:

1. "The collection and arrangement of statistical information respecting the Israelites of America.

2. "The promotion of Jewish education.

3. "The adoption of measures for the redress of grievances under which Israelites at home and abroad might suffer for religion's sake.

4. "The maintenance of friendly relations with similar Hebrew organizations throughout the world.

5. "The establishment of a thorough union among all the Israelites of the United States."

The Board's Activities: Credits

The program of the Board of Delegates reflected the social background of a young, optimistic, and relatively small Jewish community totalling approximately 125,000 in 1859. But despite these factors of youth, modest size, and the naïve faith of the day that a rising tempo of democracy throughout the globe would achieve Jewish emancipation and equality, the Board proved that a central organization, activated by competent and imaginative leadership could produce a record of positive accomplishment.

The Board's first public activity was in behalf of domestic civic protection. It set a series of notable precedents for future representations to official quarters that were necessary to safeguard the status of American Jewry. In 1861 the Board succeeded in changing a Congressional Act stating that army chaplains must be ministers of "some Christian denomination" by substituting the world "religious" for "Christian." It also brought about the appointment of the first rabbi to visit the military installations in Washington to serve Jewish personnel. Its protests to President Lincoln and Secretary of War Stanton were credited with the revocation of General Ulysses S. Grant's notorious order (December 20, 1862), expelling "Jews as a class" from his lines. In 1864 it brought about the defeat of attempts by church leaders to declare this a Christian country by an amendment to the United States Constitution. It kept persistent vigil against any infringement of the principle of separation between church and state. It was active in eliminating the application of religious tests for holding public office in North Carolina, Maryland and New Hampshire. It influenced Congress to delete from the Reconstruction Act of 1866 the requirement of a Christian oath for qualifying members of the Constitutional Convention. In 1872 it succeeded in abolishing discrimination against Jewish students at what is now the

College of the City of New York. This is an interesting precedent to the present efforts of the Jewish defense agencies to end discrimination in higher educational institutions throughout the country.

Relief and protection were other important functions of the Board. During the twenty years of its greatest activity and influence it gave relief to 3,000 destitute, homeless Jews of Tangiers and raised funds in behalf of Jews who had taken refuge in Gibraltar during the war between Spain and Morocco. It secured the cooperation of President Grant, the State Department and Congress in protecting Jews in Danubian lands, particularly Rumania. It enlisted the good offices of United States ministers in Vienna and Constantinople to defend Jews in the Balkans. In 1867 the Board successfully negotiated with the State Department on behalf of the Jews of Serbia, and ten years later prevailed upon the U. S. consul in Palestine to lend official protection to Russian Jews upon the refusal of the German consul to aid them.

The Board of Delegates also contributed to erecting a synagogue in Madrid in 1869 when the edict of 1492 expelling all Israelites from Spain was revoked. It aided the small Jewish Yishuv in Palestine, gave liberally to education in Eretz Israel, and recommended that "aid should be given to the development of industrial pursuits, and the moral, social and educational elevation of the people."

The Board also made several constructive contributions to further internal communal life. It began the first statistical study of Jews in America in 1875 and published its findings five years later; it inspired the founding of free Hebrew schools, establishing the first one in New York City in 1865; and, upon recommendation of the Board's Executive Committee, the American Jewish Publication Society was founded in 1872.

Debts

Unfortunately, however, the Board was vulnerable to the dissensions which continued to trouble the community. Because of conflicting elements in Jewish life the Board maintained a precarious impartiality in internal American-Jewish affairs.

Community disagreements were so strong that it was compelled to abandon what had been assumed as the chosen sphere of a central society of American Israelites—Hebrew education. The Board compiled a sad record on immigration. Its attitude to newcomers conformed with our current findings that the sons of aliens are generally prejudiced toward aliens. The Board succumbed to the general attitude that in a nation made up of successive layers of immigrants there was a marginal prestige in leaving Europe earlier and a marginal stigma in leaving it later. It was mistakenly fearful of being inundated by a tidal wave of refugees from eastern Europe. It did not believe the community capable of caring for the needy refugees, and underestimated the ability of the newcomers to adjust themselves. Falsely depending upon a democratic millennium of equality in Europe, the Board endeavored to halt "the abuse" of "the dispatch of poor emigrants to America" which "has long constituted a burden and an unjust tax upon our large cities." It sent emissaries to Europe to plead with Jewish committees in Paris, London and Koenigsberg to limit the numbers "to the class that could be helped," and to plan the selection, colonization and distribution of the emigrants. The Board's attitude toward East European immigrants did not change until the end of the nineteenth century.

Despite the achievements to its credit and the cooperation it extended to associations and to international conferences abroad, the Board's prestige declined in the late 1870's with the appearance of rival groups and new influences in the community. In 1875, Rabbi Marcus Jastrow tried to strengthen it by broadening the scope of its activities to include examination for the rabbinate, prizes for scholarship and the centralization of philanthropic work. But the increasing leadership of Reform Jews in the affairs of the Board and the influence of the Union of American Hebrew Congregations combined to hasten the Board's dissolution. The Union had been established in 1875 as the most important association of Reform congregations in the country. The waning interest of the Board's Reform leadership was transferred to the newer Union. After some negotiations the Board merged with the Union in 1878,

one year after the death of one of its moving spirits, Rabbi
Leeser. The Board diminished to a standing committee of the
Union, as the Board of Delegates on Civic and Religious Rights.
The new Board continued its predecessor's timid, assimilationist attitude toward Jewish problems. The Union disbanded it in
1925 because other organizations had preempted the Board's
field and this situation would leave the Union free to concentrate solely on its religious and educational program.

The Jewish Alliance

During the period of its activity Simon Wolf, prominent
Washington, D. C., attorney, became the foremost spokesman
for the new Board as well as for the B'nai B'rith, "Sons of the
Covenant," today the oldest and largest Jewish service and
fraternal organization in the United States, founded in 1843 as
an instrument for bringing together all Jews. As a zealous anti-
Zionist and bitter opponent of Jewish nationalism, Wolf opposed all attempts to organize a nationally representative Jewish agency. He depended chiefly upon his personal contacts
with "the right people," and staunchly believed that proof of
Jewish good citizenship and decency were the best answer to
anti-Semitism. Wolf's tireless and persistent efforts won him
the title of "Jewish Ambassador," although his adoption of the
ancient *shtadlan's* role of back-stair petitioning was severely
criticized.

By 1905, with an approximate Jewish population of 1,700,000,
change and unrest became manifest. The influx of large numbers of Russian and Polish Jews began to alter the complexion
of the community. Immigrant intellectuals as spokesmen for
the masses of newcomers challenged the entrenched monopoly of communal leadership, its ineffectual handling of the
growing problem of immigrant relief and its patronizing attitude. The conflict led to renewed effort to establish an over-all
community organization to represent both the old and the new
groups. The Jewish Alliance of America was the first attempt
made by the East European elements for their proper share in
communal leadership. The Alliance came into being at a convention held in Philadelphia on February 15, 1891. Nineteen

cities were represented including communities from the West and Northwest. A permanent organization was decided upon and Simon Muhr, Philadelphia philanthropist, was chosen president. The Alliance's declared purpose was to "unite Israelites in a common bond for the purpose of more effectually coping with the grave problem presented by enforced emigration." German, Sephardic, as well as Russian Jews were elected to the Executive Board.

Unfortunately, however, the Jewish Alliance was beset with obstacles which condemned it to a brief existence. It was soon undermined by obstructionist tactics employed by the German elements which had apparently given unwilling consent to the launching of an organization that brought the Russian Jews into positions of leadership heretofore pretty much of a German monopoly. The evidence emphasizes the gulf that divided philanthropic endeavor by the few, from the aspiration for democracy and self-help on the part of the masses of American Jewry. The immigration problem of the time required expenditures of large sums of money, and as the Alliance, before the days of popular campaigning for funds, could not produce the needed finances, the Baron de Hirsch Fund and rival institutions which later swallowed the Alliance came forward to father the enterprise. The trustees of the Baron de Hirsch Fund, whose purpose was to aid needy Jewish immigrants, issued a call for a meeting on September 23, 1891 to form their own organization. Delegates from several large organizations assembled to form the American Committee for Ameliorating the Conditions of Russian Refugees. According to Peter Wiernick, it was urged apparently for the purpose of heading off the activitiy of the Alliance. A controversy ensued during which the Alliance struggled to preserve its existence. It was finally forced to merge with the new body in 1892, although the Alliance still clung to the hope that "as a chartered institution it may, if it sees fit, again resume work under its own name." That same year, the danger of Russian domination of a central national agency having abated, the new united organization tendered its functions to a committee which conveniently buried it.

The American Jewish Committee

The series of Jewish persecutions in Russia under the Czars over a quarter century were climaxed by the Kishinev pogrom of 1903. Kishinev galvanized a horrified American Jewry into action. Mass meetings were held at which Christians joined Jews in sincere protest. These precedents for the mass protests against Nazism were in complete contrast to the shtadlan approach of "quietism." The voice of the people was making itself heard.

It was realized more and more that the existing defense and relief organizations were unable to cope with either the protection of Jews abroad or the needs of the community at home. In 1906, the "Year of Pogroms," the demand for a more effective organization could no longer be overlooked. Cyrus Adler wrote in the *American Hebrew* early that year:

> The affairs of the Jews in the United States as a religious and social body, are of such importance that there should be in existence a representative body which may act for all of them with authority.

Discussions of various plans ensued which led to conferences on February 4 and May 19, 1906. At the latter meeting Abraham S. Schomer, a New York attorney, set forth a plan calling for an "International Jewish Parliament." Instead, the conference committee proposed an American Jewish Committee "to promote the cause of Judaism, and to aid in securing the civil and religious rights of the Jews in all countries *where such rights are denied or endangered.*" Even this proposal met with opposition. Simon Wolf and his group of old-time leaders of American Jewry objected to the idea that American Jews should "organize as Jews" except on religious and philanthropic matters. They also feared the lessening of the influence of the B'nai B'rith and the Union of American Hebrew Congregations. So despite the opposition of the "Down-Town" poor in New York and the well-to-do "Up-Towners" in other cities, who resented the self-selected leadership of American Jewry by the New York shtadlonim, the result was that the conference set up a committee of fifty "for the purpose of cooperating with the various national Jewish bodies in this country and abroad on questions of national and international moment to the Jewish people."

On November 11, 1906, the "Committee of Fifty"—originally appointed by a smaller committee of fifteen—held its first meeting behind closed doors under the name it had adopted, "The American Jewish Committee." The number was ultimately increased, after several changes in method of selection and various efforts to "democratize" it, by adding a number of "members at large." Thus a movement for a representative organization gave birth instead to a committee of individuals with limited functions. Moreover, the committee's emergency character was recognized by its leaders. It was through the process of actual functioning that the American Jewish Committee acquired its permanent character.

In the history of the committee written by the late Louis Marshall, one of its founders and its president for many years, he says:

> Various methods of constituting such a central organization in the United States were proposed, but the only suggestion upon which a majority of the conferees agreed was that a small committee be formed of persons who, while representative of American Jewry, need not necessarily be formally accredited representatives of any organization or group, nor in a political sense of the Jews as a whole. It was not claimed by its organizers that the Committee had power to bind any constituency. The Committee expected to exercise its influence, not by virtue of power, conferred in advance, but through the support of those who might sympathize with the opinions and approve of the acts of the committee.

The activities of the Committee extend from early relief measures undertaken to meet Jewish emergencies abroad to various endeavors to protect the rights of Jews in different lands, especially in cases of crises caused by sudden political changes or upheavals. Perhaps the pinnacle of the Committee's efforts was reached in 1911 when it fought against discrimination practiced by the Russian government against American

citizens of the Jewish faith who entered Russia and whose
passports were not honored. The long agitation against this
injustice and the final course of action led to the abrogation
of the American treaty of 1832 with Russia, but it should be
noted parenthetically that the original public protests against
this discrimination were initiated by Jews outside of the Committee. However, while the Committee established a notable
record of useful undertakings "to prevent the infraction of
civil and religious rights of Jews" in many lands, its approach
to other vital Jewish questions, such as its opposition to the
registration of Jews as Jews when they entered this country
as immigrants, was largely negative. In the course of years,
the Committee endeavored to obtain more popular support
for its program. It began by cooperation with the Jewish Community (Kehillah) of New York in 1908, and Philadelphia in
1909-10. It also set up committees and chapters in different
sections of the country.

But the challenge to the Committee throughout the years
was based not only upon criticism of its work, concerning which
there was much difference of opinion, but upon its self-consti-
tuted character and its assumption of authority without any
popular elections or widespread representation of any kind.
The practice of naming its members in communities near and
far without the people of these communities having a voice
in the selections of those committee members continued and
continues to this day to be a source of irritation and censure.

The subsequent developments and activities of the Committee are recorded in the annual editions of the *American Jewish
Yearbook* from 1907 to date.

The American Jewish Congress

Like the Kishinev crisis, World War I was another emergency
which revived attempts to organize a central representative
Jewish body. The overwhelming majority of American Jews
were by this time of eastern European origin. These Jews
were no longer a formless mass, submissive to community control by the earlier arrivals and their descendants. The aftermath
of the 1905 Russian revolution had brought to this country

many intellectuals thoroughly acquainted with modern nationalism and socialism, and as a consequence, the Yiddish-speaking
community lived a vibrant intellectual life of its own. Recent
arrivals from Russia and Galicia—then the laboratories of social
democratic movements among minorities—emphasized democratic representation of the Jewish community in the United
States. The vigor of their agitation, supplemented by the
influential Yiddish press, almost forced through their point of
view. The slogan, "a Congress for and from all Jews," was
first voiced by the author in the *Jewish Daily News* of May
10, 1914, and was soon echoed throughout the country.

This demand for a democratically elected Congress, to act
and speak for all classes of Jews in the United States, was
spearheaded by the American Zionist movement. The common
denominator of Zionism, acceptance of the peoplehood of
Israel, gave cohesion to otherwise diverse groups, and on
August 30, 1914, an emergency conference of American Zionists held in New York adopted a resolution signed by N. Syrkin, B. Zuckerman and B. G. Richards calling for the conven-
ing of an American Jewish Congress.

There was a dual leadership in communal life: the paternal,
philanthropic leadership of the wealthy, Americanized, English-
speaking Reform Jews of German origin who came a generation
or two before the East European Jews; and the leadership of
the Yiddish-speaking community, then just beginning to assert
itself.

The non-Jewish world looked upon the first group as the
spokesmen of the Jewish community, but a great number of the
East European Jews, who were in the majority, resented this
leadership as undemocratic.

In 1914 the anti-nationalist and non-Zionist factions were
grouped around the American Jewish Committee, most of
whose members were Reform Jews. The outbreak of war emphasized the sharp divergence of opinion within the community on Jewish group rights and the Jewish future; and when
discussion about Jewish postwar rights became widespread
ideological differences crystallized. The Zionists considered the
Jews to be a people with a common history and destiny and a

distinctive group personality with attributes of nationhood, believing in rebuilding Palestine as the Jewish homeland.

The anti-nationalists were mostly Reform Jews with a tradition of assimilation, who looked upon the Jews not as a people or a national group but as individuals who differed, or should differ from their fellow citizens only in religion.

They also feared that any other interpretation of Jewishness might impugn their loyalty to their country in the eyes of many non-Jews and thus menace their status and security. They believed Zionism would accentuate anti-Semitism.

Cooperation in relief activities among the Orthodox, Reform, Zionists and radical Jews was insufficient to bridge deep-seated ideological divisions. In the face of such a cleavage the problem was "How were the Jews to present a united front at the forthcoming peace conference?"

Should a democratic congress formulate and make known the desires of American Jewry, or should a conference, limited in scope and not directly responsible to the community, be convoked in order to act for the Jews of the country?

There was a great popular demand to set up a permanent congress to represent all Jewish organizations and to function as the American unit in a worldwide organization of a similar type. The widely read Yiddish press and the Zionists were especially vigorous in demanding such an organization.

The American Jewish Committee was opposed since it argued that existing organizations could adequately handle postwar problems. In April, 1915, Louis Marshall said the committee could "only behold the possibility of infinite mischief" in a congress such as the one contemplated. Jacob Schiff said a conference "composed of conservative and thoroughly trained leaders is sure to accomplish more than a congress such as the Zionists and others seek to force upon American Jewry."

The Congress group objected to the continued committee oligarchy which made wealth, influence and conservatism the criterion of leadership. They challenged the Committee's desired limitation upon the purposes and scope of the Congress as undemocratic. However, the Committee insisted that an unlimited conference would prove "futile and dangerous."

The Committee wanted this conference to meet "in executive session" but Justice Louis D. Brandeis denounced this committee policy of secrecy as the very means of breeding suspicion and misunderstanding. He insisted that only through "frank and open discussion" of Jewish problems could the cooperation of non-Jews be secured.

Unable to reach an understanding with the American Jewish Committee, the nationalist elements launched an intensive popular campaign to force the hand of the anti-nationalist leadership.

After more than a year of fruitless negotiation the Congress advocates called a preliminary conference in Philadelphia on March 27 and 28, 1916. Here the movement for an American Jewish Congress, supported by Brandeis, first took shape.

The preliminary conferences gave the Congress advocates community standing and a position from which to negotiate with the Committee. The drawn-out negotiations finally resolved themselves into compromise proposals:

1. The Congress was to serve as a temporary, wartime organization to represent the Jewish people at the forthcoming peace conference.

2. The Congress was not to commit itself or any of its constituent bodies "to the adoption, recognition or endorsement of any general theory or philosophy of life."

The following year on June 19, 1917, 335,000 Jewish men and women, participating in a national election, chose 300 delegates to represent them at the Congress. Selection was made on the basis of rules prepared by a special congress board of elections. This board represented all organized groups within American Jewry. National and central organizations were given special representation enabling them to appoint 100 delegates at large.

Because of conditions created by the war, the Congress was unable to meet until one year after the elections. Then, on December 15-18, 1918, the 400 delegates met in Philadelphia. Resolutions calling for the full rights of the Jews in eastern

Europe and for the recognition of the historic claim of the Jews to Palestine were adopted.

A delegation to the Versailles peace conference was elected with the following personnel: Julian W. Mack, chairman, Stephen S. Wise, Louis Marshall, Harry Cutler, Jacob de Haas, B. L. Levinthal, Joseph Barondess, Nachman Syrkin, Leopold Benedict (Morris Winchensky) and Bernard G. Richards, secretary. The delegation succeeded in having clauses guaranteeing international protection to racial and religious minorities included in the treaty with Poland which became a model for all the other treaties.

The delegates, on their return from Versailles, reported to a second session of the Congress held again in Philadelphia on May 30 and 31, 1920. Some of the delegates, in keeping with the motives of early advocates of the Congress, urged a motion to perpetuate the Congress, but the officers and leaders of the organization insisted upon fulfilling the agreement to disband that had been reached at the "compromise of 1917." They forced an adjournment of the session. However, delegates remaining in the hall moved to form a provisional committee for the purpose of establishing a permanent Congress. This plan was ultimately realized when an election and convention was held in 1922.

The organizations originally opposed to the Congress project and which had joined it only on the condition of a restricted program, withdrew from the first temporary congress at its second session of 1920. Seeking its support from the broad masses of the people, the new American Jewish Congress now attempted to re-establish an authorized, representative Jewish body that would include those national and central organizations and local committees in every community which were willing to join it in a frank, open program of action in behalf of the American Jewish community. Congress also was to continue the defense of Jewish rights abroad, and it remained in contact with the leading European Jewish organizations and the Committee of Jewish Delegations in Paris which Congress had previously helped to establish.

Aware of the ever-pressing need for greater cooperation be-

tween existing Jewish bodies, the American Jewish Congress
at its 1929 session in Atlantic City adopted a resolution providing for consultation and possible cooperation with the American Jewish Committee and other bodies. Out of this resolution
grew a joint consultative committee which met from time to
time to review conditions affecting the Jewish people. This
committee was empowered to consult with other groups in
order to provide for unity of action in the solution of common
problems. These consultations took place intermittently until
Hitler's assumption of power in Germany in 1933.

In the 1930's, as a result of community pressure, several efforts were made to coordinate the defense activities of the "Big
Four": the American Jewish Congress, the American Jewish
Committee, the B'nai B'rith, and the Jewish Labor Committee.
But, as before, these were essentially negative efforts aimed at
eliminating waste, duplication of work and competition in
fund-raising. They were not the result of positive conviction
that a national representative or consultative organization was
needed at that time.

To meet the dire threat of Nazism, the first three organizations
formed a joint consultative council on which each had three
representatives. But the long history of factionalism continued
from the beginning, with disagreement on the tactics to be
used in the counterattack on Hitlerism. Conflict particularly
centered on the proposed boycott of German goods and services, now recognized to have been an important tactic. The
joint council dissolved in 1937.

New sentiment for cooperation brought into being an organization which this time included all the "Big Four." It was
due to the initiative and pressure of thirty communal leaders
from outside of New York, led by Edgar G. Kaufman of Pittsburgh, Pennsylvania.

General Jewish Council

On June 13, 1938, these efforts resulted in a conference of
Jewish organizations at Pittsburgh. A general Jewish Council
was formed with the American Jewish Congress, American Jewish Committee, B'nai B'rith, and the Jewish Labor Committee

participating. Headquarters of the Council were established in New York. Originally intended as a truly authoritative, over-all body, the Council soon turned out to be a purely consultative group. The proviso that no steps could be taken by the Council unless it had the unanimous approval of all the participating organizations, reduced it to helplessness in dealing with the grave problems threatening world Jewry. Relations between the partners deteriorated progressively, chiefly because of organizational rivalries and disagreements on the methods of combatting assaults upon the Jewish people. Again there was a division between quietism and overt action—between the behind-the-scenes diplomatic approach by a few and the more aggressive and completely open and democratic method of social action. Ultimately, the appalling destruction heaped upon Israel left little room for discussion, although much of the division of counsel prevailed until World War II and Pearl Harbor.

When the war broke out the American Jewish Congress invited the leading organizations to form a conference on the Jewish situation in Nazi Europe. This became the temporary Joint Emergency Committee for European Jewish Affairs. But it was still inadequate to accomplish the urgent task of rescue and to plan to meet the serious problems that were sure to confront Jewry at the war's end. The Council passed out of existence in 1944 with the establishment of the National Community Relations Advisory Council. In addition to the Big Four, the NCRAC included the Jewish War Veterans of America, the Union of American Hebrew Congregations, and community relations bodies in nineteen cities. At present the NCRAC appears to be a clearing house rather than a coordinating body. The American Jewish Committee and B'nai B'rith no longer belong.

American Jewish Conference

The need for a thoroughly representative national body to deal with postwar problems could no longer be denied. At this point a conference of the leading national organizations was called. It met at Pittsburgh, on January 23-24, 1943, to lay the foundations for a new alignment of organized Jewry in the United States. The new body called itself the American Jewish Conference.

Once again the history of the American Jewish Congress was repeated.

Once again a compromise agreement on the purpose of the Conference was reached:

1. The conference was to deal with postwar Jewish problems *abroad*.

2. The conference was to dissolve after its work had been completed.

An election of 500 delegates to the Conference was to take place throughout the country in June, 1943. Representation was to consist of delegates from both the various communities and the outstanding central and national organizations.

The American Jewish Conference was organized August 29-September 2, 1943, in the shadow of the continuous mass murder of Jews, "to plan immediate rescue of European Jewry, to take action upon the postwar Jewish problems in Europe, and to implement the rights of the Jewish people with respect to Palestine." The conference represented the overwhelming majority of affiliated American Jewry, but like the previous efforts to establish a central organization, it had to be founded in the face of a masked, rather than a frank opposition by some important community groups. These were reluctant to submit to prevailing majority opinion because of ideological differences or vested organizational interests.

This covert opposition revealed itself at the session's climax —the adoption of a resolution for a free Jewish commonwealth in Palestine. As a result the American Jewish Committee withdrew from the Conference, although in 1946 its president, Judge Joseph Proskauer, implied that the Committee did not object to an independent Jewish political entity in *Eretz Israel*. The Jewish Labor Committee left the Conference in December, 1944. Nevertheless the conference continued its efforts to rescue the remaining Jews in Europe, particularly the displaced persons. It was fully represented at the Peace Conference in Paris, June-October 1946, and was able to present the strong voice of a relatively united American Jewry. Together with other major Jewish organizations, among them the World Jewish Congress, it helped formulate Jewish demands at the Peace Conference. It continued to make representations on problems affecting the status of Jews overseas and then disappeared into limbo.

Like their predecessors in the earlier Jewish Congress of 1916, the chief advocates of the American Jewish Conference chafed under the burden of a compromise agreement by which the program of a conference was restricted to foreign affairs and was prohibited from taking up problems on the "American scene."

Within the last fifteen years the United Jewish Appeal has become an important unifying factor within the community. The UJA was formed from an amalgamation of three major funds—the Joint Distribution Committee, the United Palestine Appeal and the National Refugee Service. It brought cooperation in a vital area of fund raising. Similarly the Federation of Welfare Funds has brought unity where duplication had been before.

There is now a Presidents Conference made up of the presidents of eighteen national Jewish organizations, including every major body with the exception of the American Jewish Committee. Label Katz, president of B'nai B'rith, has succeeded Philip Klutznick as chairman of this conference. It is meeting the need for an interorganizational dialogue on matters of common concern, and the necessity of securing a community consensus for decisions and actions affecting American Jewry, so that its communal voice and actions may be united rather than anarchic and dissonant.

The 1960 annual meeting of the Rabbinical Assembly, the Conservative rabbis, in response to appeals for the establishment of an over-all body for American Jewry by its executive director, Rabbi Wolfe Kelman and Rabbi Israel Goldstein, called upon the Synagogue Council of America to act upon this proposal. At the 1960 Third General Assembly of the Council, which is the coordinating agency of the principal rabbinical and congregational branches of Judaism in the United States, in affirmative response to this call, Jewish lay and spiritual leaders urged the establishment of such an over-all representative Jewish organization to cope with pressing Jewish problems in America and overseas.

Abraham N. Heller, chairman of the assembly, said: "The promotion of a cooperative American Jewish community representing the interests of Jews in relation to the general population and before governmental agencies is the great Jewish need of the hour." While cognizant of "the existing legitimate differences in ideology and modes of expression" among national Jewish organizations, "the Synagogue Council and its constituent organizations strongly believe that American Jewry must possess a community interest with a democratic, collective voice reflecting the will of the various Jewish groupings."

Albert Vorspan, director of Reform Jewry's Joint Social Action Commission, contended that such an over-all body must include civic as well as religious bodies. Sidney B. Hoenig, Professor of Jewish History at Yeshiva University, proposed "the revival of a system of regional communities uniting diverse groups of congregations and denominational branches of Jewry into one body of general identification. The creation of such a unified community," he said, "would not only revitalize Jewry internally but would also, by eliminating present-day pseudo-spokesmen for Judaism, result in setting up an authoritative voice for the Jewish people in America."

The Presidents Conference and the initiative of the religious bodies of Judaism are the two most hopeful efforts now in gestation for a permanent, representative organization for American Jewry. The American Jewish Conference, which expired in 1949, was the last permanent group.

Now and Tomorrow

Today some 80 percent of the Jews in this country are native-born Americans who have moved away from those struggles and schisms of their fathers which had made a house divided of American Jewry. The trend, as expressed by the Synagogue Council of America, is toward Jewish unity. Differences of opinion in all problems of Jewish life and a plurality of organizations to express these differences are not only inevitable, but are in a very real sense also desirable. But these differences are increasingly tending not to stand in the way of an over-all organization through which they can be harmonized so that a greater measure of cooperative action is possible.

Whether this development will find expression in something more concrete than the present Presidents Conference by creating an actual, central, over-all democratic body, remains to be seen. The ability to meet this problem intelligently will be a measure of the degree of maturity of the American Jewish community in our time.

CHAPTER TWENTY-TWO

JEWRY BETWEEN EAST AND WEST

by MOSHE SHARETT

Practical statesmanship cannot avoid taking zigzag courses, and diplomacy, in order to overcome difficulties, must very often make a temporary compromise between fundamental principles and the exigencies of the moment. An ideological analysis, on the other hand, cannot rest content with half-truths, nor can it shirk far-reaching conclusions. In other words, it can claim the privilege of complete straightforwardness.

The rift between East and West which is tearing the world asunder confronts Jewry with a fateful issue.

On the face of it, Jews as Jews can afford to be—or rather ought to be—neutral in the conflict. As human beings, or as citizens of the world, they may take sides—that is, throw in their lot in ideological theory or political practice, with this or that system of thought and action. Yet the Jewish people as a whole, so it would seem, need not, and indeed should not, become involved in the dispute by identifying itself with either side. Inasmuch as by accident or history, Jews dwell in both camps and can only hope to live in peace and enjoy reasonable prosperity by remaining loyal to their respective governments and by adhering to their respective regimes, it should be the paramount principle of universal Jewish policy to steer clear of any clash of entanglement with either party.

This is a solution of the problem which might at first sight appear elementary and self-evident. In actual fact, and on deeper probing, things will by no means be found to be as simple as that.

Let us try to go to the core of the problem and do so, as far as possible, with complete objectivity. *What is the most immediate, basic and universal Jewish interest? Surely it is the perpetuation of the Jewish race and the preservation of Jewishness—both by the development and strengthening of the State of Israel and by the maintenance and enrichment of Jewish life throughout the Dispersion.* How can these goals be attained? How have they indeed been attained so far? First and last, by the freedom of Jewish self-expression, in word and in deed. Many external forces bear upon the fate and future of the Jewish people, over which the Jews have no control. But the mainspring of Jewish salvation lies in the free exercise by the Jews themselves of their collective will power.

No freedom in the world can be absolute or unlimited. In the case of Jewish minorities the world over, freedom of self-expression in all processes of life is of necessity subject to most far-reaching objective limitations. Yet there is every difference in the world between regimes which provide a reasonable latitude for independent collective Jewish action and those which by their very nature completely deny it—stifle it, so to speak, in advance or nip it in the bud.

Democratic regimes, governments and societies are not inherently pro-Jewish. They certainly do not in most cases pursue an actively pro-Jewish policy. Yet under democracy, as a result not of any positive intent but of the general application of a certain set of basic principles, Jews enjoy full freedom of expression, by word of mouth and in writing, of meeting and association, of religious practice and study, of communal organization, of education and literary activity, of contact with Jewish communities in other lands, of affiliation with world Jewish organizations, and last but not least, of attachment to the State of Israel, spiritual and practical, ranging from visiting it and supporting it financially to permanently settling in it.

Democracy and Jewish Self-Expression

It is all these freedoms taken together, that constitute the guarantee of Jewish spiritual survival, and it is democracy which, as a rule, automatically provides for these freedoms and, if they are occasionally curtailed, makes possible the struggle for their restoration. The democratic climate of general liberty affords Jews the chance of exerting themselves for the preservation of their identity.

A totalitarian regime, on the other hand, is not intrinsically or deliberately anti-Jewish when it strikes at the very roots of Jewish existence. This is not because the totalitarian order of government necessarily conflicts with nationalism: On the contrary, it was under totalitarian auspices that nationalism attained its most excessive forms. It is rather because the supreme dominance of a highly centralized state power, based on the denial of freedom to individuals and to freely constituted groups, tends organically to buttress up the exclusively dominant position of the majority race. Inasmuch as a totalitarian state grants a measure of autonomy to national groups, it does so only in respect of compact territorial units in each of which the ethnic majority again holds supreme sway, the entire federal structure being held together by rigid party control exercised from one omnipotent center. A national minority consisting of scattered individuals and yet striving to assert itself, can expect no quarter from the operation of such a system. The outstanding peculiarity of the world position of the Jewish people as a ubiquitous minority with the sole exception of Israel makes the totalitarian regime a menace to its survival. This is not a matter of ideological bias or preference, but the inexorable operation of a patent fact.

In purely abstract theory one might conceive of Israel going totalitarian, as a result of either internal upheaval or outside intervention. In such an eventuality, Israel's essential character as a Jewish state need not be impaired by the change of regime. This again is a purely arbitrary theoretical assumption—hardly likely to materialize against the background of the fierce enmities impinging upon Israel from near and far—but let us pose it merely for the sake of argument. Given the continued prevalence of a strong Jewish majority, Israel of a totalitarian brand would still remain a Jewish state. One might deplore the collapse within it of certain spiritual and social values and the resultant degeneration or distortion of Jewishness—but, dehydrated and distorted, such Jewishness as might remain, would still be assured of self-perpetuation. Let it be pointed out again that in actual fact the inveterate and violent character of certain hostile political trends renders the very survival of Israel under such conditions extremely improbable, yet theoretically the point is perfectly valid. For that matter, and in this case without the slightest uncertainty, America would remain American, Britain British, and France French, were they to don or be forced into a totalitarian strait jacket. But the institution of such a regime in all those countries would subject their Jewish communities to a process of miserable vegetation, dooming them in the course of time to complete disintegration and extinction. To repeat, the doom need not be decreed out of arbitrary malice, directed specifically against the Jews; it would come about as an automatic by-product of a general denial of elementary freedoms of speech, association, education, travel, etc. None of these denials would affect the continued existence of the American, British and French peoples. They would merely transform—some would say degrade, but this is a matter of opinion—certain vital aspects of these peoples' national and cultural lives. The Jewish community, however, would under such conditions be left without any air to breathe, and it might only be a matter of time before it would cease to exist.

In Dictatorial Regimes

In fairness to history, it should be recalled that what has been termed here the freedom of Jewish life and the preservation of Jewishness has on occasion been vouchsafed not only under the enlightened rule of democracy. Even in the darkest periods of the medieval era—which has been extended in certain Islamic countries down to our days—for all the oppression, segregation, humiliation, waves of persecution, and even massacres which fell to the lot of the Jews, they invariably enjoyed the elementary chances of spiritual liberty: the freedom of communing with one another, educating their children together and in accordance with their tradition, pursuing their religious studies, cultivating their spiritual values and maintaining contact in most cases with their brethren in other climes. Under the later Czars, when within a matter of a quarter of a century two fierce waves of anti-Jewry pogroms swept Russia, with local massacres breaking out in between; when practically the entire Jewish population, about five million strong, was confined to the Pale and subjected to a most elaborate system of disabilities, Russian Jewry was most potently alive, produced a rich crop of Hebrew letters and rabbinical lore, threw out a whole gallery of outstanding writers and thinkers, gave birth to Hibbat Zion and then to a mighty Zionist movement, laid the foundations and fostered the growth of the Yishuv in Eretz Israel, gave a powerful impetus to the revival of Hebrew as a modern language, and served as the central pivot of Jewish spiritual and political renaissance throughout the world.

In more recent years, under a dictatorial regime in Argentina, the local Jewish community enjoyed full opportunities of free communal and cultural life, expressed in a highly diversified pattern of social, educational and literary institutions, as well as in intense Zionist activity. No obstacles were set under that regime to the development of intimate ties between the local Jewish bodies and the Embassy of Israel, or to Jewish financial efforts on Israel's behalf. Emissaries from Israel could always come to Argentina while Argentinian Jews were completely free to visit and settle in Israel.

It would be ludicrous and grotesque to read into these assertions of historic fact any nostalgia for Czarist oppression in Russia or for reactionary regimes elsewhere, whose disappearance was hailed by Jews everywhere with a sigh of relief. All it is intended to stress here is that the negotiation of liberal democracy need not necessarily degenerate into those forms of ruthless, doctrinaire totalitarianism which spell suffocation for the Jewish soul.

For nothing short of this is today the tragic lot of Soviet Jewry. That nearly three million strong Jewish community—the word community is here a misnomer, for reasons which will soon be explained—is completely cut off from the main body of the Jewish people. The same fate is shared by the Jews of Rumania, Hungary and Czechoslovakia, only Poland being now to some extent an exception to the rule. A total of over three-

and-a-quarter million Jews of the Soviet bloc—a full one-third of the Jewish people outside Israel—can at present be likened to an amputated limb. They take no part whatsoever in universal Jewish life. They can derive no direct inspiration from any creative manifestation of the Jewish spirit anywhere in the world. No Jewish literature or press produced outside the bloc is within their reach. No Jewish emissary from abroad can address their meetings or take counsel with their representative bodies. For their part they cannot travel abroad to establish and maintain contact with Jewish communities and institutions. They are debarred from affiliation with any Jewish organization in the world outside, even if it be purely religious or cultural. They can certainly maintain no ties with the State of Israel.

Isolation and Dismemberment

But all these negative statements are liable to be misleading to the uninitiated, for they may be read as implying that within the Soviet bloc Jews are free to form societies and communities, to gather at meetings and engage in other collective activities, but that they are only precluded from any association with their fellow Jews in the non-Soviet world—and this simply because under the Soviet system of government contact with the outside world is an exclusive state monopoly. In actual fact nothing is further from the truth than such an assumption. No chance of any communal activity whatsoever is afforded to the Jews of the Soviet Union—no representative bodies, no meetings, no schools, no lectures, no celebrations or memorial gatherings, no press, no literature, not one single attribute of normal Jewish life in the free world, nor even such rudimentary forms of it as have always been tolerated by retrograde regimes in most backward countries—nothing but the synagogue and the cemetery, and in those two last ditches of Jewish collectivity, nothing but the essential technical purpose of each: the prayer and the burial.

This plight, compounded of external isolation and internal dismemberment, is utterly unprecedented in the whole age-long history of Jewish martyrdom and struggle for existence.

Equally unprecedented is the fact that this whole system of restrictions and prohibitions, which must look utterly diabolical to the uninitiated, is, as has already been emphasized, the result not of any sinister anti-Jewish design, but of the normal operation of a political order—of principles of policy and administration which have nothing whatever to do with the Jewish problem. Jews cannot meet of their own accord because no group of Soviet citizens is allowed to do so. They cannot run their own schools because no private schools of any kind are tolerated. They cannot affiliate with the outside world because no such right of free affiliation is enjoyed by anyone. Yet the realization that no harm has been deliberately meant is extremely cold comfort to the victims of a process which is tantamount to progressive spiritual asphyxiation.

The question must now be faced whether any Jew concerned with his people's survival can assume a position of neutrality toward a regime which has proved so implacably destructive of Jewish life. Still more, can any politically minded and socially conscious Jew, who at the same time is a faithful son of his people and a fighter for its salvation, square with his Jewish conscience an attitude of sympathy with, and protagonism of, this objectively anti-Jewish regime?

This analysis deliberately refrains from widening the scope of the Jewish indictment of the Soviet regime by reference to the accumulation of evidence pointing to the operation within it of trends purposefully and specifically directed against the continued existence of a Jewish collectivity in the Soviet Union. This body of evidence begins with the denial, in the teachings of Lenin and his colleagues, of the Jewish people's right to exist, or even of the very fact of its existence as a national entity. It invokes the basic and singular contradiction between, on the one hand, a political system enjoining complete isolation from the outside world, and, on the other hand, the only one among its many national groups which forms part of a people scattered throughout the world. It sets forth the unmistakable, if ineffectual, attempts undertaken by the Soviet regime to dissolve the Jewish group within its environment or deter it from asserting its distinctiveness. The charge-sheet reaches its climax when it exposes the atrocity of the physical liquidation of the Soviet Jewish writers—a unique act of extermination, perpetrated not in suppression of a certain school of thought but aimed at beheading, so to speak, an entire national unit by annihilating its intellectual élite. The file of evidence also contains the infamous doctors' libel and other similar monstrosities. Yet, even without unfolding this roll of horrors, we find the purely objective or automatic effects of the regime as such, far-reaching enough to confront us with the problem in all its utter gravity.

One might well ponder what would have been the course of Jewish history and the fate of the Zionist endeavour had Russian bolshevism triumphed in 1905 instead of in 1917, and where we would have been today without the historic contribution to Zionist achievement of the Second Aliya or the remarkable efflorescence of Hebrew literature and education in Russia in the decade preceding World War I. Conversely, one might reflect how much greater and quicker progress our effort here and Jewish life everywhere would have made if Russian Jewry had remained an integral part of the Jewish world and its primary dynamic force; if, on the morrow of the Balfour Declaration and in the crucial and formative years of the 1920's, our work in this country could have drawn on the reservoir of idealistic manpower, pioneering energy, and financial support which Russian Jewry would have mustered; or, as the late Dr. Weizmann once put it, if we had not been condemned by history, exactly at a time when broader vistas opened before us, to start working "with our right arm bound tightly behind our back"; finally, if upon the proclamation of Jewish statehood, Russian Jewry could have played its tremendously significant part in Israel's defense, growth and development.

To recall a less hypothetical eventuality, and one more modest in its historic dimensions, was it possible for true Jews to remain indifferent to the outcome of that recent phase in the contest between democracy and communism in which the destiny of France seemed to hang in the balance? Could they contemplate with equanimity the prospect of French Jewry being reduced to that condition of progressive anemia and paralysis which Russian Jewry has endured for the last forty years?

We thus reach perforce the complete reversal of the original, seemingly so plausible, proposition. As citizens of the world—simply as thinking men and women—Jews may take a position of ideological neutrality, some kind of a philosophical wait-and-see attitude, in the face of the titanic conflict raging all over the globe. As conscious and responsible Jews they are irresistibly driven to take sides. Communism may well appear to some persons to be a short cut, or the only sure road, to the reign of justice and equality among men. Furthermore, the attainment of such a lofty goal may well justify in the view of such persons a prolonged period of denial of elementary freedom resulting from the institution of a supposedly transitory regime, which by all normally accepted standards cannot but be regarded as inhuman. Both propositions can be the subject of differences of opinion or of political or intellectual speculation. What is patent and incontrovertible is that during this stage of alleged transition, a value, which an entire people, and not a spiritually insignificant one, holds supreme—namely its own preservation and progress—is bound to be submerged and go under. For Judaism and Jewishness this is an issue of life and death.

From the Standpoint of Israel

We have so far considered the problem essentially from the standpoint of the Jewish people as, for the most part, it is today; we have been assuming the continued existence of the Jewish Diaspora and brought in Israel only as an incidental element of Jewish life. Yet Israel is now the focal point of world Jewish consciousness and the most outstanding and momentous reality of present-day Jewish existence. It must, therefore, be brought fully and emphatically into the context of our analysis.

Israel is a democracy. Her democracy is older than her independence. From its very inception Jewish settlement in this land assumed democratic forms. The new society had no barriers to pull down, no feudal privileges to liquidate, no vested interests to overcome. On the positive side, democracy was enjoined by the desire of Jews to live freely and together, which was the mainspring of the entire historic enterprise of the Return and which made all returning Jews equal in worth and status. It was impelled by the necessity of joining hands to provide for essential services through mutual help, and of creating a minimum of civilized existence through collective effort. It was rendered indispensable in a society which, devoid of any state power or other means of compulsion, could claim from its members only voluntary allegiance, which in its turn could be forthcoming only if all members were placed on a footing of equality and enabled to take part in the election of their representatives. All these democratic trends were manifested in the growth of each basic cell of the national system—each village, town quarter and city—as well as within the wider framework of the national organization which in the days of the British Mandate came to be known as Knesset Israel.

The democratic spirit and practice of the Zionist movement, resulting from its voluntary and progressive character, for its part, did much to shape the Yishuv's democratic tradition. But democracy in our pre-state existence did not remain confined to municipal and political organization. Through processes of growth from below and from within it went beyond that province to the social and economic spheres. It did so because what was essentially a state structure could be maintained and developed without state powers only by the development of a cooperative movement, which is nothing but democracy in its social and economic aspects. The independent spirit of the Jewish settler, his creative impulses, and his urge to free initiative on the one hand and to mutual assistance on the other, have supplied the motive power of Israel's cooperative dynamism. It is these characteristics of the Jewish settlement process here which produced a unique phenomenon in the history of colonization—the organized application of democratic principles to mass settlement on the land. The principles so applied consisted of the recognition of each settler's right to self-determination in the choice of the social forms of his life and work; the adoption of a system whereby the composition of each group of settlers is based on mutual choice and joint responsibility; the complete self-government of the settlements from their very inception; and the fixation of settlement conditions by agreements negotiated between the elected representatives of the settlers and the national institutions.

The growth and ramification of the Yishuv's labour movement, by its very nature democratic, which had solidified its position and become the backbone of the national system prior to the attainment of independence, played an outstanding part in impregnating the entire community with a democratic spirit. As a combined result of all these processes, democracy struck deep roots into the people's soul long before totalitarianism as a world phenomenon became a menacing alternation. When the State was born it adopted as a matter of course an emphatically democratic constitution, and integrated itself, both sociologically and in its political spirit, into the fabric of the democratic world. At the same time, in its democratic evolution Israel did not try to copy foreign models but, in the main, developed patterns and practices of her own. Israel prides herself on having maintained the system of full freedom.

Israel and the Democratic World

Statehood has generated for Israel further powerful gravitational pulls toward the democratic section of humanity. Israel's ambitious immigration and development programs have caused her to depend to a most decisive extent upon external financial and technical assistance, which could only be forthcoming from the West. As a focus of universal Jewish concern and pride and as a vanguard of the Jewish people constantly in need of support and reinforcement from its worldwide reserves, Israel has become increasingly aware of the vital importance for her present well-being and future destiny of the prevalence of that political system which alone gives her freedom to forge links with the Jewish communities of the Dispersion.

Above all, the striving of Israel to make the most of the new chance of creative life vouchsafed by history to the Jews assembled in it—the new challenge and opportunity with which destiny has here presented the Jewish genius by creating a material and political framework for its free self-revelation —has definitely and indissolubly wedded this new society to

the ideals and practices of free democracy. The very continuation of the ingathering of the exiles—the process of the
voluntary immigration and settlement of large numbers of
newcomers and their willing integration—is conceivable only
in the context of a free society, the central aim of which is the
elevation of the worth of man's personality and from the life of
which any avoidable state coercion is absent.

It may be argued that the ideological orientation of a state
need not necessarily determine its political position in the tan-
gle of international relations. This may be so in abstract theory.
Practical experience has proved the far-reaching impact of
ideology on politics. In any case, ideologically Israel has never
attempted the absurdity of steering a middle course between
democracy and the very negation of it. In the evolution of
her foreign policy, Israel likewise drew the inevitable consequences from her political philosophy, which reflects her basic
articles of faith as well as her vital interests. To cite one major
example, it is only democracy that has enabled American Jewry
time and again to throw its weight into the political scales and
join issue with its own government in order to uphold Israel's
vital interests.

The contrast between the political articulateness of the Jewish community of the United States and the complete political
obliteration of the Jews of the USSR is a most telling illustration
of what free democracy, on the one hand, and totalitarian absolutism on the other, signify for Israel in her constant struggle.
And democratic revolts against official policies affecting Israel
have by no means been confined to the Jewish public or to the
United States. Quite naturally, Israel's sense of dependence upon
free Jewish or non-Jewish reactions under the aegis of democracy has not been without its counterpart in terms of her foreign policy. In particular, the decisive part played by American
Jewry in Israel's rebirth, survival and progress perforce exerted a profound influence upon Israel's stand on many an
international issue. The growing intimacy of the bond between
Israel and American Jewry—the sense of responsibility which has
developed therefrom upon Israel for American Jewry's standing and reputation—has gone a long way toward precluding the

adoption by Israel of attitudes and policies in the international arena which would have subjected that fruitful and indispensable association—fruitful and indispensable for both sides —to an unbearable strain. Putting it at its lowest, this association has imposed on Israel the utmost possible sensitiveness to the susceptibilities of American Jewry in the international sphere.

Conversely, Israel's vigorous democracy and the proven importance for Israel both of her democratic affiliations and of her connection with the Jews in the Diaspora, which in its turn could only thrive in a democratic climate, could not but influence the stand of Jewish communities on the issue of dedication to democracy and of its defence.

Having tried to place Israel in its proper setting against the background of the subject under discussion, let us return to the predicament of those large numbers of Jews within the Soviet system who are isolated both from other sections of Jewry and, in effect, from one another. Assimilation has made deep inroads into their ranks, but their hard core has exhibited remarkable powers of moral resistance and elementary self-preservation. In recent years, as a result of wartime and postwar developments, which unleashed old hatreds against them with renewed fury and made the Jews again a target for distrust and discrimination, Jewish consciousness throughout the length and breadth of that community has been revived and sharpened. The rise of Israel, her struggles, ordeals and achievements, have had a tremendous uplifting effect on Soviet Jews' morale. Their longing for a reunion with Israel, physical and spiritual, has become the main passion of their lives.

Israel and Soviet Jewry

Israel has never forgotten her torn-off brethren. Here, too, state-consciousness has enhanced the sense of Jewish responsibility. The concern about the future of Soviet Jews, the eagerness to learn more about their present condition, the efforts to use every conceivable opportunity of coming into contact with them, the speculation about the chances of their gaining freedom of exit to Israel, are among the central themes of Israel's public life. It was largely due to the initiative of Israel and of the forces and personalities closely allied with it in the Jewish world that the problem of Soviet Jews came of late to occupy so prominent a place on the political agenda of national and international Jewish organizations.

Israel's concern for the fate of those Jewish communities has also exercised its influence upon her foreign policy. This consideration, more often of a restrictive than of a formative nature, could not prevail against the compelling pressure of Israel's direct and decisive interests. *It was not possible for Israel to forfeit vital advantages of defense and development, still less to incur tangible losses in those two fundamental respects, on the extremely problematical chance of gaining something for Soviet Jews at the cost of such sacrifices.* Such measure of consideration as was shown by Israel on certain occasions for the Soviet viewpoint in the international arena, failed to elicit a reaction which might have encouraged further advances in that direction. On the face of it, by permitting its Jewish subjects to establish contact with Israel, the Soviet Union was at liberty to play exactly the same card which in the same respect the United States may be said to have used with such marked effect. But the Soviet Union did not choose to do so. It is not that it originally decided not to play the card, just as the United States did not, in all probability, ever consciously decide to play it. The striking divergence in behavior between the two countries in regard to this paramount Jewish interest of free contact with Israel does not necessarily reflect their respective attitudes to the Jewish problem. What comes to light here is the glaring contrast between their political systems.

The crucial question which faces Jewry, as it does indeed the entire free world, is whether the Soviet system is basically immutable, or is susceptible to fundamental change.

Much has been talked about and read into the changes which are supposed to have evolved in the last few years in the relationship between citizen and government inside the Soviet Union on the one hand, and between the Soviet Union and the so-called "Popular Democracies," on the other hand. The question which remains to be answered is whether these changes, if they are at all significant, indicate a real difference in kind or merely a difference in degree.

Reflecting the general evolution, certain feeble rays of light seem of late to have occasionally pierced the gloom surrounding the communities of the Soviet bloc. Here again the decisive question is whether the very few slight departures from former negative rigidity are mere sops thrown to assuage public feeling in the outside world, or whether they really indicate the initial stage in a more hopeful process. The fact that the "new look" of the USSR has coincided with the savage intensification of its hostility toward Israel does not augur any substantial relaxation of its forbidding attitude on the twin issues of Jewish communal autonomy and of Jewish ties with Israel. The present Soviet campaign of hate and slander against Israel is in itself indicative of the peculiar brand of power politics pursued by the Soviet Union. Unmitigated by any free expression of independent public opinion, its trend is to seek alliance along the world front with physical factors of decisive quantitative superiority, in utter disregard of the moral forces and qualitative issues involved.

It is human—and Jewish—to refuse to reconcile oneself to an utterly bleak outlook. Unwittingly one falls prey to wishful thinking and tries to hope against hope. Yet there is merit in rationalizing speculation and achieving the utmost possible clarity if not on the prospects then at least on the nature of the issues at stake. Neither Israel as a state nor the Jewish people as a whole should regard themselves as statutory allies —certainly not as obedient vassals—of any democracy simply because it is a democracy. They cherish the political climate of democracy not because it is a Jewish paradise, but because it leaves Jews free to work out their destiny by their own self-reliant efforts and in accordance with their own lights. Will that kind of freedom ever be accorded to the Jews in the Soviet Union and its associate states? Can it be accorded to them by way of an exception, while the regime as a whole remains substantially unchanged? Or is the entire social order of the Soviet bloc likely to be completely reconstructed on the foundations of individual and collective liberty so that the specific kind of freedom without which Jewish life is bound to perish, emerges as a by-product of the new dispensation?

These questions go to the very root of Soviet philosophy and state structure—to the very core of Soviet world outlook and internal policy. It is from that angle that the clash between communism as a political system—such as it has been known until now—and the cause of the survival and freedom of the Jewish people appears to be absolute and irreconcilable.

The Basic Concept at Stake

What is at stake is the basic concept of the virtue of freedom and the intrinsic worth of human values freely shaped.

Orthodox international communism has always regarded the world as one centralized battlefield and conceived of human history as essentially a single continuous war. The battle must have one supreme command, and the war one overriding objective. National distinctions and peculiarities can only be tolerated and taken into account as long as they do not interfere with the execution of the master plan of grand world strategy. Nations joining or forced to join the communist fold must know in advance that their first duty is unreserved obedience to its central world authority. Independence is not their inherent and inalienable right, though a certain measure of it can be granted to its claimants by the world directorate. Those national constituents who take their independence too seriously and assert it to the point of defying the supreme authority pay the kind of penalty to which the outraged world was witness not too long ago. Similarly, within each communist state, liberty is not the exercise of an intrinsic and inalienable right of the individual which stems from his personality and is subject only to a certain measure of regulation by a democratically elected government. The subject of a communist state owes absolute obedience to the dictatorial state power, which may at will hand out or withdraw certain limited doses of freedom, whilst closely watching and checking their use in practice. Between the careful rationing of freedom as a commodity from above and the emphatic assertion of freedom as a virtue from below, there is a difference in kind of a most far-reaching character. Between the varying latitudes of liberality in the rationing of freedom, which may include a return to its complete absence, the difference is but of degree and, therefore, relatively insignificant.

Whatever may be said on broad human grounds about the merits of communism, both as an international organization and as a state system, its incompatibility with Jewish life is self-evident. For Judaism can maintain itself and develop either as long as it is walled up within a spiritual ghetto which remains internally free, or, after the ghetto walls are pulled down, only in a society in which every group is free to foster and enjoy its spiritual values. Yet ruthless communist efficiency has never shown much appreciation or patience for unregimented forms of human creativeness. In its march toward its goal, it trampled them underfoot. Is the Soviet regime capable of a change of heart in this fundamental respect?

Let it be repeated that elementary postulates of Jewish life are: freedom to associate, freedom to study and educate, freedom to determine the substance and scope of communal activity, freedom to maintain contact with other Jewish communities, freedom to visit and settle in Israel.

If these elementary Jewish freedoms become a reality in the Soviet world—that is, if Soviet life is so far-reachingly transformed as to permit of their inauguration—then indeed a new era will dawn.

But the advent of that new era seems today an extremely remote contingency. It is often argued, with a fair measure of logic, that the grant by the Soviet government of one item in the list of Jewish desiderata—freedom of emigration to Israel—may be more compatible with the maintenance of the Soviet regime than the fulfilment of the rest of the program, and that therefore it is more likely to materialize in the foreseeable future. Since the problem of Soviet Jewry does not lend itself to the uniform solution applied by the USSR in regard to all its ethnic minorities which form territorial units—so it is contended—sooner or later the sheer irksomeness of a problem unsolved will force the Soviet rulers to allow Jews to go to Israel. Many an optimistic forecast by leaders of Jewry and Israel

have been based on this largely theoretical assumption. One
or two enigmatic utterances of leading Soviet personalities,
apparently blurted out, have supplied the semblance of practical justification for these conjectures. Yet the adoption of such
a course by the USSR remains utterly unlikely as long as it
pursues with unabating fury its present violently anti-Israel
and militantly pro-Arab orientation. Hence the exposure of
the cultural strangulation of Soviet Jewry cannot lag behind
the demand for the freedom of exit to Israel.

The Jewish people has no interest formally to appear on the
international scene as an uncompromising antagonist of the Soviet Union. Israel has every interest to restore her normal relationship with that major world power. The tactical problems
facing Jewish statesmanship and Israel's diplomacy in these
regards are highly delicate and complex. But whatever the
tactics, in internal Jewish circles there should be complete
clarity and a growing unity of opinion on the essence of the
problem to be faced.

CHAPTER TWENTY-THREE

THE NEXT STEP IN ZIONISM

by MORDECAI M. KAPLAN

Our present task is not to indulge in the interplay of ideas for its own sake, but to bring some order into the variety of philosophies and plans which agitate the Jewish world, to achieve a broad perspective on what goes on in it, and to show our people the way that leads to creativity and life eternal. We do not intend to deal with abstract theories but with ideology. The term "ideology" denotes a pattern of ideas which, as a way of life, is intended to direct and regulate group action. As such, it may embrace the tradition or philosophy of the group and ideas concerning its structure and functioning. That term has come into use only recently, because only of late have large bodies of people, whether as nations or classes, begun to act as units on the basis of a deliberately accepted way of life instead of on the momentum of long-standing habit or tradition. As Zionists we sense the need for reexamining our Zionist ideology. We wish to find out whether or not it suffices for our present situation, and, if not, to extend it so as to meet that situation.

We subscribe to the unity of all Jewish people and the striving and obligation of Jews of our day to help maintain the State of Israel as the central factor in the present and future existence of the Jewish people. Our concern is: "The place of Judaism and of the Jewish people in the conflict of universal ideologies in the areas of politics, religion, economics, and sociology." Stated simply, that topic indicates the need of Zionism to go further than to affirm in a general way the unity of the Jewish people and its dedication to the mainten-

527

ance of the State of Israel. It implies that Zionism should reaffirm that unity in the face of the political, religious, economic and sociological forces that threaten to undermine it. This is specifically what I shall try to prove.

Ideology in Jewish History

First, a word about the role which ideology, in the sense defined above, has played in Jewish life. Each time our ancestors in formal assembly knowingly and deliberately accepted certain principles and duties as governing them as a people, Judaism entered upon a new stage in its career. Whether those principles or duties were of long-standing and self-evident or of recent illumination, the very act of deliberate acceptance transformed them as a people and had the effect of a spiritual metamorphosis. We should therefore not be surprised, if, as a result of a fully developed Zionist ideology that would be generally accepted by the Jewish people, it would experience a genuine renaissance.

In Jewish history, the outstanding case of a formal public act that transformed the Jewish people into a new kind of human society was the covenant by which the Jews, in the days of Ezra and Nehemiah, bound themselves to keep the Laws of the Mosaic Torah. They became also a *Knessiah*, or ecclesiastical body, which served later as a model for Christendom and Islam. We might, perhaps, also treat the various covenants prior to the one in Ezra and Nehemiah's time, namely the one which Moses enacted at Sinai, Joshua re-enacted at Shechem, and King Josiah at Jerusalem, as cases of public adoption of a way of life. Having been solemnly subscribed to and accepted as an act of choice, the way of life so adopted functioned as a bond of unity among our ancestors, withstanding the disintegrative forces of time.

Except for the Karaite schism during the period generally known as the Dark Ages, neither the unity nor the status of the Jewish people was a problem. The Jews constituted a nation, in the ancient sense of an ethnic or kinship group. Their being exiled from their homeland and dispersed among other nations, in no way altered their status.

During the last two centuries, however, events have rendered the Torah tradition inoperative as a uniting factor among the majority of Jews. Consequently their group status has by this time become an enigma. Insofar as we Jews are nowadays without a definite group status and a common basis of unity, we are without a pattern of ideas, or way of life, to direct and regulate whatever cooperative efforts we have to engage in, whether it be the building of Zion, the organization of general life in the Diaspora, or the fostering of an identifiable and distinctive way of life for the various segments of our people throughout the world. Whatever has been achieved is the result of impulsive reaction to danger rather than of planned and purposeful initiative. *Without an ideology or way of life, how long can we be expected to exercise the will to continue living as one united people and to transmit to our descendants our common cultural and spiritual heritage?*

Zionism owes its existence to one of those critical events in the life of our people which almost cut its history in two. Each of those events placed our people at the edge of an abyss, nearly putting an end to its career, but, fortunately, at each such critical juncture a new idea emerged and served as a bridge that carried our people across the abyss. Each such idea may be termed "salvational," in that it saved the Jewish people from extinction and provided it with a new awareness of its destiny.

The Four Crucial Events

The first event was the migration of Jacob and his family to Egypt. Ordinarily, that would have put an end to the existence of the patriarchal group and to the tradition that had grown up in association with a deity named Shaddai. This outcome was prevented by the advent of Moses who came to the Israelites with the mission from the God of their fathers to redeem them from Egypt. The fact that redemption came from the God of their fathers saved the patriarchal history from oblivion and confirmed the destiny to which it pointed.

The second event was the destruction of the First Commonwealth. The exile which followed might have put an end to the Jewish people, had not the prophets anticipated it with an idea which interpreted that exile as only a temporary hiatus. The third event was the destruction of the Second Common-wealth. That, too, would have marked the end of Jewish history, had not Yohanan ben Zakkai conceived the idea of "a portable state," by making of the Torah a substitute for the state. That is a form of self-government known as Nomocracy.

The fourth event was the confluence of modern nationalism and modern naturalism. An offshoot of modern nationalism has been anti-Semitism; an offshoot of modern naturalism has been materialist secularism. The one has sought to destroy the body, the other to disintegrate the soul of the Jewish people. Once again a salvational idea has come to the rescue. That salvational idea is Zionism.

Thus at each critical juncture in our career as a people, whenever some cataclysmic event threatened to write "finis" over that career, a new idea emerged. It not only spelled the resurrection of the Jewish people; it also elicited from it new creative powers that had lain dormant. It is therefore not unreasonable to look to Zionism as the salvational idea that will give our people in its present crisis a new lease on life. To meet that expectation, however, Zionism has to be viewed from a much larger perspective than that of the establishment of the State of Israel.

The Second Stage in Zionism

What Zionism has achieved thus far is basic and indispens-able, but is only the first half of its task. Were it to stop at this point, it might undo the good it achieved and bring on new dangers to Jewish survival. We should heed the warning sounded by the British Zionists at one of their conventions not long after the establishment of the State of Israel:

The State of Israel has solved the problem of the home-lessness of the Jewish people. On the other hand, there is now the real danger that the existence of the State might divide Jewry into two separate camps, the Jews of Israel on the one side, and the Jews of the *Golah* on the other, with each camp speaking a different language and entertaining different ideas from the other, and absorbing cultural influences independently of each other. Should such a situation develop, it will be possible to say that while Zionism succeeded in creating the State, it has lost the people of Israel.

Nahum Goldmann put the matter less bluntly but in effect expressed a similar warning when at the First American Zionist Assembly, held in New York in December, 1953, he stated:

> It may sound paradoxical, but it may be true, nevertheless, that Zionism will hereafter be judged by its efforts for Jewish survival outside Israel more than by its efforts on behalf of Israel . . . no less than our obligation to see Israel through its difficult period is our obligation to defeat indifference, arrest assimilation, combat disintegration, for these dangers are more imminent today than in any previous period in our history.

Thus the second stage in the fulfillment of Zionism has to be as revolutionary in spirit as was its first stage. It has *to reconstitute the Jewish people, to reunify it, and to redefine its status vis-à-vis the rest of the world.* To do that, Zionism has to release world Jewry from the inhibitive influence of the traditional conception of redemption. That is the conception which pervades all our traditional writings, from the Bible down to modern times, and which is summed up in the prayer which Jews have been reciting for the last two thousand years: "Gather us from the four corners of the earth and lead us proudly to our land." Were Jews to take that tradition seriously they would have to regard themselves as aliens in every country of the world outside Eretz Israel. The fact is that it is not taken seriously by Jews who are citizens of other countries and who are treated there as equals with all other citizens. Nevertheless, that tradition is potent enough to stand in the way of world Jewish unity and the needed reconstruction of Jewish peoplehood.

Prior to the era of the Jewish emancipation, Jews accepted the status of alienage without demur. With the granting of civic rights, however, that status was no longer tolerable. The problem then arose as to what was to become of their status as exiles, which their religious tradition expected them to retain. The Reform movement tried to solve the problem by breaking not only with the tradition concerning that status of Jews, but with the tradition concerning the return to Eretz Israel: that solution has proved completely mistaken. What has Zionism on its part had to say with regard to the exilic status of Jews outside Eretz Israel?

The truth is that there is nothing in Zionist ideology as hitherto formulated that challenges the traditional belief concerning the impossibility of a normal Jewish existence outside the Land of Israel. To attempt to read into Ahad Ha-Am's cultural Zionism the idea of a permanently normal Jewish life in the Diaspora is entirely unjustified. All Ahad Ha-Am had in mind was the restoration of Eretz Israel, as more than a haven of refuge for displaced Jews and as nothing less than an instrument of a thorough-going Jewish renaissance, calling for a process of re-education of the Jews in the Diaspora. The spiritual radiation from Eretz Israel, on which he counted, was to serve as a means of awakening the national spirit which had been dormant for centuries in the Diaspora. That awakened national spirit would then impel the Jews in the Diaspora to migrate to Eretz Israel and qualify them to contribute to the Jewish renaissance there.

The weight of Zionist opinion throughout the world and in Israel is emphatically on the side of the "negation of *Galut.*" The reason is certainly not reluctance to deviate from a long-standing tradition. Breaking with the supernaturalistic idea of a miracle-working Messiah required far more courage than breaking at the present time with the traditional "negation of *Galut.*" There is, it is true, a dangerously mistaken notion that harping on this will accelerate the secure establishment of the State of Israel. It is no doubt true that the security of the State of Israel requires as large a Jewish population as the land can absorb. At present, the required and feasible number is said to be four million Jews. Likewise, it is essential that many Jews from free countries who are expert in forms of modern technics migrate to Israel. While all that is true, the assumption that by stressing the hopelessness of trying to salvage Jewish life in the Diaspora Jews will be persuaded to settle in Israel, is a tragic illusion.

Zionism's Negation of the Diaspora

Zionists who promulgate the doctrine of *shelilat ha-galut* (negation of the Diaspora) usually supplement it with the warning that even in the United States anti-Semitism might reach the proportions it attained in Europe during the Nazi regime. How little such arguments can prevail might well be inferred from what happened in Europe itself before the rise of the Hitler regime. Despite all the evidences pointing to the inevitability of what Herzl foresaw as the outcome of the growing Jew-hatred on the Continent, Zionism, even as a salvaging movement, made very little headway in Central Europe. Only East European Jews who had had a taste of pogroms and boycott, took Zionism seriously and responded to Herzl's appeal. How unrealistic, therefore, is it to expect American Jews who constitute more than half of world Jewry, to be intimidated into migrating to Israel by warnings of a possible outbreak of anti-Semitism in America? All that is true, independently of the question whether the American environment is so radically different from the European as to make the violent outbreak of anti-Semitism even thinkable. Besides, if, God forbid, the cedars catch fire, how can the hyssop by the wall escape?

If the purpose of the doctrine of *shelilat ha-galut* is to prove to Jews that Judaism cannot possibly survive outside Israel, all that it will accomplish will be to discourage those who are making herculean efforts to keep Judaism alive in the Diaspora. The Jewish layman on the whole is ignorant of Jewish tradition, is not worried about the future of the Jewish people or its religion. The Jewish future, whether in Israel or outside, is a matter of active concern only to about one-fifth of the Jewish population. Their rabbis, teachers, writers and social workers know from first-hand experience that Jewish life has not yet taken root in the free world, nor has it as yet given evidence of being able to thrive in the modern climate of opinion outside Eretz Israel. The so-called religious revival in the United States, with Jews as well as with Gentiles, is true to Mark Twain's description of the Platte River as "a mile wide and an inch deep." Fewer and fewer Jews are entering the fields of Jewish service and leadership. Far more disintegrative of Jewish life than any of the external forces in the free world is the suicidal procedure whereby each of the four denominations— the Orthodox, the Reform, the Conservative and the Secularist —is sectorianizing itself and becoming completely estranged from the other three, so that we do not have one Judaism, but four.

Nevertheless, telling Diaspora Jews that their efforts to maintain Jewish life are sure to fail will not help matters. It will certainly not bring about a greater influx of American Jews to Israel. On the contrary, it will definitely lessen the interest of American Jews in the fate of the State of Israel, to say nothing of reducing the likelihood of their migrating to Israel. It will only add to the growing spiritual crisis of Diaspora Jewry. No sensible doctor ever tells a patient that it is useless for him to exert his will to live, even if he has only one chance in a thousand—particularly if the ailment is one in which the will to live is a determining factor. In the matter of Jewish survival, the group will to live is a determining factor. Instead of trying to discourage it, common sense dictates that it should be reenforced by whatever legitimate means are at hand or can be contrived.

Jews in Israel make a serious mistake when they keep on reminding the Jews in the Diaspora that in failing to bear the brunt of the struggle and the dangers incurred in Israel, they forfeit their share in the destiny of the Jewish people. Israeli Jews should recall the story in the Bible concerning David's fight against the Amalekite bandits who carried off the women and children and considerable booty from the village of Ziklag. When David returned to Ziklag, those who had fought the Amalekites refused to give those who had remained behind a share in the booty. But David ruled: "As is the share of the fighting man, so is the share of the man who stays by the stores." The Jews in the Diaspora have served, so to speak, in the capacity of staying by the stores, and they will not be denied their share in the achievements of Israeli Jewry.

But, of course, a greater issue is at stake than that of sharing the credit for the achievements of the Jews in Israel. The real problem is how to prevent the Jews in Israel from being so blinded by short-sighted considerations as to write off the Diaspora Jews from a share in the future of the Jewish people, because they insist upon remaining where they are. The Jews of Israel should be made to understand that in the long run the future of the State of Israel itself is bound up with the future of World Jewry. Israel will, for a long time to come, have to count for its security and growth upon the manpower, the resources and the influence of Diaspora Jewry. But if they are to be counted upon, Diaspora Jews will have to see evidence in the Jews of Israel of a reciprocal feeling of fraternity and spiritual kindship.

Such feeling of fraternity and spiritual kinship cannot last or be an active factor in Jewish life, unless there be a common understanding on the part of the Jews both in and outside Israel with regard to the ultimate character and destiny of the Jewish people. The purpose of my writing this essay is to explore the realities—particularly political and spiritual—and to determine upon the basis of those realities what kind of social structure or pattern the Jewish people must adopt in order to be able to maintain a genuine sense of continuity with the People of the Book.

That We May Be a People Again

Without going far afield into the cultural, economic and nationalist forces that have been breaking up or transforming ancient peoples and calling into being new peoples, suffice it to say that each one of those forces carried to its logical conclusion is a threat to Jewish survival. Fortunately, however, they never operate in disparate fashion, and when they interact, as they must, they are liable to neutralize one another, as far as their injurious effect on Jewish life is concerned. That fact has been amply demonstrated in general life by the failure of the attempt on the one hand, in the nineteenth century, to

isolate nationalism as the all-decisive factor of human groupings, and in the twentieth, to isolate economic determinism as
the decisive factor. During the early decades of this century,
similar potency was ascribed to culture, as was the case with
those who promulgated the principle of political minority rights.
In Jewish life Dubnow was the outstanding advocate of that
principle.

When, in addition, there enters, as has been the case with
the Jewish people, the factor of deliberate choice and commitment, all attempts to base any predictive judgment on this
operation of cultural, economic or social forces have proved
entirely futile. This does not mean that we can afford to ignore
the disintegrative influences upon Jewish life, particularly in
the Diaspora, of the cultural, economic and nationalist forces
that dominate in the world today. But reckoning with them
does not mean submitting passively to them. Given the will of
Jewry, as a body, to win for itself a place in the sun, those very
forces can be mastered and made to serve that will.

In the past, we constituted a unique kind of society that
possessed an intense self-awareness. Every individual in that
society was permeated with the sense of unity and mutual
responsibility. That feeling was the substance out of which
were molded our beliefs, our values, and our hopes. That feeling is by no means dead. It is our task, however, to revive it,
so that we may again become what we were in the past, a
people as described in a statement by J. Pedersen:

> A people is not a collection of human beings, more or
> less like each other. It is a psychical whole, and in so far
> an ideal quantity. "The people" is not visible. All common
> experiences are merged into the common soul and lend it
> to shape and fullness. Thus, a psychic stock is created
> which is taken over from generation to generation, being
> constantly renewed and influenced by new experiences. It
> is lived wholly in every generation, and yet it is raised
> above it, is something which is given to it and makes
> claims to it. The connection between the generations of
> a people is just as intimate as that between the generations
> of a family. The soul of a people and the soul of the family

belong equally to the individual; only their subject matter
differs. (*Israel*, p. 475).

The prayer recited every fourth Sabbath ushering in the
new month concludes with the statement: "All Israel form one
fellowship or community." According to the description of such
a community by an American philosopher, it

> includes both intellectual understanding of one another
> and the feeling of one another's feelings, the ability to cor-
> rect and criticise one another understandingly and con-
> structively. It includes the ability and the will to cooperate
> in such manner as to conserve the good of life achieved to
> date and to provide conditions for its increase. (Henry
> Wieman, *The Source of Human Good*, p. 64).

The leaders of the Zionist movement, both in Israel and outside, should be urged to enlarge the scope of the movement, so
that it embraces as its objective not only the security and growth
of the State of Israel but also the reaffirmation of the unity
of the Jewish people throughout the world, the redefinition
of its group status, and the revitalization of the Jewish spiritual
heritage as a bond to unite the scattered Jewish communities
with one another and with the Jewish community in Israel.
These larger purposes of the Zionist movement require a radical change of heart toward Diaspora Judaism and a release
from the assumption, whether based on tradition or on mistaken expediency, that the refusal to migrate to Israel, when
one is in a position to do so, constitutes an act of spiritual
disloyalty.

Zionism's primary function is to call those Jews in the Diaspora who are of adventurous spirit, who are expert in some
practical or theoretic technique, to come to Israel and help in
its upbuilding. But it should also seek to motivate those who
remain behind to perpetuate their Jewish group individuality
and foster their spiritual heritage. They should be encouraged
to resist in their communal life the operation of forces which
tend to break up minority groups. Traditional Jews, to be sure,
do not need such encouragement. They merely have to be

asked to live up to what they profess. But the ones who need encouragement are those who are wholeheartedly eager to find a way of keeping Judaism alive wherever they happen to be, but who cannot come to terms with the traditional version of Judaism. They constitute by far the majority of survivalist Jews. If their adherence to Judaism is to be retained and their Zionist interest kept alive, they have to be made to realize that no matter where they live, they need the Jewish people and the Jewish people need them.

Aliya and Diaspora

To exercise that mutual need the following considerations have to be kept in mind:

Diaspora Jews need the Jewish people, because the state of which they happen to be citizens does not claim to provide its citizens with the affiliations which are essential to their being morally and spiritually oriented. One such type of affiliation is the family, the other is the religious community. The state leaves it to the individual citizen to choose the one as well as the other. No normally minded Jews however, can possibly satisfy his need for moral and spiritual orientation in any non-Jewish group. He must naturally look to the Jewish people to serve him in that capacity.

That is to a large extent equally true of the Jews in Israel. The State of Israel is at present already far removed in its relationship to religion, from the type of state represented in Spain, Italy, or any of the Catholic nations in South America. It is modeled largely on the type of democratic states like England, which recognizes an established church but grants equality to other churches. Whether in time state and religion will be completely separated in Israel as in the United States is questionable. However, the democratic character of the State of Israel is enough to preclude it from being able to provide even its Jews with the affiliation that is essential to their being morally and spiritually oriented. That kind of affiliation only the international Jewish people which has its core in Israel can provide them.

For the Jewish people, however, to serve Jews in that capacity both in and outside Israel, it should offer them something more than an ancient tradition or a creedal religion. It cannot afford to echo O'Neill's despair: "There isn't any present or future, there is only the past over and over again now" (*A Moon for the Misbegotten*). It has to provide them with the ability to make of its tradition a civilizing and humanizing force not only in interpersonal relations, but also in international relations. To do that, two conditions must be met: (1) *The core of the Jewish people must be situated in its own homeland, in Eretz Israel,* and (2) *the tradition itself has to be made relevant to the very ideologies, cultural, economic and sociological, which challenge it.* Out of those ideologies there can well arise—to use an analogy from music—both a harmonic and a contrapuntal system of ideas concerning God, men and the world, which would continue the tradition, enhanced in content and vision. That would then be the tradition that would mark the renaissance of the Jewish people and render it morally and spiritually indispensable to the individual Jew, regardless of where he lived.

The Jews—a Religious People

On the other hand, it does not require too much coaxing to convince the individual Jew that the Jewish people needs him, that its chances of survival are lessened if he deserts it. If the Jewish people is to have a claim on the individual Jew, it has to submit to the process of self-renewal to meet his spiritual needs and complexities which happen to be without precedent in its tradition. If the Jew has his mentality formed by the Torah tradition and has come to feel what the Jewish people has always felt and to think what it has always thought, he may even disapprove, deny and repudiate much of what has been communicated to him, without severing his spiritual kinship with it. On the contrary, his very dissent may contribute to the scope and depth of his oneness with his people.

Secondly, if the Jew is to realize how much the Jewish people needs him, it must not demand exclusive possession of his personality, by insisting that he reside in Eretz Israel. It should grant him the right, if he so chose, to live in two civilizations, in the Jewish civilization and in that of the state of which he is a citizen. The spiritual allegiance he would owe to the Jewish civilization would necessarily have to be of universal scope, and would therefore be entirely compatible with the allegiance he owes to the state of which he is a citizen. "The attachment of Jews throughout the world to Israel," once said Premier Ben-Gurion, "is based on a joint spiritual and cultural heritage and on a historical sentiment toward the land which was the birthplace of the Jewish people and of the Book" (New York Times, June 26, 1957). It devolves upon Zionism now to recognize that attachment as a spiritual or religious bond which can exercise a dynamic and beneficient influence wherever and whenever it expresses itself.

A people of which each individual is fully aware that he needs the people for his moral and spiritual well-being, and that the people needs him for its self-perpetuation and the achievement of its destiny, is in the truest and deepest sense of the term a religious people. Hitherto it was assumed that to constitute such a religious people, its members had to abide by a uniform code of beliefs and practices. With the rise of the demand for freedom of thought and the right of individual self-expression, a religious people will have to find ways and means of achieving unity without uniformity. That should not be difficult for the Jewish people, because of its inexhaustible tradition which, however diversely interpreted and applied, can nevertheless function as a unifying influence. *That means that Jewish peoplehood is not a political category but a moral-spiritual category and has to be accorded the same status as that of the world religious bodies.* The Jewish people will thus constitute an international people, whose spiritual center—since it has no political center—is to be located in its ancestral home.

In an acute article in *Hapoel Hatzair*, Israel Cohen describes the first Zionist settlements of fifty years ago. He calls attention to the experiences of the early settlers in Degania. "They could have failed completely," he says, "had they not possessed the fundamental trait of pioneers, that of rejecting conventional ideas which had behind them the authority of the most illustrious leaders of their own people: similarly, they emancipated

themselves from Socialist principles which also had behind them
the authority of great masters of economic theory." I would
add that we now should revive that trait and shake ourselves
free from the traditional assumption that the boundaries of the
State of Israel are essentially the boundaries of the Jewish
people.

All our endeavors to find solutions for our problems as Jews
are bound to be frustrated, unless we possess the courage to
create new concepts which can help us deal with conditions
that are without precedent in our history. We should not expect Jewish life under conditions of dispersion in the past,
even those during the so-called "Golden Periods," to serve as
a precedent for the future. In the past, Judaism was all of
one piece, because of the uniformity that obtained in the
thought habits of Jews. This situation cannot be repeated. I,
therefore, propose that we discuss the possibility and legality
of a Judaism that lends itself to various degrees of one's identification with it, that is, a Judaism which, in its home in Israel,
finds its embodiment in *all* aspects of life, from those of politics and culture to religion and everyday affairs, but which,
in the Diaspora must, of necessity, omit some of those aspects,
without thereby losing the right to identify itself with the
Judaism of history. All this means that the type of people, community or fellowship which we Jews have to constitute henceforth is a novum, both structurally and ideologically. Structurally, it has to resemble a hub with spokes. The hub is to
be the Jewish community in Israel; the spokes are to be the
organic Jewish communities in the Diaspora. Ideologically, the
rim which is to hold together the entire structure, must itself
consist of different strands of belief and practice which have
their source in the Jewish tradition.

What the Jewish tradition means to the Jewish people has
been realistically set forth by Buber. "We Jews," he writes,
"are a community based on memory. A common memory has
kept us together and enabled us to survive. This does not
mean that we based our life on any one particular past, even
the loftiest of the pasts; it simply means that one generation
passed into the next a memory which gained in scope—for new

destiny and new emotional life were accruing to it—and which realized itself in a way we can call organic. The expanding memory was more than a spiritual motif; it was a power which sustained, fed and quickened Jewish existence itself. I might even say that these memories realized themselves biologically for in their strength the Jewish substance was renewed."

Religion in the Free Nations

Of particular relevance to the group status of Jews in the Diaspora is the place that the traditional religions occupy in the policy of modern nations. Some nations like Russia and its satellites officially repudiate the traditional religions altogether, not only because they are traditional, but also because they are international. They therefore ban whatever activity Jews living in other countries engage in to assert their corporate individuality. In all our efforts at survival and enhancement of Jewish life we must reckon with the understanding and good will of those nations which have worked out a *modus vivendi* between the traditional religions and their own ways of life. Most of them, like England and the Scandinavian nations, recognize as preferred some particular traditional religion and as permissive all others, and some like the United States show no preference, but treat all traditional religions with respect. These various accords between the modern national ways of life and traditional religion are actually compromises between conflicting ideologies, one based on naturalism and this-worldly salvation and the other on supernaturalism and other-worldly salvation.

Apart from the question whether these compromises are satisfactory and permanent, it is a fact that only those nations which have adopted them have granted full civic rights to the Jews in their own countries and unqualified recognition to the State of Israel. That fact has to be borne in mind when we wish to find an appropriate social category for our international Jewish peoplehood. Any solution of our problem which would ignore those compromises entirely, would hardly contribute to our being understood by the nations upon whose good will we depend for our well-being and survival as a people. If, for example, Zionism were to spell the radical reconstruction of the Jewish people into a secular nation confined to Eretz Israel, with no room whatever for traditional religion with its supernaturalism and other-worldly salvation, or if it were to go to the other extreme and spell the revival of a theocracy with the restoration of the Temple, the priesthood and sacramental cult, or if it were to adopt the position that it is impossible for any fruitful life to thrive in the Diaspora—if Zionism were to adopt any one of these three ideologies, it would undermine the good will of the Western nations upon which it depends both in and outside Israel.

The Western nations are the only ones whose political structure and ideologies are such as to be compatible with the will of Jews to constitute an international people with its core in Eretz Israel. Communist nations do not tolerate the international character of Jewry. That is why it is important for Jewish peoplehood to be identified as a religious category, and for the Jewish people to be known as a religious community. Only as such a community can it fall into the familiar pattern that smooths the way for friendly intercourse with those nations without whose friendship we would find ourselves completely isolated—a condition that has to be averted at all costs.

The question, of course, is: How is it possible for a group to be designated as "religious," which is not based on a uniform system of belief and practices? The answer is, that it is not only possible to find a common element in various manifestations of a religion, but that the common element is actually the essence of the religion and that it was the passionate purpose of all our prophets and sages to call the attention of people to that common element. I refer particularly to the attitude of mutual responsibility which unites individual men and women into a group and obligates them to strive for the achievement of freedom, righteousness and peace in the world. That attitude of mutual responsibility is bound to find expression in feelings of holiness and in acts which symbolize those feelings.

The feelings of holiness are those which give rise to the concepts of divinity and messianism. Evidently, one must ex-

pect that there would be a difference between the way of life
of those who conceive divinity and messianism in keeping with
our tradition, and the way of life of those who conceive those
concepts in terms of modern thought. Nevertheless, if the
leaders of our various parties and denominations are animated
by the desire to fortify the unity of our people, wherever it
happens to live, they will be able to find the way to retain
the individuality of their respective groups, without tearing the
body of our people into tatters. We should not ask them to
break down completely the fences that divide one group from
another. All that they have to do is to permit openings to be
made in the fences. Those openings would make it possible for
the members of the different groups to work together as one
body for purposes which transcend all partisanship and which
are cherished by all Jews.

How Zionism May Unite Jewry

Let me, in conclusion, suggest some of the practical measures
we ought to decide on as essential to the consummation of
Zionism as a movement that is to give unity, status and high
purpose to the Jewish people throughout the world:

1. A decision to establish a conference on a continuing
basis. It should be convened as frequently as deemed advisable
and disbanded only after the main issues are agreed on by
majority vote.

2. The following are some of the issues to be discussed:

(a) The relationship of the Jewish people to the State
of Israel.

(b) The relationship of the Jewish people to other
states to which Jews belong.

(c) The establishment of organic Jewish communities
in the Diaspora to counteract the internally divisive forces.

(d) The adoption of measures that shall keep all segments of the Jewish people in touch with one another,
and the Jewish community in Israel in touch with the
rest of the Jewish people.

(e) The formulation of a code or constitution, or general principles or laws that should help Jews maintain their unity, status and high purpose.

3. The publication in two or three languages, besides Hebrew, of the proceedings of the conference and their wide distribution, for the purpose of having them studied and discussed among Jewish circles.

4. The culminating purpose of these conferences should be to have Jews throughout the world covenant themselves to accept their final decisions, and to have such covenant entered into formally and with great éclat after a sufficient number, to be agreed on, have accepted it.

5. In the meantime, the anticipation of such a covenant should itself be made part of the universal Jewish consciousness by means of a ritual analogous to the one observed on the attainment of the *Bar Mitzvah* age. The ritual should set forth the significance of Jewish unity, status and high purpose, and should be observed on the attainment of full maturity or thereafter.

The foregoing are only some of the specific measures which, I hope and pray, the conference may adopt.

Our conference should be conceived in the nature of a constitutional convention. All discussions should aim to formulate the specific *Halacha* or way of life, which might help our people to live and grow as *one* people throughout the world. With that in mind, we should give heed to the concluding statement made by Bialik in his well-known essay on *Halacha* versus *Aggada:*

A people which is not trained to translate its *Aggada* into *Halacha* delivers itself into (the power of) endless illusions, and is in danger of straying from the only direct path that leads from willing to doing and striving to achieving . . .

A Judaism which is only Aggada is like iron heated in the fire but not cooled thereafter in water. Yearning of the heart, stirrings of the spirit, profound love—these are beau-

tiful and helpful provided they lead to action that is steeled
and to duty that is stern.

If you really wish to build, do what your ancestors did
(in the days of Ezra and Nehemiah). *Make a firm covenant and write it . . . and lay obligations upon yourselves.*

The Jews of the Diaspora definitely refuse to serve merely
as the scaffolding for the House of Israel. They insist on constituting an integral part of that entire House. The time has
arrived when we must realize that one God has created us,
one past has formed us, and only one future has preserved and
will preserve us. If we will live up to that realization, the words
of the prophet Malachi will come true: "Your own eyes will
behold, and you yourselves will say 'The greatness of the Lord
is manifest beyond the boundaries of Israel.'"

CHAPTER TWENTY-FOUR

JUDAISM IN THE WORLD
OF OUR DAY

by NATHAN ROTENSTREICH

My concern is with the position of the Jewish people in
the world of our day. I propose to make some observations
with regard to a number of questions which should occupy a
central place in the Jewish thinking of our time.

The starting point of our inquiry is the decisive change
which took place in Judaism in these last generations, in an
attempt to lay bare the human meaning at the bottom of this
critical turn of events.

We would not be far wrong in saying that the essence of this
fundamental change within Judaism in these last generations
lay in the fact that the Jewish people took its place in the history of mankind, that is, was given a place in the ordinary,
daily course of historical events. It is difficult for us today
to reconstruct the meaning of this marked change which took
place three or four generations ago, for we are placed, without
time to reflect, in the midst of a swift-moving current of events
which draws us deeper and deeper into the vortex of world
history. It suffices to note that the face of world history
changed completely at that point when it felt prepared, knowingly or unknowingly, for good or ill, to receive the Jewish
people in its midst. The face of history changed in the sense
that it ceased to be *Christian* history, in the specific meaning
of this term, and became the *political* history of nations and
political blocs. It is true that for generations events had taken

547

place on a mundane level, including the political level. But the Christian world, insofar as it remained loyal to its original Christian principles, insisted on interpreting these events not in accordance with their political significance, on a political level, but only insofar as they were based on principles of Christian faith. To put it more bluntly, we might say that the events were prosaic but the meaning given them was Christian. With the historical changes that took place within the Christian world itself, the duality between events and their meaning was abandoned, and the meaning thenceforth interpreted in its national and political sense.

This gave the peoples of the world, historically speaking, the opportunity to accept the existence of the Jewish people in their midst together with all the events bound up with it. It is clear that this slow change was a painful process for the non-Jewish world and its attempts to withdraw have not yet ceased. Nevertheless, it is possible to say that the dominant trend was to interpret historical processes in non-theological terms and view them more and more as the interplay of social and political forces. From this point of view the least that can be said is that the ground was prepared to absorb Judaism or to include it in the world order.

But the historical picture of Judaism changed as well. The Jewish people ceased to look upon itself as walking a lone road which stretches from the foot of Mount Sinai to the end of days. The Jewish people ceased to regard its existence among the peoples of the world as a factual existence *beside* the nations without any essential relation to them or as a kind of punishment imposed upon it, a punishment devoid of positive meaning. The fact of Jewish existence beside the peoples of the world was imbued with positive significance.

As soon as the Jewish people realized that its road was not a by-path removed from the beaten track of world history but belonged and, what is more, had to belong to that history, the changes that took place in the Jewish pole coincided with those in the non-Jewish pole. And when these two changes met or, at any rate, became entangled with one another, the meeting was, as is to be expected, in the nature of a historical

crisis and we arrived at the juncture where we now find ourselves: we belong to the history of the world. It does not matter whether our belonging expresses itself in large or in small
figures; the important thing is the position we have assumed
and not the weight of numbers, the consciousness of our independence and the adjustment others make to this consciousness.

This crisis revealed itself in definite forms among the nations
of the world and among ourselves. One form finds expression
in the position of the Jews in the modern state as a result of
the equal rights granted them or which they desired to wrest
for themselves. The truth of the matter is that if the Jews acquired an equal status in the state, they attained it chiefly
in those places where they did not struggle for it. It was given
them as a result of the structure and character of these states
and not because of any native movement within the Jewish
people itself. The struggle for emancipation was crowned with
success not as a result of Jewish exertions but because destiny
brought the Jews to those countries in which the struggle did
not take place, like the United States, for example. Nevertheless,
the fact of equal status was one of political and legal status of
the Jewish people in the modern world composed of separate
states.

Another expression of this actual crisis was the participation
of the Jews in the intellectual and social movements of the
nations of the world. This participation did not take place hap-
hazardly on an individual basis by those who separated themselves from the Jewish group to take part in the world's work,
such as was the case in the Middle Ages. The force of events
themselves made it possible for Jews to take part in social and
intellectual movements, movements which were the end-result
of historical processes as well as those which gave them their
initial impetus. The most striking illustration of this aspect of
the crisis is the part Jews took in the revolutionary movements
of Europe.

The third and most impressive expression of the profound
change was the establishment of an independent Jewish state
as a political and legal entity in the history of the world. The

establishment of this state was a kind of end-product of a historical process, a confluence of various historical streams. The state was the expression of the Jewish will to become part of the flowing circle of humanity as it is, part of its structure and organic character and imbued with its prevailing concepts. The establishment of the state consummates in the new form, the political and legal status of the Jews, for the status of the Jews as a political unit extends and elevates the position of the individual Jew within the modern state. This fact of statehood represents the highpoint in Jewish participation in the intellectual and social movements of the modern world and in the attempts to shape Jewish historical existence in conformity to these ideas —in short, attempts to form Jewish existence with reference to the historical processes of the various states, and not in disregard of them. Considering these various phases, we may say that in the Jewish state this process of historical change within the Jewish people finds its consummation, a consummation which raises Jewish existence to a new level, a "new" but not necessarily a "higher level"—to content ourselves with a statement of the bare facts. Like all elevations of this kind, this brings in its wake a number of problems.

The Reaction of the Nations

Nevertheless, the question which arises in this connection is: how did the non-Jewish world take this change? To be sure, even within the Jewish group this change was accompanied by a certain amount of wavering, which has not yet entirely ceased; we shall not be far wrong, however, if we say that the main course of events, looked at from a more general point of view, was determined by the longing of the Jews to break through into world history. Can this possibly be said of the attitude and reaction of the nations of the world? The answer to this question cannot be unambiguous if we examine the facts, and we cannot reply with a simple "Yes" or "No." If we keep in mind the broad outlines of the situation, it may be said that the non-Jewish world admitted us into its history chiefly in those aspects which concern the automatic results of a process, the most striking example which comes to mind in this regard being the granting of equal rights to Jews in lawfully constituted states. The division of opinion created by the French Revolution whether to confer equal rights upon Jews or not was decided essentially by granting Jews those rights as a matter of course which the modern world considered to be automatic; that is, if equal rights were part and parcel of the structure of the state and embedded in its character, then the Jews also were permitted to enjoy them. We can therefore say that in all those matters which concern the automatic end-results of the changes which took place in the world we were admitted by the non-Jewish world.

This was not the case in the non-automatic processes, particularly in those processes which depend on our own initiative, in maintaining our own ground, or in those things which are still representative of an independent Jewish existence, so difficult to define, or in those matters where the spiritual and political interests of the peoples of the world were interwoven in the very texture of Jewish life. In this area we see how the political unit of the Jewish people, the State of Israel, served as a seismograph indicating to what degree the non-Jewish world has not yet acknowledged our existence as a separate unit or, at any rate, to what degree our existence is still subject to dispute or doubt. True, there are times when the heart does not reveal its doubts to the mouth; and the wavering reactions of the non-Jewish world to our existence remain inarticulate. At any rate, in all those processes where we were not usufructuaries or a *tertium gaudens* but stood our own ground and struggled in the light of our own ideals—in all these things we cannot say that the differences between us and world-history have been reconciled and that we have been accepted by it in the same way as many other nations have been.

This critical turning-point may be summarized by saying that the basic factor was the desire to seize the opportune historical moment to safeguard the physical and social existence of the Jews among the historical forces of the world. This tendency has presented us and the world with the question: how to reconcile Jewish existence among the forces of the world with the specific character of the Jewish people and with its heritage which is the crystallization of generations.

The Independent Jewish Way

Is the essential meaning of the Jewish aspirations to be found in this change, in its attainments and in its problems? Or is there meaning in the independent Jewish way even in its encounter with world history? And when we speak of an independent Jewish way we refer not only to the political and legal level but to a dimension over and beyond this.

Or to put it differently: can the singular character of the Jewish way of life in the common world whose gates we stormed, be summed up in its mores and folklore or does it have some additional significance? Matters of mores and folklore are no doubt important. But the question is whether the culture of Israel is exhausted by them or whether it has additional features. It is exactly in this matter that our generation finds itself confronted with the gravest problems of Jewish existence and it is these that must be analyzed.

Far be it from us, at a time of earnest deliberation, to falsify Judaism by portraying it in colors that do not comport with its historical character and internal problems. It seems that the central problem is this: Judaism is on the one hand universalistic but on the other hand, in its embodiment and actual dependence on the historical human group, it is not universalistic: Judaism is concerned with the world and its Creator, with the relation between man and God and between man and man in his dependence on God, that is, with questions of man as man. But its actual embodiment as a way of life and as an order of reality is to be found in a specific human group—the Jewish people in its historical form. There is no need for evaluating this character pro or con. It suffices only to establish the fact that it is so. But this fact is bound up with the spiritual questions of this generation.

Since Judaism is embodied in the historical confines of the Jewish people alone, it felt itself in a certain sense absolved from the responsibility of world affairs and confined itself to the cultivation of its own vineyard. But because of the historical change, which is the point of departure of these reflections, it is no longer possible to attend to this vineyard without coming to grips with the contemporary problems of humanity and the world, for our entrance into the historical process brought us face to face with these questions. The acid test that Judaism in its historical heritage must undergo in our generation is: has it the strength or not to measure up to the world problems; in other words, whether it is enough that it be a life preserver for the Jewish people or perhaps whether it can even be that, unless it meets the challenge of these world problems.

That is not to say that the answer to this question must be in simple, positive terms, as: Judaism is attempting to do this, is attempting to become a world force that would deal with the actual present-day human reality from the historical place in which it actually finds itself, within the confines of its national home. A certain correction must be made at this point: we have not yet reached that level of human history, for we are still engaged in the struggle for the most elementary needs of human existence. We may have reached that level of world history in our consciousness and in our wills but we have not reached it actually by securing for ourselves a place in the world. Therefore, as long as we are faced with this problem of extracting the human meaning out of our Jewish heritage, we are bound to remember that our actual Jewish existence has not yet been consolidated. But on the other hand it is impossible not to see that this is one of the signs of the recognition of Jewish reality in our generation, that we are living on many different levels at one and the same time. It is true that we are struggling for elementary political goals in matters of security and population, but nevertheless we desire to reach the level achieved by the rest of humanity, which has either survived these early struggles or had no need to engage in them. Insofar as we are anxious to attain the bases for these elementary acquisitions we cannot restrict ourselves to one level but are obliged to live at the same time on all the levels on which men dwell.

Here again in this simultaneity of Jewish existence we meet with many difficulties, including social difficulties. An example of one such difficulty is bound up with the life of the State of Israel. The community of this state is a poor one which is still unable to supply its needs and yet the human conscious-

ness of this community does not correspond to its poor standard of living. It is imbued with a desire for a social order and
welfare and a just government which, to a large degree, has
already solved elementary problems in the field of agriculture
and industry. One of the difficulties of Israeli society pertains
to its desire to establish a righteous social order with only scant
means at its disposal and without a highly developed industrial
background which could facilitate such an order.

In considering these corrections it is necessary to return to
the question: Can Judaism become a power capable of shaping
our human existence while meeting the challenge posed by the
problems and ideologies of our time, even when it does not
strive to expand beyond the limits of the historical Jewish
group?

The Heritage of Judaism

This question can elicit different answers. It is possible to
say that we are not at all interested that Judaism should become a force of this kind, that we are content with our social
existence based on the sociological models created for us and
with the ways of life which are part and parcel of the sociological basis of our existence. This is an answer which cannot
be dismissed without more ado. It can briefly be answered
as follows: this road is possible in theory but is not open to
us in practice, whether we desire it or not. The inevitability
of an encounter with our Jewish heritage, our dwelling within
it and the challenge it presents, these are decisive facts of our
existence. They are imposed upon us by reason of this country
and by reason of the Hebrew language. The Hebrew language
gives us the key to the treasures of Judaism and casts us willy-
nilly into the life of the generations and their bases: these are
bound up with a definite meaningful heritage and no interpretation will be able to obscure this simple meaning. Further:
we are becoming more and more aware of the various interpretations which seek to obscure the simple meaning of our
historical heritage and to emphasize its nonessential aspects.
It is therefore paradoxical but a fact that the traditional framework of our existence restores us to the generations. However

much Zionism may seek to establish Jewish existence on a basis
of present-day reality alone, it is unsuccessful in confining it
to such an exclusive foundation. If we do not see the dialectic
involved, we fail to see the facts as they are. It need not be
said that Jewish existence within an external framework only, is
impossible in the Diaspora, because it is exactly such a closed
sociological existence that the Diaspora lacks and to emphasize
the exclusiveness of such a framework is to open the gates to
assimilation and extinction.

The question should therefore be formulated as follows:
since our attachment to our heritage and the challenge it presents to us is a matter of destiny, is it a matter of destiny
alone or is it also willed?

Before coming to a consideration of this question, it should
be noted that when we speak of Judaism as a world force, we
do not refer to a Judaism which is wrapped up within itself,
without any windows on the world, but to a Judaism which is
vital, open to the world by virtue of its independence. A polem-
ical note must be inserted at this point! There is a theory which
enjoys great vogue in present-day Jewry which holds that
Judaism in the State of Israel is faced with the prospect of
being reduced to the four ells of nationalism whereas the
Judaism of the Diaspora, by virtue of its physical intermin-
gling with the world and with the great societies within it, will
continue to develop. There is no basis for such a theory; at
any rate, the facts do not support it. Not only because an
open Judaism in the Diaspora will be exposed to assimilation
and the advantages of being open would be offset by the losses
incurred, but for another reason, and that is: Judaism in the
Diaspora suffers from an inherent dualism due to the very
nature of its constitution, for it is immersed within itself and
at the same time is constrained to lead an existence beyond its
Jewish confines. Such a Judaism by its very nature is not calculated to produce a complete Jewish world, since such a complete world would do away with the duality, that is, with the
Diaspora itself. Diaspora Judaism cannot give rise to a complete Jewish realm and yet participate in the course of historical
events. Hence, only in a Jewish area, i.e., the State of Israel,

can the attempt be made to preserve a Judaism that is open and yet not vulnerable or constricted.

Forces Inimical to Judaism

When we deal with the possibility of establishing Judaism as a spiritual force of world significance, it appears that our inner question is also our outer question, that is, the question that arises among ourselves is also the question that obtrudes between us and the world. Judaism by its very nature does not desire partitions: a partition between faith and deed, between world and nation, between society and the individual. Yet, though it does not acknowledge such demarcations, the historical fate of the Jewish people has compelled it to erect just such partitions. Christianity, by its very nature is inclined to set up partitions: faith in one compartment and politics in another, the heavens up above and the earth here below, history on the one hand and faith on the other. But although the Christian nations, by virtue of the fact that they were the arena of historical events, were compelled to come to grips with actual world problems, Christianity is able to regard them, theologically speaking, as existing beyond itself. This does not mean to say that the manner in which it coped with these problems is necessarily to be recommended, but merely to indicate the fact that Christianity did meet the challenge presented by these world problems and that Judaism did not. And so long as it makes no attempt to do so, that is, so long as it makes no effort to be a complete world of ideas, faith, and spiritual values, it will not be a power capable of shaping its own ends.

The actual world with its objectives and ruling ideologies, this world with which we must come to grips, wears a definite aspect. There are forces at work in this world which are inimical to Judaism but there are also forces which can be turned to its favor.

The inimical forces are first of all inherent in the fact that we are living in an ideological world. In this world, ideas, whether they are exalted or shallow, scientific or popularized, have become the common property of all men. These ideas have a specific character: in a certain sense they are neutral with respect to the great historical issues. Ideas such as the abolition of poverty, a more equitable economic distribution, a decent standard of living for all men, making the state an instrument for social welfare—these ideas it may be said are the possession of man as man but not of a man as a member of a community, a faith, or a specific people. These ideas made it possible for the first time in history to mingle with the world and at the same time not leave Judaism, to receive the ideas of the world without a bad conscience and without becoming entangled in the great historical disputes, such as those between Judaism and Christianity. These facts constitute a destructive force from the standpoint of Judaism because every obliteration of distinctions is a threat to the existence of a separate people. But this is the price we pay for being admitted into the modern world.

Another force which carries within it seeds of destruction is connected with world politics, and particularly in our generation when politics is ostensibly concerned with social felicity and redemption which it has achieved or which it is about to achieve. In this matter there is no difference between the West and the Soviet Union. Both maintain that they are the historical embodiment of liberating principles and have indeed already incorporated them, either in a free society or in a welfare state. What has not been incorporated is on the road to improvement; there is no other road because there is no need to establish a new human kingdom. Ideas introducing redemption into politics are also found in our midst, the best example being given by David Ben-Gurion.

Hence, there is a pronounced intellectual impatience in the world of our day. The modern state, however modern it may be, requires a credo of its citizens. This credo is not always explicitly formulated as it was in the Middle Ages or as it is customarily in the Communist world. A dependence on a kind of credo is also prevalent in the Western world which requires that homage be paid to its institutions, laws and so forth. The demand to acknowledge a credo must necessarily impair Jewish existence (to the degree that it seeks to safeguard its specific functions over against the world around it).

The world in which we live and move is a technological one. It leaves little room for direct contact between man and the natural world. It sets up fixed prefabricated patterns of human experience and reduces experience to the least common denominator. This arrangement by technological means removes man from the Jewish sphere, the historical sphere, which as such does not lend itself to transformations through technological stereotypes.

The basic fact that the modern world has become an open public arena for its struggles of existence, for its modes of organization, the nature of its housing and daily manner of living has brought with it its own reaction: one is no longer inclined to find a real refuge in another social world—the world of Judaism—but desires to escape from every kind of society and make his home his castle. The modern reaction to organized rule is a withdrawal from community interests and social life. It is therefore possible for a Jew not to seek an answer for his problems in Jewish public life, but be more inclined to retire to the privacy of his home.

The Chief Modern Intellectual Movements

If we consider the intellectual movements of the modern world, we find three that are most prominent: the first movement typical of our generation goes under the name of Positivism. It asserts—in the context of our analysis—that social life and reality have no meaning; or, at any rate, the one meaning life has lies in feelings and accompanying emotions. The second movement, which enjoys great popularity, is Existentialism, particularly in its French garb. This movement goes so far as to assert that not only has social existence no meaning, but that existence in general is in its very nature absurd; not only is it bereft of all meaning, but is opposed to it.

The third movement is Marxism in its bolshevist form. True, its attraction for our generation is not as strong as it was, but it is still to be reckoned with. This movement owed its attraction to its nature. The basic principle of modern politics was formulated by Machiavelli. This political philosophy regards man as residing in a world of hostile forces. Man has been deprived of Christian grace and even the Greek *fatum*. In the world that revolves about man, caprice reigns, what Machiavelli calls *Fortuna;* and hence the only reaction of man to this world which affords him no protection, is violence—subduing nature by force and consolidating it by force. In the political sphere this meant a policy of violence in governing society by force. In a fundamental historical sense Marxism desired to be a counter-force to the Machiavellian conception, to put politics in the service of over-arching human goals, to demonstrate that the course of history itself is ruled by law and not caprice, and not devoid of reason and moral ends. Politics is the hand-maiden of history—that is, made to serve the ends of reason and ethics. In this sense Marxism desired to be the adversary of Machiavellianism and this was the message of its gospel. But historical fate dealt cruelly with Marxism. It turned the bolshevist revolution into the full embodiment of Machiavellianism itself and adopted a policy of violence and caprice such as the world has never seen, a policy where heart and lips were at such odds with each other. Bolshevist Marxism, unlike Machiavelli, does not preach in the name of violence and in the name of a *Fortuna* which governs the world. On the contrary, it preaches reasonableness and this gives it the opportunity to indulge in excesses, to govern as a dictatorship and wear an impenetrable, sphinx-like mask. Thus did Machiavellianism conquer its historical rival.

What has this, then, to do with our theme, with Judaism? All this is, first of all, designed to indicate those forces in the world with which we shall have to come to grips if Judaism intends to become a world force. To be sure, there are forces which cannot be changed, for example technological forces or the tendency to create common denominators for human existence in its cultural and psychic aspects. But in the realm of ideas it may be possible for Judaism to make a contribution.

It is not possible to discuss these questions without saying a word about Orthodox Judaism. The terms of credentials—if we may here use legal terminology—the status of Orthodoxy in Judaism, are so explicit that they require no proof. Even though a historical study of Jewish life should reveal a multi-

plicity of diverse layers and currents, and even though sociological studies should reveal rifts and factions within Orthodox
Judaism itself—this would not shake the authoritative basis of
its credentials. For the important thing is not the number of
factions or movements but how Orthodox Judaism interprets
itself today. And its interpretation is that it is the lawful heir of
Judaism. At the same time is has no desire to become a world
power and it states explicitly that it is not concerned with
mundane affairs. Orthodox Judaism has therefore no other way
out but to give us all a breathing-spell, a moratorium. It has
a right to refrain from coping with world problems but this
should not prevent others from trying to do so. Even if Orthodox Judaism believes that after all is said and done we shall
all return to her, it is still not free to withhold this respite
from us.

Variations in Judaism

The question of our generation may perhaps be put thus:
is it impossible to have ideological variations of a common Jewish theme? If this is not attempted, Jewish culture will be
exceedingly constricted and deprived of its power to be a constructive spiritual factor for future generations. This does not
mean that we must attempt to define the essence of Judaism
in systematic or dogmatic form, but we should disclose the
roots of a Jewish approach to the world—roots which are hidden
deep in Jewish history but which should now receive special
attention. We cannot interpret Judaism as former generations
interpreted it: we cannot naïvely maintain that we are a direct
continuation of the generations, for we have become too sober
historically speaking, philological criticism has made too deep
an impression on us for us to adopt the same views as our
fathers. A certain amount of freedom within dependence—this
is the only standpoint possible for this generation. How to
reconstruct our basic Jewish existence is the question which
confronts us, and the possibility of such a reconstruction will
decide whether Judaism is to be a fruitful and vital factor
capable of coping with the ideologies of our time.

When Judaism succeeds in effecting such a basic reconstruction, it will be obliged to return to the question of the place of man in creation and find an answer to the question as to whether existence is devoid of meaning as Positivism asserts, or opposed to meaning as maintained by the Existentialists, or merely a historical and political phenomenon, as held by Marxists. Judaism will be able to take a stand on these questions when it shall have discovered itself anew. In meeting this challenge Judaism will be obliged to take a stand over against Christianity and the world of Asia. It will be able to say a word about Christianity by virtue of the fact that it does not see the world as compartmentalized but seeks, by its very nature, to shape it into one whole. And it will have a word to say with respect to Asia; for the religions of Asia have now been divided by a rift which has plagued Judaism for generations. These religions are chiefly concerned with the redemption of the soul and must nevertheless now try to build an actual political world, a social order built on European concepts, not their own.

In this involved complex of affairs Judaism has no other way out than to take an Archimedean point intellectually, which will be faithful to its own principles on the one hand and open-minded to the world on the other. Such an Archimedean point can be derived from a basic Jewish outlook: that man's life does not belong to himself. In his life he is dependent on Him who gave it. In the sense man is not master of the world, and yet his attitude to the world is not a passive one. This Jewish attitude makes sense even when man's inability to dominate is not interpreted as a dependence on God, that is, even when it is not given a religious interpretation. That part of the Jewish viewpoint can be conserved which sees the world in which man lives not as subject to his caprice, not as absurd, nor yet as only historical. This view can be interpreted from the standpoint of faith or from that of non-faith. There are speculative variations within Judaism which lend themselves to controversy pro and con. But it is of utmost importance that there should be within Judaism itself enough room to give free play, actually if not theoretically, to the various possible interpretations of this attitude.

The latitude thus given would acknowledge man's dependence

on the created world and its history. Over against this world man stands as a maker and shaper in accordance with fundamental principles or in accordance with commandments dictated by faith. To shape reality is the function of Judaism, and in this it stands opposed to the salvation of the soul in Christianity and in the religions of Asia. This constant labor over against our existence, over against the actual world of society, will afford the opportunity of returning to the sources of Judaism. This Archimedean point will enable us to understand the Halacha, historically speaking, for the roots of the Halacha go deep down to this view itself and to the same active desire to shape reality. From this point of view Judaism stands opposed to secular movements which deprive the real world of meaning and to those religions which draw a sharp line between faith and the actual world. A reserved acceptance of the actual world, an acceptance united with the attempt to shape it in the light of principles not derived from man alone, this is perhaps the Archimedean point on which we shall be able to stand. In this manner perhaps it will be given to us to make Judaism a living seed for our sake, and thus perhaps it will be possible for us to exist in history, to continue along the separate road of historical Judaism and at the same time be dependent on a world that is not only historical.

CHAPTER TWENTY-FIVE

VISION AND REDEMPTION

by DAVID BEN-GURION

I will begin with some questions:

What are the Jews—a nation like all the nations, a nation with a unique character of its own, a religious community, the fragments of a disintegrated nation? What is Judaism and in what does its uniqueness lie? Is Judaism petrified, rigidly defined and unchangeable in all generations and all countries, or does it change through contact with others, and assume different forms according to the needs of a particular time and place? How was Judaism preserved in the Diaspora when the Jews were scattered among the nations, and will it be preserved in the future? What has brought about the revival of the Jewish State in our day? Is the State of Israel no more than a state like any other, or has it an ideal or a uniqueness of its own? What has the establishment of the State of Israel changed in world Jewry, and what is the mutual bond between Israel and the Diaspora? Which problems has the State solved, and which new problems has it created? What light does the State shed on our past, and what does it promise for the future?

I would not venture to offer a reply to all the questions I have put, nor am I certain that there is any definite and certain reply to historical questions in general. Besides, insofar as there are replies to certain questions, every answer arouses new questions. I will try, however, to reply to some of the questions, and if I succeed in clarifying them to some little extent, I shall feel amply rewarded.

If a Jew had been asked two centuries ago: "What is a Jew?"

563

he would have answered simply and with complete inner confidence: "A Jew is a descendant of Abraham, our Father, who obeys the commandments and hopes for the coming of the Messiah." At that time this answer would have been satisfactory to any Jew wherever he might live, but today it would not satisfy a large part of our people, perhaps the greater part. Ever since the Emancipation, the Jewish religion has ceased to be the force which joins and unites us. Nor is the bond with the Jewish nation now common to all Jews, and there are not many Jews in our time who hope for the coming of the Messiah.

If those who fought for Jewish emancipation in Germany and France had been asked a hundred or a hundred and fifty years ago: "What are the Jews?" they would have replied: "A religious community—the Jews are Germans or Frenchmen of the Mosaic faith." Most of the Jews of Russia, Poland, Galicia or Rumania would have replied a century ago: "The Jews are a minority in exile, completely different from the people among whom they live"; and fifty years ago many of them would have added: "And they aspire to return to Zion." Not many of the Jews of America, even those who continue to call themselves Zionists, would give the last answer today, for it is their desire to become rooted in their new country, as an organic part of America, like all the other religions and national groups which reached America a generation or a few generations ago.

Nor is religious Jewry any longer an integral and internally united entity. The *Neturei Karta* in Israel and the United States hardly recognize as Jews those who do not think and behave as they do. National religious Jewry of the Mizrahi school does not separate itself from the rest of the nation, and recognizes that all Jews belong to the Jewish people, but it believes that it alone observes truly original Judaism, and it aspires to impose its opinions on all other Jews by all possible means. Many observant Jews who do not belong to the Mizrahi believe that the maintenance of religious parties in Israel is extremely harmful to Judaism. They are afraid that the exploitation of religion for political purposes is a danger both to the purity of religion and to the unity of the Jewish people. Then there is Agudat Israel, which stands between the *Neturei Karta* and the Mizrahi, and there are various shades of Reform Judaism. Free-thinking Jewry is no less divided, and the division was particularly great in the period before the rise of Israel, not only in regard to religion and faith, but in the sphere of political concepts in connection with the settlement and the future of the Land of Israel.

Change and Continuity in Jewish History

Change and continuity are the lot of all nations, just as they are the lot of every human being from childhood to old age. There are nations which have known unbroken continuity and few changes, and there are others that have had the opposite experience. Our share of both change and continuity is perhaps greater than that of any other people, and the vicissitudes did not begin in recent times.

The people that went out of Egypt and wandered in the wilderness was different from the one that conquered and settled Canaan. The people that was split up into tribes in the days of the judges was different from the people that was united under the rule of the three first kings; nor was the people united under one king, the same as the people that was divided after the death of Solomon and established the kingdom of Judah and the Kingdom of Israel. There is a great difference between the people in the days of the first kings of Judah and Israel and the people in the period of Uzziah, King of Judah, and Jeroboam, son of Joash in Israel—the two great kings in whose days there appeared the prophets, Amos, Hosea, Isaiah and Micah. And the Jewish people in all the periods which I have enumerated, from the Exodus till the Babylonian exile, was not at all like the people that returned from exile in the days of Zerubbabel, Ezra and Nehemiah and founded the Second Temple.

There is a great difference between the period of Persian rule and the period of the Greeks and the Hasmoneans and the later Herodian and Roman periods. And the greatest changes were yet to come. After the destruction of the Second Temple came servitude to Rome, the great revolts that ended in defeat, and over eighteen hundred years of exile and wandering, generations of persecution and conversion, forced and voluntary, in the lands of Christianity and Islam; wandering from one country to another, from regime to regime, tongue to tongue; compulsory and ever renewing adaptation to the conditions of life, the spiritual climate, and the constantly changing political and economic frameworks in all the countries of the Diaspora in every one of the five continents; unceasing political, economic and spiritual pressure by superior forces. Throughout these prolonged and numerous transformations and tribulations, which have not yet come to an end, the continuous *ego* of our people was preserved to no smaller extent than the national *ego* of stable peoples which were never separated from their own land. What was the nature of this *ego*, and how was it preserved throughout all these internal and external changes and transformations, such as no other people has known in the annals of humanity?

One of the most original thinkers and profound scholars who have dealt with the history of the faith of Israel, Professor Yehezke'el Kaufmann, states in his book, *Golah Venechar*, that "the great rule of history is that every people, when it lives under conditions of exile, is absorbed among its neighbours." And he asks: "How, then, is it possible to explain the fact that the Jewish people clung to the forms of its national existence and maintained its unique national character in spite of the natural effect of social conditions?" And his reply is: "The fact of popular psychology that the Jewish people saw in its *religious character* the only internal reason for its fight for uniqueness, is of vital importance for the solution of our problem. It was no external factor, nor even the so-called biological urge to survive, but *the special power that was latent in Israel's religious culture that was responsible for its unique place among the nations.* The *true basis* for its uniqueness was its religion, for the sake of which it preserved its separateness from the nations . . ."

"The idea which acted in the depth of the nation's soul, compelled it to follow its own special path, and marked with its stamp all the aspects of its life, was a *religious* idea." And Professor Kaufmann emphasizes: "A *religious* idea—and not religion as a régime of laws and commandments, as people are accustomed to think. Hence it was religion (in the sense of faith, i.e., the faith in one God), which was the only source of their national will."

Professor Kaufmann accentuates the point of his interpretation still further and declares that "Judaism must not be considered a national religion in its essence because of the national symbols with which it is bound. . . . If we examine the outlook of later Judaism, that a convert became entitled to the name of 'Israel' in its true meaning by accepting the Jewish religion, we shall see that it was a true expression of *complete liberation from every ethnic bond.*"

If this interpretation of Professor Kaufmann's were correct, it would be impossible to understand the reason for the uniqueness of Jewry after the faith in one God had spread to other nations, especially by means of Islam, and to a large extent by means of various Christian sects as well, and even among the adherents of the Vedanta in India, according to the interpretation of Shankara and Ramanuja. For Professor Kaufmann emphasizes that it is not the practical commandments, but the religious idea of Judaism, namely the faith in one God in opposition to the faith in idols, that united Israel and preserved it in the Diaspora.

Monotheism and Morality

I have no doubt that many have, like myself, eagerly read Professor Kaufmann's monumental work on the history of the faith of Israel, in which he contradicts with convincing force most of the conjectures of the Bible critics of the school of Graetz-Welhausen, and proclaims—justly in my opinion—the originality and antiquity of Israel's faith in one God.

Professor Kaufmann is, of course, aware that the monotheism of Israel is different from the conception of the Vedanta, which in the books of Shankara arrives at an extreme doctrine of pure unity. The difference is in the nature of the One and Only supreme God. According to Shankara's doctrine, Brahma is a purely metaphysical entity; he has to be known and understood, and the redemption of humanity depends on this knowl-

edge and understanding. But while the supreme God of the
Vedanta imposes no obligations for right action and he himself has no moral qualities, the supreme God of Israel is the
personification of righteousness, justice and mercy, and only he
that cleaves to these qualities is near to God and is a truly religious man.

In Kaufmann's controversy with Ahad Ha'am, in which he
insisted that not only justice but kindness and mercy as well,
are basic elements of Judaism, the truth is certainly on the side
of Kaufmann, although in my humble opinion Kaufmann is
mistaken in imputing the ethics of lovingkindness and mercy
only to later Judaism and not to the Judaism of the Bible
(p. 203). Insofar as the qualities of lovingkindness and mercy
are concerned, there is no difference between the prophetic
morality and that of later Judaism, as Kaufmann implies. The
God of Israel in the Bible is long-suffering and of great mercy
(Numbers, 14: 18). Micah the Morashtite asks: "He hath
showed thee, O man, what is good; and what does the Lord
require of thee, but to do justly, and to love mercy, and to
walk humbly with thy God?" (6: 9). Hosea denounces Israel
because "there is no truth, nor mercy, nor knowledge of God
in the land" (4: 1), and when he wishes to comfort this people
he says: "And I will betroth thee unto me in righteousness,
and in judgment, and in lovingkindness, and in mercies" (2:
21). Jeremiah, the prophet of the destruction, proclaims in the
name of the Lord: "I am the Lord which exercises lovingkindness, judgment and righteousness, in the earth: for in these
things I delight, saith the Lord" (9: 23), and the Psalms constantly repeat and emphasize the quality of mercy: "The Lord
is merciful and gracious, slow to anger and plenteous in mercy"
(103: 8); "For Thou, O Lord art good and forgiving and plenteous in mercy to all them that call upon thee" (80: 51);
"For I have said: The world shall be built in mercy" (89:
3); and Zechariah, the prophet, calls to his people: "Execute
true judgment, and show mercy and compassion every man
to his brother" (8: 9).

For this reason it is surprising to find Professor Kaufmann
stating that "it was not morality but religion that served as

the basis for the uniqueness of Israel in the Diaspora." The distinction between morality and religion is foreign to the spirit and the character of the faith of Israel, both that of the Bible and that of later times, in my humble opinion, but the fundamental error of the author of *The History of the Faith of Israel* and of *Golah Venechar* lies in the fact that he does not adequately appreciate the central national factors which were active in the life of Israel, both while it lived in its own land and while it was in exile, aside from "the religious idea," i.e., monotheism, which after the spread of Christianity and Islam was no longer specific to Israel.

Professor Kaufmann, who sees the the uniqueness of the Jews in monotheism, was unable to ignore entirely the national factors active in Jewish history, and says that "in the consciousness of the Jewish people the racial religious concept indeed occupied a considerable place," and "Israel was not merely a religious community but also a nation, a specific racial and national entity." But even with this addition, it seems to me that this great scholar in the faith of Israel misses the target of historic truth. Kaufmann apparently completely ignores the profound spiritual attachment of the Jewish people to its ancient homeland even while it lived in exile; he does not realize the bond of the nation to the Hebrew language; and, what is even more remarkable, he does not appreciate the Messianic vision of redemption, which fills the very air of Jewish history, which in various periods aroused mighty, tempestuous movements in Israel, and which in our own day has led to a revolution in the history of our people.

On the threshold of Jewish history stood three central events, the memory and the influence of which have not passed away among us even to this day—the Exodus from Egypt, the revelation on Mount Sinai, and the conquest of the Land of Israel. The will for redemption preceded these three decisive events. According to tradition, which undoubtedly contains a grain of truth, our people spent its infancy in exile, in the Egyptian house of bondage, and without the will for redemption the departure from Egypt would have been impossible. Without this will, they would not have conquered the Promised Land.

As for the prophets who moulded the ancient character of our people, the will for redemption and the vision of redemption pulsate in all their prophecies, ideals, commands and visions.

The Vision that Revived Israel

We are now in the thirteenth year after the renewal of the Jewish State in our ancient homeland. In our days we have seen a number of nations that have emerged from bondage to freedom, in Europe, Asia and Africa. India, Burma, Ceylon and other countries gained their independence almost simultaneously with the State of Israel. But everyone knows the fundamental difference between the rise of Israel and that of those countries. The nations of India, Burma and Ceylon lived on their own territories all the time; but at certain periods they fell under the domination of foreign conquerors, and when they cast off foreign rule, they were left independent. Not so with Israel. Nor does the rise of Israel resemble the rise of the United States, Canada, Australia, or the Latin American countries. These countries were rediscovered by conquering voyagers from Spain, Portugal and Britain. The metropolis in Europe sent them emigrants whom they settled, and after the settlers had arrived at a certain degree of development, they split off from the metropolis by force or by agreement, and took over command of their own affairs. The rise of Israel, like the survival of Israel in exile, is a unique phenomenon in world history, and it can shed light on the riddle of the survival of Israel in exile.

The Jewish State was revived in a period when the House of Israel in the Diaspora was not as wholehearted and united as it was two hundred years ago in its faith; neither in the observance of the laws and commandments nor in the "religious idea," in which Professor Kaufmann sees the secret of the survival of Judaism. There is no doubt, however, that without the forces which preserved Judaism in the Diaspora we would not have achieved the revival of Israel. It was not a conquering and settling power, nor an enslaved nation in its own land casting off the foreign yoke, that revived Israel. *In the beginning of our revival was the vision.*

The State of Israel was established in a country which had been inhabited by Arabs for 1,400 years, and it is surrounded on the south, the east and the north by Arab countries. The Land of Israel itself was ruined and impoverished and the standard of living in it was lower than that of the countries from which the Jews who began to rebuild it came. As late as 1918, at the end of World War I, there were fewer than 60,000 Jews in this country, i.e., less than 10 percent of its non-Jewish inhabitants. And yet in this land there has arisen in our days the Jewish State. The second thing that has happened is also unique: the Hebrew language, which the people appeared to have laid aside for two thousand years, came to life again, and became the language of speech, life and literature, and of the revived State of Israel. Nothing like this has ever happened in the history of languages. We know of the tremendous effort which the State of Eire has been devoting for decades to the revival of the Gaelic tongue, and yet all these efforts have utterly failed, although the Irish people has been living in its own land all the time, and this nation—which is not yet entirely free from its profound hatred of the English who ruled it so long—continues to speak the English language. Still a third thing has happened in Israel: in this country the Jews have fundamentally transformed their economic way of life and taken up manual labor and the tilling of the soil.

What, therefore, is the explanation of this extraordinary political and cultural phenomenon, which has no parallel in human history?

The Messianic vision of redemption, the profound spiritual attachment to Israel's ancient homeland and to the Hebrew language, in which the Book of Books is written, were the deep and never-failing springs from which the scattered sons of Israel in the Diaspora drew for hundreds of years the moral and spiritual strength to resist all the difficulties of exile and to survive until the coming of national redemption.

Anyone who does not realize that the Messianic vision of redemption is central to the uniqueness of our people, does not realize the basic truth of Jewish history and the cornerstone of the Jewish faith. The spiritual and political transformations that have taken place in the Jewish people in the course of thousands of years have affected the characteristics and the expression of this vision. It did not assume the same form at all periods, just as Judaism as a whole assumed different forms at different times. But through all these changes the inner kernel was preserved, the kernel whose first germination we see in the State of Israel.

Within the consciousness of the Jewish people, there were indissolubly combined special and distinctive national elements, confined to the Jewish people, and cosmic, human elements which are outside of any national, or even human framework, for they embrace the entire universe. The supreme expression of this combination was the Messianic vision of redemption; the people's prophets and teachers aspired to complete national redemption in the Promised Land, but this aspiration was not limited to the Jewish people. It brought tidings of peace, justice and equality to all the peoples—tidings of complete redemption for humanity and the ending of all cruelty and tyranny the world over.

In the Messianic vision of redemption an organic bond was woven between Jewish national redemption and general human redemption. The inner necessity of this combination will be fully understood in our own days. In this generation more than at any other previous period in the history of mankind, nations are interdependent, and even the mightiest of nations cannot safeguard its sovereignty, security and peace without bonds with other nations. Although the world is in a state of division and disintegration, it is in fact one world, and in spite of numerous and bitter conflicts, its oneness and its unification are gathering strength with the achievements of science and technology, and modern means of communication which abolish distance. The redemption of our people, therefore, is impossible, and its peace and security cannot be safeguarded without the redemption of the world as a whole, without the achievement of general international peace, and unless peace and equality are established between the nations. For this reason the prophets and teachers of Israel did not promise redemption alone, but demanded that their people be a chosen people. The prophet Isaiah denounced his people with all the implacability of a man who was bound to the truth, and foretold the destruction of cruelty and tyranny in the world and the exaltation of all men, when he said: "And I will punish the world for their evil, and the wicked for their iniquity; and I will cause the arrogancy of the proud to cease, and will lay low the haughtiness of the terrible. I will make a man more precious than fine gold; even a man than the golden wedge of Ophir" (13: 11-12). Yet he believed in the great mission of his people, and said in the name of God: "I, the Lord, have called thee in righteousness, and held thee by the hand, and made thee a covenant for the peoples."

These two motifs—the vision of redemption and the chosen people—are repeated in the books of the Bible and the Apocryphal literature, in the Mishna and the Midrash, in the Jewish prayers and in Hebrew poetry. The greatest of Jewish philosophers, who seemed to have become estranged from his people after he had been excommunicated by the Amsterdam community, who denied religious tradition and laid the foundation for the criticism of the Bible on the basis of reason and logic, even he expressed in his *Tractatus Theologicus-Politicus,* three hundred years ago, his absolute confidence that the day would come when the Jewish people would re-establish its state and God would choose it afresh. In other words, on the renewal of its national sovereignty the Jewish people would again be a chosen people, showing the way to the world. The men who saw the vision of the Jewish State in the nineteenth century, Moses Hess and Theodor Herzl, also believed that it would be a moral state.

Naturally, so long as all Jewish communities were immersed in religious life, both the vision of redemption and the idea of a chosen people, as well as the attachment to the Land, also took on religious characteristics. The history of our days has shown that neither the vision of redemption nor the attachment to the Land and the Hebrew language are conditional to attachment to tradition and religious law. In the building and defense of the Jewish State, religious and free-thinking Jews took part with equal devotion, and the opposition to the work of settlement which brought about the creation of the State came with considerable force from both orthodox and non-religious circles.

The former saw in the attempts to establish the State by natural means a dangerous divergence from the traditional faith in the coming of the Messiah, while the latter saw in the return to the ancient homeland a danger to emancipation and the status of the Jews in the Diaspora. Although the anxieties of both sides were not entirely baseless, the revival of Israel aroused joy and pride in all sections of the Jewish people, wherever they lived, and apart from the opposition of the two extremes—*Neturei Karta* and the Communists—there was no Jew in the world who did not enthusiastically welcome the establishment of the State.

On this occasion I will not renew the argument as to whether the State was created by the immigrants or by the Zionist Organization. I will say only that it is now the greatest asset, and perhaps the only common asset, of the entire Jewish people; for in most of the values of Judaism, the Jewish people in our day is divided and disintegrated. In the Diaspora, Jews have no common language, no specific way of life, no general attachment to the Jewish law and tradition, no common conception of the nature and the future of Judaism.

In order to understand the function of the State in Jewish history from now onwards, it is necessary to discuss two further changes which radically altered the nature of the Jewish people in the first half of the present century, before the rise of the State.

At the beginning of the twentieth century there were ten and a half million Jews in the world. More than 80 percent of them (8,673,000) were concentrated in Europe, and less than 10 percent lived on the American continent: about one million in the United States, and about 50,000 in the other countries of the New World. At that time about 700,000 Jews lived in Asia and Africa, and about 55,000 in the Land of Israel. Before the beginning of World War II, the Jewish people numbered about 16,500,000, and although in the meantime millions had emigrated overseas, the great majority of the Jewish people, almost nine million souls, lived in Europe. European Jewry, especially that of eastern Europe, had been for the previous three centuries the Mother of Jewry. It housed the centers of learning; within it there arose the Emancipation movement; in it there were born the *Haskala* and modern Hebrew and Yiddish literatures. In its midst *Jüdische Wissenschaft* flourished, from it there grew the *Hibbat Zion* movement and the Jewish workers movement, and when the First Zionist Congress was convened at the end of the nineteenth century by the creator of political Zionism, Dr. Theodor Herzl, European Jewry was the major part, the fortress and support, of the Zionist movement.

In the Zionist movement we must distinguish between ancient sources, almost as ancient as the Jewish people itself, and new circumstances and factors which grew on the soil of the modern era in Europe in the nineteenth century and the beginning of the twentieth. These ancient sources are the profound spiritual attachment to the ancient homeland and the Messianic hope. Their beginning is bound up with the life of the first Hebrew, to whom, according to tradition, the promise was given: "And I shall give thee and thy seed all the land of Canaan for an everlasting heritage." It was neither Herzl, nor Hess nor even Baruch Spinoza, who invented the idea of a Jewish State. For thousands of years Jews prayed three times a day: "Blow the great trumpet for our freedom and raise the banner for the ingathering of our exiles, and gather us together from the four corners of the earth, and may our eyes behold the return to Zion in mercy." The sporadic waves of immigration from various countries, the visits of emissaries from Palestine to the various parts of the Diaspora, the Messianic movements that arose from time to time, from the period following the destruction of the Temple to the eighteenth century—all these were a real and living expression of the attachment and the longing for the homeland, and the hopes that throbbed in the hearts of the people for national redemption and salvation. Until the beginning of the emancipation in the nineteenth century, all Jews wherever they were, knew that the places where they lived were only a temporary exile, and it did not even occur to them that they were a part of the peoples among whom they lived, just as such an idea was foreign to those peoples themselves. This feeling of being foreign existed in East European Jewry till the last moment. The Jewries of Russia, Poland, Rumania and the Balkans knew all the time that they were a minority people in a foreign land, and in the eighties of the nineteenth century there began a mass migration from the countries of the East to lands overseas.

This feeling of foreignness, which was expressed in the word "Galut" existed in all the generations after the destruction of the Second Temple. The Jewish faith, the Messianic hope, and the feeling of moral superiority, enabled the Jews to overcome all the troubles and persecutions and sufferings that were their lot in most countries and in most historical periods. In this capacity for resisting external pressure, there was a kind of great moral heroism, but it was a passive heroism, for it was accompanied by a submission to fate and a feeling of helplessness. The longed-for redemption was to come by supernatural means.

The Modern Movement of Redemption

The revolutionary events of the nineteenth century, the movements of national revival that rose among several European countries, aiming at unification and independence (in Italy, Germany, Poland and the Balkans), the wakening of a working class to fight for a new social system, the mass migration from Europe to countries overseas—all these opened up in the nineteenth century a new road for the vision of Messianic redemption, straightened the backs of the Jews, strengthened their consciousness of their own value and standing, and revealed the possibilities of redemption that were latent in Jewish migration. Faith grew in the capacity of the Jew to rebel against his destiny, to liberate himself by his own strength from the bonds of exile, to bring the redemption nearer by natural means, by a planned effort of settlement. A new phenomenon appeared which changed the course of Jewish history: the phenomenon which we call *halutziut* (pioneering)—the creative and revolutionary capacity for action which brings into play the human faculties for the realization of the ideal without recoiling from any difficulty or danger, which brings into action all the physical and spiritual powers, and strives with every ounce of energy toward the goal of redemption. This creative and active faith was at first the heritage of a few, but the life's example of those who began the work of implementation slowly influenced hundreds, thousands, and later even tens of thousands, and the impetus of *halutziut* transformed *Hibbat Zion* and the Zionist movement into historic forces.

There were also pioneering phenomena in previous centuries; in the days of Don Josef Nasi in the sixteenth century, in the days of the immigration to the Land of Israel of Rabbi Judah Hasid and his companions at the beginning of the seventeenth century, and in the days of Rabbi Hayim Abulafia in the middle of the eighteenth century. These, however, were sporadic phenomena, which were not continued. Only in the last quarter of the nineteenth century did the pioneering spark flame up and grow and incessantly gather strength, until it arose like a pillar of fire, lighting the way for the loyal sons of the Jewish people in all parts of the Diaspora, to the establishment of the Jewish State.

Without the guidance of a social ideal, which was also born in the nineteenth century, the pioneering impetus would have lost its way and wasted its efforts, and the Jewish State would not have been established: this was the idea that labour is the principal foundation for a healthy national life. Not only did the Jews in the Diaspora live in exile and depend on the decisions of others, but the structure of their economic and social life was different from that of any independent people living in its own land and controlling its own destiny. The Jews were landless and were not employed in the principal branches of the economy on which the self-supporting existence of a nation depends. Without a mass return to the soil and to labour, without the transformation of the economic and social structure of the Jewish population in the Land of Israel, we would never have arrived at a Jewish State. It is impossible to conceive of a state the majority of whose people does not work the soil and carry out the types of work required for its economic survival.

The feeling of foreignness, either as a reaction to anti-Semitism in central and western Europe, or as the outcome of the consciousness of a specific Jewish character and the absence of a traditional bond with the gentile nation and its culture, as in eastern Europe; the example of the national and social liberation movements; and the recognition of the value of labour as the main basis for national life—all these were common to large parts of European Jewry, and almost only of European Jewry. It was there that there appeared the pioneering movement which transformed the aspiration of generations into an act of daily implementation; it was this movement that laid the foundations for the Jewish State, the most wonderful event in the life of the Jewish people since the conquests of Joshua, son of Nun.

But during the twenty-eight years between the end of World War I and the end of World War II, European Jewry was visited by two appalling disasters: one-third of East European Jewry was cut off from world Jewry by force about forty years ago, at the end of World War I, by the bolshevik régime in Russia; and about two-thirds were slaughtered by the Nazi butchers during World War II.

This was a double disaster, unparalleled even in the history of our people, which visited us in the first half of this century, before the establishment of the State. Only scanty fragments of European Jewry were left in freedom, and the period of European Jewry in the life of the Jewish people came to an end, never to return. In the second half of this century, however, there was a second change, a fruitful and beneficial one, in the growth of the great Jewish center in the United States of America, from one million at the beginning of the century to over five millions in our own day. And this was not only a quantitative growth. In the foremost country of the New World there grew a Jewish center, the like of which was never seen in the Diaspora for wealth, influence and power, for political and spiritual capacity. And this Jewry, which had first considered itself a spiritual "colony" of European Jewry, has become in our own day the political, material and cultural metropolis of Diaspora Jewry. Here there arose a great labour movement, though it is now shrinking as the second and third generations of immigrants shift to trade and industry and the free professions. Here there arose important centers of Jewish scholarship, Jewish universities and academies for teachers and rabbis; here the feeling of exile and foreignness grew weaker and disappeared completely, and although the ideology of assimilation struck no roots in American Jewry, assimilation in practice—in language, culture, manners, economy and political life—is constantly growing. The Jews of America, including the Zionists among them, see themselves as a part of the American people, while at the same time they consider themselves a Jewish community; their hearts are alert to every Jewish cause, and their material and political assistance for the building of the Yishuv and the establishment of the State has been of inestimable value.

When the Jewish State arose in the middle of 1948, the character, status, distribution and conditions of life of the Jewish people were completely different from what they were at the end of the nineteenth and the beginning of the twentieth century.

The State—a New Chapter

The rise of Israel opened up a new chapter not only in the history of this country but in the history of Jewry as a whole. It straightened the back of every Jew wherever he lived; in the course of a few years it redeemed hundreds of thousands of Jews from poverty and degeneration in exile, and transformed them into proud, creative Jews, the builders and the defenders of their country; it poured new hope into the hearts of the helpless and muzzled Jews of the Soviet bloc; it revealed the extraordinary capacity of Jews for accomplishment in all spheres of human creative work; it revived Jewish heroism; it assured every Jew who enjoys freedom of movement in the land where he lives, of the opportunity to live in his independent homeland if he chooses to do so, thus insuring potentially, if not in practice, a life of independence for the entire Jewish people. On the international scene there appeared a free Jewish nation, equal in rights with the rest of the family of nations. It is not remarkable that all parts of the Jewish people in the Diaspora, whether they called themselves Zionists or non-Zionists, orthodox or non-religious, whether they lived in lands of prosperity and freedom or in lands of poverty and enslavement, welcomed the rise of the State with love and pride, and the State became the central pillar on which the unity of Diaspora Jewry now rests. Let us not, however, be overconfident; the vision of redemption brought forth the State, but the State is still far from the realization of the vision.

The State has solved a number of problems, and also produced new ones. Jewish sovereignty enables the Jew in Israel to mold his own life as he wishes, according to his own needs and values, in loyalty solely to his own spirit, his historic heritage, his vision of the future. In Israel, the barrier between the Jew and the human being has fallen. The Jews in their own state are no longer subject to two opposing and conflicting authorities: on the one hand to the authority of the gentile people in all economic, political and social matters and in most spiritual and cultural questions, as citizens and subjects of a state with a non-Jewish (or even anti-Jewish) majority; and on the other hand, their own authority in the one small and poor corner which draws its sustenance only from the past, in which they function as members of the Mosaic faith or of the Jewish people in the world. Israel has restored to the people living in its midst their wholeness as Jews and human beings; the sovereign Jewish authority covers all the needs, acts and aspirations of man in Israel. In Israel the profound cleavage, which in the Diaspora split, and still splits, the lives and souls of Jews, has been healed—the cleavage which impoverished both the man in the Jew and the Jew in the man. Our lives have again become, as in the days of the Bible, a complete unity of existence and experience, which embraces in a Jewish framework all the content of the life of man and people, all his acts, needs, aspirations, cares, problems and hopes.

In Israel there has been created not only the Jewish field, the Jewish sea, the Jewish road, the Jewish factory, the Jewish laboratory, Jewish science and research dealing with all that the world contains and not only with *Jüdische Wissenschaft.* Here there has arisen a Jewish armed force and Jewish political life; and Jewish literature, poetry and art once again draw their sustenance from all the natural and living sources that sustain us. The single, complete authority makes everything human Jewish, and everything Jewish human. Only here, where we have become free citizens in the State of Israel, have we become citizens of the world with equal rights, who must adopt an attitude of our own on all the problems of the world and the relations between nations. This sovereignty also imposes on us heavy responsibilities which were unknown to Jews in the world for many centuries: we bear the full responsibility for our fate and our future, and we have a heavy price to pay for this responsibility.

On this occasion I will not go into Israel's political and economic problems, but I must deal with its internal problems and its bonds with world Jewry. I will say only a few words on the decisive and fateful political problem of Israel: the problem of security. The solution of this problem does not lie in the organization of a first-class army—and no one will suspect me of any desire to belittle the value of the Israel Defense Forces. The survival and the peace of the State of Israel will be safeguarded by one thing and one thing alone—large-scale immigration. For the safeguarding of its security the State requires an addition of at least two million Jews in the coming period.

The State's Two Supreme Laws

This State has been established by the strength of the entire Jewish people, and not only that of the Jewish people who live in our own generation; I have no doubt that all generations of Jewry have a share in the extraordinary and tremendous accomplishment of our day: the State has been established for the entire Jewish people. But *in practice* the State is today inhabited by only 1,700,000 Jews, about 14 percent of the Jewish people. For this reason alone, the State considers itself no more than a beginning. The State of Israel has two central objectives that were laid down in the Proclamation of Independence and in two special laws, which—although they are not called laws—I consider to be the supreme laws of the State of Israel, destined to be a light for the generations. Until these are fully implemented the work of the State of Israel will not be completed. The first is the Law of the Return, which contains the objective of the ingathering of the exiles. This Law decrees that it is not the State that grants a Jew the right to settle in Israel, but that this is his right by reason of the fact that he is a Jew, if only he wishes to join the population of the country. In Israel a Jewish citizen has no privileges over the non-Jewish citizen. In the Proclamation of Independence we laid it down that "The State of Israel will uphold the full social and political equality of all its citizens, without distinction of religion, race or sex," but the State sees the right of Jews to return to the Land of Israel as preceding its foundation, and having its source in the historic and never-broken bond between the Jews and their ancient homeland. The Law of the Return is not like those immigration laws existing in other countries which lay down the conditions under which the State receives immigrants from abroad. The Law of the Return is the Law of the historic permanence and continuity of the bond between the Land and our people; it lays down the principle of state by virtue of which the State of Israel has been revived.

Within the few years in which the State has been in existence, complete exiled communities, from Asia, Europe and America, have returned to Israel, but we are still at the beginning of the process of the ingathering of the exiles. None of us can foretell the potential scope of the ingathering of the exiles. There are Jewish communities which wish to come here and are not permitted to do so. There are Jewish communities which have the permission, but do not have the will. But there is not a single Jewish community in the world which does not send some Jews to Israel, whether the number is small or great. The two forces which were active in the process of *aliya* before the rise of the State—distress and the visions of redemption—have now been reinforced by the attractive power of Israel, its freedom and independence, and its creative momentum. Only the future will show what parts of our people will return to the homeland, but we are certain that the millions of Jews who long to come to Israel, and who for decades have been deprived of the right to do so, will surely come in the end.

The second law determines the social direction of the State and the character to which we aspire for the people of Israel— and it is contained in the State Education Law. Paragraph Two of this Law says: "The object of State education is to base elementary education in the State on the values of Israel and the achievements of science; on the love of the homeland and devotion to the State of Israel and the Jewish people; on training in agricultural labour and handicraft; on pioneering implementation, on striving for a society built on freedom, equality, tolerance, mutual assistance and love of humanity." This law lays down the main lines for making us into a model people and a model state, and asserts our unfailing bond with the Jewish people in the world. Our historic goal is a new society built on freedom, equality, tolerance, mutual assistance and love of humanity—in other words, a society without exploitation, discrimination, enslavement, the rule of man over man, the violation of conscience and tyranny. This law also expresses our aspiration to develop in Israel a culture built on the values of Judaism and the achievements of science. And the Law demands devotion not only to the State but also to the Jewish people.

Both this Law and the Law of the Return are far from a state of complete realization; they are only signposts by which the State wishes, and is bound, to be guided, so that it may survive and achieve its historic aim.

We cannot boast that the people of Israel are today a model people, although within our short period of independence we have perhaps made more progress relatively than any other country in a similar period. Our society is far from perfect, and it needs reforms. Nor can we congratulate ourselves that by adding a million Jews to our population after the rise of the State we have carried out the ingathering of the exiles. But I shall try briefly to describe both the historic necessity of making this country into a model state, and the qualifications we have to carry out such a great ideal, as well as the need and the prospects for the ingathering of the exiles to the maximum extent.

Israel's Faithful Ally

Israel has one faithful ally in the world: the Jewish people. Israel is the only country in the world which has no "relatives" from the point of view of religion, language, origin or culture, such as are possessed by the Scandinavian peoples, the English-speaking peoples, the Arab peoples, the Catholic peoples, the Buddhist peoples, etc. We are a people that lives alone. Our nearest neighbors, both from the geographical point of view and from the point of view of race and language, are our bitterest enemies, and I am afraid they will not speedily be reconciled to our existence and our growth. The only loyal ally we have is the Jewish people. There is no doubt that no inconsiderable parts of scattered Jewry will join us in the near future: both Jews from the Islamic countries and Jews from Europe, as well as no small number from the Jewries of the prosperous countries. But there was a Jewish Diaspora as early as in the First Temple, which preceded the Babylonian exile; this Diaspora was in Egypt. During the period of the Second Temple the Diaspora grew, and it is hard to imagine that the Third Commonwealth will absorb the whole of the Diaspora of our days. *The survival of Jewry from now on is inconceivable without the State of Israel and an inner attachment to that State. But the survival of the State is also inconceivable without a loyal partnership between it and all the Jewries of the Diaspora.* Without a moral, cultural and political illumination that will go out from Israel to all parts of the Diaspora, this partnership may be undermined. The War of Independence and the Sinai Campaign aroused Jewish pride and raised the status of Jews among the Jewish people and in the whole world. But the State of Israel was not created to be a Jewish Sparta, and it is not by military heroism that it will win the admiration of the Jewish people.

Only by being a model nation, of which every Jew, wherever he is, can be proud, shall we preserve the love of the Jewish people and its loyalty to Israel. Our status in the world, too, will not be determined by our material wealth or by our military heroism, but by the radiance of our achievements, our culture and our society—and only by virtue of these will we acquire the friendship of the nations. And although there is no lack of shadows—most of them heavy—in our lives today, we have sufficient grounds for the faith that we have it in our power to be a model people. And it is already possible to point to three elements in Israel today which give clear indications of the moral and intellectual capacities latent within us; they are the labor settlements, the Israel Defense Forces, and our men of science, research, literature and art, who can bear comparison in their relative quantity and high quality with those of any other people in the world.

The labor settlements have marked new roads toward a society built on liberty, equality and mutual assistance, which have no parallel in any country, in the East or the West. The Israel Defense Forces are not only a loyal and effective instrument for defence, but an educational framework that raises human standards, breaks down communal barriers, and gives the youth of Israel self-confidence, responsibility to the community, and a vision for the future.

And although in the few years of our sovereign independence we have been compelled to invest tremendous resources in defence, the absorption of immigrants and the building of our economy, and we shall have to continue to do so for many years to come, we have succeeded in establishing institutions of science and research and development, literature and art, on a level as high as that of the most developed countries.

I am not one of those who engage in destructive criticism of science, as if the law of causality had been abolished and there was a doubt of the existence of matter, and the undermining of science had restored us to faith in the miracle of revelation. I am one of the "conservatives." Einstein, it will be remembered, continued to believe in the law of causality even after the quantum theory. And in my humble opinion, if I may say so, matter has not been abolished, but the identity of matter and energy has been revealed. It may be said that in a way the duality of matter has been broken down by science, and we still remain within the bonds of experience and the reign of material laws. Science, however, does not tell man what path to choose in life, for science is beyond good and evil. Without religious or moral or spiritual values man has no reliable guide in life, and the human race has no more exalted values than those bequeathed to us and to the world by the prophets of Israel.

Just as we must not belittle the tremendous difficulties which face Israel in the political and economic spheres, so we must not ignore the moral difficulties that are strewn in our path: the habits of Diaspora life, the lack of education and political capacity, our over-fragmentation, our exaggerated partisanship, the undermining of tradition, absorption difficulties, the influence of inferior books and periodicals from within and without, the numerous crimes among immigrants who have not become integrated and Israeli youth who have lost all spiritual and social values. We shall not consolidate our national standing and security in one day, nor shall we achieve our economic independence without difficulty, and certainly we shall not become a model people without constant effort and social struggle. There is also a mutual influence between our economic position and our political status on the one hand, and our capacity for spiritual and social advancement on the other. Matter and spirit are not two separate realms. The creation of the body and soul are dependent on each other. We have in store a difficult and prolonged effort in all spheres—economic, political, social and cultural. But the history of the Jewish people in all periods, and the capacity that has been revealed since the establishment of the State, the extraordinary transformation that has been achieved among hundreds of thousands of immigrants in a short space of time—all these may strengthen our faith that in the end we shall accomplish our aim, though much depends on the attitude, the cooperation, and the will of the Diaspora.

The Diaspora of Today

We are now faced with a Jewish Diaspora which is radically different from that which existed fifty years ago. The two largest and most important centers of Jewry in the Diaspora are in the United States and the Soviet Union. The greater part of the Jewry of the Moslem countries has already come

to Israel, and it may be assumed that most of the remainder
will also come here within the next few years. American Jewry
is different from any Jewish community we have known so far
in our history, from Babylon Jewry in ancient times to Russian
Jewry in the days of the Czars. It has grown up in freedom and
equality, and all those among whom American Jews live are
descendants of immigrants like themselves. In one thing alone
does it resemble all the other Jewish communities in the Diaspora: its economic and social structure is different from that
of the majority of American people. The Jews of America belong more and more to the middle and upper classes; the number of farmers is almost nil, and the number of workers is
constantly declining. Jews are being absorbed in trade, industry and the free professions, and they are making great material
progress in these vocations. How this will influence their situation and the attitude of the majority to them, time alone will
tell.

   In all other respects there is no difference between Jews and
non-Jews. There is no ideology of assimilation among the American Jews, but there has been an increase in assimilation in
practice, although this assimilation does not involve the denial
of Jewishness. This Jewishness, however, has few and feeble
foundations. There is an increase in religious worship, but it
is doubtful whether it involves an intensification of religious
consciousness. Membership in a synagogue or a temple is not
identical with an attachment to traditional law or to the spiritual values of the prophets of Israel. Members of the bodies
that belong to the Zionist Organization are no different from
those Jews who do not belong to that Organization. Zionism
in America is not based on the consciousness of exile and foreignness, and on the will and the need to turn to Zion. Any
comparison between the fate of European Jewry and that of
Jewry in the United States—whether for good or for ill—is
baseless. There is nothing to prevent the Jews in America to
preserve their Jewishness and their bond with Zion, but at the
same time there is no internal or external obligation to do so.
Any scientific prognosis based on historical necessity—if scientific prognoses are possible at all in history—is liable to be

disproved. There is no particular usefulness in abstract discussions of the future of Jewry in America—*but we should discuss what is to be done to safeguard its future in accordance with our Jewish aspirations and needs.*

The position of Jewry in the Soviet bloc, and especially in the Soviet Union, is different. This Jewry has been condemned to disintegration for about forty years by a hostile, totalitarian regime. The generation that has grown up under bolshevik rule cannot receive any Jewish education, and it has been forcibly severed from its historical tradition and its bonds with the Jewish people and the Land of Israel. It cannot read and write either Hebrew or Yiddish. It is forbidden to leave Russia. And had it not been for the rise of Israel, it would have been condemned sooner or later to disappearance in the Jewish sense.

But even a totalitarian regime is neither all-powerful, nor safe against changes and fluctuations. In contradiction to the declared theory of self-determination for all the peoples in the Soviet Union, the Jews, although they officially belong to a Jewish nationality, do not enjoy this right. The Birobidjan experiment was a complete failure, and anti-Semitism in the Soviet Union, although it is forbidden by law, has neither ceased nor weakened. This fact, no less than the fact of the existence of the State of Israel, encourages and strengthens Jewish feelings, although under the conditions of the Communist régime they have no organized or cultural expression. The Jewish problem in Russia becomes more and more troublesome even from the point of view of the Russians, and it is not impossible that ultimately, and perhaps even in the next few years, they may arrive at the only real solution: the opening of the gates for the *aliya* of the Jews to Israel. According to reliable information, the number of Jews in Russia is three to three and a half millions. If the gates are opened, it may be assumed that at least half of Russian Jewry will come to Israel, and the State of Israel and the entire Jewish people must prepare for this possibility, which involves both tremendous difficulties and beneficial prospects such as we have not yet known, for the State and the future of the Jewish people as a whole.

Even though over 80 percent of Diaspora Jewry is concentrated in the two great world powers, we must not neglect the Jewish communities in the other prosperous countries, in western Europe, Canada, Latin America, South Africa, Australia and New Zealand. Conditions in these countries are not exactly identical with those in the United States, but there is a considerable resemblance. Here, too, there is no point in engaging in abstract prognoses. What we have to deal with is methods of work and the means of deepening the consciousness of the Jewish mission and Jewish unity. In my opinion these methods are threefold:

1. Hebrew education, the central place in which will be held by the study of the Book of Books.

2. The intensification of the personal bond with Israel in all forms: visits; investment of capital; education of children, youth and university students in Israel for longer or shorter periods of time; training for the best of the youth and the intelligentsia to fit them to join the builders and the defenders of the country.

3. Deepening the attachment to the Messianic vision of redemption that is the vision of Jewish and human redemption held by prophets of Israel.

These three elements are the *common denominator* which can unite religious, orthodox, conservative, reform and free-thinking Jewry, and give Jewish meaning, purpose and significance even to those Jews who will not join in the process of the ingathering of the exiles. These are the three elements that can serve as a moral and cultural bond between Diaspora Jewry and Israel. Attachment to Hebrew culture, and first and foremost to the Book of Books, in the original; to Israel; and to the Messianic vision of redemption, redemption both Jewish and human; that is the threefold cord which can unite and bind together all sections of Jewry, of all parties and of all communities; and—if we will it—it shall never be broken.

CHAPTER TWENTY-SIX

JUDAH AND ISRAEL

by ROBERT GORDIS

To understand the future of the free Jewish communities
in the Diaspora we must reckon with the past of the Jewish
people, for the nature of these populous and influential centers
can only be understood in the context of the historical experience of our people from its early days to the present. In George
Santayana's words, "He who forgets the past is doomed to
repeat it." Not a few widespread errors are to be attributed to
this disregard of history.

During its long experience, the Jewish people evolved three
forms of group life. The first was the *natural community*, in
which Jews lived in their own land, either under conditions
of full independence or under alien rule with partial autonomy
in the fields of culture and religion. During that era, which
comprises by and large the periods of the First and Second
Temples, every Jewish child in the land felt himself an integral
part of his people, without need to reflect or doubt his status.
From the life of his people each individual drew all his being, to his people he contributed all his efforts and capabilities,
and within his people all his aspirations and desires found their
expression. The idea of separating from his people could not
occur to him, except in such rare cases of willful defection, as
that of the historian, Josephus Flavius.

Then there came the days of the Destruction and the Exile.
The Jews were scattered among the nations, and their temporary
residence among them became permanent. In most places, the
Jews had the special status of an alien group, which existed

solely by leave of the dominant power or the supreme ruler. The "host" nation officially recognized the government organs of the Jewish community, such as the Archons in Alexandria, the Exilarch in Babylon, the Aljama in Moslem and Christian Spain, the Council of the Four Lands in Poland and its counterpart in Lithuania, and the *parnasim* and community leaders in the ghettos of Italy and Germany. Here the Jewish community assumed a new form, that of the *compulsory community*. Now the individual Jew could not rid himself of his obligation toward Jewry as a whole, unless he was prepared to sever the connection entirely by a religious conversion, an extreme step beyond the realm of possibility for the great majority of the people. So long as a person had not ceased to be a Jew, the government imposed community discipline on him, compelled him to comply with the communal laws, to pay the taxes and fines levied on him, and also to accept all communal penalties, ranging from excommunication to whipping, and in some cases, even to the death penalty. In the eyes of the external government, the individual Jew did not exist at all— he was merely a cell of that alien and singular organism which was basically and profoundly different from its surroundings and followed its own particular customs in its internal life. As regards its external relations, the Jewish community in the Diaspora was a kind of state within the state; it was permitted to remain because of its economic usefulness as *servi camerae,* "slaves of the exchequer," or in other respects.

There were basic differences between the natural community, which lived an independent life on its own land, and the compulsory community, which spent all its days in temporary quarters, which was dependent on the will of others, and was reminded at every turn that it was in exile. Nevertheless, these two types of groups resembled each other in several basic respects. In both, the authority of the state prevailed over the will of the individual, insisting that he should not evade his obligations toward the community. Despite this, it is important to stress that the loyalty of the individual to the community sprang from an inward, and not merely an outward, source. The inner desire of every Jew to share in the

heritage of Torah and the faith it enshrined, operated power-
fully within the compulsory group and thus paralleled an important element of the natural community. On the other hand,
in the natural community the element of outward compulsion
was not entirely absent. The two forms thus bore some resemblance to each other, despite their fundamental differences.

Organic Communities

Another conspicuous similarity between the two types of
Jewish community concerns their life-content. Both were all-
inclusive, that is to say, the community created, fostered and
controlled all the interests of the nation and all the needs of
the individual. It was the community that established and
maintained all those aspects that we today classify as religion,
culture, education, civic defense, charity and social services,
family life, economic organization and the administration of
justice. Both types of group life, therefore, may be defined by
the sociological term "organic community," i.e., a community
dealing with all matters relating to the life of the individual
and the group as such, and, consequently, entitled to demand
the support and discipline of each of its members.

This common feature produced yet another trait characteristic of both types of group—a complete unconcern with the basic
problem which has preoccupied the modern Jew during the
past two hundred years and which is still far from resolved:
What is the nature of the Jew and the character of the Jewish
group? This issue never arose anywhere during those two stages.
Neither the Bible nor the Talmud contains any discussion of
the nature of the Jewish group—whether it is a race, a religion
or a nationality—and the reason is not far to seek. In its classic
periods the Jewish people did not differ from other nations
in regard to the scope of its group life. For everywhere in the
ancient world, the nation included religion, culture and the
tradition of a common ethnic origin. These were so organically
interrelated that the destruction of the state meant the extinction of the people, the religion and the culture as well.

Nor did the medieval Jewish philosophers raise the question
of the nature of the Jewish people and its spiritual heritage.

A short definition is given by the Gaon Saadia in his famous dictum, "Our nation is a nation only by virtue of the Torah," and this generally accepted approach found a succinct expression in the familiar utterance of the Zohar, "The Holy One, blessed be He, the Torah and Israel are one." In sum, from the beginning of Israel's existence to the end of the Middle Ages, the nation, the religion and the culture formed a single entity, not susceptible of separation either in theory or in practice.

There was indeed one important feature in which the two types of community parted company. In the compulsory group, the Jews were always dependent on the will of others and always liable to persecution, expulsion, expropriation and massacre. In view of the permanent crisis hanging over them, the community felt compelled to demand total obedience from all the members, since any deviation was likely to weaken the shaky position of a group that lived by the sufferance of others. Diaspora Jewry therefore developed a tendency toward intolerance, including even the suppression of dissenting views. To a certain extent, the fierce struggle of Christianity against the heretical sects arising in its midst also served as an example to Jews in dealing with heterodox opinions and practices. Whenever a breach threatened in the ramshackle wall of defense, the entire community was mobilized for the battle. In this respect, medieval Judaism is fundamentally different from biblical and talmudic Judaism, upon which it is based. Thus, when the Karaite sect in the early Middle Ages denied the authority of the Oral Law, Rabbinate Jewry used all its weapons, including the ban, in order to fight it.

An instructive difference is apparent in the attitude of the Pharisees to the Sadducees in the days of the Second Temple, when the latter, too, opposed the validity of the Oral Law. The sages of the Mishna polemized against the Sadducees, but did not resort to the minor ban or to excommunication. It is evident that the spirit of authentic Judaism, as reflected in the biblical and talmudic periods, did not favor the use of force and coercion in matters of conscience. This tendency gained momentum only in later ages, when the pressure of the *Galut* was very strongly felt and the existence of the people hung by a thread. Freedom of thought and expression constitutes a precious legacy from the most creative epochs of Jewish history, the periods of the First and Second Temples.

To be sure, the ban as a coercive institution has its origin in the Book of Ezra (VIII, 8), but its development in the days of the Mishna and the Talmud was slow, and it does not seem to have occupied an important place in law or in life until the Middle Ages. During that difficult period, the ban served as the most important defensive weapon against those seeking to destroy the institutions of autonomous communal government or to undermine the law of the Torah, the source of the authority of the leadership.

A detailed survey of the history of the ban in the Middle Ages shows that in the overwhelming majority of cases the ban was used not in the sphere of faith or opinion, but in the practical domain: (1) to protect the dignity of the communal courts; (2) to discipline those who had contravened practical precepts, e.g., not observed the "second day of the feast" in force in the Diaspora, sold non-kosher meat or offended against morality; and (3) to punish leaders who had abused their offices. Even in the case of the famous excommunication by the Amsterdam community of Uriel Acosta and Baruch Spinoza, the principal motive was not religious-philosophical intolerance, although this factor, too, was of course not lacking, but the desire to prevent the spread of heterodox ideas from the Jewish ghetto to Dutch circles, which might have led to the abolition or the restriction of the Jewish rights of residence and activity in Holland.

Even the Middle Ages, however, did not cause a complete eclipse of the tradition of freedom of thought and of the right to dissent, the clear imprint of which is visible in all the books of Scripture and on every page of the Talmud. So long as the authority of the *halacha* and of the practical precepts was not challenged, medieval Judaism left fairly wide scope for difference in the sphere of faith and opinion. The reborn State of Israel should hold high this precious Jewish tradition of freedom of the spirit.

As we have noted above, the natural and the compulsory communities have many features in common. The third type of community, on the contrary, which is the product of the latest period, differs from its two predecessors in almost every respect. This new type of group-structure is the basis for the permanent crisis in the life of the modern Jew—during the last two hundred years in western Europe and America, and in the last half century in eastern Europe, as well. Its marks, moreover, are highly evident in Israel.

The Mighty Revolution

The eighteenth century saw a mighty revolution in the life of the Jewish people, originating in France, spreading to Germany and the other Western countries, and eventually reaching the populous communities of eastern Europe. The thinkers of the "Age of Reason" shook the foundations of traditional culture, generally, and of religion in particular. Their view penetrated also into the seemingly closed world of the Jewish community and gave intellectual confirmation to a process of surrendering the Jewish tradition that had already proceeded apace following the tremendous changes in the economic and political structure of Western society. The "philosophers of reason" helped justify the Jews of the younger generation in their denial of the authority of the Torah and its precepts as a way of life. The French Revolution, which destroyed the remnants of the feudal system in the West, following the Industrial Revolution and the rise of the bourgeoisie, adopted the slogan of "the rights of man" *qua* man and declared all differences of race, religion, social status, and economic class, to be artificial and immaterial. From this flowed the logical conclusion that the Jews, too, deserved equality of rights and were to be accepted as citizens, and not as members of a foreign organism living on sufferance within the confines of the state.

In brief, the "Enlightenment" propagated by the philosophers undermined the authority of religious tradition, and the "Emancipation" espoused by the statesmen granted equality of rights to the individual Jew, at least in a legal and economic sense.

The horizons of existence within the economy, culture and society, widened immeasurably for the individual as Western Jews penetrated into the life of the countries in which they dwelt. It is not surprising that most Jews enthusiastically offered up the "sacrifices" demanded of them: abolition of the authority of the Jewish community, weakening of the feeling of group solidarity and renunciation of the traditional way of life based on the Torah.

Both the benefactors and the beneficiaries in this granting of equal rights understood that the process was not a gift, but a matter of *quid pro quo*. In the words of one of the great advocates of Jewish emancipation, Clermont-Tonnerre, "to the Jews as Jews—nothing; to the Jews as men—everything." The famous Sanhedrin convened by Napoleon also showed a clear tendency toward surrendering Jewish communal existence for the sake of the emancipation of the individual. Since the total extinction of the Jewish group was no easy matter, it was hoped at least to reduce its power and scope and to minimize the authority of the tradition upon which it rested. Only isolated individuals and a few groups, such as the Jews of Holland, opposed the Emancipation and rejected both its benefits and its drawbacks. Extreme assimilation, which expressed itself especially in conversions and mixed marriages, soon began to wreak havoc in the settlements of the West. This went so far that a hundred years later a sociologist like Felix Theilhaber predicted the "disappearance of German Jewry" in the near future, as the result of an irreversible bio-sociological process.

Reactions against Assimilation

But life does not obey the laws of logic, and sometimes sets at naught even the doctrinaire decrees of "historical necessity." After retreat before the first vigorous onslaughts of assimilation, forces latent within the Jewish people reasserted themselves against the danger of extinction. Not all Jews were seduced by the mess of pottage offered by assimilation. Various factors, in part subconscious ones, played their part in this reaction, such as a deep, unsuspected loyalty to ancestral tradition, a reverence for the Torah and its way of life, scarcely appropri-

ate for modern living in an age of progress, but of which they
were unable to divest themselves. Deeply rooted childhood
memories, shamefaced affection for parents and grandparents
whom one did not want to hurt—these, too, played a part.
There were not a few who were troubled by qualms of conscience: their sense of self-respect could not reconcile itself
to the idea of repudiating a spiritual heritage for the sake of
material gain. The famous Jewish stiffneckedness refused to
surrender to adversaries whose ill-will was scarcely disguised.

Beyond all these subtle motives must be added the crassest
and most conspicuous factor—the growth of anti-Semitism—
which emerged in the very days of progress and precisely in
the enlightened countries of the West. A series of sensational
events stimulated a process of re-education for the modern
Jew. The Damascus Blood Accusation in 1840, the abduction of
the Mortara boy in 1855, the organized massacres and legal
discrimination in Russia from 1881 onwards, ritual murder
trials in Russia, Bohemia, Hungary and Germany between
1882 and 1911, the rise of parties and factions that glorified
anti-Semitism as a philosophy in Germany and France, and
above all, the Dreyfuss Affair in France—these events taught
thousands of Jews in western Europe that the emancipation
and assimilation were not identical with the Messianic age and
that a long road lay ahead before the establishment of brotherhood and peace among men would become a reality.

Of course, the advocates of "Emancipation" within Jewry
and without did not hope for the complete extinction of Judaism. They were content with less, with its restriction to the
sphere of abstract religious and ethical doctrine and the practice of a limited number of rituals, especially those which
did not stress the particular character of the Jewish group.
The Emancipation era gave rise to the third type of Jewish
group life, that which may be called the "voluntary community," for everyone was now at liberty to join the Jewish community or to secede from it. It was no longer a natural and self-
evident fact that every individual Jew belonged to the Jewish
community, nor did the government force him to accept the
community's discipline. On the contrary, a thousand influ-

ences were steadily at work, consciously and unconsciously, to draw him away from its orbit.

True, important elements in Jewry opposed assimilation, continued to identify themselves with the Jewish community and tried to maintain the age-old spiritual heritage to the best of their ability and understanding. Genuine devotion and outstanding talent created various philosophies of Jewish survival, but the *status quo ante* could not be restored. Jews no longer lived together in separate compact areas of their own. By accepting citizenship in their various countries of residence, they renounced the authority of their traditional legal and administrative institutions. Linguistic assimilation was an essential prerequisite for admission into the society of their Christian fellow citizens; in brief, they were compelled to accommodate themselves to a new culture and way of life, of which their forebears had never dreamt. *Two goals now motivated the Jew in the modern period: the preservation of his Jewish identity on the one hand, and the defense of his political and social rights on the other.* The maintenance of Jewish existence was all the more difficult as the values of modern culture, science, philosophy, literature and art found a strong echo in his heart; beyond the practical *necessity* of integrating himself in the new society, he felt an inner *desire* to be spiritually at home in the modern world.

Attempts at Survival

To safeguard Jewish survival in this new, enthralling and perilous world, various modes of approach were evolved with one characteristic in common—they all created a *fragmentary Judaism,* in place of the organic all-embracing totality which had prevailed in the past. When a ship is sinking, every sailor tries to save one or another object from destruction. Thus, several attempts were made to rebuild Jewish loyalty by propagating a *secular Jewish culture.* The founders of the Science of Judaism in Germany at the beginning of the nineteenth century hoped that the revelation of the rich cultural values created by the Jews in the past would induce Jewish youth

in the present to associate itself with the people, instead of
being carried away by the alluring tide of assimilation and
personal advancement. The futility of the "Society for the Science of Judaism" soon became apparent when most of its
leaders themselves changed their religion, and only Leopold
Zunz—in the words of Heine—"remained faithful to the sublime caprice of his soul." The Science of Judaism, which continued to develop until our day, became an important and
even indispensable instrument utilized by other movements
dedicated to Jewish survival, but it was unable per se to step
into the breach.

Other fruitful attempts were made to preserve the Jewish
group by creating a rich secular literature and culture in both
Hebrew and Yiddish. To a lesser extent a German-Jewish,
French-Jewish and English-Jewish literature emerged. These
cultural achievements entered the treasure house of the Jewish
spirit but their original purpose was not achieved. Culture
by itself is not capable of building and preserving a people.

More consistent were the attempts to refashion *Judaism as a
religion* and transform Judaism into a sect parallel to the ruling Christian denominations. Here Germany served as an excellent experimental laboratory. Enormous differences existed
between Abraham Geiger and Samuel Holdheim's Reform on
the one hand, and Samson Raphael Hirsch's Orthodoxy on
the other, but both renounced the national character of the
Jewish group in the present. Both believed that a Jewish people had existed in the past; they disagreed as to whether it
would be reconstituted in the days of the Messiah; but they
were not at all divided as to the present. Even the positive
historical school of Zechariah Frankel—known in our day as
Conservative Judaism—which proclaimed the importance of the
national elements in Judaism, such as the Hebrew language
and the aspiration of a return to Zion, was not entirely free
from a tendency to confine Judaism largely within the framework of a religious cult. Since all the religious tendencies of
the nineteenth century sought primarily to buttress the civic
and political equality of the Western Jew, besides reckoning

with new ideas and attitudes in the fields of philosophy and science, they all attempted to create a Judaism *kechol hadatot,* "like all other religions."

The weakness of religion generally as a result of the new ideas of the nineteenth century, strengthened the tendency toward relinquishing Judaism, while in addition there were the advantages the individual Jew expected from absorption into the majority. In the second half of the nineteenth century, it appeared that the famous slogan "German citizens of the Mosaic persuasion" had indeed succeeded in providing a firm basis for the rights of the modern Jew by the side of his fellow citizen of the Catholic or Protestant faith. But this was so only in theory. In point of fact, this approach was unable to eradicate the feelings of religious hostility, racial hatred and economic jealousy which now assumed "scientific" forms. On the contrary, along with the progress of assimilation, anti-Semitism increased.

The nineteenth century was marked by the rise of nationalism and the creation of unified states, such as Italy and Germany. This stimulated the idea in the minds of many Jewish leaders and thinkers that Jewry, too, should secure its existence through *Jewish nationalism on a secular basis,* so that Jews might again be a people "like all the nations." The advocates of Diaspora nationalism, such as Simon Dubnow and his adherents, demanded for the Jews minority rights to parallel those of the numerous other ethnic groups intermingled in eastern Europe. Zionism, which drew more directly from Jewish tradition in the past and was more deeply rooted in the realities of the present, demanded the return to Zion and the upbuilding of the homeland. Not one miracle has taken place in our generation, but miracle upon miracle: the ingathering of the exiles, the regeneration of Jewish creative power in the spiritual and material sphere, the re-establishment of the State and its heroic defence against its enemies. We, who are privileged to see the vision of a rebuilt Jerusalem growing before our eyes, are both thrilled and awed by this manifestation of Israel's eternal life; and before this miracle and mystery, only silence is seemly. . . .

It is important to emphasize that these various attempts to save one or another aspect of the Jewish heritage were all rooted in the tradition and to a considerable extent represented its development. Enormous achievements of permanent value must therefore be credited to the cultivators of the Science of Judaism, to the creators of modern Hebrew and Yiddish literature, to the spokesmen for the various modern religious philosophies of Judaism, and above all, to the pioneers of Zionism and the builders of the State of Israel. Nevertheless, we should not overlook the fact that none of these approaches succeeded in creating a *complete, integrated* Jew, such as had existed in earlier generations. The reason is self-evident—the modern period, which began with the French Revolution, created the *voluntary community,* which aspired to nothing more than a *fragmentary, non-organic* conception of Judaism for its members. This basic feature of Jewish life during the last two hundred years has produced all those numerous instances of groping and inner contradiction, fragmentation and inconsistency in the soul of the modern Jew. "Thou shalt be whole"—this biblical commandment has been largely neglected in the life both of the individual and of the community in our time. The numerous manifestations of decadence, evasion and spiritual impoverishment which characterize modern Jewish life have their origin in this dissection of a once-living organism.

This situation cannot be allowed to continue, for we are standing on the threshold of a new epoch. The old slogans, only partially successful in the past, are totally inadequate today. In the past twenty years, a triple revolution has taken place in Jewish life: the extermination of the great majority of Eastern Jewry through Nazism, the rise of American Jewry and the establishment and consolidation of the State of Israel.

In the Revolutionary Modern Period

This momentous period requires a new approach. As we have seen, there have been three stages in the history of the Jewish people: the "natural community" of the period of independence, the "compulsory community" of the Middle Ages, and the "voluntary community" of the modern period. *We must recognize that none of these is appropriate to our present situation.*

At first blush, it would seem that in the State of Israel the "natural community" has been re-created, for each individual member in the State of Israel naturally feels himself to be part of the community. But the similarity with the "natural community" of ancient times is far from complete. In the modern world, a man may change his nationality at will, group membership cannot be imposed on him, in spite of the rabbinic principle that "an Israelite, although he may have sinned, is still an Israelite." Not a few of those leaving the State of Israel sever their connection with it. Moreover, the State of Israel is a democratic country and the Israeli Arab, therefore, is a full-fledged citizen, who rightly demands full and equal rights, and is increasingly being integrated into the national life. The question arises as to the nature of the relationship of the Israeli Jew to the Israeli Arab. This problem cannot be permanently evaded.

Even more serious is a second problem: what is the nature of the relationship of the Israeli Jew to the Diaspora Jew? It seems to me that the universally accepted position in the State of Israel—perhaps the only principle shared by all the parties, from the right to the left—is that *the State of Israel is a state like all other states, and that the Jewish people is like all other peoples, neither less nor more.* From this position the conclusion is derived that the Jews of the Diaspora are essentially a part of the Israeli nation, with rights and duties related to the State. Moreover, due to his remoteness from the homeland, the Diaspora Jew faces complete extinction, either through a slow process of assimilation or because of violent outbreaks of persecution. The State of Israel and its citizens are therefore in duty bound to "utilize" and "salvage" Diaspora Jewry as effectively as possible, while there is still time. Individuals who can be persuaded, must be brought to the Land of Israel; but the others, who cannot be moved from their countries of residence, should be urged to serve the State by their material means and political influence, before they fall prey to extinction and oblivion. It should be noted that most Israeli activity in the realms of education and propaganda, that is directed to Diaspora communities, is conducted largely in this spirit.

The interminable debates on "the affirmation or the negation of the Diaspora" have convinced neither the negators nor the affirmers. What is incontrovertible is that the theory of the inevitable doom of the Diaspora communities through assimilation or persecution is not accepted by even an insignificant minority of the Jews of the free world, especially in America.

It has not been noted that this approach is also inadequate for dealing with the attitudes of world Jewry to Israel. The term *moledet* (literally "birthplace") usually applied to the State of Israel is totally inappropriate. The five million Jews of the United States regard the State of Israel with pride and affection, but they do not see it as "the old country" (in Yiddish *die alte heim*), the phrase that their fathers, immigrants from Russia, Poland, Austria and Hungary, applied to the lands of their birth. Moreover, the attitude of American Jews to Eretz Israel is completely different from the attitude of Irish, German and Italian immigrants who have left the lands of their birth for the New World, and who have no attachment to the former except for a number of receding memories, which grow weaker every day. The American Jew did not come from Eretz Israel, nor does he wish to erase it from his memory as part of a dead past. Eretz Israel occupies in the consciousness of the Jew abroad a special place, which cannot be expressed by the term moledet.

The Nature of American Jewry

But this is not all. American Jews know well that assimilation is an ever-present peril, fraught with sacrifice and heartache. But they nevertheless do not expect total disappearance. Unlike other ethnic minorities which within a few generations become fused with the real or imaginary Anglo-Saxon majority and vanish in the American "melting-pot," American Jews see every indication of their permanent survival as an identifiable group in America. This conviction stems from two sources:

the nature of the Jewish community in the United States as it is now crystallizing, and the structure of American society as it has developed since the establishment of the United States. American history demonstrates that every ethnic-cultural minority coming to America is eventually absorbed and disappears. This happened to the Dutch, Swedes and Hugenots in the seventeenth century. In the same way, assimilation has made considerable progress in the case of the German, Scandinavian and Irish elements that immigrated in the nineteenth century, and the same tendency is increasingly present in the most recent groups of immigrants, the Italian and the Polish. Swimming against the stream is possible only to a few who are willing to be regarded as aliens. American society does not contemplate the existence of a multiplicity of ethnic groups, except for a brief transition period of one or two generations. On the other hand, a basic feature in the life of the American people is the principle of the permanent existence of many religious groups, large or small, *de jure* and not merely *de facto*. An American who belongs to a small sect, such as the Mennonites, the Quakers or Jehovah's Witnesses, is not inferior to a member of one of the large groups, such as the Catholics or the Methodists. Moreover, although Jews make up only about four percent of the total population, the idea of the equality of religions is so deeply rooted in the heart of the American people that Judaism is recognized as an equal partner of Catholicism and Protestantism, forming a "religious triad" with them. As a result, its influence and prestige are greater than its proportion in the general population.

The American Jew, therefore, looks forward to the permanence of his Jewish life in the country, not as an alien or on a temporary basis, but as an established member of the American nation. He also sees several positive *internal* factors making for group survival which can be mentioned here only briefly. One is the fact that so large a group, numbering over five million, can bear the loss of thousands and tens of thousands, through secession and total assimilation, without the loss of the collective Jewish identity. Another is the concentration of the vast majority of American Jews in communities of considerable extent, which permit the establishment of religious, educational and cultural institutions that deepen the sense of Jewish loyalty in the hearts of children, youth and adults. More than half of the Jewish population lives in New York and environs, while over two million others live in the thirteen largest cities of the country. That is to say that 75 percent live in Jewish communities of 10,000 or more members, sufficiently large and viable to guarantee survival.*

During the last ten years, there has been a growing tendency to settle in suburbs around the large cities. Far from encouraging assimilation, these attractive areas stimulate in the Jew a need to belong, at least officially, to the Jewish community by joining a synagogue, a Jewish community center, or Jewish organizations, such as the Zionist Organization, the B'nai B'rith and the like. There is, of course, no lack of prophets of woe who regard this "suburban" Jewry as utterly superficial and vacuous. They deny that there is any spiritual awakening to be discerned in the emergence of hundreds of newly organized communities in all parts of the country. It is true that psycho-sociological factors play no small part here—the human wish to adapt oneself to one's environment by belonging to a community, as well as the urge to strike roots in the new settlement where these residents have established themselves by the purchase of houses and gardens.

This is true, but it is not the whole truth. If the significance of the religious revival on the basis of such external manifestations was at first exaggerated, we should not make the opposite mistake of minimizing realities and dismissing them out of hand. The extensive and far-flung movement to the suburbs, which is leading to the establishment of congregations, the opening of schools for children and classes for adults, the founding of Jewish youth organizations, the appointment of rabbis and social agencies and the setting up of countless organizations for various Jewish causes, cannot fail to have some influence on the life and thought of the participants. There is considerable evidence of a new attachment to Jewish customs,

* See Dr. Goldberg's essay.

which expresses itself at least in the observance of the most salient features, such as the kindling of the Sabbath lights, *kiddush,* Hanukkah and Purim, the High Holy Days and the Pilgrimage Festivals, *Bar mitzvah* and marriage rites, and also, in growing attendance at synagogue services by tens of thousands of men, women and children.

In the last few years, there has been a considerable increase in the number of children attending Hebrew schools, and the percentage of youth receiving some education is steadily growing. Even the most superficial education—the majority of American-Jewish children have not yet passed beyond this stage—serves at least to strengthen the pupils' feeling of belonging to their people. It should be noted that the educational situation has improved qualitatively as well. The number of day schools (yeshivot) is increasing, and although their students still constitute only a small minority, there are already thousands who devote anywhere from ten to twenty hours a week to Hebrew studies.

Interest in Judaism is noticeable also among the adults, and the reading of literature on Jewish religion, history and current problems has grown. There are an increased number of courses in religion and Jewish culture at general universities and Jewish educational institutions. Altogether, the intellectuals are displaying an interest and respect for the values of religion and its manifestations in life that would have been inconceivable twenty years ago.

Jews and the American Religious Revival

The much-discussed general "religious revival" in America is a complex and variegated phenomenon, which cannot be disposed of by a snap judgment. It may best be described in the shape of a pyramid. The base represents an *abstract interest* in the content of religion which has developed in recent years among the people at large, as well as student youth, the intellectuals and progressive circles. The narrower, middle section of the pyramid represents the smaller number of those who have risen from abstract interest to *theoretical acceptance* of the principles of the religious world-view and to a positive attitude toward religious practice. The apex of the pyramid represents the minority which has reached the highest level of *personal commitment* both to the religious world-view and adherence to its way of life.

Some observers of the Jewish migration from the congregation of the large cities to the spaciousness of the suburbs insist that the move will increase the trend toward superficiality, ignorance and extreme adaptation to the non-Jewish environment. One such observer has already eulogized the quality of Jewish life in the ghettos of the cities during the past generation. No one truly familiar with the facts concerning these areas of settlement thirty or fifty years ago, will fall prey to the error of exaggerating the degree of Jewish knowledge and loyalty prevalent there. On the contrary, the urge toward adaptation and assimilation was by no means absent among children of teeming tenements in a crowded city. As for the danger of the loss of Jewish identity by contact with non-Jewish neighbors in the new suburbs, an interesting and unexpected sociological phenomenon has become evident. Even in these districts, a social distinction exists between Jew and Christian. They meet in business, at school, in cultural institutions and in the political sphere. But these relations, while friendly, rarely go deep. At six o'clock when the working-day is over, each of them returns to his own house and to the fellowship of his own group. There seems to have emerged a "maple-lined ghetto." Whatever attitude may be taken toward this phenomenon, it is clear that its existence will reduce the impact of assimilation among most of the new suburbanites.

As a member of a recognized religious community, the American Jew feels at home in the American nation, and this feeling of "at homeness" is nurtured by the lessening of organized anti-Semitism following the fall of Hitler. It is not without significance that despite the discovery of Communist spies in the United States during the recent period, many of whom were of Jewish origin, the preachers of anti-Semitism have not succeeded in exploiting this situation and whipping up a large-scale anti-Semitic movement in the United States.

At the same time, the Jew has a feeling of kinship toward

his Jewish brethren everywhere in the world, and contributes toward their rescue and the satisfaction of their needs. He is especially proud of the achievements of the State of Israel in peace and war, and does not hestitate to voice his opinion concerning political developments that are prejudicial to the interests of the new State, which, he profoundly believes, is the natural ally of the free world and the United States. How is he to explain his relationship toward another country as an American citizen? No other religious community has a similar attachment for a country outside the borders of Amercia.

Unlike All Nations and Religions

Just as the Jew in the State of Israel encounters difficulties if he wishes to define his Jewishness within the limits of conventional nationalism, so the Jew in the Diaspora cannot exhaust his Jewish consciousness within the formula of conventional religion. The secular nationalist approach ("Jews like-all-other nations"), no less than the Simon-pure sectarian theory ("Judaism—like-all-other religions") is totally inadequate for comprehending the realities of Jewish life. The Jewish people is unique—this is both the teaching of tradition and the key to its future. Ever since its emergence, the House of Israel was taught that it was a peculiar people, a people that "dwells alone and is not reckoned among the nations." The Talmud did not hesitate to describe God as wearing phylacteries bearing the legend, "Who is like unto Thy people Israel, one nation upon the earth." *The Jewish people is unique in the world.* The believing Jew will see in this attribute the will of God, who has elected Israel from all peoples for His service. The secular Jew will seek to explain this uniqueness by the extraordinary events that have befallen the Jewish people during its long pilgrimage through time, but he will still be confronted by the miracle and the mystery of a unique and eternal people.

A vital Jewish life for our age requires two factors: (1) *the recognition that the Jewish people is a unique group-phenomenon in the modern world;* and (2) *the creation of an organic group life, containing the elements of peoplehood, religion and culture in an indissoluble bond.* Because of its uniqueness, the

Jewish people cannot be compared with any other religious or racial group. By restoring the all-inclusive, organic character of Jewish life, we do not mean to turn back the clock of history. For in contrast to the Middle Ages we shall establish an organic Judaism based not on external compulsion, but on free choice, so that every individual wishing to sever his connection with his people will be at liberty to do so.

Jews do not constitute a religious community or a "race" or a cultural group, or even a nationality, in the ordinary sense of these terms. If we want a term, there is the well-known traditional term "people" (*am*), which denotes a religio-cultural ethnic group. The members of the Jewish people all over the world differ among themselves in their social and economic position, their political nationality, their religious views. Nevertheless, they belong to one people sharing a common history, a sense of kinship going back to the Patriarchs, a loyalty to the tradition of Judaism as the source of their being, however they may modify it, and a profound conviction of a common destiny.

Only such an approach can serve as a bridge linking the Jews of Israel and of the Diaspora, which is the supreme task of our generation. If Diaspora Jewry recognizes solely the religious aspect in Judaism, while its attachment to Hebrew culture remains weak and superficial, the present warm feeling of brotherhood toward the Jews of the State of Israel is bound to decline. It is therefore vitally necessary to intensify educational and cultural work in the Diaspora, to develop the knowledge of the Hebrew language among the youth and adults, and generally to encourage the will to survival in Jewish groups everywhere. The State of Israel has already contributed a considerable number of teachers and group-leaders for the Diaspora communities, especially outside the United States. Unfortunately, they have not always approached their task with a correct appreciation of the realities of Jewish life. If their efforts are to bear fruit, they must not approach their work in the spirit of a salvage operation or as a temporary extension of life for dying Jewish communities. They must be imbued with the realization that there are prospects of genuine, contentful Jewish life in the free world, at least in the present and in the near future. As to the more distant future, no prophets bearing patents of authority have yet arisen in our generation.

Of course there are many who predict the ruin of the free centers on the basis of the bitter fate of the European Jewish communities. But they are overlooking one basic truth. American Jewry is a *novum*, a new experience, a unique phenomenon in the long history of the Jewish people. This large, powerful community has two forbears from which it stems, western Europe and eastern Europe, and it resembles each of them in certain features. Like every child, however, it is not completely identical with its progenitors: it has a character of its own.

American Jewry—Unique Phenomenon

American Jewry resembles western European Jewry in its modernity and its adoption of the culture of its environment, but it differs from it in most respects. First and foremost, it far surpasses western European Jewry quantitatively, both absolutely and relatively. German Jewry, the largest group in the West, never numbered more than 600,000, i.e., one percent of the total population. American Jewry numbers five and one half million, i.e., 4 percent of the total population; its density of settlement has already been mentioned. But this is not all. The great majority of American Jewry has a feeling of being at home, as free and equal citizens rooted in the land and the nation, such as was rare even in western European Jewry, which always had to be on the alert against organized, arrogant and powerful anti-Semitism. And lastly, America has an active Jewish life with all its facets, a host of organizations and movements, with elaborate programs, for the inculcation of Jewish ideals and sentiments in the youth—instrumentalities which western European Jewry possessed scarcely at all before Nazism.

It cannot be denied that America has not developed a Jewish way of life of rich and varied content, matching that of eastern European Jewry, but one trait American Jews have inherited from their eastern European parents which they are transmitting to their children, a warm feeling of Jewishness, a deep sentiment of identification with their brethren. One more detail deserves to be noted. The widespread European attitude which regarded the negation of religion as the hallmark of culture and was particularly noticeable among modern Jews, finds no counterpart in America. It goes beyond the fact that there are no important anti-religious movements there. So long as religion is the main foundation for Jewish survival, we cannot overlook the advantage of Jews living in an environment which regards religion with respect. And the fact that both fascism and communism have failed to strike deep roots in America diminishes beyond measure the danger of the physical extinction of American Jewry.

In a famous article, Ahad Ha'am defined the life of Western Jewry in his time as "bondage in freedom," and that of Eastern Jewry as "freedom in bondage." For that new entity called American Jewry, there is hope that at least a sizeable minority of it will be vouchsafed "freedom in freedom."

One condition emerges from Jewish history: *There is nothing eternal about the Jewish people but the people itself. Not only were the Diaspora centers destroyed countless times, but the center in Eretz Israel came to an end on three occasions; in the days of the Patriarchs, with the destruction of the First Temple and with the destruction of the Second Temple.* If each individual soul is a universe, we dare not condemn to extinction any community within the Jewish people.

Education—the Vital Task

The Jews of the free world, who have already succeeded in establishing themselves socially and economically, are beginning to realize that Jewish education in its widest sense is their most vital task. If the achievements of Hebrew education in America are so far not satisfactory, history teaches that modest beginnings may ultimately produce glorious fruits. Along with education, we must revive the ancient *mitzva* of *Aliyat regel*, pilgrimage to the Land of Israel, emphasizing that every Jew should visit Israel at least once in his life. This mitzva must be treated not as the clever idea of an enterprising tourist agency, but as an instrument for the renewal of the spirit and faith of the people. Students should be encouraged to spend one year of their studies in Israel. Honeymoons, wedding anniversaries and other happy events should be marked in the same manner. In 1956, we proposed to the Israeli Government Tourist Bureau the creation of congregational tours, with sight-seeing and educational programs worked out in advance. From these would come some who would settle permanently or at least return again, for the spell of the land of Israel is irresistible.

The mutual influence between Israeli and world Jewry does not end here. We should discard the notion that in things material the Diaspora is to be the giver and Israel the recipient, and in matters spiritual Israel is to be the giver and the Diaspora the recipient. Mutuality is a law of nature; vital influence is always reciprocal. The various international conferences held in Israel have already sufficed to show that the important creative forces in the country will gain by contact with the creative scholars, scientists and thinkers abroad. It is necessary, therefore, to seek means to bring talented sons of Diaspora Jewry to Israel, so that they may teach and bring the fruits of their spirit to their brethren in the homeland.

The participation of creative forces from abroad in Israeli life may obviate a deplorable feature now to be observed in the land: the attempt to dismiss the long history of Diaspora Jewry as a meaningless, uncreative and even unworthy interlude, to be blotted from the national consciousness. Precisely in a period of national progress and self-confidence it is necessary for Israel to remember that we are "the smallest of all peoples," and that national arrogance and vanity does not befit us. *In the interaction between Israel and the Diaspora, Israel can make an important contribution by stressing the particularist aspect of the Jewish tradition and thus deepening the Jewish content in the life of the Diaspora. Diaspora Jewry, on the other hand, by virtue of its situation, is fitted to emphasize the universalist tradition which Israel must not lose sight of.* Many non-Jewish scholars have been unable to understand the existence of these two tendencies in the Jewish spirit—universalism and nationalism—and the vitalizing and fructifying tension between them. They have therefore proceeded to reject or deny one or another

as inauthentic. It would be unforgivable if we destroyed one
of these two indispensable elements of our tradition—reaching
from the Bible to the Talmud, from medieval literature to the
thinkers of our own time—which obligates everyone of us to be
at once a man and a Jew, both in his own home and outside.

Israeli Jewry Must Search Its Soul

If Diaspora Jewry is thus faced with important tasks in the
shaping of "one people throughout the world," then Israeli
Jewry, too, must enter upon a searching of soul and reconsider
its attitude both to the Diaspora and to the Jewish tradition.
If Israeli Jews restrict the spiritual content of their life to the
Hebrew language and the common experiences involved in the
upbuilding and defence of the country, they will achieve creation of a limited culture, devoid of worldwide value and universal significance. What a tragedy, if the people which for
thirty centuries has been a prime builder of world culture, in
the hour of its national regeneration, became content to be
a small, narrow-minded nation, having no purpose in life beyond the struggle for survival—survival for mere survival's sake!
Such a Levantine culture would perforce lead to alienation
from the roots of the Jewish spirit, to a contraction of the individual Jewish soul in Israel and to a complete dissociation from
World Jewry. Fortunately, this peril is far from immediate
today; it may not be so remote tomorrow.

It should be noted with sorrow that in contrast to the wonderful revival of the spirit in most spheres of Israel's life and
action, religion has not yet experienced such a renewal. A deep
chasm yawns between the official supervisors of religion and
the broad mass of the people, who have moved away from religion not only in practice, but even in theory. An antagonistic
and even contemptuous attitude toward tradition is far from
infrequent. The chief blame for this rests upon those official
custodians of the Torah who have not risen to the needs of
the hour. There is need for a renewal of Israel's faith on Israel's soil, not for the sake of the Diaspora, but in the vital
interest of the State of Israel itself.

A renewed religious tradition will be able to give the youth a rationale for ethical living. It can nurture its spirit on a philosophy of Judaism which regards man as God's image and his partner in the Creation, thus bringing him closer to the Divine Presence for which he longs in his sublimest moments. The spiritual physiognomy of the adult generation in Israel, even of the freethinkers among them, has been shaped by the religio-ethical principles of the tradition which they imbibed in the house of their parents and the environment of their youth. The charming, gifted and heroic youth now growing up in Israel lacks this background. There is, therefore, not a little danger that the cult of power and the worship of material enjoyment may come to be the main determinants in the life of the individual and the community. Another basic problem in Israel is a widespread factionalism, which has gone so far that there is no common, unbiased forum and meeting-ground where the problems of the individual and of the community may be considered free from party viewpoints. Vital religious institutions would supply this need.

In spite of the criticism and scorn some observers have heaped upon it, the American synagogue, which is a spiritual center of the community, and not only as a house of prayer, has much to teach its Israeli counterpart, both as regards the scope and the nature of its activities. The mechanical transfer of the eastern European rabbi to the radically different conditions of the State of Israel has left him bereft of any significant function and without any genuine influence on the people. The role of the American rabbi would prove a far better model for Israel.

Lastly, only a revival of religion in a form appropriate to our generation can implant in the hearts of the sabras in Israel the realization that a strong link binds them to their brethren in the Diaspora and that four thousand years of suffering, heroism and achievements are not to be dismissed as meaningless. The danger of the emergence in Israel of "Hebrew-speaking goyim" is not purely imaginary.

There is no time to be lost, for only in the present generation, when personal links still exist between the Yishuv and the Diaspora, is there an opportunity to bridge the gulf.

The renewal of Jewish religion in Israel in all its manifestations and the strengthening of Jewish culture abroad in all its expressions are the obverse and reverse of the medal which is the future of the Jewish spirit. These two purposes can only be achieved if Jews are imbued with the conviction that the Jewish people is an entity, *sui generis.* Its children must be inspired to accept the burden of a fate both tragic and sublime, imposed upon them by destiny, with a mission to the world, far from fulfilled. Thus they will be willing to be living links in the eternal chain of a unique people. This faith will flower into an appropriate way of life for Jews the world over, as they build a voluntary community, devoted to an organic, creative Judaism.

The following Ten Principles seem to us fundamental for the meaningful survival of the Jewish people and should become part of the world-view of Jews dedicated to the Jewish future:

1. *The unity of world Jews as one people,* with a common history in the past, a common culture in the present, and a common destiny in the future.

2. *The centrality of Jewish religion and ethics within Jewish culture* as the supreme manifestation of Jewish creativity and the main basis for Jewish existence in the future.

3. *The central position of the State of Israel,* not only as a haven of refuge for our oppressed brethren, but as the necessary environment for a full Jewish life, and for the creation of lasting spiritual values for the Jewish people and all mankind.

4. *The duty of every Jew in the world to take part in the upbuilding of the land of Israel and defence of its legitimate interests and aspirations* by the standards of justice, freedom and peace.

5. *The possibility and the necessity of continued Jewish existence in the Diaspora,* and the need to encourage Diaspora Jewry to deepen the content and creative character of its Jewish life.

6. *The legitimacy of national loyalties* among men which to be sure, have turned into a destructive force in the life of civilization in our day, but which must be conceived in the spirit of the Jewish prophets, who were the authentic creators of the ideal of nationalism in world history. The prophets saw national loyalties within the framework of international law and morality to which they must be subordinate. When nationalism is conceived of in the light of prophetic teachings there is no problem posed by so-called dual loyalty, when Jews of the free world are patriotic citizens of their respective countries and on the other hand, loyal to the Jewish people, of which they are an organic part.

7. *The mission of the State of Israel* is to work shoulder to shoulder with World Jewry to "reorder the world after the Kingdom of the Almighty," keeping alive the Messianic vision, until all mankind enters upon its heritage of justice, freedom and peace, and every human being is free to dedicate himself to the striving for perfection.

8. *The right of every Jew to be recognized as a brother in the household of Israel,* and to accept and interpret Jewish tradition and culture in accordance with his own insights and attitudes.

9. *The vital need to build everywhere voluntary communities dedicated to organic Judaism,* which will include loyalty to Israel, the values of the Jewish religion and the content of Jewish culture.

10. *The recognition, in practice and not merely in theory,* that the most fundamental enterprise in the life of the people is the improvement and enhancement of *Jewish education* for young and old, so as to mold its life through loyalty to the Jewish people and its heritage.

If we will it, it is no idle dream.

CHAPTER TWENTY-SEVEN

THE DIALOGUE BETWEEN ISRAEL AND THE DIASPORA

by SALO W. BARON

We all have a feeling—a correct feeling—that both the Zionist movement and Jewish life generally are passing through a great crisis which calls for solutions not previously offered either by Zionist literature, the Zionist movement or life itself. The situation is new and the solutions must also be new.

As far as can be foreseen, the Jewish Diaspora is an enduring phenomenon, destined to last for generations. I am not saying that it is eternal—no one can make predictions as to eternity—but we are going to have a Diaspora for many generations to come. Likewise, I feel certain of the permanence of the State of Israel, so that there is bound to be a continuing dialogue between the State of Israel and the Diaspora.

To put the matter paradoxically, let us assume, for the sake of argument, that all Diaspora Jews decide unanimously (imagine Jews deciding unanimously on anything, but let us assume that they do this time) to vanish out of existence, to liquidate Diaspora Jewry, except for those intending to emigrate to Israel. And let us assume even more paradoxically that in order to implement their decision they resolve to adopt the ruling religion, to become Catholics in Catholic countries, Protestants in Protestant countries, Moslems in Moslem countries. Would this mass conversion put an end to the Jewish group?

It is still possible for an individual convert to be absorbed in the majority, though this is now more difficult than it was in the Middle Ages and in the earlier part of the modern

617

period, when a man became a Christian and no questions asked. Today there is hesitancy even after the man has become a convert, but it is nevertheless still possible for his descendants to become members of the majority group. However, if all Jews were converted simultaneously, what would happen, according to all historical experience, is that we should before long witness the emergence of new communities, a Hebrew-Catholic Church, a Hebrew-Protestant Church and even a Hebrew-Moslem Community. That is to say, there would be the same separate groups, the same Jewish minorities in the countries, but with this difference: that the Jewish tradition, the Messianic idea, the Jewish religion—the fine things that justify the existence of the Jewish minority—would vanish from the world. This process occurred in Visigoth and Almohad Spain, with the Marranos in Spain and Italy, the Donmeh in Turkey. Whenever Jews changed their religion simultaneously, as a group, they were not absorbed into other nations.

We have heard repeatedly of Jewish assimilation, cataclysmic assimilation, or anonymous assimilation, or whatever other name you wish to call it. Assimilation is widespread, and I shall yet revert to it, but assimilation will not mean complete disappearance. The Jews will remain.

This, then, is our initial premise. The Jews will remain in their various Diaspora countries for many generations. True, Diaspora communities may be lost through extermination, such as occurred in the great Holocaust. No sane person will deny such a possibility. Thirty years ago, the idea of anything like the European Holocaust would have seemed fantastic. It would have been inconceivable that nations in the twentieth century should exterminate their Jews. And yet it happened, it happened on a much larger scale than ever before, and so it is possible. But it has to be made clear that from the point of view of the Zionist movement, a great change has occurred as far anti-Semitism is concerned.

Anti-Semitism and Zionism

From the days of Pinsker and Herzl to our own days, anti-Semitism has been a main factor in Zionist ideology. We have always stressed the idea that because of anti-Semitism there was no hope for Jewry in the Diaspora and that the Jewish State, therefore, was the only solution. Even today there are people who believe that this threat can induce Jewish youth in the United States, Canada, South Africa or anywhere else to come to Israel *en masse.*

This belief is sadly mistaken. The threat of anti-Semitism is not capable of influencing many people. Nuclear war constitutes a much more immediate threat: thousands of people fear that such a war may break out in the near future. There have been times of international tension in recent years, when indeed, it seemed almost imminent. Nevertheless, have people in their thousands left New York, Washington, London, or any other city threatened by atomic war and gone to settle in smaller places? I have met only a few, a select few, if I may say so, who changed their residence by reason of that ever-real threat.

This means that if we speak of mass emigration then I am sorry to say that it is a great historical truth that mass emigration is almost always the result of pressure, usually economic, or both political and economic. One does not have to be a Marxist to know that precisely in such matters the economic factor is the strongest, while political pressure also plays an important part. This was illustrated long ago by the nomad Bedouin tribes of antiquity. When there was a famine in their country, they migrated elsewhere. And so people have migrated at all times under economic pressure. Even in our Zionist history most of those emigrating to Eretz Israel came from Russia under pressure from the Czars, from Poland under pressure from Grabski, from Germany and other countries under overwhelming pressure from Hitler, and are coming at this hour from Arab countries under pressure from the Arab governments. In all these cases, there has been both political and economic pressure.

Of course, there have always been a number of notable exceptions: there have always been pioneers, both in this country and elsewhere, who emigrated from their homes for idealistic reasons, in quest of spiritual values. And I hope there will be many thousands of them both in this and in coming generations, who will come to this country* in order to find spiritual satisfaction, not because they are compelled to leave their own country. But to hope that there will be a mass emigration of this type, an emigration of millions—two millions, as Ben-Gurion said—is contrary to all past history, to all experience not only of the Jewish people, but of all peoples.

Therefore, now that we are discussing the Zionist movement and a possible reassessment of its values, it seems to me that the movement should abandon its view that anti-Semitism is the main motive for the exodus of the children of Israel. Under the impact of everyday life, the anti-Semitic threat has lost much of its force as a living reality in the minds of the young, whether in the United States or in other free countries.

I will tell you of my personal experience. I came to the United States in 1925. I live in a small community, not in an illustrious Jewish community such as that of New York, but in a tiny place in Connecticut. There are very few Jews there; when my daughters went to school, they were the first Jewish children in twenty years. I have been living for twenty-two years in that completely Christian locality, which, moreover, lies in an area considered in that part of the world to be anti-Semitic. Nevertheless, I have told my friends that if I were asked to testify before a Senate Investigation Committee, not from hearsay, but from personal experience, I would have to say that neither I nor my family have been exposed to any anti-Semitic incident or anti-Semitic expression during the twenty-two years of my residence in that locality and all the thirty-two years that I have been in the United States. I have read about such incidents in the press or heard about them from others, but I cannot recall a single thing of this kind as an actual witness.

Not that there is no anti-Semitism there. There certainly is anti-Semitism in America. But "hearing is not like seeing." Those who have not had some actual, personal encounter with anti-Semitism will regard it as something remote. There are youngsters in America who may feel that they have not been admitted to a certain school, especially a medical school, be-

* Israel.

cause they are Jews. This is quite possible. Others may have applied for a job and not obtained it because they were Jews. But even these people are becoming fewer. If, under these circumstances, you come and tell the young that anti-Semitism is on the march, they will regard it as something remote. It will not affect them psychologically either today or tomorrow.

The Lachrymose View of Jewish History

It thus seems to me that Zionism will do well to leave the matter of anti-Semitism to those organizations which concern themselves mainly with the protection of Jewish rights—the American Jewish Committee, the Anti-Defamation League, etc. The Zionist movement has a more fundamental issue to concern itself with.

Perhaps I am coming here to something even more fundamental. The theme of anti-Semitism and Jewish distress is so common among Jews that even the Foreign Minister of the State of Israel, Mrs. Golda Meir, could not help using very emotional language in discussing it. In this respect, there was hardly any difference between Ben-Gurion, Mrs. Meir, Dr. Goldmann, and Jacob Pat. They were practically unanimous in stressing this theme.** Now, I have felt increasingly all my life that this emphasis keeps the youth away from us both in Israel and in the Diaspora. Present-day youth is impatient of hearing that all Jewish history is a tale of woe and nothing more. Present-day youth feels that there is more to Jewish history. Perhaps that accounts for the fact that youth here takes greater interest in the Bible than in the Middle Ages or in the modern period. All descriptions of the Middle Ages and the modern period present a sequence of tribulations, of expulsions and persecutions, of what Graetz calls the *Leidensgeschichte* of the Jews. This *Leidensgeschichte,* he says, is the only thing that happened to the Jews, apart from the history of our sages.

Since my early days, I have insisted that the lachrymose conception of Jewish history is not correct from the point of view of historical truth, but neither is it congenial to our generation,

** At the "Jerusalem Ideological Conference on the Problems of Zionism, World Jewry and the State of Israel," August, 1957.

a generation not of ghetto Jews, but of Jews living a young life, who are free and active in various countries.

It seems to me that the sooner we abandon this conception, the better it will be both for the understanding of Jewish history and for the education of the present generation. There is much greatness in Jewish history—creative greatness. There was pioneering in every sense in the days of the Babylonian Exile, when many Jews played an important part in the Babylonian economy, and in the days of Hellenistic Egypt, and there were pioneers in Europe and America. Those merchants of the nineteenth century, those great nuclear scientists of our days, all these were and are pioneers, pioneers of the mind and the body, who found and paved new ways for themselves and for civilization.

The same analysis applies to the great epic of our martyrs, and as far as I can see, even to the history of the Holocaust in our days. When Shlomo bar Shimshon told of the martyrs of Mayence in his *Scroll,* he spoke of one thousand victims slain in one day, who silently suffered the fate decreed by heaven. But in the case of the Holocaust of the six million, we hear chiefly of the fighters of the Warsaw Ghetto and far less of those who suffered their fate in silence. In fact, I have been told that both in this country and in the United States it is difficult to find young scholars to study the Jewish history of the Nazi period. They admit that it is an important subject, but it is not one they wish to go into very much. It has been said at this Conference that our great writers both in Israel and in the United States have not yet given us an artistic-literary account of the Holocaust, the greatest disaster in the whole of Jewish history. This, too, seems to me a symptom of a new feeling, a new approach. It appears that we want to create, to be pioneers, to be fighters, to be active, and not a passive Jewry of distress and tribulation.

Hence, the Zionist movement must tread new paths, stressing neither anti-Semitism nor the past and present suffering of the Jewish people, but the great beauty of the new creativeness, the new life that is developing here. It is this great creativeness, which is indeed without parallel, that will captivate the hearts of youth abroad, and it is similar creativeness that will make our Middle Ages and our recent past appear as something vital and attractive.

The Enduring Dialogue

The dialogue between the Diaspora and the State of Israel is not something newly arisen. It is what distinguishes Jewish history from that of all other peoples. I am not going here into the question of the "chosen" people—these are religious beliefs which one accepts or not—but I have no doubt whatsoever that the history of every great people is something "new under the sun." Has there ever been in world history anything like the history of the U.S.A. or the U.S.S.R. or the British Empire, or even of the French or the German peoples? Every people has its own peculiar history. Jewish history, too, is unique, all the more so because it dates further back, 3,500 years or more. Its importance lay originally in the significance of the religion engendered by it for a large part of mankind. It became still more unusual as a result of the dispersion of the Jewish people throughout the world.

I remember that in my youth several opponents of Zionism came to me and said: "You Zionists are mere dreamers. Can a colony be created without a mother country? If the English, the Dutch, the French, the Greeks, the Sidonites, etc., established colonies, there was in each case a mother country behind them. There was an army, a powerful fleet, a government treasury behind them. You wish to reverse the order and have the Diaspora build itself a mother country. This is the opposite of what is normal."

I said to them: "You are right. It is generally true that colonies are created by a mother country. But in our history, in Jewish history, it has already happened twice that the Diaspora built the mother country. The Jews from Egypt built the First Temple, and the Babylonian exiles built the Second Temple. Why should not the exiles of the twentieth century build the Third Temple?"

This is precisely what has happened. We have reversed the order. Why? Because from the very outset, from the days of our ancestor Abraham, there has been a unique relationship between the world at large and this country.

I am now coming to the grave and fundamental question of our nationalism. We must remember that world nationalism has undergone a great development during the past hundred years. Gone are the days of Fichte's *Menschheitsnation,* of Mieckiewicz' and Mazzini's Messianic nationalism, that is to say, of nationalism that assigned to itself a cultural task, the task of building up a nation for the sake of mankind, and not a nation for its own sake. When the Zionist movement first emerged at the end of the nineteenth century, it was largely nurtured on that Messianic nationalism. It added of course an ingredient of its own, something of the age-old, traditional Messianic idea, which represented precisely that same combination of nationalism and humanity. The greatness of Zionism lay in this universal Messianic idea it stood for.

In the twentieth century, nationalism as a whole deteriorated considerably. It became more extreme, more radical, until it reached its peak in fascism and Nazism, in all the totalitarian slogans of the state, the national state or the racial state, as the be-all and end-all.

I sometimes warn my Arab friends and my friends from the Far East, saying: "See that you do not make your new states purely political bodies, centers of political power and political entrenchment, keeping out the human-cultural element."

I remember that a few years ago an Arab at Columbia wrote a thesis on the part played by the Arab States at the U.N. While examining him, I remarked: "You have written a whole book about how the Arab delegates have represented their States, doing this and that, almost always in connection with the Israel question, that is to say, in a matter where your own interests were involved. What would you have done if you had had to write such a book on the Scandinavian peoples, who are also members of the U.N.? They, too, have taken part in every General Assembly, but they have not had such a question, they have not always been concerned with the interests of Denmark or Sweden, for or against which the U.N. can do very little. You would not have been able to write a book then."

This confirmed to me something that I had known in advance: that the Arab nations were in fact concerned almost exclusively with political questions. This may perhaps be a lesson both for the State of Israel and the Diaspora. Let us not forget our own age-old nationalism which has always been both national and human, but which is now appearing in a new shape, under new conditions. The danger of our forgetting it is very close.

Lesson from History

I am not here criticising Prime Minister Ben-Gurion. He is a man on whom a heavy burden rests, the tremendous task of building a State *today*, not tomorrow, not in the course of twenty years. He holds the office of Minister of Defense and he feels that he needs two million more Jews immediately for security reasons. In this case, one cannot say: "Wait for Messianic nationalism, human nationalism." But we others, who stand somewhat outside, should always remember certain things. Let us not forget that our ancestor Abraham, who lived a long time before Joshua the son of Nun, left Ur of the Chaldaeans and came to Eretz Israel, left Egypt and returned to Eretz Israel. In a sense, he symbolizes for us the combination of the greatest cultures of the ancient East—Babylonian, Assyrian and Egyptian—the cultures which made world history together with Eretz Israel. When anti-Semites speak of the "international Jew," there is something to it. The Jews have been and are scattered all over the world; they were so scattered in the days of the Second Temple, when the greater part of Jewry already lived outside Eretz Israel. Evidence of dispersion may perhaps be found even in the days of the First Temple. There are numerous indications that some Jews remained in Egypt and did not go to Eretz Israel: Papyri of the thirteenth and twelfth centuries show that there were still Hebrews in Egypt then. There were some there again, in Tahpanhas and Elephantine, even before the destruction of the First Temple.

If even during the period of the First Temple, we were not exclusively in Eretz Israel, in the days of the Second Temple, most of the nation seems to have remained abroad. It seems to me that one of the most important things I have to say concerning the period of the Second Temple is that, in my opinion (I am not here following the latest view), two-thirds of the nation lived abroad then. This two-thirds, except for those in Babylonia and later in Egypt, did not make Jewish history. They were content to let Eretz Israel make history. They were helpers, but not partners. They certainly made pilgrimages, they paid the Shekel, the holy Shekel, to Jerusalem, they collected money and sent it through groups of emissaries to the Holy City. All this was very well, but they left it to the leaders in Eretz Israel to make fundamental decisions for them, without consulting them. Of course, there were political conflicts even then. In the Diaspora, the Roman government protected the Jewish minority; in Eretz Israel, it protected the Greek minority against the Jews. "Divide and rule" was the motto. The difference in Rome's attitudes to the two groups was so great that after the destruction of the Temple, Vespasian and Titus told delegates from Alexandria and Antioch that they did not wish to deprive the Jews there of their equal rights on account of the Jewish treason in Eretz Israel. In Alexandria the Jews were convenient to the Romans, whereas they were not at all so convenient in Eretz Israel. The position was different later on, during the revolt under Trajan, when the Jews of Egypt rose up in arms.

Historical developments might perhaps have been different if the Diaspora had taken a more immediate part in the destinies of the State of Israel in the days of the Second Temple. Of course, it is not worth speculating what would have happened in history in such-and-such a hypothetical case. But the great tragedy of the destruction of the Temple is at least half to be ascribed to the split. The Sadducean leaders in Jerusalem, in particular, did not pay attention to the Diaspora, and the Pharisees did not stress the State so much as religion. They felt that it was they who understood the requirements of the nation, they who had brought about its rebirth. Let us remember these facts. We can learn no end of lessons from this historical experience.

The Beginning of Worldwide Emancipation

Lastly, I wish to tackle one more basic problem, which is bound up with all these matters: the problem of emancipation. If we speak of the assimilation of American, British or French Jews, the expression is perhaps not strictly correct. Assimilation is a program, a party program, such as there was in Germany or in Poland. But we should remember that assimilation—i.e., becoming a part of the people in whose midst one lives—is one of the basic objectives of every emancipation movement. If emancipation has any meaning, it is that from now on the Jews will not be a minority in the face of the national majority, but a part of the national majority itself. This is a situation the like of which there has never been in Jewish history and which has accordingly led to a great crisis in Jewish life, a crisis due to utterly new conditions.

In the days of the First Exile, the question was whether Jews would be able to survive without a state, without a country, without a Temple. Then Ezekiel came, and later the men of the Great Synod and many others down to Hillel and the Pharisees, and decided that the Jews could live in segregation from the other peoples, be a separate people in the midst of the peoples, a minority, the same sort of minority in all countries, with the same synagogues, the same *batei-midrash,* for which it makes no great difference whether they are in one country or in another. All this ceased in the period of the Emancipation.

However, I wish to remind you that the crisis is only beginning. True, emancipation was first proclaimed by the American Revolution, by the French Revolution, as early as the eighteenth century, but in truth, in historical fact, it is not a reality even today. For it is sufficient to remember how only fifty years ago half the Jewish people lived under Czarist rule, with its Pobiedonochevs and its Porichkieviches, utterly without equality of rights. Another important part of the people lived in Rumania, in the Ottoman Empire, etc. Perhaps two-thirds of the entire Jewish people did not enjoy emancipation. And as for the free countries, where they had formal equality of rights, most of the Jews who lived, say, in 1907, in the

United States, Britain or France, had been born and bred
in Russia, Rumania or the Ottoman Empire and were not free
Jews in the full sense of the term. A man does not change
overnight merely by passing from one country to another.
He does not stop being what he is. Even in America, after a
hundred years or more, the present generation of Jews is the
first almost wholly born and bred in the country. This is
something new.

There is even more to it. After 1917-18, it seemed that
equality of rights would be given to Jews in the whole world.
But it was not. Poland did not keep her promises, Rumania
did not keep her promises. Then the Nazi movement arose,
which not only did not grant equality of rights, but wanted,
and proclaimed as its object, the total destruction of the Jews.

Therefore, future historians will perhaps admit that the emancipation of the Jews, even on paper, did not really began until
1946. It is a very new phenomenon. Worldwide emancipation
has only just begun.

Turning-Point in History

Thus, we are indeed faced by a great crisis. We are no longer
able to accept the answer given for five hundred years, from
Ezekiel to Hillel, which was basic to the whole existence of the
Jewish people in the Diaspora down to our own days. We
now have to think of a new life, a life to lead, as Americans
and Jews, Britons and Jews, Frenchmen and Jews. This is
something new. If this crisis finds no solution, then Diaspora
Jewry will perhaps indeed, in the course of time, vanish from
the world. However, as I said at the outset, there is no reason
to believe that for many generations to come the Jews would
be able to vanish from the world even if they wanted to. The
great majority of Diaspora Jews wish to survive as Jews. What,
therefore, does this turning point in Jewish history mean?—That
is the question.

*I think it is one of the great tasks of the State of Israel, in
partnership with the Diaspora, to find new ways in which
Jews living in the countries of equality of rights, can at the
same time be creative and fruitful as Jews.* Since as a matter

of historical necessity it is impossible for Jews to vanish from the world, let us not make the mistake of thinking that ways will not be found.

In my address at the Congress of Judaistic Studies, I discussed the great degree of pioneering ability American Jewry has demonstrated not only in the economic sense, not only in the spiritual-human sense, but also in the sense of communal achievements, new organizational achievements. I had in mind all those "Jewish Centers," all those summer camps and even charitable institutions, all those new approaches of a free people. If it has the pioneering spirit, if it has the will to strengthen the community, it will find the way. Jews in America have in part already found it, not only for themselves, but also for several other Diaspora countries.

In conclusion, then, it would be well for us to make up our minds:

First, that both the State of Israel and the Diaspora have come to stay for the foreseeable future—not eternally, but for as long as we can foresee;

Second, that the dialogue between the State of Israel and the Diaspora will go on for a great many generations to come, though its form may vary from time to time;

Third, that the Zionist movement should not lay so much stress on the anti-Semitic menace, but leave this matter, as well as the practical fight against anti-Semitic phenomena, to other public bodies;

Fourth, that it must be constantly stressed that the Zionist movement does not regard the emancipation movement as an internal rival but that, on the contrary, Zionism confirms the demand that the Jews in all their countries of residence should enjoy full civic rights.

It has generally been held in Zionist circles that there is a rift between emancipation and Zionism. Ahad Haam spoke of "auto-emancipation," as opposed to emancipation. Conversely, many fighters for equality of rights regarded it as their duty to oppose Zionism. Now, in historical perspective, we can see that emancipation and the national movements, including Zionism, are in fact one. It was emancipation that made possible the emergence of a modern, non-ghetto nationalism. Moreover, it was only through emancipation that a generation or generations of Jews grew up, knowing how to use arms, familiar with industrial technology and government administration. Emancipation has given Diaspora Jewry economic plenty and political influence. Without all these things the rebirth of the Jewish State in this era and form, would have been inconceivable.

Actually, it was precisely emancipation that demonstrated the need for a Jewish State, more than all the Messianic ideas did. In our time the greatest danger to Jewish existence was and is the possibility that the Jews may cease to be one people. There was a danger that there would be a separate Jewry in the United States, another in the European countries, another in Russia. In fact, in the 1920's, it seemed as if two Jewish peoples already existed: one in Russia, Yiddish-speaking, brought up on Sholom Aleichem, without religion, without Zionism, without Hebrew, without a Messianic idea, but recognized as an ethnic group; and another in the West, educated in English or French schools, mostly not speaking a language of its own, not constituting a national minority in the legal sense, but having a religion, having the Hebrew idea, the Zionist idea, the longing to return to Zion.

If this situation had lasted a long time, different sects might have arisen in Judaism, different territorial sects, perhaps more than the twenty-four sects which in the opinion of our sages brought about the destruction of the Second Temple. This is the reason why it was particularly necessary that a modern state should arise, a place where it would be impossible for the Jews to assimilate to anyone else, where they would be Jews, not American Jews, British Jews or Argentine Jews, but Jewish Jews. Such a place, the only such place, is Eretz Israel. Even in the days of the Mandate, there was no question of the Jews in Eretz Israel assimilating to anyone.

The fifth point I wish to make is—in recapitulation of what I said before—that the Zionist idea should no longer base itself to so great an extent on the long succession of our tribulations, but should also stress that which is beautiful and auspicious, the great achievements of the Jewish people in the past as well as those yet to come.

My sixth point is this: The future economic, social and spiritual achievements of the State of Israel will without doubt give it a strong magnetic power even for countries where there is no political or economic pressure.

Meanwhile—and this is my seventh and last point—let us continue building a great world culture which for all its historic antecedents is essentially new, the culture of an eternal people scattered throughout the world, which is at the same time a partner in the world's cultures and a partner—a real partner, not a mere helper—in the political, and even more, the cultural and religious achievements of that increasing part of Jewry which is concentrated in the State of Israel.

CHAPTER TWENTY-EIGHT

DEMOGRAPHIC CHARACTERISTICS OF AMERICAN JEWS

by NATHAN GOLDBERG

EDITOR'S INTRODUCTION

The voluntary nature of Jewish life under the conditions of American democracy has been inimical to the transplantation of the Kehillah of the European dispersion. It does not follow, however, that conspicuous planlessness in vital areas of communal concern is therefore necessary. Ignorance of what the American Jewish population has been, what it is, and what it is tending to be, blocks intelligent planning of communal programs and policies.

Nathan Goldberg's important population studies are illuminating the vast demographic dark continent of American Jewry's vital statistics, and its past, present and possible future. Just as Arthur Ruppin and Jacob Lestchinsky did for Diaspora Jewry, so contributors to American Jewish demography are now supplying fundamental data on the Jewish people and the basic conditions of its communal life in the United States—explaining the who, what and why of Jewish growth and existence in America. Demographic reports in the American Jewish Yearbooks, and studies such as Dr. Goldberg's, are necessary to furnish reliable answers to such significant questions as: How many Jews are there in the United States, and where are they located? What is the proportion of children, adults and old people? What about intermarriage? What's happening to the size of the Jewish family? What insights do population trends afford for communal planning?

A community which discriminates semantically between *Galut*, meaning "exile," and *Diaspora*, meaning "dispersion," which denies the Israeli thesis of *shelilat hagalut*—the negation of the Galut-Diaspora, which argues the possibility of creative Jewish survival in America, must have answers to those questions if those concerned with the future of Jews and Judaism in the United States are to make wise provision for the years to come. Also, the restricted immigration quotas and the destruction of the population and cultural centers of Central and East European Jewry not only affect the Yiddish press, theatre and schools. They also require the community to rechannel Jewish philanthropy formerly devoted to the adjustment of the immigrant to the American environment.

In his essay here, Dr. Goldberg makes a significant contribution to the necessary inventory of the American Jewish community's population trends. He presents here, for the first time, as the result of a remarkable research, a significant sample of Jews in America (immigrants from Russia, the great majority of whom were Jewish), which overcomes the lack of such information in the Census reports that has been the bane of American Jewish demography. The provision of such a sample permits fruitful investigation, analysis, and interpretation in many vital areas affecting the age structure, marriage pattern and health of American Jews. This is a signal achievement by Dr. Goldberg in behalf of American Jewry's self-understanding and future planning.

The aging of the American-Jewish population emphasizes the need for community concentration on geriatrics, degenerative and chronic diseases and first-rate homes for the aged. Community provision, planning, counseling, vocational, cultural and recreational programs for the aged must go far beyond the puerile Golden Age concept in making possible the creative and productive use of old people and their fruitful application of their leisure time.

Dr. Goldberg's study of the psychological characteristics, familial adjustment and sociological problems of the Jews in the United States has a twofold purpose. The results of such a study aim to give the Jews a better understanding of the behavior, attitudes, values, aspirations and problems of the Jews. To the extent, however, that the Jewish group is a component of the human race, the results of this and similar studies of the Jewish group are likely to lead to a better understanding of the social behavior of human beings in general. Methodologically speaking, the Jews, being a minority, are a kind of laboratory or experimental group. The findings of such studies have practical implications and can be used by those who are engaged in social and communal planning as stated. There are, however, other valid reasons and justifications for such investigation. Whatever the practical values of the results of such inquiries may turn out to be, we should not overlook or even minimize the fact that such studies, if properly planned and conducted, are likely to lead to a better understanding of the Jew, which is of great importance from the point of view of the Jew. Equally important is the fact that studies of the Jews, like studies of any other ethnic, religious, political and economic group, are likely to result in a better understanding of human beings in general. The sociological study of the Jews, for instance, is likely to be a contribution to sociology in general, and to the sociology of the Jews, or Jewish sociology, in particular. In all these respects Dr. Goldberg's essay is an outstanding example of a meaningful demographic study.

Dr. Goldberg's study of the occupational pattern of the

Jews in the United States in 1900 was based on the assumption that most of the Russians in 1900 who lived in the very large cities were actually Jews from Russia. His proof or evidence has been accepted as sound and convincing. He has, therefore, applied similar reasoning to the 1950 census results. It was, however, much easier to show that most of the Russians in 1900 were actually Jews than in 1950. In view of this, Dr. Goldberg used various sources of reliable information to show that even in 1950 most of the Russians in certain parts of the country were Jewish.

As far as the fertility of the American Jews is concerned, Dr. Goldberg is neither pessimistic nor optimistic; he expresses no value-judgments.

Dr. Goldberg does point out, however, why fertility-rate conclusions based on the comparison of the number of Jewish children under five years of age, with those of non-Jewish children of the same age—are falsely premised and wrong. His findings show a continuing downtrend in the fertility rate of American Jews, and must be weighed in determining the validity of the opinion that Jews have shared in the present general population explosion, so that, therefore, the fear that the Jewish family is not now reproducing itself is unfounded. Certainly American Jewry is faced with a crucial challenge to provide the conditions that will make possible a positive survivalist answer to the question: "Will the Jewish population be able to expand, or at the least, maintain its numerical strength by natural growth?"

This study has analyzed as much of the data as is available. The Jewish birth rate now is probably higher than in the 1930's. The data at hand do not show, however, that there was as much of a "baby boom" in the Jewish community as in the country at large.

Dr. Goldberg has tried to do three things: First, he has paid considerable attention to methodological problems. As a matter of fact, his discussion of sources of information is actually a discussion of methodology. He calls attention to the shortcomings of many of the methods used, including the Census Bureau Surveys and national samples. He has evaluated many other studies from a methodological point of view.

Second, he has tried to present up-to-date facts on various demographic processes and phenomena. His essay has data on the geographical distribution, metropolitanization, age and sex composition, marital status, family pattern, inter-marriage, planned parenthood, fertility, morbidity and mortality of the Jews.

Third, his interpretations of the several demographic processes and phenomena are of considerable interest, importance and value. They are a kind of a bridge between the past and present, offering as they do essential information for a synthesis of past and present experiences of the Jews.

Dr. Goldberg has attempted to show the impact of the culture of the Jews on the contemporary American Jewish community. This culture is, however, being modified and adapted to present-day needs. In brief, Dr. Goldberg has endeavored to give a cultural-historical-sociological-psychological interpretation of demographic processes in the Jewish community. Most of the literature on the demography of the Jews here and in other countries is primarily descriptive. This is probably the first attempt to give such an interpretation and as such is of inestimable significance.

The increased incidence of divorce points up the need for family counseling and service. The incidence of psychoneurotic and character disorders poses the moot question of whether the continuing achievement of more equality of opportunity and civil rights for American Jewry will result in a greater feeling of security and consequently, less functional disturbances.

These and other findings in Dr. Goldberg's essay are indispensable if Jewish public service is to plan providently the answers to future questions: How many hospitals will we need? How will an aging population affect our health and social welfare institutions? How many child recreation centers and schools shall we have? What is the number of vocational guidance counselors and teachers of different subjects required? How extensive should our program of adult education, teacher training and rabbinical preparation be? With such information American Jewry need not guess in the dark.

What of the future? Will the growth of the Jewish population in the years to come be affected by the suburban hegira, and the realization that the one-child family is not good for the child and not good for the family?

The hope that the size of the Jewish family will increase in the suburban era must be tempered by the fact that the move to suburbia is part of the quest for a better life for the children, an objective that is completely consistent with a small family. Also, suburban and urban woman's emancipation from kitchen and childbed, and her increasing entrance into the world of business, career, sisterhood and community clublife and cultural and social interests will compete strongly with domesticity and motherhood.

Dr. Goldberg's facts and figures are essential source material. Their interpretation and analysis can emphasize vital trends which reveal community wants and lacks, and areas of wasteful effort, competition, overlapping and duplication. Further, Dr. Goldberg's essay, as an example of outstanding methodology, content and interpretation in Jewish demography, emphasizes the dire need for American Jewry to subsidize such scholarship and research as paramount for its intelligent and creative survival.

CHAPTER TWENTY-NINE

DEMOGRAPHIC CHARACTERISTICS OF AMERICAN JEWS

by NATHAN GOLDBERG

The demographic pattern of the Jews in the United States is not quite the same as of other ethnic and religious groups. Human beings reproduce themselves; they marry; they migrate; they die. The universality of these and other demographic processes does not, however, mean that marriage, fertility, morbidity, migration, and mortality rates are constant. They vary from country to country and from generation to generation. Within any given country, differences are almost always found among its various religious, ethnic, occupational, and income groups. Demographic differences between Jews and others in the United States are presumably of a quantitative rather than a qualitative nature; some vital processes occur more or less frequently in one of these two groups. The observed differences are to some extent the result of differences in values, modes of living, socio-economic status, past experiences, aspirations, and other psychological, sociological and cultural factors.

Methodological Problems and Sources of Information

The observation that there are demographic differences between Jews and others is based on several sources of information. Unlike those of other countries,[1] the U.S. Bureau of the Census does not make any attempt to ascertain the ethnic origin or religious composition of the population. The

638

only time it did collect data on the religious preferences of the population was, as we shall see, in its sample survey in March, 1957. Several groups objected to it. It is, therefore, doubtful whether the Bureau of the Census will soon make another attempt to determine the religious composition of the population and the demographic, economic, cultural, and social characteristics of the several religious groups. Those who object to the inclusion of a question on religion in the census population schedule and in the registration certificates of births, deaths, marriages, etc., maintain that it would (a) "violate the constitutional guarantee of freedom of religion," (b) "violate the constitutional guarantee for the separation of church and state," (c) it would "constitute an unwarranted impingement upon the privacy of Americans," (d) it would "create a dangerous precedent," for if the government can compel Americans to disclose their religion, it can also compel them "to disclose their political, economic, social and all other beliefs."[2] Those who advocate the inclusion of such questions emphasize the practical and theoretical value of such information. Planning bodies of religious organizations, social service agencies, manufacturers and distributors of certain commodities, and governmental agencies would find data on the demographic, economic, social, and cultural characteristics of the local units of the various religious denominations very helpful and useful. Such information would help sociologists, demographers, and other scholars in their efforts to understand and interpret human behavior and social and cultural trends and changes. Whatever the merit of the pros and cons may be, the Bureau of the Census does not collect such data.

The situation is not, however, as hopeless as it may at first appear to be. The unavailability of census data and vital statistics on religious and ethnic groups has induced Jewish communities to make surveys of the demographic, occupational, social, and cultural characteristics of their members. A number of such studies were made within the last twenty-five years or so. Some communities attempted to enumerate each and every Jewish family or household; others used samples of the Jewish population in their respective localities. Some used interviewers to collect the data, others asked the prospective respondents to fill out questionnaires. The scope of these surveys varies, some have tried to collect more information than others. There is now and then a lack of uniformity in the definition of terms and classification of responses or respondents. Very important is the fact that such surveys are more likely to be made of small and medium-sized Jewish communities than of the largest ones, where most of the American Jews live. We do not have, for instance, reliable data on the Jews in Boston, Chicago, Cleveland, New York, Philadelphia, St. Louis. The fact that most of the surveys are made for practical rather than scholarly purposes often means that the surveyors *summarize* rather than *analyze* their data. The surveys are made at different times. Not many of the communities have been surveyed more than once. It thus appears that the results of such surveys cannot always be used for purposes of comparing Jews and others who live in the same city and Jews who live in different localities.

Nationwide surveys of social, demographic, occupational, political, and cultural characteristics of the population are another source of information. Those of them which set out to compare ethnic or religious groups now and then have some valuable information on the Jews. One has to bear in mind, however, that the results of such surveys are usually based on very small samples. The number of Jewish respondents in many of them is rather small, in some instances less than 100. By way of illustration, in the recent nationwide study of the fertility of American couples only 66 of the 2,713 white married women who were interviewed were Jewish women whose husbands were Jews, eight Jewish women were married to non-Jews, and the husbands of nine non-Jewish interviewees were Jews.[3] In each of two nationwide sample surveys made by the National Opinion Research Center less than 75 Jewish households were included.[4] The results of such small samples are subject to large sample errors. Moreover, even if small probability samples are representative of the general population, it is not known to what extent the Jewish respondents are representative of the Jewish population. It is doubtful whether those who conduct such sample surveys ever attempt to obtain samples of the several social, religious, occupational and other subgroups in the Jewish community. Equally important is the fact that the Jewish group included in such samples is very often too small for purposes of analysis.

The sample survey of the religious composition of the civilian population made by the Bureau of the Census in March, 1957, has information on characteristics of Protestants, Catholics, Jews, and others. "This survey was the first in which the Bureau asked a nationwide sample of persons a question on their religion."[5] The question, "What is your religion?" aimed to obtain information on the religious identification or preference of the respondents rather than to ascertain their religious beliefs or observances or church or synagogue affiliation and attendance. Although the information was obtained on a voluntary basis, the results "are subject to biases due to errors of response and to nonreporting . . . a few persons may have misreported their religion for one reason or another."[6] The observation that the "sampling variability of a religious group which is concentrated in a part of the United States (that is in a few states or in urban areas) may be somewhat larger" than in the case of those who are not so concentrated and urbanized, undoubtedly applies to the Jewish group. And it is quite possible that the shortcomings of nationwide sample surveys discussed above equally apply to the sample of the Census Bureau. Its sample was, however, much larger, about 35,000 households in about 330 sample areas. About 3 percent or around 1,100 of these households were Jewish. Some of the results of this survey were not made public because "it is most consistent with the public interest to make no further publication of data on this subject at this time."[7] This was probably due to the pressure of those who were against the inclusion of a question on religion.

Our fourth source of information—used here for the first time —is the report on the nativity and parentage of the population at the time of the 1950 census. This report actually has, although indirectly, information on the Jewish immigrants from Russia (U.S.S.R.) and their American-born children. As we shall see, most of those who reported in 1950 that they were born in what is now the Union of Socialist Soviet Republics and lived in several of the largest cities, were actually of Jewish descent; the same applies to the native-born children whose parents came from Russia.

One of the reasons for this statement is the fact that 765,531 of the 1,749,075 immigrants from the Russian Empire, 43.8 percent, who came to the United States in the years 1899-1910 identified themselves as Hebrews. If we assume that practically all of the 788,300 Polish, Lithuanian, and Finnish immigrants from Russia came from those parts of the Russian Empire which subsequently became Poland, Lithuania, and Finland, the number of immigrants from Russia is reduced from 1,749,075 to approximately 960,800. By the same token, some of the 765,531 Jewish immigrants from Russia came from those parts of the Russian Empire which later on became Poland, Lithuania, and Finland. What proportion of these Jewish newcomers were from Soviet Russia?

If we assume that the ratio of Yiddish-speaking immigrants from Russia to such newcomers from Poland, Latvia and Lithuania was approximately the same in 1899-1910 as in 1930, then 72.7 percent of the Jewish immigrants from the Russian Empire in the years 1899-1910 were from Soviet Russia. According to the 1940 census, 76 percent were from Soviet Russia. The percentage was probably larger in the years 1899-1910. Some of the Yiddish-speaking immigrants from Poland in 1930 were actually from Galicia. Secondly, it was probably easier for Jews from Poland and Lithuania to reach the shores of the United States in the years following World War I than for their brethren from Soviet Russia, so that the ratio of Russian to Polish-Lithuanian-Latvian Jews in 1930 was actually less than in 1890-1910. Differences in the age composition of these two groups is another consideration. In 1940 the percentage of Yiddish-speaking women from Russia and Poland 15-74 years old who were in the age group 55-74 was 30.8 and 25.7, respectively,[8] a difference of about 20 percent. This suggests that the Jewish immigrants from Soviet Russia were older than those from Poland and that a smaller percentage of the former who had come in the years 1899-1910 were still alive in 1930 and

1940 than of those who had come from Poland. It thus appears that the ratio of Jewish immigrants from Russia to those from Poland and Lithuania was much higher in 1899-1910 than in 1930 and 1940. On the other hand, some of the Polish, Lithuanian and other Jews probably continued to report that they were born in Russia. At any rate, if we assume that three-fourths of the Jews from the Russian Empire who came to the United States in the years 1899-1910 were from those parts which were in 1950 Soviet Russia, then they constituted approximately 60 percent of the Russian immigrants.

The percentage of immigrants from Russia admitted in the years 1911-1932 who were Jews was 64.5. All in all, the Jews probably constituted about 62 (61.7) percent of those who came in the years 1899-1932 from those parts of Russia which subsequently became parts of Soviet Russia. This being the case, we may assume that about 62 percent of those who reported Russia as their country of birth at the time of the 1950 census were Jews.

It is quite possible that some of the Jewish immigrants did not identify themselves as Jews at the time of their arrival. Calling attention to the sudden increase from approximately 58,000 in 1910 to 392,000 in 1920 in the number of immigrants who reported Russian as their mother tongue, the Bureau of the Census observed: "In particular, it is probable that a large proportion of the persons reported in 1920 as Russian in mother tongue were in reality Hebrews; and it is possible also that the very great increase between 1910 and 1920 in the number of persons thus reported is due in some measure to the return of certain persons in 1910 as Yiddish and in 1920 as Russian in mother tongue." Ten years later, the Bureau remarked that "many Jews of foreign birth report German, Russian, or other languages as their mother tongue."[9] Some Jews, in other words, tried to conceal their ethnic or religious identity.

Equally important is the fact that the geographical distribution of the Jewish and other immigrants from Russia in the United States was not the same. The 1899-1910 ratio of Jewish to other immigrants from Russia whose places of destination were New York, Massachusetts, Pennsylvania, Illinois, or Ohio was 5:1. This does not at all mean that the Jewish and other immigrants actually remained in these places. It is, nevertheless, a fact that these two groups of immigrants were not randomly distributed and that a much larger percentage of the Jewish than of the other newcomers settled in the largest cities.

Rank correlation coefficients were computed to see to what extent the rate of concentration of Yiddish- or Hebrew-speaking immigrants in large cities was similar to the concentration pattern of those who were born in Russia. Polish, Irish, Italian, Russian, Jewish and other immigrants settled for some reason or other in the large American cities. This being the case, the question was not whether there was any similarity, but rather whether the correlation coefficients were in some cases higher than in other cases. Rho or Spearman and Tau or Kendall correlation coefficients of their degree of concentration in 1930, 1940 and 1950 in Boston, Chicago, Cleveland, Detroit, Los Angeles, New York, Philadelphia, Pittsburgh, and San Francisco and in the 14 largest cities in 1940—these nine and Baltimore, Buffalo, Milwaukee, St. Louis, and Washington, D.C.—were computed. The results are in both cases very similar.

The correlation coefficients suggest that there is a higher degree of association or similarity between the Yiddish group and those born in Russia than between those whose mother tongue was Russian and those born in Russia. The principal reason for this is the fact that the overwhelming majority of the Russian-born immigrants who lived in these nine cities in 1950 or before were of Jewish descent. The same is also true in the case of the native-born of foreign or mixed parents who were born in Russia.

Finally, a careful study of the demographic, occupational, and educational characteristics of immigrants from Russia and their American-born children, who lived in 1950 in the nine standard metropolitan areas[10] which were reported in the census volume "Nativity and Parentage" suggests that we are actually dealing with those who are Jewish rather than Russian. In his discussion of the Russians in the United States, Professor Bogue observes: "The foreign-born population of Russian origin surpasses all other ethnic groups, both first and second generation,

TABLE 1.—*Correlation Coefficients of the Concentration of Jewish and Russian Immigrants and of Their American-Born Children in Nine Cities*

	RHO	Dif. (%)	TAU	Dif. (%)
Yiddish and Russia, 1930, immigrants (a)	1.00⎫	33.3	1.00⎫	63.9
Russian and Russia, 1930, immigrants (b)	0.75⎭		0.61⎭	
Yiddish and Russia, 1940, immigrants	1.00⎫	33.3	1.00⎫	63.9
Russian and Russia, 1940, immigrants	0.75⎭		0.61⎭	
Yiddish and Russia, 1940, American-born	0.97⎫	29.3	0.89⎫	45.9
Russian and Russia, 1940, American-born	0.75⎭		0.61⎭	
Yiddish 1940, and Russia 1950, immigrant	0.83⎫	0	0.83⎫	0
Russian 1940 and Russia 1950, immigrant	0.83⎭		0.83⎭	
Yiddish 1940 and Russia 1950, American-born	0.93⎫	20.8	0.83⎫	15.3
Russian 1940 and Russia 1950, American-born	0.77⎭		0.72⎭	
Jews 1937 and Russia 1940 (c)	0.95		0.85	
Jews 1937 and Yiddish 1940	0.95		0.85	
Jews 1950 and Russia 1950	0.95		0.89	

These are a few illustrations of how to read this table:

(a) Correlation between rank of concentration in 1930 of Yiddish-speaking immigrants and immigrants from Russia.

(b) Correlation between rank of concentration in 1930 of immigrants who reported Russian as their mother tongue and immigrants from Russia.

(c) Correlation between rank of concentration of Jews in 1937 and of immigrants from Russia and their American-born children.

and also surpasses the native white stock, in socio-economic status. . . . The second generation is especially outstanding. This differential may be explained in part by the fact that the Russian group contains large refugee and Jewish components, and that a large proportion of such immigrants place great value on obtaining an education and a white-collar position."[11] Actually, a very small proportion of them are not Jewish;[12] it is even less in the nine standard metropolitan areas than in the other parts of the country.

In view of these facts, *a conservative estimate would be that more than seventy percent of the immigrants from Russia and of their American-born children who lived in 1940 in Boston, Chi-*

cago, Cleveland, Detroit, Los Angeles, New York, Philadelphia, Pittsburgh, and San Francisco, were of Jewish descent. If we assume that the same was also true in 1950 (there are no data for estimates), it follows that most of the Russian immigrants and their native-born children who lived in 1950 in these nine standard metropolitan areas were actually of Jewish origin. It is interesting, in this connection, to note that the 1951 survey of the Los Angeles Jewish community reported that there were approximately 42,960 Jews from Russia and that according to the 1950 census the Los Angeles standard metropolitan area had 44,575 immigrants from Russia. Thus these Jews comprised 96 percent of the Russian immigrant population of Los Angeles. Whether the territorial unit was in both instances the same or not, it is safe to assume that very few of the Russians there were not Jews. *The 1950 census report on the Russians and their American-born children in these nine standard metropolitan areas is therefore a very important source of information on the Jews from Russia and their native-born children.*

While this is so, there are also several limitations. At best, the information in the 1950 census report is on Russian Jews and their American-born children. It has no data on Jewish immigrants from other countries and their native-born children. Equally important is the fact that there is nothing in the report on the American-born of native-born parents. The Russian Jews and their American-born children are, however, a very important component and very large segment of the Jewish population. Secondly, the present analysis is restricted to those who lived in 1950 in nine standard metropolitan areas. Although a large percentage of the immigrants from Russia and their American-born children in the other parts of the country were Jewish, the percentage was probably not as large as in the nine metropolitan areas. Probably more than seventy percent of the American Jews were concentrated in these areas. The census report is based on a twenty percent sample of the entire population. Estimates based on samples are, however, subject to sampling errors. In view of the fact that the estimates in this case are based on a relatively large sample, the standard errors are likely to be very small. Finally, some of this group were not of Jewish origin. The census report is, nevertheless, an important source of information on the Russian Jews and their descendants in the United States.

In view of what has been said about the sources of information on the demographic characteristics of the Jews in the United States, the answer to the question "How large is the Jewish population?" will vary with the sources of information and assumptions on which the estimates are based. It was estimated, on the basis of the March 1957 sample survey of the religious composition of the American population, that there were at that time 3,868,000 Jewish men and women 14 years old and over. They constituted 3.24 percent of the civilian population 14 years old and over. If we add those under 14 years old, both of whose parents were Jewish, then there were in March 1957 approximately 4,975,000 persons whose religion was Jewish.[13] They constituted 2.96 percent of the total civilian population. As we shall see, the drop from 3.24 to 2.96, a decrease of nine percent, is a very important fact; it suggests that the Jews have a significantly lower birth rate than the other ethnic and religious groups.

It was estimated that as of May 1, 1961, the civilian population numbered 180,661,000.[14] If we assume that, first, the March 1957 estimate of the relative number of Jews was well founded, and, secondly, that the rate of increase of the Jewish population in the years 1957-1961 was approximately the same as of the general population, it appears that there were about 5,347,600 persons of Jewish descent. If we include those in the armed forces both here and abroad, then there were on May 1, 1961 following the same reasoning as before, 5,422,000 persons whose religion was Jewish.

This number is somewhat less than Alvin Chenkin's estimate. Using an altogether different method, he concludes that there were about 5,531,500 Jews in 1960.[15] According to the previous method, one would have expected on July 1, 1960 approximately 5,347,800, a difference of 183,700 or 3.3 percent. In general, these two estimates are not too far apart. The surveys made by the National Opinion Research Center in 1953 and 1955 suggest that the Jews constituted three percent of the population.[16] In May 1961 this would mean 5,419,830 Jews in the United States.

The geographic distribution of the Jews seems to be significantly different from the regional distribution of the rest of the population. Most of the former concentrated in the Middle Atlantic States, in parts of New England, and in several North Central States. Estimates of the regional distribution of the several religious groups vary.

The geographic distribution or concentration of a religious minority varies, among other things, with the economic opportunities its members anticipate, attitudes toward them, historical events, past experiences, and socio-cultural values. Most of the Jewish and other European immigrants landed in New York or in nearby ports of entry. A larger percentage of the Jews than of the others remained in the Northeast (Middle Atlantic States and New England) because of its educational and economic opportunities, their preference to live in large cities, the attitude toward them, the presence of communities of their co-religionists, and the hope to be able to preserve and transmit their socio-cultural values.

It was, therefore, to be expected that they would be more concentrated in certain states than in others. A. Chenkin reports 11 states in 1960 with a Jewish population of at least 100,000. About nine-tenths of the total Jewish population and only 52 percent of the general population lived in these states. According

TABLE 2.—*Estimates of the Regional Distribution of Protestants, Catholics and Jews (Percentages)*

Region	March 1957			National Opinion Research Center			Chenkin, 1960
	Protestant	Catholic	Jewish	Protestant	Catholic	Jewish	Jews
Northeast	16.8	46.0	69.1	17.6	46.0	61.2	66.6
North Central	30.4	28.0	11.9	29.2	29.8	11.4	13.8
South	38.3	13.9	7.7	40.0	7.7	9.4	8.8
West	14.5	12.1	11.3	13.2	16.6	18.0	10.8
Total	100.0	100.0	100.0	100.0	100.1	100.0	100.0

Sources: Current Population Reports, Series P-20, No. 79, p. 6; Bogue, *op. cit.*, p. 699; Chenkin, *op. cit.*, pp. 62-63.

to this estimate, almost 46 percent of the total Jewish population were in New York and one-tenth in California.

Although each of these states has a relatively large Jewish population, they constitute in each one of them, except New York, a very small percentage of the total population. Only 5.3 percent of their inhabitants were Jewish. Even in New York they constituted not more than fifteen percent. As far as the other states are concerned, in twelve they constituted one-quarter of one percent or less, in ten between 0.25-0.49 of one percent, in six between 0.5-0.74 of one percent. All in all, in 33 states they constituted less than one percent of the total population and in 39 states they accounted for not more than two-thirds of one percent of the residents. In general, Jews are found in industrial, commercial, and highly urbanized states.

The geographic distribution of American Jews has changed in recent years. The percentage of Jews in California and Florida has increased. As in the case of the general population, these states attract older persons. Florida as a vacation or resort place offers some business opportunities. The percentages of Jews in Pennsylvania, New York, Massachusetts, and several other states has dropped. Some of them have settled in Califor-

TABLE 3.—*Estimated Number of Jews in Selected States, 1960*

State	Number	Percentage of Jewish Population	Percentage of General Population
California	530,300	9.6	3.4
Connecticut	101,300	1.8	4.0
Florida	112,100	2.0	2.3
Illinois	297,300	5.4	2.9
Maryland	118,100	2.1	3.8
Massachusetts	226,100	4.1	4.4
Michigan	102,700	1.9	1.3
New Jersey	326,300	5.9	5.4
New York	2,533,900	45.8	14.9
Ohio	162,200	2.9	1.7
Pennsylvania	454,600	8.2	4.0
Total	4,964,900	89.8	5.3

Source: A. Chenkin, *op. cit.*, pp. 62-63.

nia or Florida; others have moved because of business or professional opportunities and considerations.

The largest cities have the largest concentration of Jews. The March 1957 survey reported that seven-eighths of them lived in urbanized areas[17] of 250,000 or more, about fifty-four percent of the Catholics, and almost one-fourth of the white Protestants. According to the surveys of the National Opinion Research Center, eighty-four percent of the Jews, about forty-five percent of the Catholics, and almost twenty-three percent of the Protestants live in metropolitan areas with a million or more inhabitants.[18]

According to A. Chenkin's survey, in 1960 there were five cities or metropolitan areas with a Jewish population of at least 100,000. Next to New York,[19] the Los Angeles metropolitan area had the largest Jewish concentration in 1960. Its population increased from approximately 323,000 in 1951 to 391,000 in 1959,[20] a gain of twenty-one percent in less than ten years. This rather phenomenal growth was due primarily to the settlement of Jews from other parts of the country for economic, health, and other reasons. Other large Jewish communities are Chicago, Philadelphia, and Boston. The estimated 3,199,000 Jews in these five cities and Essex County, New Jersey, constituted in 1960 almost fifty-eight percent of the total Jewish population.

There were six cities or metropolitan areas each with a Jewish population between 50,000 and 99,999. Five of them—Baltimore, Cleveland, Detroit, Miami, and Washington, D.C., had between 80,000 and 89,000 Jews. It is estimated that the San Francisco Jewish population increased from 40,900 in 1939 to 46,600 in 1959,[21] a gain of about 14 percent in two decades. This is in striking contrast to the growth of the Jewish population in Los Angeles. About 19,400 were in the surrounding areas of San Francisco. One-twelfth of the Jewish population was in these cities. Finally, in five cities or metropolitan areas—Buffalo, Cincinnati, Hartford, Milwaukee, and Pittsburgh—the number of Jews ranged between 25,000 and 49,999.[22] It thus appears that 69 percent of the Jews in the United States lived in 17 cities or metropolitan areas each of them having a Jewish population of not less than 25,000.

Jews in other countries are also concentrated in large metropolises. Almost three-fourths of the Canadian Jews are in Montreal and Toronto. It is estimated that 280,000 of the 400,000 Jews in Argentina are in Buenos Aires. Most of the Jews in Brazil, about seventy percent, live in Rio de Janeiro and São Paulo. About four of every 10 Jews in Morocco are in Casablanca. Johannesburg probably has one-half of the Jews in the Union of South Africa. About fifty percent of the French Jews live in Paris. About sixty percent of the English Jews are in London. Approximately one-third of the Jews in Israel are concentrated in Haifa, Jerusalem and Tel-Aviv.[23]

The concentration of the Jews in large cities is not a new phenomenon. They have lived in urban centers for many centuries. Their concentration in cities was partly the result of the attitudes of non-Jews toward them. If they were denied the right to own land and to cultivate the soil, they moved to cities where they hoped to find other sources of income. If their property was subject to confiscation, they hesitated to invest in real estate. If they were subject to expulsion, they tried to have cash on hand. Jews became craftsmen, traders, and distributors. They moved to towns and cities where they manufactured and exchanged goods; they used the local market place for purchasing and selling goods. Moreover, they preferred to be urbanites for religious reasons. Religious-minded Jews settled in places where there was a sufficiently large number of their co-religionists to enable the Jewish community to have a synagogue and a school for the Jewish education of their children, a Kosher butcher shop and a Jewish bakery, a Jewish tailor and barber, and many other agencies and institutions which they needed as Jews. Small communities could not very well support a rabbi, ritual slaughterer, teacher, cantor, and many other religious and communal functionaries. In a sense, it was easier for an urban Jew to be an observant Jew than for the rural Jew. Some preferred those economic activities which offered them a good opportunity to be able to pursue their Jewish studies. Jewish merchants and storekeepers, for instance, could more easily set aside part of the day for study and religious purposes than other Jews. Psychologically, they felt more secure and were

more at ease among their own, especially in those places where
there was a marked anti-Jewish sentiment. The Jews, in brief,
generally preferred to live in relatively large Jewish communities for religious, psychological, social, and other reasons. The
town or city was practically the only place where such communities could actually emerge and exist.

The concentration of the Jews in the large metropolises has
its advantages and disadvantages. Large Jewish communities
offer very good opportunities for the transmission and revitalization of their socio-cultural heritage. They can have their houses
of worship, schools for children and adults, libraries and museums, newspapers and periodicals, social service agencies and
hospitals, community centers and summer camps, and many
other agencies and services which facilitate the perpetuation
of the Jewish community. Urbanites have better opportunities
to make good and effective use of their talents, abilities, and
skills. Large Jewish communities are reservoirs of energy which
can be used for the promotion and advancement of Judaism and
Jewishness. Demographically, they have better health services
and medical care. Politically, the presence of a relatively large
number of Jews may result in legislation aimed to protect the
rights of religious and ethnic minorities.

There are, however, counteracting effects. American, European, and other Jewish communities are by no stretch of the
imagination self-contained, self-sufficient, and independent economic units. There is economic interdependence between the
Jews and the other ethnic and religious groups. The former
render professional and other services to their non-Jewish neighbors and vice versa. Protestants and Catholics normally employ
Jewish craftsmen, clerks, salesmen, and other workers. This
being the case, the large Jewish community is located in cities
where the non-Jews invariably outnumber the Jews. Although
the Jews are concentrated in the large Jewish communities, they
constitute a small percentage of the total population. The
March 1957 survey reported that not more than 7.7 percent of
those in urbanized areas of 250,000 or more were Jewish and
only one percent in the other urban centers. Miami and New
York are probably the only two cities where the Jewish com-

ponent constitutes about one-fourth of their inhabitants. The Jewish density in all the other large cities is much less. It thus appears that even the large Jewish communities are surrounded by a non-Jewish population several times their size.

Agencies of social control are generally less effective in large cities than in other communities. There is more anonymity and less face-to-face or personal contacts in large metropolises than in smaller communities. Even the primary groups, including the family, are not very effective. Sociologically speaking, "city air makes free" means that there is more individualism and more personal freedom in the large city than in other places. There is less conformity and uniformity in the metropolis. It follows that the large Jewish communities do not have as much control over their members and are not as cohesive as the smaller communities. This is particularly so in the United States, where the large Jewish communities have no overall central Jewish organization, and affiliation with any Jewish agency is on a purely voluntary basis. The existence of myriad organizations, each competing for the support and sympathy of the members of the Jewish community, not infrequently results in confusion, apathy, and disorganization. The effectiveness of public opinion and social control in the American Jewish communities seems to diminish as their size and that of the cities in which they are located increases. It not infrequently results in duplication and waste as well as in failure to make effective use of the large reservoir of good will, talent, and energy.

The structure and functions of the neighborhood today are not the same as in the recent past. Not many work in their own neighborhood. The shorter workday, longer weekend, improved transportation facilities, and changes in socio-cultural values have in many instances resulted in a decrease in interpersonal contacts among neighbors. The patterns of social interaction and communication have changed in the sense that the neighborhood has ceased to be a very effective agency of social control. The Jew of today does not have as many interests in common with the coreligionists who live in his neighborhood as the Jew in the past. On the other hand, the neighborhood, as in the case of members of other groups, has become an important social symbol. The architecture of the house, its size, the neighborhood where it is located, and the rent one pays indicate the social status of the owner or occupant of the house. Many of them are more interested in enhancing their social prestige than in preserving their cultural heritage. Like many others, Jews prefer to live in prestige neighborhoods. The processes of invasion and succession are in full operation in Jewish and other neighborhoods. The old Jewish sections are gradually disintegrating and disappearing; new Jewish neighborhoods—gilded ghettos—are emerging. There is, however, less concentration in any given territorial unit than in the past and more dispersal, less voluntary segregation and more desegregation. Except probably for those who own their dwelling units, there is less rootedness in the neighborhood. The mobility of the Jews raises many problems. It takes time and it costs money to build and maintain houses of worship, schools, centers, and hospitals.

Jewish suburbia has had some effect. There is more interpersonal contact and more effective interpersonal communication in small and medium-sized suburban communities than in large cities. This in part accounts for the fact that more suburban Jewish families are affiliated with religious and other Jewish organizations than those living in large cities. This is also one reason for the fact that a larger percentage of Jewish children in the suburbs than in large cities are enrolled in Jewish schools. Affiliation is, however, only one of many possible indicators of one's Jewish values and ideals. Nor is the erection of an imposing and expensive synagogue or temple proof positive that the members of the Jewish community are genuinely interested in Jewish culture. Such structures are only a means to an end. It happens not infrequently that the same motives and means are actually being used for radically different ends just as different means are now and then used for obtaining the same ends. The suburb probably has many potentialities. It could to some extent result in a revival and revitalization of the interest in Jewish values and culture. Jewish suburbanites are, however, just as much influenced by general trends as others.

One of them is that our contemporary urban-industrial society has evolved a man-made oriented philosophy of life. Man's success in his efforts to have more control over natural forces has resulted in the emergence of a man-made and man-centered orientation—that is, man is the real creator and producer; he can make things and change them. Very few are inquisitive enough to ask how man has become what he is, what are his ultimate goals and place in the universe, what he really does hope to achieve. The man-made orientation tends to emphasize the importance of this-worldliness and of the relativity of values. This has resulted in a kind of intellectual rootlessness. Although the present generation has virtually unlimited confidence in man's ability to continue to unlock many of the mysteries of life and secrets of nature, it probably suffers from a feeling of insecurity. It is doubtful whether the Jews in the American metropolises are different in this respect. Their values, ideals, and aspirations do not seem to be quite the same as those of their ancestors who lived in the pre-industrial city. They do not seem to have the serenity and fortitude, peace of mind and confidence, hope and self-assurance of their ancestors. The Jew in the American metropolis has many of the traits and characteristics of his non-Jewish neighbors. Some of the values and ideals of the American Jews are incongruous with their socio-cultural heritage. The pre-industrial city was a place where Jews came to live as Jews; the contemporary metropolis has in some respects a de-Judaizing effect on members of the Jewish community.

Demographically, those who live in large cities generally have a low birth rate. Some of them have a very low replacement rate. As we shall see, the Jews have fewer children than some of the non-Jews who live in the same metropolises as they.

The Vanishing Immigrant

The immigrant in the American Jewish community is not being replaced any more; most of the Jews in the United States are native-born of immigrant and American-born parents. They constituted in the years 1936-1938 about 65 percent of the Jewish population in Buffalo, Minneapolis, New London, New Orleans, Norwich, Passaic, Pittsburgh, San Francisco and Trenton.[24] According to surveys made in 1949-1954, almost seven-tenths of the Jewish population in Jacksonville, Los Angeles, New Orleans, Passaic, Pittsburgh, Port Chester, and Trenton were American-born with a range of 68-83 percent. Surveys made in 1956-1959 show that the native-born constituted about 76 percent of the population in Canton, Charleston (W. Va.), Des Moines, Houston, Los Angeles, Portland (Oregon), San Francisco, and Washington, D.C.,[25] with a range of 71-85 percent. Whether the use of different communities accounts to some extent for changes in the proportion of immigrants or not, there is, as we shall see, other evidence that the ratio of natives to immigrants is undergoing a change.

There is now a relatively smaller number of immigrants in the United States than at the end of the nineteenth century. They constituted one-sixth of the white population in 1890 and only 7.5 percent in 1950.[26] The immigrant is gradually disappearing.

The communities which were studied in the 1930's and in more recent years can be used for measuring the approximate rate of increase of the native component. Almost 63 percent of the Jewish population in Passaic, Pittsburgh and Trenton in 1937-1938 were American-born and close to 74 percent in 1949-1953, an increase of 17.5 percent. San Francisco reported an increase from 68 percent in 1938 to 71.5 in 1959. Los Angeles had a much higher rate of increase: the native-born constituted 68 percent in 1951 and 75 percent in 1959. There was probably no change in New Orleans, where the native component accounted for about 81 percent of the Jewish population both in 1938 and 1953.

New Orleans is not the only Jewish community where less than one-fifth of the population are immigrants. The natives constituted 83 percent in Jacksonville and Washington, D.C., and 85 percent in Charleston, W. Va. Cities which originally attracted a relatively large number of Jewish immigrants apparently still have higher ratios of immigrants to natives than other Jewish communities. Changes in the ratio of these two population groups is in some cases due to differences in their rates of migration.

By far the largest group of Jewish immigrants is from Russia. They constituted in 1938 about 48 percent of the immigrants in

Buffalo, Pittsburgh, and San Francisco. More recent surveys show that close to 44 percent of the Jewish immigrants in Canton, Los Angeles, New Orleans, Passaic, Port Chester, and Washington, D.C., are from Russia or probably were born in those parts of Russia which subsequently became Poland, Lithuania, or some other independent state. The percentage of Jews from Poland was practically the same at the time of these surveys, 15.2 and 14.7, respectively. There is probably now a larger percentage of Jews from Germany among Jewish immigrants than in the 1920's because of the anti-Jewish policy of Nazi Germany.

There is no similarity between the age structure of the immigrants and natives. Only 2.5 percent of the immigrants in Canton, New Orleans, Passaic, Pittsburgh, Port Chester, and Washington, D.C., were under 15 years of age while approximately one-fourth were in the age group 65 and over, which is extraordinarily large. Their median age was 54. It thus appears that very few of the Jews under 15 are immigrants, and that a substantial proportion of those 65 and over were not born in the United States. Clearly, the immigrant component has a larger proportion of persons who are no longer in the labor force than do the natives. Some of these aged persons may need financial assistance, others are in need of medical care. A relatively large number of the immigrants are widows and widowers. The extremely small percentage of those under 15 is due to the fact that not many of them are still in the child-bearing age; only 17.7 percent of 16,100 immigrants were 20-44 years old, which is not even one-half of the usual proportion.

There were more women than men among the Jewish immigrants. There were on the average 925 men per 1,000 women in Canton, New Orleans, Passaic, Pittsburgh, Port Chester, and Washington, D.C. One basic reason for this is the fact that women live longer.

The American immigration policy is the principal reason for the gradual disappearance of the immigrant. The immigration laws of the 1920's have drastically reduced the number of newcomers. The drop in Jewish immigration actually dates back to World War I, when it became virtually impossible for the

Russian and the other Jews to emigrate and to cross the Atlantic. The immigration laws of the 1920's, which aimed to reduce the number of newcomers from Poland, Lithuania, Russia, Italy and other countries, account for the fact that a very small number of Jews has been admitted since then. The annual average of Jewish immigrants admitted, dropped from approximately 92,850 in 1899-1914 to 18,000 in 1920-1959.[27]

The American Jewish community is gradually becoming a community of native-born of American-born parents. This is so because it is doubtful that the United States will change its immigration policy radically in the foreseeable future. It is also doubtful that Russia will soon begin to let Jews emigrate. *The American Jewish community is thus becoming culturally a very homogeneous community.* The native-born Jewish men and women have been exposed to the same educational system, to the same or similar social, cultural, ideological, and other stimuli and values.

The gradual disappearance of the immigrant is likely to have some impact on the Jewish community. He was, among other things, a bearer of Jewish culture; he was interested in Hebrew or Yiddish literature; he supported the Jewish theater; he studied Jewish history. His arrival had revitalized Jewish life. Some of the Jewish immigrants became eminent Jewish scholars and distinguished communal leaders, others made important contributions to the physical and social sciences as well as to literature and art. How many of their American-born children and grandchildren are likely to follow in their footsteps, and will continue to be as much interested in Jewish culture as their immigrant fathers and grandfathers?

SEX RATIO OF JEWS IN
THE UNITED STATES

The sex-ratio—the number of males per 100 or 1,000 females—of any population varies with the number of males and females born, number of survivors of each of the sexes at any given time, and migration. Man cannot, for the time being, determine or control the sex of his children. Generally speaking, the sex ratio at birth is about 1,060 males per 1,000 females, meaning that more boys than girls are born. The number of survivors varies with the mortality of each sex. This is to some extent affected by the culture and social conditions under which they live. War, for instance, results in an imbalance of the sexes. Occupational hazards result in a higher mortality of man. More men than women generally migrate across countries or continents. As far as the Jewish immigrants in the United States are concerned, there was a larger proportion of women and children among them than in the case of other newcomers. One of the principal reasons for it was the fact that most of them came with the intention to stay. They therefore tried to bring the members of their family as soon as it was possible.

According to the March 1957 survey, the sex ratio of the Jews

TABLE 4.—*Sex Ratios*

	March 1957 Census Bureau Survey (a)			10 Cities (b)		5 Cities (c)	
	Jewish	Protestant (White)	Roman Catholic	Jewish	Non-Jewish (White)	Jewish	Non-Jewish (White)
Under 5				1,059	1,036	1,139	1,034
5-9				1,339	956	1,064	1,030
10-14				1,230	985	1,110	1,004
15-19	842 (d)	944 (d)	961 (d)	1,284	878	1,595	913
20-24	1,198	785	825	780	956	507	929
25-34	880	926	932	867	920	956	919
35-44	860	936	948	914	922	1,121	923
45-54) 55-64)	1,004	909	957	1,070	937	1,095	934
65 & over	842	790	853	873 911	985) 749)	922	808
Average	927	894	927	983	930	1,038	927

Source: (a) U.S. Bureau of the Census, Current Population Reports, Series P-20, No. 79; (b) Camden, Charleston (S.C.), Los Angeles, Miami, New Orleans, New York, Passaic, Pittsburgh, Port Chester, Trenton; the surveys were made in 1948-1953; it is assumed that no significant changes occurred; data will be found in the reports on the results of the respective community surveys; (c) Canton, Des Moines, Houston, Lynn, Washington, D.C.: the surveys were made in 1955-1956; data will be found in the reports on the results of the respective community surveys. (d) 14-19.

according to age was not at all similar to the age sex ratios of
the white Protestants and Catholics. The Jewish sex ratios fluc-
tuated upward and downward, while the age sex ratios of the
others seem to have followed an orderly downward trend. As
a matter of fact, the Spearman rank correlation coefficient
between the age sex ratios of Jews and Protestants and of Jews
and Catholics is −0.53 and −0.36, respectively, while in the
case of the Protestants and Catholics it is +0.83. Is the observed
difference due to sampling errors or is the sex ratio of the Jews
really different? If the latter, is it because of differences in
socio-cultural conditions or biological factors?

Further analysis shows that there is a negative correlation
between the age sex ratios of the Jews as reported by the surveyors of Jewish communities and the March 1957 data on the
Jewish group. The rank correlation coefficient (rho) between
the sex ratios according to age (five age groups) of the Jewish
population in the five communities surveyed in 1955-1956 and
the age sex ratios of the Jews according to the March 1957
survey is—O.G. On the other hand, the rank correlation coefficient between the age-sex ratios of the Jews in these cities and
Protestants and Catholics in March 1957, is in each instance
+O.G. This would suggest that the differences between Jews
and others as reported by the Bureau of the Census are likely
to be due to sampling errors, although it is not at all easy to
understand how this could have happened as far as the sex
composition of the Jewish group is concerned.

Turning now to the Jewish community surveys, we find that
the rank correlation coefficient between the sex ratios according
to age in the ten and five communities is −0.67 in the case of
the Jewish population and −0.92 in the case of the white non-
Jews living there. One possible reason for the difference in the
correlation coefficients is the fact that the sex ratios of the
two non-Jewish groups are as of 1950, whereas the ratios of
the two Jewish groups do not refer to the same year; one
group was surveyed in 1948-1953 and the other in 1953-1956.
It seems, however, that there is a greater similarity between
the non-Jewish population in the several cities than in the
case of the Jews. Furthermore, the rank correlation coefficient

between the Jews and white non-Jews in the ten and five cities is −0.018 and 0.37. There seems to be more similarity between the age-sex ratios of the Jewish population surveyed in 1955-1956 and the non-Jews in 1950 than in the case when both were surveyed almost at the same time. Table 4 shows that the sex ratios of the Jews fluctuate much more than that of the non-Jews.

Once again, why are the age sex ratios of the Jews subject to such fluctuations while this does not seem to be so in the case of the non-Jewish population? Are the oscillations in any way the result of sampling or are the age-sex ratios of the Jews really not the same as of the other religious groups? And granted that they are different, why does the non-Jewish group have a sex ratio pattern and the Jews not?

What are some of the implications of the sex ratio? If one sex outnumbers the other, it may result in an increase in interfaith marriages or in the proportion of single persons. The ten communities reported that they had 47,000 men 20-24 years old and 77,350 women.[28] In the case of the five communities there were 7,970 and 10,200 respectively. This age group has a very high marriage rate. An appreciable numerical excess of one sex over the other may reduce the fertility rate. Enrollment in Jewish schools varies with the sex ratio; so does the demand for certain kinds of recreational, social, and other services.

The age structure of a country varies with the fertility and mortality rates of its inhabitants and their migration. If we divide the population into three principal age groups—dependent children or those under 15 years, those who are in the labor force, and those 65 years and over—we find that those under 15 constitute a larger proportion of the population in countries with a high birth rate than in those with a low birth rate. A larger percentage of the population is in the age group 15-64 in countries which do not have a high fertility rate than in those countries where parents tend to have many children. Although man is mortal, he has some control over his life span or expectancy. The mortality rate varies, among other things, with conditions of work and standard and style of life, medical knowledge and care, sanitation and hygiene, relaxation and recreation patterns. As the life expectancy goes up, the per-

TABLE 5.—*Age Distribution of Jews and Others, March 1957*
(*Percentages*)

	MALE			FEMALE		
Age	*Jewish*	*Protestant (White)*	*Roman Catholic*	*Jewish*	*Protestant (White)*	*Roman Catholic*
14-19	8.6	11.8	12.3	9.5	11.2	11.9
20-24	6.8	7.2	8.2	5.3	8.2	9.2
25-34	16.6	19.2	21.4	17.5	18.5	21.3
35-44	18.1	19.3	21.1	19.5	18.4	20.7
45-64	37.5	29.7	27.4	34.6	29.2	26.5
65 and over	12.4	12.8	9.5	13.6	14.4	10.4
Median Age (years)	44.9	41.1	38.8	44.1	41.6	38.7

	10 Cities (a)				5 Cities (b)			
	MALE		FEMALE		MALE		FEMALE	
Age	*Jewish*	*Non-Jewish (White)*	*Jewish*	*Non-Jewish (White)*	*Jewish*	*Non-Jewish (White)*	*Jewish*	*Non-Jewish (White)*
Under 5	9.2	9.2	8.6	8.2	10.6	11.1	9.7	9.9
5-9	9.6	6.8	7.1	6.6	10.6	7.7	10.4	7.0
10-14	6.3	5.7	5.0	5.4	9.1	5.5	8.6	5.1
15-19	6.1	5.6	4.7	4.0	6.0	5.6	3.9	5.7
20-24	3.7	8.0	6.0	7.8	2.9	8.7	6.0	8.7
25-34	13.0	17.0	14.7	17.2	16.1	19.3	17.6	19.5
35-44	16.5	15.8	17.8	16.0	19.7	15.9	18.3	16.0
45-54	16.2	13.7	14.9	13.6	12.9	12.1	12.2	12.0
55-64	9.1	11.0	10.2	10.4	12.0	14.2	13.4	16.3
65 and over	10.2	7.1	11.0	8.9				
Median Age (years)	36.2	33.6	37.2	34.4	31.6	30.9	31.5	32.0

a) The cities are: Camden, Charleston, S. C., Los Angeles, Miami, New Orleans, New York, Passaic, Pittsburgh, Port Chester, Trenton; the surveys were made in 1948-1953; it is assumed that the percentage distribution before 1950 and soon thereafter was practically similar.

b) The cities are: Canton, Des Moines, Houston, Lynn, Washington; they were surveyed in 1955-1956.

centage of the aged increases. Young men and women are more likely to migrate than young children and aged persons. The former are looking for economic, social, and other opportunities. There is a relatively larger number of persons 15-64 years old in countries of immigration than in places of emigration.

The March 1957 survey shows that the Jews have a relatively smaller number of those 14-24 years old than the Protestant and Catholics, and a much larger proportion of those 45 years and over than the two largest religious groups. The median age of Jewish, Protestant and Catholic men 14 years of age and over was 44.9, 41.1, and 38.8 years. The median age of the Jews was about 9 percent above the one of the Protestants and 16 percent above the median age of Catholics. The median age of the Jewish women was 6 percent above the median of Protestant women and 14 percent above the median age of Catholic women. This suggests that the life expectancy of the Jews is not quite the same as of Catholics and white Protestants. A study of the expectation of life of Jews and others in Canada shows that Jewish males had in 1940-1942 a life expectancy of 67.53 years at time of birth and the total male population only 62.95, a difference of about 7 percent; in the case of the females it was 69.89 and 66.29, a difference of about 5 percent. The differences are reduced with advance in age.[29] The mortality experience of the American Jew is probably similar to the life expectancy of their brethren in Canada.

AGE STRUCTURE

According to the March 1957 survey, the Jews had fewer children under 14 years than the Protestants and Catholics. The percentage of such children of each of them was 22.2, 26.7, and 27.7 respectively. The Jewish percentage was 83 percent of the percentage of Protestants under 14 and four-fifths of the Catholic percentage. There are at least two possible reasons for the smaller percentage of Jews under 14 years. One is that Jewish children under 14 have a higher death rate than other children. It was estimated, however, that Jewish children in New York City under 15 years had in 1953 a death rate of 142 per 100,000 and non-Jewish (white) had a mortality rate of 233 per 100,000; the Jewish rate was only 61 percent of the non-Jews. Similarly, Jewish boys under five constituted 9.5 percent of all the Jewish male decedents in New York City in 1931; in the case of the non-Jewish males the boys under five accounted for 13.7 percent of the deaths. The difference was not so marked in the case of the female decedents, the percentages were 9.1 and 10.8 respectively. As far as those under 15 years are concerned, the Jewish boys and girls constituted 12.7 and 12.2 percent respectively, of the decedents, the non-Jews 16.8 and 13.7 percent respectively. Similar results were obtained in Canada and Berlin, Germany.[30] It thus appears that a larger percentage of Jewish children at any age under 15 survive. (As we shall see, the principal reason for the small percentage of Jewish children under 15 is the lower birth rate of the Jews in the United States.)

The median age of the Jewish men and women in the ten cities was practically the same as of those surveyed in 1957— 36.7 and 36.9 years respectively. But the median age of the non-Jewish (white) population in these 10 cities did not coincide with the 1957 median age of Catholic and Protestant (white) men and women—34 and 31 years, respectively. It did coincide with the median age of the non-Jewish population in the five cities—31.5 years. The median age of the Jewish men and women was the same as of the non-Jews. Why, then, is the median age of the Jewish population in the five cities who were surveyed in 1955-1956 at variance with the results of the 1957 survey but not the median of the Jewish men and women in the ten cities surveyed in 1948-1953? Is it due to sampling errors or to some other reason?

The Jewish population in the ten cities seems to have been older than their brethren in the five cities. The former had a larger percentage of those 55 years and over and the latter had a larger proportion of those under 10. One possible reason for the larger percentage of older persons in the ten cities is that Los Angeles, New York, Pittsburgh, and Miami have a larger proportion of immigrants than the other communities.

The proportion of children under 10 years has increased. They constituted in Passaic and Trenton 12 percent in 1937 and 15.7 percent in 1949. Their percentage in New Orleans increased from about one-tenth in 1938 to 17 percent in 1953. In San Francisco the percentage of the Jewish population under 15 years increased from approximately 15 in 1938 to almost one-fifth in 1959. The increase suggests, as we shall see, an increase in the birth rate.

There was a similar increase in the percentage of the senior members. In Passaic and Trenton the percentage of those 55 years of age and over increased from about 11 percent in 1937 to 17 percent in 1949. Those 65 years of age and over who lived in New Orleans in 1938 constituted one-twelfth of the local Jewish population and 13 percent in 1953. In San Francisco the increase in the proportion of those 65 years and over was from nine percent in 1938 to 16.5 percent in 1959. The Jewish community now has a larger proportion of senior members than in the past.

TABLE 6.—*Age Composition of Native-Born Russians (Jews)
and Others of Immigrant or Mixed Parentage in Nine
Standard Metropolitan Areas, (a) 1950
(Percentages)*

| | MALE | | FEMALE | |
Age	Russian (Jewish)	Other	Russian (Jewish)	Other
Under 5	2.4	4.1	2.3	3.7
5-9	3.6	4.5	3.4	4.0
10-14	4.9	5.2	4.4	4.6
15-19	6.8	6.7	6.5	6.3
20-24	10.1	8.9	10.1	8.8
25-29	12.6	10.7	13.7	10.6
30-34	14.7	11.6	15.7	11.8
35-39	14.9	11.2	15.5	11.0
40-44	12.2	9.3	11.5	9.0
45-49	7.1	7.3	7.0	7.2
50-54	5.5	6.4	5.3	6.4
55-59	3.1	5.1	2.7	5.2
60-64	1.3	3.6	1.1	3.9
65-69	0.5	2.3	0.5	3.0
70-74	0.2	1.5	0.2	2.1
75 and over	0.1	1.5	0.1	2.4
Median Age (years)	33.3	33.1	34.2	35.1

Source: U.S. Bureau of the Census, Census of Population: 1950 Population, Volume 4, Nativity and Parentage, Table 16.

(a) The standard metropolitan areas are: Boston, Chicago, Cleveland, Detroit, Los Angeles, New York, Philadelphia, Pittsburgh and San Francisco. As explained before, most of these Russians were of Jewish origin.

The suburban Jewish communities have a larger percentage of young persons than the metropolises. Those under five years constituted in 1949 about 15 percent of the Jewish population in the Trenton suburban area and only 7.5 percent in the case of those in Trenton. The percentage of those 65 years and over was 1.8 and 6.6 respectively. The percentage of those under 5 years increased in 1959 from 5 percent in San Francisco to almost 9 percent in Marin County, and one-tenth in the peninsula communities. As far as those 65 years and older are concerned, the percentages decreased from about 16 in San Francisco to eight in Marin County and 6.6 percent in the Peninsula communities.

The age composition varies from city to city. One-tenth of the Los Angeles Jewish community in 1959 were under 5 years and only 5 percent in San Francisco in the same year. San Francisco had a larger proportion of those 65 years and older than Los Angeles—16 and 7 percent respectively. Those under 5 years constituted 7.2 percent of the Jewish population in Passaic in 1949 and 7.5 percent in Trenton in the same year; those 65 and over constituted 3.5 and 6.6 percent respectively. Apparently certain persons are more likely to settle in one type of city than in another.

The age composition varies from area to area in the same city. Generally speaking, the older areas are more likely to be inhabited by senior members and the newer neighborhoods are more likely to attract the younger generation. The older folks may prefer to remain where they are because of financial reasons, relatively low rent, as well as sentimental considerations. The younger generation is more interested in comforts and in prestige symbols.

Table 6 shows the age distribution of the native-born Russians, most of whom (as shown before) were Jewish, and others of immigrant or mixed parentage who lived in 1950 in the following standard metropolitan areas: Boston, Chicago, Cleveland, Detroit, Los Angeles, New York, Philadelphia, Pittsburgh, and San Francisco. Almost 11 percent of the Russian (Jewish) males were under 15 years while close to 14 percent of the others were in this age group. The percentages of those 15-19 were 87 and 77.2 respectively. The Russian (Jewish) group had fewer of those 6 years and over than the others. The age distribution of the Russian (Jewish) and other females was along similar lines. The age distribution of these Russians was in many respects similar to the age composition of those known to be Jewish. The differences are to some extent due to the fact that the Jewish community studies included the entire population, natives of immigrant and American-born parents as well as immigrants and this Russian (Jewish) group consisting only of native-born of immigrant or mixed parentage.

The age composition of any group is an important consideration. Fertility and mortality rates and marriage and divorce rates vary with the age structure of the population. Widowhood is more prevalent among certain age groups. School enrollment, the need for certain recreational facilities, summer camps, homes for senior members of the community, houses specially built to accommodate elderly persons, the incidence and prevalence of certain diseases, these and many other social, cultural, economic, and psychological problems, phenomena and processes vary with age. Any effective community planning must take the age structure of the population into consideration.

MARRIAGE AND FAMILY

There are several significant differences between the attitude of Jewish and other men and women toward marriage and family life. The former generally marry at a later age than Protestants and Catholics. They have fewer bachelors and spinsters. Jews have fewer broken homes or families.

A study of one thousand students from Connecticut high schools shows that a smaller percentage of Jewish than Protestant and Catholic respondents intended to marry their steady and that very few have already committed themselves to marry their steady. Only 11 percent of 55 Jewish students intended to marry their steady compared to about 14 percent of 365 Protestant and 549 Catholic respondents. More significant is the fact that only about one out of 14 Jewish respondents, about one out of seven Protestant and almost one out of five Catholic students had committed themselves already to marry their steady.[31] Jewish high school students apparently intend to marry at a later age than their non-Jewish classmates. The same study shows that a smaller percentage of those who plan to go to college have agreed to marry their steady than those who do not intend to continue their studies. Similarly, a relatively smaller number of the very good students have committed themselves already to marriage. Generally speaking, a larger percentage of Jewish than other high school students plan to go to college. This being the case, many of them find it rather difficult to commit themselves at a relatively early age to marry their steady. There is usually a correlation between a student's high school grades and his or her intention to go to college.

More Jewish than other men and women generally marry, although the former are likely to marry at a later age. A study of college graduates reports that "among Jewish coeds the proportion of unmarried career women is only 23 out of 100. Among Protestants, the proportion is the same as for all coeds—that is, 31 out of 100. Among Catholic women the proportion jumps to 48 out of 100." Further analysis shows that age, family, college attended, and course of study do not account for the low marriage of Catholic coeds. The conclusion is that the chances of a coed to marry "will depend more than anything else upon her religion."[32] L. M. Terman's follow-up study of his group of geniuses reports that by 1940 about 78 percent of the Jewish men and almost 74 percent of the Jewish women were married against 68.5 and 71 percent respectively of the non-Jewish geniuses. In 1945, however, the margin between them was narrowed.[33]

Jewish students are more likely to say that their parents are happily married than other children. Approximately four-fifths of 247 Jewish students enrolled in several colleges thought their parents to be happily or very happily married. Only seven out of ten Protestant and Catholic students gave such reply. Although this Jewish group rated low in religiousness, they rated very high in marital happiness. This suggests that "little relationship between religiousness and parents' marital happiness appeared for the Jews in this study."[34]

A much smaller percentage of this group of Jewish than other college students were children of divorced parents. Only 3.3 percent of the Jewish respondents, 7.7 percent of the Catholic and one-tenth of the Protestant students had divorced or separated parents. A study of Detroiters shows that the "Jewish families had the lowest divorce rate of all, with only 4 percent of the 26 Jewish respondents who had ever married reporting a divorce." Of the 206 Catholic respondents, 8 percent were divorced and the 247 white Protestants had a divorce rate of 16 per 100 ever married.[35] This suggests that the Jewish family is more stable than the family of the members of other religious groups.

The marital status pattern of the Jews and others was in several respects similar and different. Very few Jewish and other males under 20 years were married. A larger proportion of the Jewish than of the other males under 24 were single. This was not so in the case of those 25 years and over. Apparently more Jewish than other men eventually marry, although they start family life at a somewhat later age. Age at marriage of bridegrooms generally varies with their education and occupational preferences. About 41 percent of men with four years of high school who were married between January 1947 and June 1954 were at least 25 years old at the time of their marriage, but 57 percent of those with at least four years of college were in the same age group. Those who go to college or a professional school usually do not have an income of their own and therefore marry at a later age than those who start working as soon as they leave high school. There are also other reasons for the difference in age at marriage between those who are and those who are not college graduates. There are, among other things, differences in their levels of aspiration, standard and style of living and their social status. Similarly, those who are in wholesale and retail trade or in service industries generally marry at a later age than those who are in manufacturing, construction, transportation, etc. The study referred to above showed

TABLE 7.–*Marital Status of Jews* (A) *and Others*
(*Percentage Distribution According to Age*)

	Single		Married		Separated-Divorced		Widowed	
	Jewish	Non-Jewish (White)	Jewish	Non-Jewish (White)	Jewish	Non-Jewish (White)	Jewish	Non-Jewish (White)
MALE								
15-19	99.98	97.6	0.02	2.0	–	0.2	–	0.2
20-24	77.3	72.0	21.2	27.0	1.5	0.9	0.01	0.1
25-34	19.5	28.4	78.8	69.0	1.8	2.3	–	0.3
35-44	6.2	15.1	93.5	79.7	0.3	4.1	–	1.1
45-54	3.5	13.8	95.2	77.2	0.3	5.0	0.9	3.4
55-64	2.5	11.5	94.4	74.4	1.2	4.2	1.9	9.9
65 and over	6.4	10.8	75.8	55.5	1.2	3.5	16.6	30.3
FEMALE								
15-19	90.0	92.4	10.0	7.4	–	0.5	–	0.1
20-24	34.3	51.1	62.1	46.6	3.6	1.9	–	0.4
25-34	13.6	20.6	83.7	73.8	2.1	4.5	0.6	1.1
35-44	4.3	15.8	92.4	72.6	3.2	6.8	0.1	4.9
45-54	4.9	12.9	79.9	68.8	5.2	6.1	10.0	12.2
55-64	0.7	13.8	71.5	53.2	4.0	4.3	23.8	28.7
65 and over	13.9	11.6	41.2	24.7	2.0	1.7	42.9	62.1

Source: the data on the Jewish men and women were from the respective Jewish community studies; the information on the non-Jewish groups is from the U.S. 1950 Census of Population. (A) Data was available on the Jews in New Orleans, New York, Pittsburgh, and Washington, D.C.

that 48 percent of men in service industries and 46 percent of those in wholesale and retail trade were at least 25 years old at the time of their marriage; in the case of those in construction or manufacturing the percentages were 42 and 40, respectively.[36]

It so happens that more Jews are college graduates and are in the several professions and in wholesale and retail trade than non-Jews. This, then, is one reason why Jews marry at a somewhat later age than non-Jews. A larger percentage of the former than of the latter eventually marry because Jews are, for historical, cultural, psychological, and other reasons more family-centered than other groups.

As far as broken families are concerned, a smaller percentage of Jewish than of other husbands were separated or divorced.

Although this does not necessarily prove that separations and divorces are less prevalent among the former, because a larger percentage of the Jews than of the others might have, for some reason or other, remarried, there is some evidence, as it was shown before, that there are probably fewer broken homes among Jews than among other groups. Moreover, a smaller percentage of Jews than of white Protestants and Catholics in Detroit thought that divorce was "always or usually wrong from the moral standpoint." The percentages who expressed such a view were 11, 34, and 66 respectively.[37] Equally important is the fact that these religions stress the importance of family life, family purity, and mutual devotion to the spouses. Furthermore, Judaism has a more tolerant attitude toward divorce than Catholicism and perhaps even Protestantism. It will also be recalled that the Landis study showed that the Jewish group "rated low in religiousness but high in marital happiness when compared with the other faith groups."[38] This being the case, it is very doubtful that the difference in the incidence of separation and divorce is in any way related to differences in religious teachings and degree of religiousness of Jews and others.

JEWISH PARENTAL DEVOTION

One possible explanation is the fact that the Jews have for centuries been subjected to all kinds of discriminatory practices, anti-Jewish legislation, inquisitions, degradations, forced ghetto life, persecutions, pogroms, and mass massacres. In a sense, their neighbors declared a war against them. But in time of war the warring parties are not infrequently more united against their common enemy than at any other time. Conflicts and crises tend to have an integrative effect, at least as long as they last. The Jewish family was therefore a more cohesive unit than the family of other groups. Husbands and wives were more likely to be united in their struggle for existence and defense of their rights than other spouses, who were not singled out for such merciless treatment as the Jews. Similarly, Jewish fathers and mothers could not very well ignore the fact that their children were less protected and secure than those of non-Jewish parents. They therefore felt inner-bound to care for and shield their offspring. Their children, they thought, would sooner or later be treated in the same way as any other Jew. Why, then, not try to make their life as pleasant as possible and as long as possible? More than any other parents, Jewish fathers and mothers became child-oriented and their offspring became the focus of their attention. In the course of time they became very solicitous over their children, extremely devoted parents, and very much concerned about their future. Jewish fathers and mothers developed such a strong feeling of responsibility that they were willing to make supreme sacrifices for their children who would have to live in a hostile society. Jewish parents tried their utmost to provide their children with emotional, economic, and social security. The Jewish home was gradually transformed into a veritable castle and real fortress; neither non-Jewish parents nor children were so much in need of security as the young Jewish children. The Jewish community naturally encouraged such attitudes of parents toward their children and of the spouses toward one another. These attitudes soon became deeply rooted and ingrained; they became one of the distinguishing characteristics of Jewish family life. Although conditions have changed, these attitudes have not. There is still a feeling of insecurity. Jewish parents still think that their children do not have the same opportunity as the offspring of other parents.

The quest for self-validation is another reason. Every normal human being wants to convince himself that he is in one way or another as good as, if not better than any other member of the group, and tries to convince others that this is actually the case. This, however, presupposes a fair opportunity to be able to demonstrate his talent and dexterity, ability and skill, devotion and loyalty, knowledge and understanding, and so on. The Jew, however, did not always have the same chances for self-expression and self-validation as others. Burdened with many economic, political, and social restrictions, the Jew tried to make effective use of the few opportunities now and then available to him in such a way that he could at least expect a favorable reaction from his coreligionists. The family was one of them. Here he was a free man, no one could interfere with him. He endeavored to be a good and faithful husband and a devoted and solicitous father. His efforts to take good care of the members of his family were greatly appreciated by them and they were a source of real satisfaction, joy, and happiness for him. His devotion to his family, his self-sacrificing attitude, his strict adherence to the principle of family purity—these were some of the things the Jew did in his quest for self-validation and social prestige. Although American Jews now have other opportunities for self-validation than their ancestors, they still regard the family as one of the focal points in their life. This occasionally results in some intrafamily problems. Some parents are probably overprotective, an attitude which children now and then resent. Some parents are emotionally too dependent on their children and now and then are frustrated and disillusioned individuals. Whatever the results, the family is still an extremely important medium for self-validation and self-expression. This may be one of the reasons why a larger percentage of Jews than of others eventually marry. This may also be one of the reasons why Jews marry at a somewhat later age than others. The way they see it, family life entails, among other things, many obligations and responsibilities. This being the case, one must be psychologically, economically, and socially mature for his role of husband and father. All this implies is that, by and large, Jews regard marriage as a very important stage in life for which one must be adequately prepared. The fact that Jews are more likely to use the family as a medium for self-validation also explains to some extent, as we shall see, why they generally have fewer children than members of other groups.

Does all this imply that the family values of members of other religious and ethnic minorities which are in one way or another being discriminated against are very much similar to the attitude of Jews toward the family? The minority status of the Jews and their motives for using the family as a medium for self-expression and self-validation are only two of many other reasons for their present attitude toward the family. Each ethnic and religious group has a certain uniqueness and individuality. Past experiences, the influence of great men and leaders, traditions, beliefs, ideals—these and many other factors mold ethnic and religious groups and influence their family values.

Returning to the marital status of Jews and others, Table 7 shows that the former have a smaller percentage of widowers than the other groups. This would suggest that Jewish women generally live longer and therefore Jews become widowers at a later age than others whose wives die at an earlier age. It may also be due to the fact that Jewish widowers are more likely to remarry than others. Surveyors generally want to know what the marital status of the individual is at the time of the inquiry rather than whether the respondent was ever widowed or divorced and subsequently remarried. In both groups there is a positive correlation between age and the proportion of widowers.

The Jewish and other women married at an earlier age than the men. One reason for this is the fact that man is the supporter and provider, he has economic responsibilities both as husband and father. Also, for some reason he wants his wife to be somewhat younger than he. For biological, psychological, and other reasons, the woman prefers to become a wife at an early age. As in the case of Jewish men, a larger percentage of Jewish than other women are married. The Jewish group has a smaller percentage of widows. As pointed out before, Jews generally live longer. It is also quite possible that a larger percentage of Jewish than other widows remarry.

Table 8 shows the marital status of Russians, most of whom are Jewish, and others in nine standard metropolitan areas, where most of the Jews live. A smaller percentage of the Jewish male immigrants than of the native-born group were single. The same is also true in the case of the other male groups as well as in the case of Jewish and other women, both immigrant and American-born. One reason for it is that the social values, standard of living, and style of life of the immigrant are somewhat different from those born and raised in the

TABLE 8.—Marital Status of Russians (Jews)(a) and Others in Nine Standard Metropolitan Areas,(b) 1950 Percentages

IMMIGRANTS

Marital Status	MALE Russian (Jewish) 14-24	MALE Russian (Jewish) 25-44	MALE Russian (Jewish) 45	MALE Others 14-24	MALE Others 25-44	MALE Others 45	FEMALE Russian (Jewish) 14-24	FEMALE Russian (Jewish) 25-44	FEMALE Russian (Jewish) 45	FEMALE Others 14-24	FEMALE Others 25-44	FEMALE Others 45
Single	75.5	12.0	5.6	81.6	16.7	9.3	48.0	10.8	3.1	55.1	11.3	6.2
Married	23.1	85.8	82.9	16.9	80.9	77.3	45.8	83.0	64.5	43.5	82.9	60.8
Widowed	1.4	2.2	11.4	1.5	2.4	13.5	6.1	6.2	32.3	1.3	5.8	33.0
Separated												
Divorced												
Total	100.0	100.0	99.9	100.0	100.0	100.1	99.9	100.0	99.9	99.9	100.0	100.0

NATIVE-BORN OF IMMIGRANT OR MIXED PARENTAGE

Marital Status	MALE Russian (Jewish) 14-24	MALE Russian (Jewish) 25-44	MALE Russian (Jewish) 45	MALE Others 14-24	MALE Others 25-44	MALE Others 45	FEMALE Russian (Jewish) 14-24	FEMALE Russian (Jewish) 25-44	FEMALE Russian (Jewish) 45	FEMALE Others 14-24	FEMALE Others 25-44	FEMALE Others 45
Single	85.5	16.3	8.0	84.8	19.6	8.0	65.0	13.3	8.1	69.7	15.2	13.1
Married	14.4	82.1	86.8	14.8	78.2	86.8	34.4	82.7	74.4	29.6	80.5	59.2
Widowed		1.6	5.2			5.2	0.6	3.9	17.5	0.7	4.4	27.7
Separated	0.3			0.4								
Divorced												
Total	100.0	100.0	100.0	100.0	100.0	100.0	100.0	99.9	100.0	100.0	100.1	100.0

Source: U.S. Bureau of the Census, Census of Population: 1950, Population, Vol. 4, Nativity and Parentage, Table 22.

(a) As shown before, the large majority of the Russians were of Jewish descent.

(b) Boston, Chicago, Cleveland, Detroit, Los Angeles, New York, Philadelphia, Pittsburgh, San Francisco.

United States. Some of the immigrants undoubtedly came here with their wives.

The immigrant groups had a relatively larger number of broken families than the native-born Jewish and other men and women. We do not know, however, to what extent this was caused by the death of one of the spouses. It is quite possible that immigrants do not live as long as those born in the United States because of differences in occupation, income, mode of living, medical care, housing conditions, and so on.

The Jewish women started marrying at an earlier age than the Jewish men. A smaller percentage of the former than of the latter were single. But the Jewish women had a larger percentage who were widowed, divorced, or separated than the Jewish men. Since Jewish husbands do not live as long as Jewish wives, it is to be expected that there should be more widows than widowers. It is not known, however, whether Jewish widows and divorcees are less likely to remarry than Jewish widowers and divorced men. The native-born Jewish women had a smaller percentage of widows and divorcees than the other American-born women. Differences in the remarriage rate as well as in the incidence of divorce and widowhood probably account for the smaller percentage of widows and divorcees among Jewish women.

In general, the analysis of the marital status of the Russians and others in these nine standard metropolitan areas shows that the marital status pattern of the Russians is very similar to that of those who are very definitely known to be of Jewish descent. The principal reason for this great similarity is the fact that most of these Russians in 1950 actually were of Jewish origin.

INTERMARRIAGE

Whom do Jewish men and women prefer to marry? More specifically, what is their attitude toward interfaith marriages, and what percentage of them have spouses who are not of Jewish origin? In view of the fact that there is no official record of the religion of brides and grooms, there are no reliable data on the incidence of intermarriage in the United States. The results of studies of samples of the population suggest that there has been an appreciable increase in the rate of interfaith marital unions.

To begin with, the attitude toward interfaith dating has changed. According to a study of high school students in Seattle, Washington, in 1948, Jewish boys and girls were less ethnocentric than those of other groups. There was less opposition on the part of the Jewish high school students to interfaith dating than in the case of the other respondents. The Riverton study reported that 43 percent of the Jewish teen-agers old enough to date had one or more dates with non-Jewish boys and girls. Almost as many, 42 percent, were absolutely opposed to such dating. The dating pattern of the Riverton Jewish teen-agers seems to have been very similar to the one of 387 Jewish students at Columbia College and 149 at Barnard College in 1952. Whether these respondents, who were known to the Columbia University Jewish chaplain, were representative of all the Columbia and Barnard Jewish students or not, 41 percent said they had dated a Gentile within the past six months. A more recent study of college students reported that only 14 percent of the Jewish respondents, 52 percent of the Protestant students, and 64 percent of the Catholic group were willing to interdate.[39]

Dating not infrequently results in going steady. Nine percent of the Columbia-Barnard group were going steady with Gentiles. About 28 percent of a small group of Jewish students at the University of Minnesota in 1940 said that they had love affairs with non-Jewish women, and 15 percent of Jewish women on that campus gave a similar answer.[40]

Whether Jewish men and women interdate and go steady with those who are not Jewish or not, indications are that the attitudes of the present generation of Jewish coeds in America toward interfaith marriage is not the same as of their ancestors. Landis, who collected data in 1952-1955 on the attitude of students attending colleges located in parts of the country where there is not so heavy a concentration of Jews, reports that the attitude of Jewish females varies with the religiousness of their parents. Three-fifths of those from families who were indifferent to religion and only 12 percent from devout families were willing to intermarry. About two-fifths of the Jewish male respondents had a similar attitude; 13 percent of them were willing to convert to the faith of their future spouse. About 35 percent of the Columbia-Barnard respondents expressed a favorable attitude toward interfaith marriage and 22 percent were against it. Jewish college girls at the University of Wisconsin in 1941 were not as much against marrying a non-Jew as Protestant and Catholic respondents were against marrying a Jew. Seven-tenths of the Riverton adolescents preferred not to intermarry. The results of surveys of the attitude of Jewish students at Cornell, Yale and other schools are similar. On the other hand, a study of a small group of college students reported in 1958 that only four percent of the Jewish respondents, one-tenth of the Catholic group, and 15 percent of the Protestants were willing to intermarry.[41]

A similar change has occurred in the attitude of Jewish parents toward mixed marriages. Only 57 percent of the Riverton parents thought that interfaith marriages were likely to be a failure. Four-tenths of a small group of native-born Jewish fathers were willing to accept such marital unions of their children. Although 87 percent of a group of Jewish women were not against mixed marriages, only 42 percent would have approved such marital unions in the case of their children. Three-fourths of Protestants, about four-fifths of Catholics, and 92 percent of Jews in the Detroit area thought that intrafaith marriages were preferable. Finally, a survey of Jews in Elmira, New York, suggests that the attitude of adults toward interfaith marriages varies with the extent of their involvement in Jewish life. Only 31 percent of those who belonged to Jewish-Gentile social groups and 65 percent who belonged only to Jewish organizations said it was "distasteful to have someone in their family marry a Gentile."[42]

It thus appears that the attitude toward exogamy has changed. Fewer Jewish men and women are opposed to it. Those who are against interfaith marriages are generally not as vehemently opposed to such marital unions as Jews used to be. This does not, however, imply that there has been a corresponding increase in the rate of intermarriage. It not infrequently happens that there is a discrepancy between attitude and overt behavior, between what one says and does. Not all those who are not opposed to or are in favor of interfaith marriage will actually intermarry. And it now and then happens that even those who are against exogamy marry, for some reason or other, outside their faith.

The rate of interfaith marriage of Jewish men and women in the United States has increased. According to the survey made by the U.S. Bureau of the Census in March 1957, approximately one out of 14 married Jewish men and women (7.2 per 100) were husbands and wives of non-Jewish spouses. This was in striking contrast to the results of the study of the incidence of intermarriage in New York City in 1908-1912. It was then estimated that there were 117 intermarriages per 10,000 marital unions (1.17 per 100) in the New York Jewish community. The same study showed that American-born Jewish men and women had a much higher intermarriage rate (seven times as much) than the immigrant generation—451 against 64 intermarriages per 10,000 marital unions. Moreover, the prevalence of mixed marriages varied with the country of origin of the Jewish spouses. East European Jews had a lower rate of interfaith marriages than those who were English, French, or German Jews. The non-Jewish groups had a much higher intermarriage rate. The Census Bureau estimated that the Protestants had 86 intermarriages per 1,000 marital unions and the Catholics had 216, as against 72 per 1,000 marriages in the case of the Jewish group. The New York study also showed that the non-Jewish groups had a higher intermarriage rate than the Jewish brides and grooms.[43]

Other studies show that exogamy is more prevalent in the American Jewish community than the results of the Census Bureau seem to suggest. The intermarriage rate of the Jews who were married in Iowa in 1953 was 31 per 100 marriages. Those who were married for the first time had a lower intermarriage rate than those who were married for the second or third time. Is it because those who were married for the first time were more likely to be under the influence of their parents than the others? The Iowa Jewish women had a much lower intermarriage rate than the men, 10.8 percent against 31 percent. It is doubtful, however, whether the Iowa Jewish community is representative of the Jews in the United States. A survey of a neighborhood in Manhattan, New York City, showed that approximately 18 percent of the Jewish women and one-fifth of the Jewish men had non-Jewish spouses. Once again, there is no convincing proof that this midtown area is representative of the New York Jewish community. A study of high school seniors in Boston, St. Louis, Omaha, and Denver showed that 14, 21, 23, and 27 percent, respectively, were children of Jewish fathers and non-Jewish mothers. About one-fifth of these Jewish husbands had non-Jewish spouses. According to another sample, 12 percent of Jewish husbands and about 11 percent of Jewish wives had non-Jewish spouses.[44] As stated before, these samples are not necessarily representative of the Jewish population. They seem to suggest that more than one out of 14 Jewish husbands and wives have non-Jewish spouses, as reported by the Census Bureau.

Jewish community surveys are another source of information on the prevalence of interfaith families. The 1959 Charleston, West Virginia, survey reported that 84 of 376 married couples (22%) had non-Jewish spouses. Almost one-fifth of the Jewish husbands and only 5 percent of the Jewish wives had such spouses. About one-tenth of these non-Jewish spouses converted to Judaism. The 84 intermarried couples had eight married children, six of whom married non-Jews. In Charleston, South Carolina, eight or nine of every 100 marital unions were interfaith marriages. The Charleston temple has special provisions for dues for those whose spouses are not Jewish. In some instances the non-Jewish spouse may be interred in the cemetery of the congregation. The Jacksonville, Florida, Jewish community reported in 1954 that 65 out of every 1,000 families had a non-Jewish spouse. Portland, Oregon, had in 1957, 6 percent of such families. Los Angeles reported an increase in interfaith families from 4.8 percent in 1951 to 6.3 percent in 1959. It was much higher in the San Francisco area. In about 17 percent of the families in San Francisco in 1959, either the husband or wife was not Jewish; it was estimated that such families constituted in 1938 from 7 to 10 percent. The Peninsula reported, in 1959, 20 percent and Marin County 37 percent of interfaith families. One of the spouses in one-ninth of the Jewish families in the Washington, D.C., area in 1956 was not Jewish. There was a relatively larger number of such families in its suburban communities than in the nation's capital; the percentages were 17.6 and 5.3, respectively. One of the spouses in one-third of the Jewish families in the Virginia suburbs was not Jewish.[45] The Jews living in the Washington area are probably not representative of their brethren in the other parts of the country.

There are several studies of endogamy-exogamy in the New Haven Jewish community. Interfaith marriages increased, according to one of them, from 1.2 percent in 1900, to 5 percent in 1930, 6.3 percent ten years later, and 5.1 percent in 1950. It was estimated that the wives of about 3 percent of the Jewish men who were married in 1948 were not Jewish. It was estimated that families with one Jewish spouse constituted in 1953 7 percent of all the Jewish families in New Haven.[46]

The several studies suggest that interfaith marriages were less prevalent at the beginning of the twentieth century than in the 1950's. The Jews are more likely to marry within their own group than Catholics and Protestants. Jewish men are more likely to intermarry than Jewish women. One reason for this is the fact that the man is the provider. He is therefore more likely to mingle with non-Jewish men and women than the Jewish woman. A larger percentage of Jewish boys than girls go to college where they come in contact with members of other ethnic and religious groups. It is also quite possible that a college education results in a kind of cultural relativism. Moreover, the young man is expected to take the initiative and propose. Equally important is the fact that daughters are more likely to be under the influence of their parents than sons, who, in our culture, are expected to be more aggressive and independent than their sisters.

Demographically speaking, interfaith marriages tend to lower the rate of population growth. Persons who intermarry not infrequently have fewer children than those whose marital

partners are members of their own group. According to the
1957 survey made by the Census Bureau, there were 880 children under 14 years per 1,000 married couples, both of whom
were Jewish and only 459 such children per 1,000 married couples when only one of the spouses was Jewish. The interfaith
couples had only about one-half, 52 percent, as many children
as the intrafaith group. In the case of the Protestants, the
intermarried couples had about 15 percent fewer children under
14 years than those who had married members of their own
religious group. As for the Catholics, the interfaith couples had
only about 45 percent as many children under 14 as the intrafaith couples. Students at Michigan State College, both of whose
parents were Catholic, reported a larger number of siblings than
those whose mother was Catholic and father was Protestant;
the former reported an average of 3.6 children per family and
the latter only 2.2. Those whose both parents were Protestant
reported an average of 2.7 children per family while those
whose mother was Protestant and father Catholic had an average of only 1.9 children. Similar results were reported by
Drachsler in the case of Jewish endogamous and exogamous
couples.[47] Differences in age or social status may be one reason
for the lower birth rate of the interfaith couples. Secondly,
such couples probably hesitate to have children because they
are not fully convinced that they will really succeed in their
marital adjustment. Some of them probably prefer not to have
any children or very few because the birth of a child is likely
to raise the difficult and vexing question about the religion of
the newly born. Another consideration is the fact that children
of mixed parentage now and then have unpleasant experiences,
in the sense that they do not exactly know who or what they
are in a culture that favors religious affiliation and identification.

Interfaith marriages are probably not as stable as endogamous
unions. A larger percentage of students at Michigan State College who came from interfaith families reported separation or
divorce than those who were children of intrafaith parents.
About 4 percent of those both of whose parents were Catholic
said their parents were not living together; 6 percent of the
students both of whose parents were Protestant gave a similar

reply. Of those, however, whose parents were Catholic-Protestant, 14 percent reported broken homes. A survey made in Iowa in 1953 showed that a much larger percentage of Jewish and other divorcees were inter- rather than intramarried. According to a study made in 1955, one-fourth of the marriages of Jewish husbands in Boston whose wives were not Jewish ended in divorce or desertion. The divorce-desertion rates of such marriages in St. Louis, Denver, and Omaha were about 44, 48, and 62 percent. Similar results were reported for interfaith marriages in other countries. Jewish couples in Hungary had in 1930-1932 a divorce rate of 14.5 per 100 marital unions. In the case of Jewish wives whose husbands were Catholic, Lutheran, or Calvinist, the percentage of marriages which ended in divorce was 16.8, 17.6 and 19.3, respectively. Jewish couples in Berlin had in 1892-1902 a divorce rate of three per 1,000 but it was ten per 1,000 in the case of Jewish husbands whose wives were not of the same faith.[48]

It is probably more difficult to achieve a good marital adjustment when the spouses do not have a common religion and culture than when they have the same or similar religious or cultural background. Some interfaith spouses start their family life rather inauspiciously because of the opposition of the parents to such marital unions. This not infrequently results in some uneasiness, tension, and even conflict. The birth of a child may precipitate differences of opinion about the religion of the boy or girl. The attitude of friends may now and then make their marital adjustment more difficult.

The fact that interfaith marriages are more likely to end in separation or divorce probably has a deterrent effect. Whatever their religious values and attitudes may be, some men and women prefer not to take too many risks and chances as far as their family life is concerned.

According to one study, the premarital family ties of those who intermarry are generally not quite the same as of those who marry a member of their own religious group. The former are more likely to have had tenuous ties to their family when they were young and at the time of their marriage than those who do not intermarry. Those who come from a well-integrated family will hesitate to antagonize their parents when they are about to select a spouse.[49]

The Jewish background of the family is another important factor. Other things being equal, *children whose parents have succeeded in imparting to them their Jewish values are more likely to identify themselves with the Jewish people and to marry a member of their own group than those whose parents are marginal or peripheral Jews,* provided, however, that there is a close attachment on the part of the children to their parents. Those who are under the influence of their Jewish-centered parents, have attended a Jewish school for several years, have close family ties, and are not rebellious will probably prefer an intrafaith marital union.

The interfaith marriage rate will depend on the attitude of the non-Jewish prospective brides and grooms to such marital unions and their willingness or readiness to marry a member of another religious group. Generally speaking, religious-oriented societies have very low interfaith marriage rates. Members of such societies are rather tradition-directed and are religious-centered. There is not much individualism and freedom of choice in such societies; supraindividual values regulate the preferences, aspirations, and daily behavior of the members of such societies.

The attitude toward interfaith marriage of those who live in a this-worldly oriented and man-centered society is strikingly different from the attitude of those who live in an other-worldly oriented, religion-centered and tradition-dominated society. According to the former, family life is one of the opportunities an individual has for self-fulfillment and self-expression. It is not simply a matter of cohabitation. Husband and wife are to live together as long as there is mutual understanding and they have common interests and goals. Marital happiness is of utmost importance. Whether the selection of a spouse is based on the principle of complementary needs or not, men and women form and contract marital unions because they think that they have a community of interests as well as a mutual desire for each other and a mutual respect for each other's personalities.

They marry, in other words, because they are in love. In contemporary American society men and women who plan to marry are expected to marry only if they are in love. About 80 percent of 998 engaged couples said that one should not marry if not in love and about 82 percent of 1,824 engaged persons were of the opinion that husbands and wives who cease to be in love should separate or divorce. When Jewish teen-agers were asked whether they would prefer to marry one of their own group with whom they were not in love or one who is not of Jewish origin with whom they were in love, three-fourths of them said that they would prefer to marry the one with whom they were in love, although he or she was not Jewish. Four-tenths of their parents agreed with them[50]. It thus appears that contemporary American society regards love as extremely important. Secondly, whether the Riverton Jewish respondents are representative of the Jews in the United States or not, we may assume, nevertheless, that a smaller percentage of the present generation of American Jewish men and women than of those of several decades ago are unalterably opposed to interfaith marriages. Love, individualism, and marital happiness are some of the reasons for the change in the attitude of Jewish and other men and women toward interfaith marriage and for the upward trend in such marital unions.

As far as the Jewish group is concerned, there are several other reasons. The Jewish community is not as integrated and cohesive as in the past. It is more permissive and tolerant than several generations ago. The percentage of marginal or peripheral Jews has increased. The present generation is more this-worldly oriented, individual-centered, and materialistically minded than their ancestors of several generations ago.

The percentage of Jewish men and women with a college education has increased. College graduates and professionals now and then question the validity and authority of some traditions, customs and beliefs. Such persons are likely to think in terms of cultural relativism. Moreover, their mingling with their non-Jewish classmates on the campuses on a more or less equal-status basis is likely to increase the proportion of marginal Jews.

The media of mass communication transmit messages which are not aimed at integrating the Jewish community. At best, the daily newspapers, magazines, and books have very few items of Jewish interest. The radio and television have invaded the Jewish home, formerly the Jew's fortress and castle which remained impregnable for many centuries. The Jew was never exposed as much to non-Jewish culture and values as now. Whether intended or not, the media of mass communication are instrumental in the de-ethnicization of the Jew and other minority groups.

Changes in the occupational pattern of the Jews are another contributing factor. The Jews and others now have more occupational and professional contacts than in the past. Occupational propinquity now and then results in marital unions.

The shorter workday and longer weekend is another factor to be considered. Since Jews and others have more free time, their leisure-time activities are not limited to their immediate neighborhoods. They are therefore more likely to come in contact with non-Jews in recreational and similar centers than in the past. Moreover, once they are away from their immediate neighborhood, they enjoy a certain anonymity—the agencies of social control of the Jewish community are not as effective there as in the Jewish neighborhood.

The interfaith movement has probably changed the attitude of some individuals toward out-group members. They seem to assume that the movement for the brotherhood of man implies that there are no religious and cultural differences and that such diversity, wherever it exists, should be abolished. Men and women who are exposed to such teachings are more likely to intermarry than those who wish to preserve the existing religious and cultural diversity, although they are against any form of discrimination and segregation. The same applies to those who join or sympathize with those ideological movements which tend to minimize existing cultural differences and advocate equality for all.

Our socio-cultural macrocosm consists of myriads of microcosms. The fact that a relatively small number of persons actually intermarries suggests that the impact of social, cultural, and technological changes varies from individual to individual. Our large-scale or macrocosmic explanations do not seem to be quite adequate. We therefore have to turn to the individual, or social microcosm, to see whether there is any correlation between certain personality traits and individual experiences and interfaith marriage.

It appears that the relations between parents and children are in some cases an important factor. Children whose parents are overprotective are likely to have a very strong urge to become psychologically independent; children whose parents, one or both, are of the dominating type are likely to have a very strong desire to become psychologically emancipated. Interfaith marriage is one of many ways by which one can attain his or her psychological independence and emancipation.

It has been suggested that the husband-wife or father-mother relations are of some importance. If the mother-wife is an aggressive, demanding, possessive, and controlling individual, then her sons are likely to think that most, if not all, Jewish wives have such characteristics. Such an image of the Jewish wife is likely to result in a desire to marry a non-Jewish woman.[51]

There are other personality needs which are conducive to interfaith marriage. In some cases such a marital union is an expression of a desire to dominate a certain religious or ethnic group. For others, it is an expression of a desire to take revenge on those groups which discriminate against or persecute a given minority group.[52] Exhibitionism is another motive. Some intermarry because they wish to attract the attention of relatives, friends, and others. Others intermarry because of masochistic motives. Peripheral Jews are likely to intermarry because of their desire not to be identified any more with the Jewish group, either because they think the non-Jews are in some ways superior to the Jewish people, or because being a Jew is a source of many unpleasant experiences. Some think that an interfaith marriage is likely to offer them better opportunities to climb the social ladder.

Generally speaking, there is a preference on the part of individuals for social, cultural and religious homogamy. Intragroup marriage is more likely to provide the married couple with more gratification and satisfaction than heterogamy. The needs and preferences of individuals do not, however, always coincide with the values and norms of their parents, social class, ethnic group and religious community. As long as the supraindividual norms or values are considered to be more important than the preferences and the aspirations of the individual, very few, if any, interfaith marriages are likely to occur. An increase in such marriages means that there is less conformity, group loyalty, and cohesiveness than before.

FERTILITY OF THE JEWS IN
THE UNITED STATES

One of the demographic characteristics of the Jews in the United States is their preference for small-sized families. They generally have a lower birth rate and fewer children per family than other religious and ethnic groups. It is doubtful whether this is in any way due to differences in fecundity, the physiological ability to have children. The lower birth rate of the Jews is probably a result of their social status, values, and aspirations.

The lower fertility of Jewish women is not a recent phenomenon. Dr. John S. Billings, who made a study in 1889 of approximately 10,600 Jewish families, called attention to the fact that the birth rate of Jewish women 15-49 years of age was only about 70 percent of the birth rate of the general population. He also pointed out that the native-born Jewish women probably expected to have fewer children than those who had come from Germany, Russia, and Poland. He concluded that his "figures for the births by successive years, if accurate, indicate that the birth rate (of the Jews) is tending to diminish."[53]

His prediction was correct. The Jewish birth rate continued to fall. Its rate of decrease was greater than that of the general population. The cumulative fertility rate of Jewish mothers 45-74 years old who were born in Russia dropped much more in the years 1910-1940 than did that of other immigrant mothers. In 1910, when 71 percent of the immigrants from Russia reported Yiddish or Hebrew as their mother tongue, the cumulative fertility rate of the mothers 45-74 years of age who were born in

Russia was 7,368* per 1,000 mothers. In 1940 the cumulative fertility rate of the mothers 45-74 years old who were born in Russia and reported Yiddish or Hebrew as their mother tongue was only 3,727 per 1,000 mothers. Although these two groups are not strictly comparable—some of the 1910 group were not Jewish mothers—it is, nevertheless, interesting to note that the 1940 cumulative fertility rate of the Jewish mothers was only 50.6 percent of the 1910 rate of the Russian mothers, the great majority of whom were Jewish. The 1940 cumulative fertility rate of the other immigrant mothers, some of whom were Jewish, was, however, 71 percent of their 1910 rate.[54] This suggests that the Jewish group had a higher rate of decrease than the other immigrant mothers.

An analysis of the cumulative fertility rate in 1940 shows that the size of the Jewish immigrant, actually Yiddish-speaking, family was decreasing at a more accelerated rate than the birth rate of other immigrants and the native-white population. Women 45-54 years old who were born in Russia or Poland and whose mother tongue was Yiddish or Hebrew, had in 1940, only about 63 percent as many children as those whose country of origin and mother tongue were the same, but who were then 65-74 years old. In the case of all the other immigrants, the cumulative fertility rate of those 45-54 years old was only about 86 percent of those 65-74 years of age. In the case of the native white women, the younger group had about 85 percent as many children as those 65-74 years old. The native white women in cities with a least 25,000 inhabitants who were 45-54 years old had about 82 percent as many children as those who were 20 years older than they.

Jewish women 15-44 years old who were born in Russia or Poland, and who reported Yiddish as their mother tongue, had in 1940 a lower cumulative fertility rate than the other immigrant mothers as well as native-white mothers, even those who lived at the time of the 1940 census in cities with at least 25,000 inhabitants. Although immigrant mothers generally have higher birth rates than native-white mothers, the reverse was true in

* They had an average of more than seven children per mother!

TABLE 9.—*Cumulative Fertility Rate of Jewish and Other Mothers in the United States, 1940*

Age of Mothers	Number of children ever born per 1,000 mothers born in Russia or Poland whose mother tongue was Yiddish	Cumulative Fertility Rate of Jewish Mothers as Percentage of:		
		Non-Jewish immigrant Mothers	All Native-White Mothers	Native-White mothers in cities with at least 25,000 Inhabitants
15-34	1,736(a)	77.3	83.8	95.6
35-44	2,391	75.0	77.5	93.3
45-54	3,144	77.2	89.1	107.7
55-64	4,025	91.5	104.7	125.0
65-74	5,026	106.5	121.3	141.4
15-74	3,211	83.4	106.8	126.0

Source: Bureau of the Census, Sixteenth Census of the United States: 1940 Population, Differential Fertility, 1940 and 1910, Women by Number of Children Ever Born, pp. 11-12, 127-28. This report is based on a sample of the population.

(a) 1,736 children per 1,000 mothers means an average of 1.736 children per mother, etc.

the case of Jewish immigrant mothers whose mother tongue was Yiddish. The Jewish immigrant mothers 45-54 years old had fewer children than the other immigrant mothers as well as the native-white mothers. Equally important is the fact that the Jewish immigrant mothers 45-54 years old had only about 78 percent as many children per mother as those 55-64 years of age; the other immigrant mothers had, however, almost 93 percent as many children; the cumulative fertility rate of the native-white mothers 45-54 years old who lived in cities with at least 25,000 inhabitants was about nine-tenths as much as of the same type of mothers who were 55-64 years old. It thus appears that the birth rate of the younger generation of Jewish immigrant women had dropped much more than even that of native-born mothers who lived in large cities. Since American-born women generally have a lower birth rate than immigrant women, it is very likely that native-born Jewish women had fewer children than the Jewish immigrant group. It follows that the difference in fertility rate between American-born Jewish and other mothers was probably greater than between Jewish immigrant and native-born white mothers. Secondly, although the fertility rate of the Jews and others dropped, the former had a higher rate of decrease than the others.

Similar results were obtained from the 1950 census. The Russian-born women who lived in 1950 in the standard metropolitan areas of Boston, Chicago, Cleveland, Detroit, Los Angeles, New York, Philadelphia, Pittsburgh, and San Francisco, most of whom it will be recalled, were Jewish, had a lower fertility rate than the other immigrant women in these metropolitan areas. There were about 496 children under 5 who were native-born of foreign or mixed parentage per 1,000 Russian-born women 25-44 years old and approximately 659 such children per 1,000 other immigrant women who lived in these nine metropolitan areas. The Russian (Jewish) group had only 75.2 percent as many children under 5 as the other immigrant women. Similarly, the Russian group had about 556 such children per 1,000 Russian-born women 25-44 ever married, and the other immigrants had around 743 such children per 1,000 such women who lived in 1950 in the nine standard metropolitan areas referred to above.[55] The Russian group, most of whom were Jewish, had only 74.8 percent as many such children as the other immigrant women ever married. These Russian women had fewer children than other immigrant women because most of them, as shown before, were actually Jewish, who are known to have a lower fertility rate than other women. Even the Russians who lived in other parts of the country than the nine metropolitan areas, many of whom were Jewish, had a lower birth rate than the other immigrant women; the former had only 75.3 percent as many children under 5 who were native-born of foreign or mixed parentage per 1,000 Russian-born women ever married than the other such immigrant women who did not live in the nine metropolitan areas. There is hardly any other possible explanation for the fact that the Russians had in 1950 fewer children than immigrants from other parts of Europe than that most of them were actually Jewish, especially in the case of those who lived in the nine metropolitan areas.

The Census Bureau report on the fertility of Jewish and other women, based on its March 1957 survey, shows that the former had fewer children than Catholic and Protestant women. The Jewish women 15-44 years old and ever married had only about 77 percent as many children ever born per 1,000 such women as the Catholics and about 79 percent as many children as the Protestant women ever had. In the case of those 45 years old and over, who are not likely to have any more children, the percentages were about 73 and 81, respectively. The Jewish women 45 years and older had an average of 2.22 children per woman ever married, the Protestants 2.75, and the Catholics 3.06.[56] It is doubtful whether the Jewish group had enough children for replacement, especially if we bear in mind that a larger percentage of the Jewish than of the other women were immigrants who generally have more children than native-born women.

The March 1957 Census Bureau survey has some additional information on the birth rate of Jewish and other women. The former had 717 children under 14 years of age per 1,000 women 20-64 years old, and 1,304 such children per 1,000 women 20-44 years old. It was approximately 77 percent of the number of such children Catholic and Protestant (white) had in the case of the 20-64 group and about 87 percent in the case of women 20-44 years old. Similar results are obtained when the number of children under 14 per 1,000 women 25-64 years old is computed.[57] Whatever procedure one follows, the results are similar in the sense that the Jewish group has fewer children than Protestant women, who, in turn, have a lower birth rate than Catholic women.

The results of other studies lead to similar conclusions. Pearl's study of 30,949 women, 2,866 of whom were Jewish, who gave birth to children in 139 hospitals not controlled by the Roman Catholic Church, located in or near a large city east of the Mississippi in the years July 1931-January 1933, shows that the Jewish women had fewer children than Protestant and Catholic women. The Jewish women gave birth to 35.1 live births per 100 years of married life, the Protestant group had 42, and the Catholic women 45.9 children. The Jewish women had 83.6 percent as many children as the Protestants and only 76.5 percent as many as the Catholic women.[58] It is doubtful whether the observed difference is in any way due to the fact that the Jewish women were several months older at the time they were married than the other respondents.

The Growth of American Families study shows that Jewish women expect fewer children than other women. The 74 Jewish respondents expected not more than 2.4 children, the 1,817 Protestant women wanted to have an average of 2.9 children, and the 787 Catholic wives preferred to have an average of 3.4 children.[59] If the number of children Jewish wives expect to have in any way coincides with the number of children they actually have and if this group of Jewish respondents is in any way representative of the Jewish population, it would appear that the growth of the Jewish population has practically stopped.

In the light of what has been said, it is rather surprising to find that there are more children under 5 per 1,000 Jewish women 20-44 years old than in the case of the general population. Thus, there were on the average 458 Jewish children per 1,000 Jewish women 20-44 years old in Camden, Charleston (S.C.), Los Angeles, New Orleans, New York, Passaic, Pittsburgh, Port Chester, and Trenton. The non-Jewish population there had an average of 410 children under 5 per 1,000 such women. The Jewish communities had almost 12 percent more such children per 1,000 women 20-44 than the non-Jewish population. Similarly the average number in Canton, Des Moines, Houston, Lynn, and Washington, D.C., was approximately 516 and 459, respectively. These Jewish communities had about one-eighth more children under 5 per 1,000 women 20-44 than the general population.

There are several reasons for this. To begin with, this is in a sense a measure of survivors; it shows the number of children under 5 per 1,000 women of a certain age rather than the number of children ever born; it does not include those who have died. It so happens, however, that Jewish children have a lower infant mortality rate and a large percentage of them reach the age of three, four and so on. Jewish boys under 5 who died in New York City in 1931 constituted 9.5 percent of all the Jewish male decedents there; in the case of the white

non-Jewish males, they constituted 13.7 percent of their decedents; in the case of the girls, they constituted one-eleventh and
one-ninth, respectively, of the female decedents. A survey of
several neighborhoods in New York City in 1932 showed that
the Jewish infant mortality was only 70 percent of the non-
Jewish group. It was estimated that Jewish children under 14
in New York City had in 1953 a death rate of 1.4 per 1,000
and the non-Jews 2.3;[60] the Jewish rate was only 60 percent of
the non-Jewish. The same probably prevails in other cities.
In view of this, it is doubtful whether the number of children
under five per 1,000 women of a certain age, can be used for
the purpose of comparing the fertility of Jewish and other
women.

Secondly, there is probably not much of a correlation between
the number of children under 5 per 1,000 women of a specified
age and the actual number of children ever born. It is quite
possible that a substantial proportion of Jewish women have
the number of children they desire at a relatively early age.
Thus we find that there were approximately 1,584 children
per 1,000 Jewish women 20-29 in Los Angeles in 1951 and
2,045 in 1959; there were, however, 970 such children per 1,000
women 20-34 in 1951 and 1,103 in 1959. The addition of women
30-34 resulted in a greater reduction in the number of children
under 5 per 1,000 women 20-34 in 1959 than in 1951. Similar
results were obtained in the case of Passaic. One possible reason for it is that they try to have their children at an early age.

There are, however, other factors to be considered. Because
of differences in mortality rate, it is quite possible that a
relatively larger number of Jewish than other women reach
the age of, let us say, 40-44. Also, it is quite possible that a larger
percentage of Jewish than of other mothers who have children
under five live in suburbia. For these reasons as well as for
those stated above, it is doubtful whether the number of children under five per 1,000 women of a specified age who live
in large cities is a good yardstick for comparing the fertility
of Jewish and other women.

The Jewish women who lived in 1951-1955 in the metropolitan
Detroit area had fewer children than Protestant and Catholic

wives. The Jewish women 40 years old and over reported an average of 2.07 children, the others 2.16 and 2.78, respectively. These results are slightly at variance with those reported by Lenski.[61] The Jewish sample was rather small.

There is probably a larger number of children under five per 1,000 Jewish women 20-44 in the suburbs than in the large cities. Trenton Jews had, in 1949, 271 such children per 1,000 women 20-44; the Jews in the Trenton suburbs had 573 such children per 1,000 Jewish women 20-44. The young couples, especially those who have or expect babies, tend to move to suburbia.

Have American Jews participated in the general population explosion of recent years? Has there been a consequent upward trend in the Jewish birth rate similar to the one experienced by the general population? No reliable data are available for an analysis of the trend in the Jewish birth rate. We have, however, some data on the fertility pattern of the Jews in Greater Des Moines and Passaic which seem to suggest that they have not had a "baby boom." Excluding the childless married women, about 40 percent of the Jewish women in Greater Des Moines who were 45-64 years old and married had, in 1956, three or more children and only approximately 30 percent of those 35-44. The difference is statistically significant at the 5 percent level. Even if we assume that those 35-44 years old, who probably had their children during the "baby boom" period, will have some more children, it is doubtful whether they will have on the average more children per married woman than those 45-64 years old, some of whom stopped having children before the "baby boom" started. Jewish mothers in Passaic 35-44 years old had, in 1937, an average of 2.23 children and in 1949 only 1.81, a drop of about 19 percent; in the case of those 45 years and older, the averages were 3.51 and 2.51, respectively. It is quite possible that there was a relatively larger number of immigrants, who generally have larger families than American-born Jewish women, in 1937 than in 1949. However, those 25-34 years old had, in 1937 an average of 1.25 children and 1.47 in 1949. It appears that there was no "baby boom" in these two communities. As far as the other Jewish communities are concerned, it is doubtful whether we can generalize on the basis of the fertility pattern of the Jews in Des Moines and Passaic.

The fertility pattern of the Jews in the United States is similar to the birth rate of their brethren in other countries. Jewish women in Canada 20-24 years old and married had, in 1951, an average of 258 children per 1,000 such women; the non-Jewish married women had 350 children.[62] The Jews in Holland, Germany, and other countries had fewer children than the non-Jews. Regardless of where they live, twentieth-century Jews have a lower birth rate than other ethnic and religious groups.

PLANNED PARENTHOOD AMONG AMERICAN JEWS

Is this in any way due to differences in fecundity, the physiological ability to have children, or to the preference of American and other Jews not to have many children? A study made of Jewish and other women in seven standard metropolitan areas— Chicago, Detroit, Los Angeles, New York, Philadelphia, Pittsburgh, and San Francisco-Oakland—shows that the Jewish respondents expected to have fewer children than the other women. All the interviewees had their second child in September 1956, five to seven months before they were interviewed. The interviewees were native-born, once-married, and living with their spouse at the time of the interview. One hundred and sixteen of the 1,165 couples who were interviewed were Jewish. These 116 Jewish wives desired an average of 2.7 children. The 369 Protestant wives whose husbands were Protestant desired three children and the 480 Catholic wives whose husbands were of the same religion wanted to have 3.6 children. The differences are statistically significant. The family-size preferences of the husbands were generally similar to the number of children desired by their wives. According to the Growth of American Families study, it will be recalled, the Jewish women expected to have 2.4 children, the Protestant respondents desired to have 2.9 and the Catholic interviewees wanted 3.4 children.[63]

Not only do Jewish couples desire to have fewer children than others, they are actually more likely to try not to have more children than they desire than some other couples. According to R. Pearl's study, four-fifths of Jewish women 20-39 years old were contraceptors, 55 percent of Protestant and almost 39 percent of Catholic women were in the same category. The results of the Growth of American Families study are similar; a larger percentage of Jewish than other wives were using contraceptives.[64]

More Jewish than other women begin to use contraceptives before their first pregnancy. Eighty-three percent of Jewish wives began using them before their first pregnancy, 52 percent of Protestant and only 32 percent of Catholic women did the same. According to another study, 88 percent of 125 Jewish women began to use contraceptives before the birth of their first child, 61 percent of Protestant and 37 percent of Catholic women were in the same category. There was no difference between Jewish wives of white-collar and blue-collar husbands, although a much larger percentage of Protestant wives whose husbands were white-collar than blue-collar workers became contraceptors before their first pregnancy.[65]

Equally important is the fact that Jewish women are more likely to use more reliable and effective control methods than other wives. As before, 85 percent of 64 Jewish women have limited themselves to the use of chemical or mechanical devices; three-fifths of Protestant and about one-fourth of Catholic women did the same. According to another study, nine-tenths of Jewish wives whose husbands were white-collar workers used the three most effective control methods; in the case of such Protestant and Catholic wives the percentages were 64 and 31, respectively. As before, there was practically no difference between wives of white-collar and blue-collar husbands in the case of the Jewish group.[66]

No wonder that the Jewish couples were more successful both in their attempts to plan the number of children they have desired, and in the spacing of their children! The Jewish couples had the lowest failure rate. They had 9.8 failures per 10 years of exposure to contraceptives before the first pregnancy and a failure rate of 7.8 after the first pregnancy. The failure rate of the Protestants was about three times larger and the Catholics had a higher failure rate than the Protestants. The average number of months from their marriage to the birth of their second child in the case of Jewish, Protestant, and Catholic couples was six years, five years, and 57 months, respectively.[67]

The results of the several studies show that the lower birth rate of Jewish couples is due to the fact that a relatively larger number of them are contraceptors than in the case of other groups. As far as it is known, there is no difference in the physiological capacity of having children of the several religious and ethnic groups. Members of some of these groups, however, prefer to have more children than others. Jewish couples expect to have fewer children than other husbands and wives. They are therefore more likely to be contraceptors than other couples.

WHY AMERICAN JEWS HAVE
SMALLER FAMILIES

Why do Jewish couples desire to have fewer children than other spouses? One explanation is that differences in family-size preferences are correlated with differences in the occupations of husbands, income of the family, education of one or both spouses, metropolitan character of the community in which families live, and similar social and economic factors. A larger percentage of Jewish than of other families live in large cities; a relatively larger number of Jewish than of other husbands and wives are college graduates; a larger percentage of Jewish than other husbands are in the several professions or in white-collar occupations. It was recently reported that when these and several other social and economic variables were held constant, differences in family-size preferences and fertility patterns between Jewish and Protestant couples, but not between Jewish and Catholic couples, either diminished or practically disappeared. Some are therefore of the opinion that the family-size preferences and low fertility of Jewish couples are a function of these and similar socio-economic factors.[68]

The results of other studies seem to be at variance with those of the Growth of American Families study. According to one of them, 85 percent of the Jewish white-collar class were successful planners and 66 percent of such Protestants, the difference being highly significant; similarly, 76 percent of Jewish and 54 percent of Protestant blue-collar workers were successful planners, the difference being statistically significant. Although the difference in the percentage of Protestant white- and blue-collar workers who were successful planners was statistically significant, there was no statistically significant difference between these two groups in the case of the Jewish sample. The average number of months between their marriage and the birth of their second child of Jewish and Protestant white-collar workers (including professionals, managers, officials, proprietors, salesmen, and clerks), was 71 and 63 respectively; it was 76 and 57 months, respectively, in the case of the blue-collar workers. Protestant white-collar workers desired to have more children than the Jewish white-collar group; the same was true in the case of the blue-collar workers. A survey of a New York middle-class area showed that Jewish managers, proprietors, and officials had fewer children than such non-Jews, many of whom were Catholics. Terman's Jewish geniuses had fewer children than his other geniuses.[69] These studies suggest that *there are differences in the family-size preferences and fertility pattern of Jewish and Protestant couples both of whom live in large cities, are engaged in more or less similar occupations, and presumably are not markedly different in their educational attainments and incomes.* Moreover, this theory does not account for the fact that there is hardly any significant difference in the family-size preferences and fertility pattern of Jewish professionals, proprietors, white-collar and blue-collar workers. There is apparently no correlation between the socio-economic status and birth rate in the case of the Jewish group.

Statistically speaking, the fact that two or more groups have the same average does not necessarily mean that they are similar. One has to take into consideration the range of patterns of variation of each one of them. The more homogeneous a group is, the more will the measurements of its members be clustered around its mean; the more heterogeneous a group is, the more will the individual measurements be scattered. The average is in the former case more representative of the group than when there is much dispersion. As far as the study under consideration is concerned, Dr. Freedman and his collaborators do not discuss the homogeneity-heterogeneity of the Jewish and other groups and do not compare their patterns of variation.

There are several historical, socio-cultural, and psychological factors which differentiate Jews from others and which have to be taken into consideration. Jews are probably more family-centered than other groups; they are very much interested in the welfare and future of their children. Historically, they did not have the same opportunities for self-expression, self-fulfillment, and self-validation, which are universal human traits, as others because of the hostile attitude toward them. The family was one of the few places and groups where they could act as free individuals and where they could expect to be treated with respect and dignity. The Jewish husband and father was almost as much in need of his wife and children, for purely psychological and sociological motives, as they were in need of him. This greater interdependence strengthened their family ties and intensified their devotion to their children. This tradition has been handed down from generation to generation and is still a very important factor in Jewish life.

The responsibilities of Jewish parents have in the course of time greatly increased. This-worldly minded Jews do not believe in miracles and do not believe that prayers and piety will help them and their children very much. Since they are the ones who want children, they feel that they are the only ones responsible for the mental, cultural and social development of their children. Being this-worldly minded, they are very much interested in the this-worldly welfare of their sons and daughters.

As this-worldly minded, they are also very much concerned about their own socio-economic status as well as that of their children. Traditionally family-centered, this-worldly minded and secular-oriented Jews are more likely to be future-oriented and to have the provident "rainy-day" mentality than are some other parents. This means that Jewish husbands and wives in a highly competitive individual-centered, and other-oriented society, who have the tradition of being family-centered, are more likely to desire to have fewer children than other couples.

The proverbial veneration of Jews for learning is another important factor. Whatever the reasons and motives, they have throughout their history emphasized the importance of study and scholarship. At the time when other ethnic groups and nations paid homage to their military and political leaders, royalty and nobility, the Jews held in very high esteem their scholars and spiritual leaders and offered financial and other aid to those who aspired to become Jewish scholars. Jewish parents hoped that their sons and the husbands of their daughters would be men of learning. "Torah is the best sehorah" (learning is the best thing one could aspire to have), well epitomizes their attitude toward learning. This being the case, the Jew in a society which emphasizes the importance of learning, could be expected to be more receptive to this idea and to be more ready to spend several years on a college campus and in a professional school than the children of other ethnic groups who do not have such a tradition.

Parents who aspire to a higher education for their children and who do not make adequate provisions for it, do not seem to be quite realistic about it. The sending of a child to college and to a professional school generally presupposes long-range planning on the part of the parents. From a strictly financial point of view, they are generally expected to pay the tuition fees. They have to support and take care of the child while at college or professional school. They are deprived of a potential source of income because college students are hardly expected to be able to contribute to the family chest. Those who are fully aware of the financial responsibilities that parents who plan to send their children to college and to a professional or graduate school are expected to assume, not infrequently realize that a large family is not at all compatible with their aspirations for a higher education and professional training for their children. As far as Jewish mothers are concerned, there is a negative correlation between their aspiration to have college-educated children and the number of children they desire to have. There was some positive correlation in the case of the Catholic mothers and no correlation in the case of the Protestant respondents.[70] The high respect for the scholar which is deeply rooted in Jewish tradition and life; the practical importance and value of higher education and professional training in contemporary society; their future-oriented and rainy-day mentality; their rational and realistic analysis of means and ends; their familistic values and sense of responsibility for the education and general welfare of their children—all account for the fact that Jewish mothers are more likely to think that they have to make adequate financial and other provisions for the higher education and professional training of their children than other parents. Jewish parents are therefore more likely to perceive the incompatibility between their parental responsibilities and a desire for many children than parents with quite different values and goals.

The minority status of the Jews is another important factor. The unfriendly attitude toward them makes them feel very insecure. The persecutions they have been subjected to throughout the ages cannot be easily erased from their individual and collective mind and memory. They therefore strive to attain a certain degree of economic independence, and security, and social status for themselves and their children. They are, in other words, more likely to be future-oriented than those who are not being discriminated against.

Similarly, Jewish parents are more likely to try to maximize opportunities for their children. As long as they are under the impression that their children are expected to have a better education and training in order to be accorded the same opportunities as the children of the dominant group, they will endeavor to send their children to good colleges and professional schools. As long as they think that their children are

expected to excel themselves in order to have the same professional and social opportunities as those of the majority group,
they will try to impress upon their sons and daughters the
importance of being good students. As long as they share the
view that Jews are being discriminated against, Jewish parents
will try to make adequate financial and other provisions for
their sons and daughters. This means that Jewish children are
not infrequently dependent upon their parents for a longer
period than are those of other ethnic groups. It also implies
that it probably costs more to raise a Jewish child than a non-
Jewish one. In order to enable their children to overcome as
many of the disadvantages which they are likely to encounter
as members of a minority group, Jewish parents prefer to minimize the psychological and sociological importance of a large
family so that they may be able to maximize opportunities
for the few children they expect to be able to take good care of.

If the minority status of the Jews is really such an important
factor as far as their fertility pattern is concerned, why did their
ancestors in Europe, who were less tolerated and had practically
no civil and political rights and no legal protection, have large
families? As long as Jews believe that the hostile attitude toward
them and the persecutions they are subjected to are a kind of
punishment for their sins and those of their ancestors, they are
going to look upon their persecutors with a certain degree of
equanimity. Not that they want to suffer, but they believe they
have to endure the mistreatment and persecutions they are subjected to as a kind of expiation. As far as their children are
concerned, they are, naturally, interested in their social and
economic welfare. They believe, however, that Providence will
take care of them and their children and they are therefore
against the voluntary limitation of the size of their families. The
contemporary Jew, however, is man-made oriented. Anti-Semitism is the result of certain economic, political, and social conditions. Some are anti-Jewish because of certain personality
problems and difficulties. Since discrimination is a man-made
product, man can stop it or outlaw it. Unlike their ancestors,
who were guided by their religious traditions, the present generation of Jews is change-oriented. Like many others, they think

that man can change his social structure and system of social relations, and that he can remake society to be a better place to live in than it is now. If their ancestors were not very much concerned about the views and attitudes of the non-Jews, American Jews are other-directed, in the sense that they wish to be on friendly terms with members of the dominant group and want to be treated as equals. Jews who are other-worldly oriented are more likely to be able to endure suffering and discrimination than this-worldly minded individuals. The latter want legal protection, economic independence, psychological security, and social equality for themselves and their children. To the extent that they do not have the moral strength, spiritual fortitude, religious fervor, and Messianic hope of their forefathers, one could hardly expect American Jews to have as many children as their ancestors used to have.

Is the family-size preference of Jews in any way similar to the fertility pattern of other ethnic and religious minorities? As far as American Catholics are concerned, they have much larger families than the Protestants, who, in turn, generally have more children per family than the Jews. The attitude of the Catholic Church toward birth control is one reason for it. In general, the history, experiences, values, and aspirations of the Jews are not quite the same as of the other ethnic and religious minorities. Nor is the attitude toward Jews the same as toward other minorities. Inasmuch as they are not as familistic and future-oriented as the Jews, their family-size preference is not the same as that of the Jews in the United States.

MORBIDITY AND MORTALITY

There are many biological and social determinants of disease and death. There are genetic factors as well as sex and age differences. Medical knowledge and the availability of medical care and services are important considerations. Traditions, superstitions, and social and cultural values have some effect. Conditions under which people work, periods of rest and recreation, leisure-time activities, standards of living, housing conditions, are some of the social determinants. Personality characteristics are also of some importance.

Jews have a low birth rate and a low infant mortality rate. It was estimated that Jews in several New York neighborhoods had in 1932 an infant mortality rate of 40 per 1,000 and the general population 57. Jewish boys in New York under 5 had, in 1925, a death rate of 16.4 per 1,000 and those of the general population 21.7. Montreal Jews had in 1950 an infant mortality rate of 12.9 per 1,000 live births, the Anglo-Celtic group there had an infant mortality rate of 29.7 and the French 57.7[71] One of the principal reasons for the lower infant mortality rate of the Jews is that Jewish infants are generally better cared for from the moment they are born.

A much smaller percentage of Jewish than of other decedents in 1953 were under 5 years of age. Although such children constitute a smaller percentage of the Jewish than of the rest of the population because of the lower birth rate of the Jews, it is doubtful whether this is the real reason for the much lower

TABLE 10.—*Percentage Distribution of Decedents in New York City in 1953 According to Age*

| | Jewish Decedents | | Protestant-Catholic Decedents | |
	Male	Female	Male	Female
Under 1	1.4	1.1	2.5	2.0
1-4	0.5	0.4	0.8	0.7
5-9	0.3	0.2	0.4	0.2
10-24	0.8	0.5	1.3	1.0
25-39	2.0	3.0	3.2	3.7
40-49	6.6	6.5	9.4	7.7
50-54	6.7	6.4	8.6	6.5
55-59	10.4	8.2	10.6	8.4
60-64	13.5	11.0	14.0	10.7
65-69	17.2	14.8	15.5	13.3
70-74	15.2	15.8	13.6	14.6
75-79	12.1	13.4	10.3	13.1
80 and over	13.4	18.6	10.0	18.2

Source: David M. Liberson, "Causes of Death Among Jews in New York City in 1953," *Jewish Social Studies*, 1956, Vol. 18, p. 110.

percentage of children among Jewish decedents. The principal reason is probably the fact that Jews have a lower infant mortality. They have fewer children, they try to take good care of them, they endeavor to save the life of as many of their infants and babies as is humanly possible.

There was a relatively smaller number of teen-agers and young adults among the Jewish than the other decedents. In the case of the Jewish males, those 5-24 constituted 1.1 percent and those 25-49 about one-twelfth, 8.6 percent; the corresponding percentages for the non-Jewish group were 1.7 and 12.6. The percentage of these two age groups, 5-49, in the case of the Jews was only two-thirds of the non-Jewish group. One reason for it is that Jewish children receive better medical and general care than those of other groups and that Jewish adults are more likely to use the services of good physicians. Differences in education and income, among other things, would probably account to some extent for the fact that Jews are more likely to get good medical care than others. Jewish children terminate their schooling at a much later age than non-Jewish teen-agers and are thus less likely to be exposed to certain occupational hazards and diseases at an early age. Differences in occupation, housing, standard and mode of living, drinking habits, leisure-time activities are other reasons.

A larger percentage of the Jewish than the other male decedents were 65 years old and over. This suggests that the Jews have a higher life expectancy and that a relatively larger number of them reach the age of 65. As they grow older, they begin to experience the degenerative processes over which, for the time being, man does not have much control.

The life expectancy of females is not the same as of males. A larger proportion of female than of male infants, adolescents, and adults generally survive. Differences in environmental conditions and influences are not the only reasons for the sex difference in mortality. Although male and female infants and babies live under the same environmental conditions, a smaller proportion of the former than of the latter actually survive. There is some evidence that the constitutional resistance of males to the various degenerative life processes is not as good as of females.[72] Biological factors are apparently very important. As in the case of the males, a smaller percentage of the Jewish than of the other female decedents were under 65. Jewish and other women in their childbearing period, 25-39 had a higher mortality rate than men.

The age distribution of the decedents in 1953 was not the same as in 1931. Jewish boys under 5 constituted, in 1931, almost one-tenth, 9.5 percent, of the male decedents and in 1953 only 1.9, one fifth of the 1931 percentage. On the other hand, Jewish men 70 years old and over accounted for only 19 percent of the decedents in 1931, and constituted almost 41 percent in 1953. In the case of the non-Jewish males the corresponding percentages were approximately 16 and 34. Similar changes occurred in the age distribution of the female decedents in New York City.[73] These changes were brought about by advances in medicine, increase in purchasing power, better working conditions, higher standard of living, and other social improvements.

The causes of death have changed. As the percentage of the population 65 and over increases, an increase in the incidence of the degenerative diseases as cause of death is to be expected. Cancer, heart and vascular diseases as causes of death were reported more frequently in 1953 than in 1931. On the other hand, tuberculosis, diabetes, and pneumonia were reported less frequently. Cancer, heart diseases and diabetes as causes of death were more prevalent among Jews than other decedents both in 1931 and 1953-1954. Death was more often attributed to cirrhosis of the liver, pneumonia, and tuberculosis in the case of non-Jewish than Jewish decedents. Accidents as cause of death were reported more frequently for non-Jews than Jews. This may be a result of differences in occupation. The deaths of a relatively larger number of Jews than others were attributed to hyperplasia of the prostate and suicide. The causes of death of Jews in St. Louis in 1955-1957[74] were similar to those of the Jewish decedents in New York City in 1953-1954.

Whether Jews are biologically different or not, the fact that some of the causes of death are more prevalent among them while others are less frequently reported, is in part due to their social and cultural values, occupational pattern, family life,

TABLE 11.—*Percentage Distribution of Causes of Death of Jewish Decedents in New York City, 1931 and 1953*

Causes of Death	1931	1953
Cancer	14.6	23.0
Cardio-arterio-venal diseases	40.8	61.8
Cirrhosis of liver	1.5	0.5
Pneumonia	10.3	2.8
Tuberculosis	3.2	0.3
Diabetes	4.3	3.0
Syphilis	0.6	0.1
Suicide	1.8	0.8
Others	22.9	7.7

Source: David M. Liberson, *op. cit.*, p. 114.

standard of living, mores, and past experiences. This is probably one of the reasons for the fact that organic mental disorders are less prevalent among Jews while the reverse is true in the case of functional disturbances. The feeling of insecurity of the Jews, the frustrations they experience, their levels of aspiration, the tensions under which they live—all seem to have some effect on the personality of the Jew. A survey made in New Haven in 1950 showed that psychoneurotic and character disorders were more prevalent among Jews than among those of Irish and Italian origin. Jews had a relatively smaller number of schizophrenics. There was no alcoholic and drug addict in the Jewish sample, who constituted about 5 percent of the Irish and Italian patients. As in the case of the non-Jews, mental disorders were more prevalent among the lower than upper classes of Jews.[75]

The percentage of Jewish men and women of those admitted to New York State hospitals for mental disorders was less than expected. Other things being equal, they should have constituted approximately the same percentage of the admissions as of the white population in the state. Moreover, most of the Jews live in large cities which generally have a higher rate of first admissions than those in small communities and in rural places. Because of differences in the birth rate, a larger percent-

TABLE 12.—Percentage of White First Admissions to New York State Hospitals for Mental Disorders Who Were Jewish

Period	Total		Manic Depressive		Dementia Praecox		Psychoses with Cerebral Arterio Sclerosis		Senile Psychoses		General Paresis		Alcoholic Psychoses	
	M.	F.	M.	F.	M.	F.	M.	F.	M.	F.	M.	F.	M.	F.
1920-1928*	10.9	11.7	16.3	17.4	15.6	13.4	4.9	6.9	4.9	6.9	11.3	9.1	1.1	0.3
1930-1938*	11.3	14.7	15.8	17.4	17.1	17.9	9.1	13.4	6.5	10.1	9.2	9.0	1.4	0.4
1940-1944*	12.8	16.3	19.0	19.2	18.8	19.1	12.6	16.4	9.7	12.7	7.8	7.0	1.7	0.5
1946-1952*	10.9	13.0	15.8	14.7	14.7	14.0	13.0	14.0	10.0	12.0	7.3	3.6	1.1	0.3

Source: Benjamin Malzberg, "Mental Diseases Among Jews in New York State, 1920 to 1952," Yivo Annual of Jewish Social Science, 1955, Vol. 10, pp. 279-99.

* Even number years.

age of Jews are adults who are likely to suffer from some mental
disorders. On the other hand, it is quite possible that more Jewish than other mental patients are being treated privately by
psychiatrists and psychoanalysts or are patients in private hospitals than non-Jewish mental patients. This very likely accounts
for the fact that the percentage of Jews in the New Haven
study, which included even those who were under the care
of psychoanalysts, was greater than expected—about one-eighth
rather than one-tenth.

The percentage of Jewish men and women with psychoses
with cerebral arteriosclerosis increased considerably. The Jewish men constituted about 5 percent of such patients in 1920-
1928 and 13 percent in 1946-1952. A similar increase was
reported for Jewish women. The percentage of Jewish patients
with senile psychoses in 1946-1952 was twice as much as in
1920-1928. An increase in the percentage of Jews 65 years old
and over accounts for part of the rising trend in the percentage
of Jewish patients with psychoses with cerebral arteriosclerosis
and senile psychoses. It is not known, however, whether the
increase in the prevalence of such disorders actually coincided
with the increase in the percentage of the Jewish population
65 years old and over.

Alcoholic psychoses are rather rare among Jews. They constituted less than 2 percent of the male patients with such disorders. There was, however, a slight increase in the prevalence
of such psychoses among Jewish men.

There was an increase in the percentage of Jewish patients
with dementia praecox in the years 1930-1938—the years of an
economic depression—and in 1940-1944, the war years. The
percentage of Jewish patients diagnosed as being manic-depres-
sive increased in 1940-1944. It is quite possible that the depression, Hitlerism, and World War II account in part for the rise
in these psychoses.

Some psychoses are more prevalent among Jewish women
than men. One reason for the greater prevalence of psychoses
with cerebral arteriosclerosis and senile psychoses among Jewish women than men, is the fact that a larger percent of the
former than the latter reach the age of 65. General paresis and

alcoholic psychoses are more characteristic of Jewish men than women.

In general, mental disorders have their roots in the personality traits and experiences of individuals, and in the culture of the society in which they lived Jews are not an exception to this rule. Their psychoses are to a very large extent an outgrowth of their personal experiences, social status, the attitude toward them, and their social and cultural values.

NOTES

1. Thirty-two of 52 countries which took population censuses in the years 1945-1954 included in their schedules questions on religion and 15 collected data on the ethnic characteristics of their inhabitants. Philip M. Hauser and Otis D. Duncan (eds.), *The Study of Population* (University of Chicago Press, 1959), pp. 338-41 and 347-50.

According to D. Good, 40 countries recently included at least one question on religion. *Population Index* (January, 1959), p. 3.

2. Israel Goldstein, "Religious Census: An Alien Idea?" *The Washington Post* (July 16, 1957), p. 12; D. Good, *op. cit.*, pp. 4-12.

3. Ronald Freedman, Pascal K. Whelpton, and Arthur A. Campbell, *Family Planning, Sterility and Population Growth* (McGraw-Hill Book Co., 1959), p. 105.

4. Donald J. Bogue, *The Population of the United States* (Free Press, 1959), pp. 697-98.

5. U.S. Bureau of the Census, "Religion Reported by the Civilian Population of the United States: March 1957," *Current Population Reports*, Series P-20, No. 79 (February 2, 1958), p. 1.

6. *Ibid.*, p. 4.

7. D. Good, *op. cit.*, p. 7.

8. Bureau of the Census, *16th Census of the United States: 1940*, Differential Fertility, 1940 and 1910, pp. 106-7.

9. U.S. Bureau of the Census, *14th Census, 1920, Population*, Vol. 2, p. 967; *15th Census, 1930, Population*, Vol. 2, p. 342.

10. For the purposes of the 1950 census, "a standard metropolitan area is a county or group of contiguous counties which contains at least one city of 50,000 inhabitants or more. In addition to the county, or counties, containing such a city or cities, contiguous

counties are included in a standard metropolitan area if according to certain criteria they are essentially metropolitan in character and socially and economically integrated with the central city." Criteria of metropolitan character and integration are given. In New England, "towns and cities were the units used in defining standard metropolitan areas." These definitions and the sets of criteria can be found in each of the 1950 census reports on population.

The 1950 census report *Nativity and Parentage* has data on immigrants and native-born or immigrants of mixed parentage who lived in the following standard metropolitan areas: Boston, Chicago, Cleveland, Detroit, Los Angeles, New York, Philadelphia, Pittsburgh and San Francisco.

11. Bogue, *op. cit.*, p. 371.

12. Fred Massarik, *The Jewish Population of Los Angeles* (Los Angeles Jewish Community Council, 1953), pp. 16 and 29.

13. U.S. Bureau of the Census, "Religion Reported by the Civilian Population of the United States: March 1957," *Current Population Reports*, Series P-20, No. 79, pp. 6 and 8.

14. U.S. Bureau of the Census, *Current Population Reports*, Series P-25, No. 231.

15. Alvin Chenkin, "Jewish Population in the United States 1960," *American Jewish Year Book*, Vol. 62, 1961, p. 63.

16. Bogue, *op. cit.*, p. 698.

17. An urbanized area "contains at least one city with 50,000 inhabitants or more in 1940 or according to a special census taken since 1940" and "also includes the surrounding closely settled incorporated places and unincorporated areas that comprise its urban fringe," *1950 U.S. Census of Population, Characteristics by Size of Place*, p. 5A-6.

18. Bogue, *op. cit.*, p. 700.

19. According to Chenkin, New York City had in 1957 a Jewish population of 1,936,000 and the adjacent counties Westchester, Nassau, and Suffolk 465,000. According to another estimate, the number of Jews in New York City increased from 1,996,000 in 1950 to 2,115,000 in 1957, a gain of about 6 percent, and the three neighboring counties had a Jewish population of 466,000, in C. Morris Horowitz and Lawrence J. Kaplan, *The Jewish Population of the New York Area*, pp. 108-10.

20. Massarik, *The Jewish Population of Los Angeles, 1959* (Jewish Federation-Council of Greater Los Angeles, 1959), p. 8.

21. Massarik, *The Jewish Population of San Francisco, Marin County and the Peninsula, 1959* (Jewish Welfare Federation of San Francisco, Marin County and the Peninsula, 1959), pp. 11 and 15.

22. Chenkin, op. cit., pp. 57-61, is the source of information on the number of Jews in these cities. The numbers are estimates.

23. Leon Schapiro, "World Jewish Population," American Jewish Year Book, Vol. 62, 1961, pp. 382-88.

24. Sophia M. Robison, ed., Jewish Population Studies, New York, Conference on Jewish Relations, 1943, pp. 11, 23, 39, 61, 73, 93, 156, 170; Julian B. Feibelman, A Social and Economic Study of the New Orleans Jewish Community, Philadelphia, 1941, p. 34. Here, as well as later on in other cases, it is assumed that no significant changes took place.

25. The data will be found in the respective community surveys. It is assumed that no significant changes occurred in the years 1949-1954; similarly, the assumption is that no significant changes took place in the years 1956-1959.

26. U.S. Bureau of the Census, Census of Population: 1950, Population, Vol. 4, "Nativity and Parentage," Table 1.

27. Liebman Hersch, "Jewish Migrations during the Last Hundred Years," The Jewish People, Past and Present (Jewish Encyclopedic Handbooks, Central Yiddish Culture Organization, New York, 1948), Vol. 1, p. 409; Ilya Dijour, "Jewish Immigration to the United States Since 1944," American Jewish Year Book, Vol. 62, p. 64.

28. Was the difference in any way due to the fact that some men were in the armed forces, or that those in out-of-town schools were not included?

29. Mortimer Spiegelman, "The Longevity of Jews in Canada, 1940-42," Population Studies (December, 1948), p. 296.

30. David M. Liberson, "Causes of Death Among Jews in New York City in 1953," Jewish Social Studies (April, 1956), p. 99; Nathan Goldberg, "The Jewish Population in the United States," The Jewish People: Past and Present (Central Yiddish Culture Organization, New York, 1948), Vol. 2, p. 33; Spiegelman, op. cit., pp. 298-99; Louis Rosenberg, "Births, Deaths and Morbidity Among Jews in Montreal in 1950, Jewish Social Studies (1953), Vol. 15, p. 105.

31. Jerold S. Heiss, "Variations in Courtship Progress Among High School Students," Marriage and Family Living (May, 1960), p. 168.

32. Ernest Havemann and Patricia S. West, They Went to College (Harcourt, Brace, 1952), pp. 55-56.

33. Lewis M. Terman, Genetic Studies of Genius, Vol. 4 (Stanford University Press, 1947), p. 300.

34. Judson T. Landis, "Religiousness, Family Relationships, and Family Values in Protestant, Catholic, and Jewish Families," Marriage and Family Living (November, 1960), p. 342.

35. Gerhard Lenski, *The Religious Factor* (Garden City, N.Y.: Doubleday & Co., 1961), p. 198.

36. U.S. Department of Health, Education, and Welfare, Public Health Service, National Office of Vital Statistics, *Socioeconomic Characteristics of Persons Who Married Between January 1947 and June 1954: United States*, pp. 314 and 317.

37. Lenski, *op. cit.*, p. 150; the results are based on small samples.

38. Landis, *loc. cit.*

39. George A. Lundberg and Lenore Dickson, "Selective Association among Ethnic groups in a High School Population," *American Sociological Review*, Vol. 17 (February, 1952), p. 26; Marshall Sklare and Marc Vosk, *The Riverton Study* (The American Jewish Committee, 1957), p. 41; Victor A. Christopherson and James Walters, "Responses of Protestants, Catholics and Jews Concerning Marriage and Family Life." *Sociology and Social Research*, Vol. 43 (September-October, 1958), p. 19; Hershel Shanks, "Jewish-Gentile Intermarriage: Facts and Trends." *Commentary*, Vol. 16 (October, 1953), p. 374.

40. Shanks, *loc cit.*; Clifford Kirkpatrick and Theodore Caplow, "Courtship in a group of Minnesota Students," *American Journal of Sociology*, Vol. 51, (September, 1945), p. 116.

41. Landis, *op. cit.*, p. 345; Shanks, *loc. cit.*, Thomas C. McCormick and Boyd E. Macrory, "Group Values in Mate Selection in a Sample of College Girls," *Social Forces*, Vol. 22 (March, 1944), p. 317; "The Fortune Survey," *Fortune* (November, 1942), p. 10; Christopherson and Walters, *loc. cit.*, L. D. Rockwood and M. E. N. Ford, *Youth, Marriage, and Parenthood* (John Wiley, 1945), p. 87; M. Greenberg, "The Jewish Student at Yale," *Yivo Annual of Jewish Social Science* (1946), p. 229; forty-seven percent of the respondents had no objection to interfaith marriage.

42. Sklare and Vosk, *op. cit.*, p. 36; Aaron Antonovsky, "Aspects of New Haven Jewry," *Yivo Annual of Jewish Social Science*, Vol. 10 (1955), p. 143; Morton Sontheimer, "Would You Approve Your Child's Marrying a Protestant? Catholic? a Jew?" *Woman's Home Companion* (March, 1953), pp. 30-31; Lenski, *op. cit.*, pp. 48-49; John P. Dean, "Jewish Participation in the Life of Middle-Sized American Communities," in Marshall Sklare, ed., *The Jews*, p. 314.

43. U.S. Bureau of the Census, "Religion Reported by the Civilian Population of the United States: March 1957," *Current Population Reports*, Series P-20, No. 79, p. 8; Julius Drachsler, *Intermarriage in New York City, 1921*, pp. 53-54.

44. Loren Chancellor and Thomas P. Monahan, "Religious Reference and Interreligious Mixtures in Marriage and Divorce in Iowa," *American Journal of Sociology*, Vol. 61 (1956), p. 235;

Jerold S. Heiss, "Premarital Characteristics of the Religiously Inter-married in an Urban Area," *American Sociological Review*, Vol. 25 (1960), p. 49; Carle C. Zimmerman and Lucius F. Cervantes, *Successful American Families* (New York: Pageant Press, 1960), p. 151; Freedman, Whelpton, and Campbell, *loc. cit.*

45. *The Jewish Population of Charleston, W. Va.* (1959), pp. 3-4; Charles Reznikoff, *The Jews of Charleston (S. C.)*, Jewish Publication Society of America (1950), pp. 152, 205, 239-40; Jacksonville Jewish Community Council, "All About Us!" (1954), p. 11; Jewish Welfare Federation of Portland, Oregon, *Jewish Census—Portland Urbanized Area*, p. 5; Massarik, *The Jewish Population of Los Angeles* (1959), p. 32, and *The Jewish Population of San Francisco. . .* (1959), p. 44; Stanley K. Bigman, *The Jewish Population of Greater Washington in 1956* (Jewish Community of Greater Washington, 1957), p. 124.

46. Ruby J. R. Kennedy, "Single or Triple Melting Pot?" *American Journal of Sociology*, Vol. 58 (1952), p. 56; August B. Hollingshead, "Cultural Factors in the Selection of Marriage Mates," *American Sociological Review*, Vol. 15 (1950), p. 623; Antonovsky, *op. cit.*, pp. 139, 143.

47. Judson T. Landis, "Marriages of Mixed and Non-Mixed Religious Faith," *American Sociological Review*, Vol. 14 (1949), p. 404; Drachsler, *op. cit.*, p. 77.

48. Landis, *op. cit.*, p. 403; Chancellor and Monahan, *op. cit.*, p. 235; Zimmerman and Cervantes, *op. cit.*, p. 154; Stephen Somogyi, "Differential Divorce Rates by Religious Groups," *American Journal of Sociology*, Vol. 46 (1941), p. 676; Maurice Fishberg, *The Jews* (Scribner, 1911), p. 217.

49. Heiss, *op. cit.*, p. 54.

50. Ernest W. Burgess and Paul Wallin, *Engagement and Marriage* (J. B. Lippincott Co., 1953), pp. 393-95; Sklare and Vosk, *op. cit.*, p. 36.

51. Maria H. and Daniel J. Levinson, "Jews Who Intermarry," *Yivo Annual of Jewish Social Science* (1958/1959), Vol. 12, pp. 112-14.

52. George Little, "Analytic Reflections of Mixed Marriages," *Psychoanalytic Review* (1942), Vol. 29, pp. 20-25.

53. John S. Billings, "Vital Statistics of the Jews in the United States," *Census Bulletin* (December 30, 1889), No. 19, pp. 4, 6, 8, 9.

54. Bureau of the Census, *Sixteenth Census of the United States, 1940, Population, Differential Fertility, 1940 and 1910, Women by Number of Children Ever Born*, Tables 7, 8, 11.

55. It is quite possible that Jewish mothers who reported Yiddish as their mother tongue had a higher cumulative fertility rate than

those Jewish immigrants who reported some other mother tongue, because of differences in the number of years they have been in the country and because of differences in the rate of acculturation.

The term immigrant is being used here in a political or legal, rather than in a sociological sense. Immigrants are those who were not born in the United States. The Census Bureau includes among them even those who arrived when they were only about one week old or even younger, and were thus under the influence of American culture practically from the moment they were born.

56. Bureau of the Census, *United States Census of Population: 1950,* Vol. 4, *Special Reports,* "Nativity and Parentage," Tables 7, 14, 16, 22. (See note 26.)

57. *Statistical Abstract of the United States, 1958,* Vol. 79, p. 41.

58. Raymond Pearl, *The Natural History of Population* (Oxford University Press, 1939), pp. 236-37.

59. Freedman, Whelpton and Campbell, *op. cit.,* p. 287.

60. Nathan Goldberg, *op. cit.,* p. 33; J. B. Maller, "A Study of Jewish Neighborhoods in New York City," *Jewish Social Service Quarterly,* Vol. 10 (1934), p. 274; Liberson, *op. cit.,* p. 99.

61. David Goldberg and Harry Sharp, "Some Characteristics of Detroit Area Jewish and non-Jewish Adults," in Marshall Sklare, *The Jews,* p. 109; Lenski, *op. cit.,* p. 217.

62. Louis Rosenberg, "The Demography of the Jewish Community in Canada," *The Jewish Journal of Sociology,* 1959, Vol. 1, p. 232.

63. Charles F. Westoff, Robert G. Potter, Philip C. Sagi, Elliot G. Mishler, *Family Growth in Metropolitan America* (Princeton University Press, 1961), pp. 180 and 139; Freedman *et al., op. cit.,* pp. 69, 70, 287.

64. R. Pearl, *op. cit.;* pp. 241 and 340; Freedman *et al.,* pp. 65, 66, 67, 104-5.

65. R. Freedman *et al., op. cit.,* pp. 110-11; Ch. Westoff *et al., op. cit.,* p. 72.

66. R. Freedman *et al., op. cit.,* pp. 180-81, 185; Westoff *et al., op. cit.,* pp. 79-80.

67. Westoff *et al., op. cit.,* pp. 92-97, 183; Pearl, *op. cit.,* p. 242.

68. R. Freedman, P. K. Whelpton, J. W. Smit, "Socio-Economic Factors in Religious Differentials in Fertility," *American Sociological Review* (1961), Vol. 26, pp. 608-14; E. Rosenthal, "Jewish Fertility in the United States," *American Jewish Year Book* (1961), Vol. 62, pp. 11-25.

69. Westoff *et al., op. cit.,* pp. 185-88, 215; C. S. Solomon,

"Social Characteristics and Fertility," *Eugenics Quarterly* (1956), Vol. 3, p. 101; L. M. Terman, *op. cit.*, p. 301.

70. Westoff *et al.*, *op. cit.*, pp. 254-60, 327.

71. Maller, *op. cit.*, p. 274; Spiegelman, *op. cit.*, pp. 298-300; Rosenberg, "Births, Deaths and Morbidity Among Jews in Montreal in 1950," *Jewish Social Studies* (1953), Vol. 15, p. 105.

72. Francis C. Madigan, "Are Sex Mortality Differentials Biologically Caused?" *Mailbank Memorial Fund Quarterly* (1957), Vol. 35, pp. 202-23.

73. Charles Boldaun and Louis Weiner, "Causes of Death Among Jews in New York City," *New England Journal of Medicine* (1933), Vol. 208, pp. 407-16.

74. *Public Health Reports, 1959*, Vol. 74, p. 243.

75. Bertram H. Roberts and Jerome K. Myers, "Religion, National Origin, Immigration, and Mental Illness," *American Journal of Psychiatry*, 1954, Vol. 110, pp. 759-64; August B. Hollingshead and Frederick C. Redlich, Social Class and Mental Illness (John Wiley, 1958), pp. 204-5.

CONCLUSION

by JACOB FREID

A COMMUNITY IN TRANSITION

The "miracle" of the re-creation of a Jewish state after two millennia and of the following years, coincided with the trek to the suburbs. The successful struggle for statehood and the subsequent efforts of Israel to preserve its new-won independence has had a positive effect on American Jews. It is evident in their greater willingness to be identified with Jews, to affiliate with Jewish organizations and institutions, to join a synagogue, to give generously to Jewish causes. Abraham Duker's perceptive studies from the dual vantage point of a sociologist-historian adds to the common explanations of these trends toward affiliation and identification, the growing acculturation in American society, the establishment of Israel and the impact of the Hitler holocaust.[1]

The "education of Hyman Kaplan"—which we once termed Americanization, the credo of the melting pot—to the sociologist is acculturation to America. This pattern of acculturation to America was more evident in the Jews. Jews adjusted to American life more rapidly and successfully. To them, as Nathan Goldberg detailed in his study of economic trends, America presented a ladder of economic and social opportunity which they climbed eagerly, ably and rapidly into the professions and the middle classes. They had left the old world of persecution, prejudice and poverty for the new world of the second chance.

True, in the economically impoverished and constricted Pale

---

[1] Abraham G. Duker, "Some Aspects of Israel's Impact on Identification and Culture Patterns," *Jewish Social Studies*, January, 1959.

of Settlement there was no ladder of opportunity but an obstacle course. But the Jewish community achievement norms, with plaudits and prizes of prestige, status and success, were incentives to Jewish learning for the scholar and the Talmud *chochem*. In the United States the American cash-nexus, income-bracket image of success replaced the scholar by the doctor, the businessman, the "alrightnick"; and with acculturation came Jewish deculturation.

Jewish Diaspora existence has a two millennia patina of minority status. If Jews could not change the weather they could dress according to the climate, with the result that the Jew's intercourse within the group assumed a defensive orientation. Inhibited by and conditioned to his perennial short-end-of-the-stick role in the majority-minority relationship through the centuries, the Jew's relations to the non-Jew in his land of residence did not have the spontaneity which is an unconscious expression of equality of status.

In the ghetto he was shut away from the principal arteries through which the main events coursed for the people among whom he sojourned. In the lands of emancipation the entrance fee for acceptance was high, and often exacted an additional personal toll from those who negotiated the trans-ghetto passage. Ruppin's studies of intermarriage, baptism and conversion reveal the process of osmosis toward emancipation, activated and influenced by the Enlightenment and the Haskalah.

In the United States equalitarianism, political and social, was a fact of frontier life. The year 1890, which marked the first decade of the great Jewish migration to America, also brought to a close the era of the westward frontier. The quickening pace of American industrialization and urbanization with its increasingly important dollar-sign criterion of status could not provide social equality to penniless immigrants; but it did provide opportunity and the chance to breathe the exhilarating air of freedom, citizenship and suffrage. The East Side urban enclaves which were the first areas of Jewish settlement were artificial ghettos. For residence in America was different not only in degree, but in essence. It did not have a ghetto tradition, ethos, or atmospheric psychology.

The depression years spawned demagogues and lunatic-fringe organizations whose anti-Semitic campaigns, in the degree of their vehemence and the extent of their support, were novel and frightening. Father Charles Coughlin, Catholic priest and pastor of the Shrine of the Little Flower in Royal Oak, Michigan, began his rise to political prominence in 1930 by organizing the Radio League of the Little Flower. Using the "Jewish issue" as a means to the end of achieving political power, his broadcast sermons were heavily laden with political content and strident anti-Semitic opinions, both demagogic and fascistic in character. His activist followers constituted themselves a Christian Front whose adherents bore an affinity to the *lumpen*-proletariat who became Hitler's storm-trooper bully boys of the Nazi party. He also published a street-corner-hawked and widely circulated magazine, *Social Justice*.

As the war clouds gathered, the respectable and respected isolationist movement, whose flag flew from the tower of the Chicago *Tribune*, whose organization was America First, and whose unshakeable faith was in Washington's *Farewell Address* as the be-all and end-all of American foreign policy, linked itself to anti-Semitism and anti-Semitic groups as an answer to the anti-Hitler, pro-allied efforts of the Jews and internationalists. The effect of American leadership which often confers a nimbus of authority and expertness in many areas because of a heroic achievement in one—such as leading the major leagues in home runs, or in this case, flying the Atlantic Ocean non-stop—brought Col. Charles Lindbergh to the forefront of American isolationism, with its anti-Jewish overtones.

However, Pearl Harbor and World War II discredited isolationism as well as the followers of the Nazi line and doctrines. Anti-Semitism's roots were traced to the Nazi plague which had engulfed Europe in tragedy, and thus shorn of sustenance they atrophied and perished. In 1942 Coughlin's ecclesiastical superiors prohibited his radio broadcasts, and *Social Justice* was barred from the mails under the espionage law.

As 1962 began, the record showed that the years since Pearl Harbor—while recently spattered by the spate of swastikas daubed on synagogue walls in late 1959 and in early 1961—

had not been marred by the resurrection of the hate movements
of the virulent thirties. The pseudo "facts" and "scientifically"
untenable assumptions which were the underpinnings shoring
up racism and racist theories, prejudices, and discrimination,
were knocked out by a barrage of discoveries of social and
physiological scientific research.[2] The American Jewish Committee and B'nai B'rith took the leadership and made vital
contributions in this area, while the American Jewish Congress
used Law and Social Action as a potent weapon in extirpating
the discriminatory practice which breeds and nurtures prejudice.

It is within this context that American Jewry is acting out
its present role as a community in transition. The stage is the
same, but the scenery is changing and the scene has shifted
since Namier and Ruppin were writing. The present challenge
is not anti-Semitism but wholesome acculturation without un-
wholesome Jewish deculturation and assimilation. The Jews are
a particular group whose evolution in the new world, while
in step with the general patterns of American life, yet connotes
a distinctive thread in the warp and woof of the tapestry of
American experience. And this distinctiveness stems from the
"desire of the Jews to fit into the social patterns of the United
States without losing their own group individuality—an individuality formed by an ancient culture making continuous attempts to accommodate itself in the framework of new civilizations."[3]

Vance Packard in his best-selling study of American society's
social climbers, *The Status Seekers*,[4] reported certain irrational
attitudes of some of the non-Jewish élite towards Jews. ("There
was no effort made to promote or avoid comfort or discomfort.
I merely reported what I saw.")[5] Packard made a study of the
"apartness" he found between Jews and non-Jews in the same

---

[2] Oscar Handlin and Mary F. Handlin, "Acquisition of Political and
Social Rights by the Jews in the United States," *American Jewish Year
Book*, 1955, p. 86.

[3] C. Bezalel Sherman, "The Jew in American Society," *Congress Weekly*,
December 8, 1958.

[4] Vance Packard, *The Status Seekers*, David McKay Co., 1959. Interview
in National Jewish *Post and Opinion*, December 4, 1959.

[5] *Ibid.* in National Jewish *Post and Opinion*.

communities. He did not try to specify the basis of this "apartness" as being either by choice or from discrimination. "Non-Jews frequently say it is by choice that the Jews continue being apart. Jews frequently report that it is discrimination that keeps them that way," Packard said. "I, personally, feel that both factors are involved," he added.[6] Though criticized by reviewers for certain errors and lack of sociological expertness, the book is important for the fact that so many non-Jews have read it and been influenced by its author's judgments. As indicative of non-Jewish attitudes, perceptive insights by honest non-Jewish observers such as Mr. Packard are important. He feels that today's tendency to segregate people into "population layers" will probably have two major influences upon American Jews —a centrifugal pull towards assimilation and a centripetal push towards "voluntary ghettoizing," as exists currently in the New York City area.

Based on his years of leadership together with Will Maslow and Alexander Pekelis for the struggle to legislate discriminatory practices out of existence, Leo Pfeffer contends that social discrimination is one of the least important problems facing American Jewry. Packard demurs that social discrimination of this type does constitute some threat to the Jewish community, "since so much club life today is an adjunct to business . . . as a result of the overpowering growth of giant corporations."[7] Dr. John Slawson makes this same point in a series of significant addresses.[8] This explains the different emphasis and approach of these two agencies in their civil defense activities.

A significant number of Jews in America are groping for an idiom of Jewish expression and involvement that will give them personally a comprehending and meaningful relationship to and identification with Jewish history and peoplehood. You see them at the conventions of the Union of American Hebrew

[6] *Ibid.*

[7] *Ibid.* The American Jewish Committee is making a concerted effort against the discriminatory practices of large corporations and industries which deny advancement into executive positions to qualified Jewish personnel.

[8] "Social Discrimination," 1955; "Integration and Identity," 1959; "The Unequal Treatment of Equals," 1959, American Jewish Committee.

Congregations, the United Synagogue of America, the Union of Orthodox Jewish Congregations, and Reconstructionist meetings; they are also at lectures of the Theodor Herzl Institute, the American Jewish Historical Society, the National Jewish Music Council and the Jewish Book Council, and at conferences of the Council of Jewish Federations and Welfare Funds and the National Jewish Welfare Board. Many, once anonymous, are now searching for insight, for commitment, and to do better for their children what was done so poorly for themselves, to improve and invigorate Jewish life in America.

The kaleidoscope of a community in transition has both its dark and bright color patterns. On the one hand critics find the rabbinate, the synagogues, the schools, the agencies, institutions, organizations of an atomized community unequipped to fulfill their historic responsibilities favorably. On the other hand there are assertions by careful observers full of hope for the testing period of the sixties to affirm or deny. Rabbi Albert I. Gordon voiced his opinion that "today there are more Jews —young enthusiastic Jews—who have the will to be Jews than I have noted in over three decades. There is ample reason to speak hopefully concerning their future."[9]

"Not status seeking, but genuine desire to come closer to Judaism is behind the current move to synagogue affiliation," in the opinion of the executive director of the United Synagogue of America, Dr. Bernard Segal. If the Jews going to synagogues were motivated by status or group identification seeking, other institutions were better fitted to offer it to them "at lower prices and lower personal commitments," he argues.

The factors most influential in conditioning social development during this generation were the growth of cities and the acceleration of technological changes as predicted by Henry Adams.[10] By the time of Franklin Roosevelt's first inauguration,

[9] Albert I. Gordon, *Jews in Suburbia,* (New York: Beacon Press, 1959). "The Jews of surburbia have, to date, achieved a high degree of integration into the total life of their communities. They have also succeeded in attaining a high measure of identification with the Jewish people and its way of life."

[10] Henry Adams, *The Education of Henry Adams,* (1918), (New York: Modern Library, 1931).

more than half of the population of America lived in towns and cities, and a sizeable part of it in the densely populated metropolitan areas. With the increasing "citification" of the country, the metropolis became the center of industry and business, of government, of entertainment, of education, of culture. Urban ideas and patterns of life diffused over the countryside. Under the impact of the movies, radio, television, the automobile, syndicated newspaper features, national advertising, interstate thruways, etc., provincialism, regionalism and "otherness" softened and gave way to standardization. The internal migration was from the rural to the urban areas. For the Jews the migratory pattern was from one urban area to another—in New York it was from the East Side "ghetto" to a middle-class apartment in the Bronx or Brooklyn, and then to the so-called "golden ghetto" of Central Park West, Riverside Drive, and the West Side.

With the end of World War II the push set in from the urban centers to the suburban periphery. The young married families, priced out of decent city housing after the war and aided by government loans to veterans for housing, funneled out of the areas of second and third settlement of their parents in their new or used automobiles to raise their families in the suburbs. This intramural migration from city to suburb was accompanied by an increase in the membership roles of suburban religious centers. Many who had been Jews in revolt against their parents' immigrant generation orthodoxy—Duker's anonymous, illiterate non-Gentiles of the metropolis—after their primary propulsion to the suburbs, experienced a secondary pull to the synagogue.[11] They came to fulfill social needs—to make new friends, to belong, to identify. The gregarious temple social generated an atmosphere of social warmth which thawed out strangeness and strangers, enabled the newcomer to overcome loneliness and to meet people who were either "old" newcomers of a year or two residence, or new newcomers like themselves. The synagogue was a quick and simple solution to the quest for fellowship and friendship in a new community. It was also

[11] Gordon, op. cit., Chapter 4, "The Synagogue—Center of Jewish Life."

a wholesome place for their children to meet and make friends, and affiliation with it fulfilled conformity to the current American opinion that religious affiliation is a necessary facet of respectability and normalcy in American society.

Nahum Goldmann may deplore the "tendency to concentrate Jewish life around synagogues and to turn Judaism into synagogue worship." He may reject the synagogue as the center of Jewish secular as well as religious life as a danger which "may lead to a distortion of Judaism's true character."[12] But he cannot deny it. The synagogue *is* the vital center of suburban Jewry regardless of the descriptive River Platte cliché of the shallowness of its Jewishness. However, Bernard Segal is vulnerable in his belief that the desire to approach closer to Judaism is the prime motivation for synagogue affiliation. The democracy-on-wheels of the automobile as a possession of suburban families and the compulsions of the lonely crowd had more to do with the edifice complex of synagogue proliferation. The auto was the new Conestoga which made the suburban era possible. It was the rolling liaison between job and home and the rival-partner to the commuting railroad, both competing and sharing in the transporting of suburbanite breadwinners to and from the city every working day.

Rabbi Gordon's observation concerning the will to be Jews offers hope for the future realization of Segal's view as a worthy objective. But that time is not yet. The centrality of the synagogue in America is not that of a Jewishly virile educational, cultural, intellectual and religious center—a dynamic, creative life force for Judaism and Jewry. At present it is rather a cultural-social institution where the congregational member can listen to lectures on psychoanalysis or book reviews, see the local ballet teacher present a dance recital, or watch the temple little theatre group stage a broadway musical for entertainment and fund-raising. But, the Israeli critic asks, "Does this distinguish Jews from Gentiles?"[13] How can this charac-

[12] In an address to the Council of the World Zionist Organization in Jerusalem, December 28, 1959.

[13] Eliezer Livneh, "In Critical Comment," Forum IV, p. 71; Isaiah Leibowitz, "The World and the Jews," in *ibid.*, p. 85.

terize the Jewish people and give content to its "Jewish" life?
The great question is whether the synagogue, like the Columbia
University experience, will rise to the challenge and the opportunity offered by a social constituency which is groping in
unconscious confusion, but which can respond to a purposeful
effort to transmute it into a comprehending, participating congregation of mature men and women personally committed to
Judaism as a way of life. The effort, if it is to succeed, will
adapt historical insights to an indigenous environment where
American Jews live in a Gentile world in a free, democratic
society that reaches its secular and non-Jewish apogee each
December with the total immersion baptism of the virgin birth,
and whose materialistic, psychological and intellectual frame of
reference is conditioned by the fact of living in such a world.

The fact that there have been enthusiastic attendance and
participation at conferences arranged for the rabbi and the
Jewish social worker to meet and to share ideas, problems and
insights for mutual understandings, rapport, and partnership in
serving the community and in meeting the perplexities of the
Jew today, is an indication of the step forward. In a provocative meeting devoted to the community center, a new generation
of social workers since the time of the forties revealed the
significant change in center programs toward positive Jewish
content and education. The center worker of the sixties, unlike
his predecessors, understands Jewish programming and its implementation.

This workshop on "The Relationship of the Synagogue to
the YMHA," is a measure of progress from the vacuum of the
pre-war years, as its companion session on "Jewish Content
in the Social Work Process" is in Jewish social welfare and
health agencies. Like the setting up of the first Jewish cultural
foundation by the Council of Jewish Federations and Welfare
Funds, so this first annual conference on the relationship of the
rabbi to the Jewish social worker on December 21, 1959, under
the sponsorship of the Commission on Synagogue Relations of
the Federation of Jewish Philanthropies of New York is a creative beginning in a new and positive direction for American
Jewry. The conferences in 1960 and 1961 underscored this hope.

A community in transition after three hundred years, American Jewry represents a complex people of all shades of commitment from Orthodoxy to Reform to agnosticism to atheism; from positive identification and affiliation to anonymity and assimilation. Under the impact of the Hitler catastrophe, Israel's statehood, and the intramural exodus to the suburbs, there has been an impressive increase in synagogue membership and school enrollment.

The representative and conflicting opinions in the Diaspora-Israel dialogue here indicate the debaters' differences concerning American Jewry's future. The optimists speak of "new creative forces" which will express themselves in a golden age of Diaspora Jewry rivalling those of Babylonia and Spain.[14] The pessimists speak of the negation of the Galut and the Diaspora and prophesy the western European blight of assimilation, intermarriage and disintegration. What is most apparent is that American Jewry's destiny will be *sui generis,* the result of a dynamic process of environmental challenge and response—affected by the common past, the climactic experiences of the past quarter century, from the advent of Hitler to the independence of Israel and the renaissance of Hebrew culture, the unique American environment with its own social forces, and Jewry's response to their economic and social pressures, influences and challenges.

During this period of transition there is an honest attempt on the part of a growing number to leapfrog the first stage of suburban return to the synagogue now fixated to an unfortunate extent at the level of the social club, dance-hall, "simchatorium" involvement. The mordant River Platte description of American Jewish education by Alexander Dushkin and Uriah Engelman, as a "mile wide and an inch deep" will no longer also characterize suburbia only if and when the Jewish community matures to an understanding of and a devotion to the goal of a meaningful Jewish education as presented in Dr. Engelman's essay. Else there will continue to be pin prick involvement but no depth

[14] Samuel Blumenfeld, "American-Jewry, Reflections on Social, Communal and Spiritual Trends," *Essays on Jewish Life and Thought* (New York: Columbia University Press, 1959), pp. 137, 135, *et passim.*

to Jewish education in the future. Incidents which pragmatically reveal the truth of the River Platte cliché occur even in communities preponderantly Jewish in population.[15]

Yet there are the signs of hope indicated above. Further, the day schools are also growing in number and attendance. They are preparing the cadres who leaven Jewish education, understanding, and commitment with quality and depth. They may be the leaders of a future transformation and marked improvement in American Jewish life. The summer Hebrew-speaking camps, such as Massad and the Ramah camps, make Jewish education an informed, enriched, and personally meaningful living experience of which John Dewey would heartily approve. Such an experience has vital psychological and spiritual effects in the self-development and Jewish commitment of its campers. The next generation should benefit from the contributions of the alumni of the day schools and Hebrew-speaking camps to Jewish knowledge, comprehension and creative living.

The fears that the day school is not a wholesome development are unfounded. There are aspects to private schools which trouble the liberal—the Groton-Andover-Exeter appearances of undemocratic exclusiveness, snobbishness, segregation. The liberal Jewish parent may feel in a vague sort of way that he is somehow lending comfort to those who are overtly or subtly seeking to undermine the American tradition of separation of church and state. Others feel any trend away from the public schools is unhealthy.

Based on an empirical experience with Orthodox and Conservative day schools, the editor cannot agree that the growth

[15] At Christmas 1959, in Lawrence-Cedarhurst-Woodmere school district #15, where the community is overwhelmingly Jewish, the schoolrooms had Christmas trees. In the sixth grade, with twenty-six Jewish children in a class of thirty, the class voted on whether or not to have a Christmas tree. The tally was twenty-four in favor and six against. In this area there are six synagogues (two Reform, two Conservative, two Orthodox). Several have memberships of 1,000 or more families, and among the Rabbis are nationally prominent leaders. Also, the Parent-Teachers Association is virtually entirely Jewish in this school. This is a symptom of the problem of suburban Jewry, of the "River Platte" ineptness of the religious school and the pulpit, and the ignorance and indifference of the home today.

of Jewish day schools is an "unhealthy trend." Such a belief fails to comprehend the validity of cultural pluralism in American society and in consequence commits the fallacy of considering positive Jewish education to be in conflict with American democracy, when in reality it enriches and strengthens both Americanism and Jewishness.

The seriousness of this fallacy cannot be underestimated. It reflects the worst qualities of minority existence and its attendant insecurity, and in fact, breeds an "unhealthy" form of inferiority. American culture flourishes precisely because of the contributions of its varied groups. It we dry up the vital educational sources of Jewish life, what indigenous product shall we have to contribute? To ask this question is to supply an argument for the continuing extension and strengthening of the Jewish day school for those who wish it. As for the argument of segregation, to the sociologist who sees the Jew immersed in a majority, secular, non-Jewish environment, the facts of American life make it a non sequitur. The ability to speak and read Hebrew is but one of the objectives of Jewish education so ably set forth by Engelman and Dushkin in their impressive study. But when his Hebrew learning is combined with a background of general knowledge above the average, of Jewish knowledge far above the average, and an intimate identification with the Jewish past and present based on a fund of positive and meaningful Jewish childhood memories, the graduate of a good day school will generally be a wholesomely adjusted, educated Jew who can equate Jewish and American existence and values without fear or anxiety neuroses.[16]

Dr. Solomon Grayzel sees neglect of the Jewish cultural heritage as a threat to Jewish survival more menacing than anti-

---

[16] Compared to a good day school, much of Jewish education is unimpressive. It was found impossible to integrate a child of ten who had moved and left a Conservative day school, into the afternoon weekday school of a Conservative congregation with a membership of more than fifteen hundred families, and with a distinguished school reputation. Even in the *Hay* class for thirteen-year-olds, in addition to being too young for peer group associations, the ten-year-old was the only one who could converse in Hebrew. Nor in the active youth program of this center was there one Young Judean or young Zionist group or a Hebrew-speaking group.

Semitism. "In fact the anti-Semite serves us as a scapegoat for our own sin of weakening our heritage. The real enemy is abandonment of our cultural and historic traditions."[17] Grayzel's statement is true, but only because the succeeding fight against anti-Semitism and discrimination has made it possible to heed his warning and to act upon it. Coincidentally, as if in response to this note of caution, the 1959 Assembly of the Council of Jewish Federations and Welfare Funds gave an enthusiastic reception to the report on the National Cultural Study. Reaffirming the principle of the indivisibility of equal rights, the Assembly praised civil rights progress in recent years and continued its commitment "to help secure the fact as well as the principle of equal opportunity for all." The CJFWF showed mature understanding of the fact that the civil rights struggle had reached a level of attainment against negative bars and discriminatory practices at which creative Jewish living and culture could complement it for positive American Jewish existence. In a meeting as historically pregnant for Jewish culture as the conference on the relationship of the rabbi and the social worker was for American Jewish social welfare work, the inspired delegates hailed the plan for a Jewish renaissance with "the sort of excitement that used to be reserved only for rescue and rehabilitation."[18]

A Jewish Cultural Foundation will coordinate efforts to further cultural projects, to aid and counsel local communities concerning the programs and budgets of cultural agencies, and to engage in projects which other bodies cannot encompass. A community, which like Gaul is divided into three parts religiously, has established a Council of Jewish Cultural Agencies as an expression of agreement on the cultivation of a common Jewish culture. This is an important step forward for American Jewry.

[17] Philadelphia *Jewish Exponent,* December 4, 1959.
[18] *The Reconstructionist,* November 27, 1959. "The community begins to emerge as the social structure in which all Jews can find a common life and purpose. Within that structure, diversity of theological commitment and observance may be encouraged. So long as some overarching unity is achieved, American Jewry can afford the luxury of denominationalism."

WHAT OF THE FUTURE?

Do most Jews practice Judaism today in greater or lesser degree only because they are conforming creatures of ethnocentric tribalism, tabu-conditioned against exogamy apart from the intermarriage minority, and wishing to belong to a group of their own whatever its merits or beliefs? Can the community make creative use of this fact as in the analogy of the university students at Columbia, or are the circumstances too different for similar success?

The negative influences of nostalgia, conformity, tribalism, superstition, and cultural lag are evident.[19] Hopefully there are positive factors as well. Among these are observant knowledge of the Jewish past, comprehending commitment, Jewish conviction and affirmative faith in the values of Jewish religious and secular civilization. Gradually program committees are agreeing to pay Jewish professionals, lecturers, scholars, and writers fees to lecture and teach on Jewish topics, just as the men's clubs and sisterhoods pay golf pros, magicians, hairdressers, etc. Adult education programs are increasing in quality and attendance, and entire courses and institutes are being conducted. The Theodor Herzl Institute in New York offers an excellent series of lectures and courses.

That education, both for children and adults, is a prime factor in determining the choice between assimilation and affirmation is implicit. Uriah Engleman, for the children, and Label Katz, president of B'nai B'rith, for the adults, are representative of those who wish to make it explicit. Mr. Katz rejects "community mores that relegate adult Jewish educators to a marginal status," and reduce the content of Judaism "merely to an awareness of anti-Semitism. Judaism then ceases to be a civilization. It becomes a psychological complex." Beginnings of potential significance are occurring in addition to those already noted.

[19] Sholome Michael Gelber, "Does the Jewish Past Have a Future?", *Essay in Jewish Life and Thought* (New York: Columbia University Press, 1959), pp. 255, *et passim*.

In 1960 the Union of American Hebrew Congregations established a department of Adult Jewish Education whose purpose it will be to introduce, improve and enrich such programs in its member congregations. The sponsorship of excellent books as vehicles for adult education, such as *Great Jewish Personalities* by B'nai B'rith, and *Great Ages and Ideas of the Jewish People* by Hadassah is another hopeful start.[20]

In fact, as Arthur Cohen, a young publisher contends, "in the United States today it is at last possible to choose *not* to remain a Jew."[21] Until now the Jew could not exercise this choice to be or not to be a Jew. The irresistible forces of history and circumstance compelled him "to accept what his birth had already defined," he argues.

This Jewish intellectual then answers the question of choice posed by his thesis. His reply is summed up by the title of his confessional—"Why I Choose to Be a Jew." Can we consider it an augury of an affirmative answer by the third and fourth generations of American Jews to Namier's prescription for non-survival? Is the Jewish *élan vital* of the "survivalists" who wish to remain as Jews too powerful for those whom John Slawson terms the "euthanasians" who are willing to die painlessly, to diminish significantly?[22] Dr. Slawson correctly cites Hansen's Law: what the son wishes to forget the grandson wishes to remember. "That is exactly what is happening with us, and that is why we have had the transition from the settlement houses, which were completely non-sectarian in content, to the Jewish centers."[23]

As a youth, Cohen almost took the road out of Judaism. With the dupe's path of dialectical materialism already thoroughly exposed, the exit door he was about to open was Christianity. His confession of his "conversion" to Judaism by the

[20] Simon Noveck (ed.), *Great Jewish Personalities: In Ancient and Medieval Times.* (New York: Farrar, Straus & Cudahy, 1960); Leo Schwarz (ed.), *Great Ages and Ideas of the Jewish People.* (New York: Random House, 1959).

[21] *Op. cit.*

[22] "Trends in the American Jewish Community," The American Jewish Committee, 1956, p. 9.

[23] *Ibid.*, p. 17.

late Milton Steinberg as guide and teacher, tells how the path was retraced backwards through Christianity to Judaism, "revealing the groundwork of Jewish thought and experience which supported what I have come to regard as the scaffolding of Christian 'unreason.' "[24] The editor witnessed a number of similar returns at Columbia University by this and other roads.

Mr. Cohen's conversion was effected through "study, reflection and thought" of Jewish religious principles, concepts and values. It is based on a belief in Torah and the Sinaitic revelation as the word of God. Others will not accept his belief that the Jewish people has been chosen as the special instrument of God.

But many who cannot do so are receptive, as the generation of the 1930's was not, to Judaism as a credo for living as described in these words of Cohen's gifted teacher, the late Rabbi Steinberg:[25]

> A respect for life, a sense of the rights of others, an ideal of family purity, high standards of decency and honor, a strong sympathy for the exploited and persecuted—all these were explicit in the Book and implicit in Law and custom. When the Jew compared his morality with that of the world, he felt that the contrast favored him immensely.

To lead the life of a people, a tradition, and a faith devoted to the ethical and religious ideal of the inviolability of the human spirit and the sanctity of life, to remain true to the vision of Isaiah for the peace and redemption of man in a nuclear world hovering over the abyss, is in keeping with a folk whose greeting is "Shalom," whose toast is "L'Chaim."

Will Jews in the modern world choose to be Jews? Certainly. But the quality of that choice as measured by the level of Jewish social identity, historic loyalty, cultural and spiritual expression and scholarship, intellectual understanding, secular idealism, and religious commitment is for the future to reveal.

[24] *Op. cit.*

[25] Milton Steinberg, *Making of the Modern Jew,* Behrman House, 1948, p. 96.

CONTRIBUTORS

GORDON WILLARD ALLPORT, professor of psychology at Harvard University is also chairman of its Department of Social Relations. Dr. Allport was formerly director of the National Opinion Research Center and editor of the Journal of Abnormal and Social Psychology. He is the author of the significant book, *The Nature of Prejudice*.

SALO WITTMAYER BARON is Miller Professor of Jewish History, Literature, and Institutions at Columbia University and director of its Center of Israeli and Jewish Studies. He is also the Alexander Marx Visiting Professor of History at the Jewish Theological Seminary. His monumental work is *A Social and Religious History of the Jews*.

NATHAN C. BELTH, public relations director of the Anti-Defamation League of B'nai B'rith, is author of *Fighting For America* and editor of *Barriers: A Study of the Patterns of Prejudice*. Mr. Belth has served in various editorial capacities on the staffs of the *Brooklyn Eagle* and the *New York Daily Mirror*.

DAVID BEN-GURION is the foremost contemporary Jewish statesman and the first prime minister of Israel. Prime Minister Ben-Gurion is a prolific author and a dynamic, forthright, and provocative personality. His frank views on the Zionist movement and American Jewry have set in motion a hurricane of controversy which is still seething.

MENAHEM BORAISHA was himself one of the important figures of world Yiddish literature. He published six volumes of poetic works in Yiddish including *Der Gayer*, a five hundred-page epic of Jewish life and thought. Born in 1888 in Poland, Boraisha came to the United States in 1914.

Boraisha contributed numerous articles and essays to Yiddish dailies and periodicals. He was the editorial writer of the *Congress Weekly*, published by the American Jewish Congress. He died in 1949.

DR. URIAH Z. ENGELMAN is head of the Department of Research and Information of the American Association for Jewish Education. He is the author of *The Rise of the Jews in the Western World* and has contributed extensively to scientific and general publications on Jewish demography, social history and education, written in Yiddish, Hebrew

734

and English. He is a regular contributor to the *American Jewish Year-Book*. With Dr. Alexander Dushkin, he conducted the first National Study of Jewish Education sponsored by the American Association of Jewish Education.

BENJAMIN R. EPSTEIN is national director of the Anti-Defamation League of B'nai B'rith. He has taught at the University of Pennsylvania and was a fellow of the Institute of International Education for special study in Germany at the beginning of the Hitler era. He has since revisited Germany several times at the request of the Bonn government to study anti-Semitism and the state of democracy in the West German Federal Republic. Mr. Epstein is co-author with Arnold Forster of *The Troublemakers* and *Cross Currents*, and of the report, "Germany—Nine Years Later."

JACOB FREID, Executive Director of the Jewish Braille Institute of America, is also chairman of the Political Science Department, undergraduate division, of the New School for Social Research, and has taught sociology at Rutgers University. He was editor of *Jewish Affairs*, and during World War II served as chief of the Moscow Desk of the O.W.I. and U.S. State Department.

Dr. Freid received his Ph.D. from Columbia University where he was President of the Jewish Graduate Society and chairman of the Zionist Circle. He has contributed to many general and Jewish periodicals.

ROBERT GORDIS is Rabbi of Temple Beth-El of Rockaway Park, New York. He has been an associate professor of Bible at the Jewish Theological Seminary of America and Visiting Professor of Old Testament at the Union Theological Seminary. He is the author of a number of books on the meaning of modern religion and original Biblical research, and was formerly editor of *Judaism*.

MORDECAI MENAHEM KAPLAN is religious leader and founder of the Reconstructionist movement, professor of homiletics at the Jewish Theological Seminary and a former dean of its Teachers Institute. He is chairman of the editorial board of *The Reconstructionist*, and a prolific author. Among his books are, *Judaism as a Civilization, The Meaning of God in Modern Jewish Religion, The Future of the American Jew.*

DR. BERNARD KRAMER is an associate professor of Preventive Medicine at the Tufts University School of Medicine.

Dr. Kramer received his Ph.D. from Harvard University

where he was a research assistant in social psychology. He was formerly associated with the late Professor Louis Wirth in the Committee on Education, Training and Research in Race Relations of the University of Chicago, and was a research social psychologist with the New York State Mental Health Commission in Syracuse.

JACOB LESTCHINSKY was formerly editor and research secretary of the Department of Economics and Statistics of The Yiddish Scientific Institute (YIVO), Vilna, 1925-29. He was a member of the Institute of Jewish Affairs and is the author of numerous books, articles and studies dealing with Jewish economic and sociological problems.

In "Balance Sheet of Extermination—I," Jacob Lestchinsky surveyed the terrible losses inflicted on European Jewry during a decade of Nazism and war. In "Balance Sheet of of Extermination—II," he describes what was lost in terms of Jewish institutional and cultural life.

SAMUEL H. LEVITAS was executive editor of *The New Leader* for thirty years, until his death in 1961. A Menshevik leader, Sol Levitas came to the United States to escape sentence to Siberia. In April, 1917 he was editor of the *Labor Daily* in Vladivostok, and the following year he was a delegate to the Congress of Soviets called to ratify the Brest-Litovsk Treaty. He came to the United States in 1923, joined the American Socialist party and wrote articles for the *Jewish Daily Forward*. He fought unflaggingly to expose the Communist movement, and under his direction *The New Leader* became a foremost publication of progressive thought.

WILL MASLOW is Executive Director of the American Jewish Congress. He was formerly with the *New York Times*, Associate Counsel of the New York City Department of Investigation, Director of Field Operations of the Committee on Fair Employment Practice; General Counsel of American Jewish Congress and director of its Commission on Law and Social Action.

ALEXANDER H. PEKELIS was born in Odessa in 1902, studied at the University of Leipzig and the University of Vienna for two years, then studied law for four years at the universities of Florence and Rome. In 1928 he received his law degree and spent the following year at the London School of Economics and Political Science. He returned to Italy to teach law at Italian universities, and became a full professor of jurisprudence at the University of Rome. As a refugee from Mussolini's Italy, he practiced law in Paris in 1939 and 1940. In 1941 he came to the United States and was a professor at the New School. In 1942 he studied again at Columbia University Law School.

LEO PFEFFER is General Counsel and Director of the Commission of Law and Social Action of the American Jewish Congress. Mr. Pfeffer was an editor of the New York University *Law Review* and is a foremost authority on the separation of church and state. Among his books are *Church, State and Freedom.*

HAROLD URIEL RIBALOW is an editor, author and literary critic. He was formerly managing editor of *Congress Weekly* and *American Zionist.* A noted literary critic of Jewish writing, he has edited numerous anthologies of Jewish short stories and essays, and has written book reviews and literary articles for the *New York Times, The Saturday Review of Literature* and virtually every important Jewish periodical.

BERNARD G. RICHARDS was one of the founders of the American Jewish Congress and served it as executive secretary for a number of years. He was Secretary to the American Jewish delegation to the Peace Conference of Versailles, 1919. For several years he served in various government departments in Washington. He has written extensively for the Jewish and general press and is the author of *The Discourses of Keidansky.* Mr. Richards is now Chairman of the Board of Directors of the Jewish Information Bureau.

JACOB ROBINSON, Director of Special Projects at YIVO, was legal advisor to the Israeli delegation to the U.N., and Vice-President of the Legal Committee of the U.N. General Assembly in Paris in 1950. He was formerly a member of the Lithuanian Parliament and legal adviser to its delegation to the International Court of Justice. Dr. Robinson has taught International Law at Columbia University and was Director of the Institute for Jewish Affairs. At the Nuremberg war crimes trials he was special adviser to the U.S. Attorney General. He is the author of *The Problem of Minorities; Human Rights* and *Basic Freedoms According to the U.N. Charter; Israel and the U.N.*

DR. NEHEMIAH ROBINSON is the director of the Institute of Jewish Affairs of the World Jewish Congress. Dr. Robinson is an authority on international law and human rights

and is the author of books and studies on the civil and
political rights of minorities. He has also prepared numerous important reports and memoranda to United Nations
agencies on genocide, human rights, anti-Semitism, etc.

NATHAN ROTENSTREICH, dean of the faculty of humanities at
Hebrew University, is the leading ideologist of the Mapai
party and a foremost Israeli thinker. He is the author of
numerous studies in philosophy, philosophy of history, and
Zionist theory.

MOSHE SHARETT is a former prime minister of Israel, and Minister of Foreign Affairs. He headed the Israeli delegation
to the UN General Assembly during its first years as a
member and is now a member of Knesset and of the executive committee of Mapai.

DR. JOHN SLAWSON is Executive Vice-President of the American
Jewish Committee and a member of the executive committee of the U.S. National Commission for UNESCO. Dr.
Slawson inaugurated a comprehensive program of scientific
research into the causes of anti-Semitism and methods for
combatting group prejudice. The result of this pioneering
effort was the five-volume series, *Studies in Prejudice*, a
standard reference work for social scientists. Dr. Slawson is
the author of *The Delinquent Boy*. He has taught at the
University of Michigan and at City College of New York.

GOODWIN WATSON, internationally known social psychologist,
is a professor of education at Columbia University. He
was formerly Director of Research for the National Council
of the YMCA and Director of Analysis of Broadcasts from
other nations for the U.S. during World War II. He has
written widely in the fields of psychology and education.

MEYER WAXMAN is a rabbi, educator and author. He was Pro-
fessor of Bible, Jewish History and Philosophy at Hebrew
Theological College and the College for Jewish Studies in
Chicago. He is the author of *A History of Jewish Literature*,
Dictionary of Hebrew Proverbs, *A Handbook of Judaism*.

ALFRED WERNER is a contributing editor of *Arts Magazine*, and
U.S. correspondent of *Pantheon, International Magazine of
Art*. He taught art history at Wagner College and the City
College of New York. He is the author of books on Pascin,
Modigliani, Dufy, Vlaminck and Utrillo, and a contributor to
Jewish Art, edited by Cecil Roth, and to the *Encyclopaedia
Britannica* and the *Universal Jewish Encyclopedia*.

Index

Spain, 382-83; France, 383-84; and Nationalism, 392ff.; in Palestine, 392ff.; Eliezer ben Yehudah, 392; and Zionism, 393; *melitzah*, 390; Prayer Books, 385-86; in life of Jews, 386-88; Modern, 388ff.; in Israel, 394, 399ff., 586-89; periodicals, 394; literary figures, 395-409; in America, 402-7, 441; publications, 404-5; education 405-7; list of writers, 407-9; 571, 599, 601, 611, 630, 729

Herzl, Theodor, 573-75, 618

Hillel Foundation, 177, 178, 182, 187

Hitler, Adolf: 9, 11, 14, 18, 19, 176; influence of, 186, 200, 254, 270, 316, 373ff.; and American Jewish writers, 422, 429ff., 607, 718

Inquisition, 10

Intermarriage: in Argentina, 160; in United States, 176, 187, 188, 308, 313, 676-88, 719

Ionesco, Eugene, 181

Israel: 9, 12, 14, 29n., 172; impact of, 186; pride in, 189, 194; response to, 200; democracy, 517, 521; and the democratic world, 519ff.; and Soviet Jewry, 521-26, 586-88; and Zionism, 530ff.; and Diaspora, 531-35, 563-89 *passim*, 602ff., 608, 617-31; and Jewish peoplehood, 543-46, 563-89 *passim*; statehood, 579-89, 619ff., 718

Jewish Alliance, 494-95

Jewish Colonization Association, 40, 141, 146

Jews: German, 10, 358, 360, 483-85; Diaspora, 12-13, 14, 15, 48 (*see* Diaspora); and genocide, 17-49; in Moslem lands, 50-90; Communists, 94, 172-76; and Five Year Plan, 95-96; special treatment in Soviet Union, 106, 107, 248; Pale of Settlement, 109; a "caste," 109, 302; in Soviet Union, 110, 115, 509-26 *passim;* dislocation, 141; adaptability, 153; mutual aid, 153-54; vitality, 170; status, 224; victims of prejudice,

261-63; not in executive positions, 300; in Middletown, 310-15; under democracy and totalitarianism, 509-29; unity 527, 544-46; and ideology 527ff.; a religious people, 539ff., 563-89, 590ff.

Judaism: as integrating force, 185; ethical principles of, 178, 187, 194; and religious freedom, 210, 226; and art, 319, 328ff.; and Israel, 590-616; under freedom and dictatorship, 509-26; Halacha, 545, 562; and Christianity, 547-48, 556-57, 559, 561, 566-67, 591ff.; in today's world, 547-62; Marxism and, 558-60; Messianic vision, 570ff.

Kehillah: 26-28, 32-42; in Latin America, 165; in Argentina, 156, 165; in New York, 498, 632

Khrushchev, Nikita: 9, 12, 124-26, 130, 429, 431, 434-35

Latin America: 14; Jewish population in, 139; growth, 142-44, 150; early Jews, 140; modern immigration, 141-43, 150-51; economic and social structure, 147; economic contributions of Jews to, 148; tolerance, 154, 157; anti-Semitism, 163-65; cultural activity, 167

Law and Legislation: against prejudice, 268; 279-96 *passim*; free speech, 279, 280, 281, 285; free press, 279, 280, 291 civil rights, 316

Lenin, Nikolai, 134

Lesser, Isaac, 485-87, 494

Lestchinsky, Jacob, 10, 632

Libya, 87-89

Literature: 321-27; American-Jewish 321ff.; 410-26; Yiddish, 356-76; Hebrew, 377-409

Maslow, Will, 195, 224, 310, 722

Meir, Golda, 121, 189

Mexico, 143, 147, 150-51, 155, 164, 165, 166

Migration: 136-38; to Latin America, 140-44, 150-51, 157; discouraged,

144, 493; to Brazil, 161; to United States, 483-84, 493, 494, 495, 498

Miller, Irving, 195

Morocco, 80-84

Moslem Lands: 12, 14, 50-90; state of development, 52

Namier, Lewis B., 9, 11, 13, 184, 188, 197, 721

Nazism: 17-49, 176, 193, 272, 336, 431; *Einsatzgruppen*, 432; and negators of Galut, 433; educational reaction to, 440, 449, 720

National Community Relations Advisory Council, 202, 504

Orthodoxy: 175; and prohibition of graven images, 320, 329-30, 337; *yeshivoth*, 447; day schools, 447-48, 460, 461, 463; attitudes of children in Orthodox schools, 465

"Operation Magic Carpet," 90

ORT, 41, 94

Pale of Settlement: 10, 92-93; breakdown of, 95

Pekelis, Alexander H., 195-200, 202, 279

Peretz, Yitzchok Leibush, 372

Peru, 143, 155, 163

Pfeffer, Leo, 195, 201, 722

Poland: 10, 17-49 *passim*; Warsaw Ghetto, 21-22

Population: 10-11; in Latin America, 143, 144; demography, 632-711 *passim*; urban concentration, 144, 650-53

Prejudice: 192, 193, 194, 202, 203, 224, 227; action against, 231-52, 316; modification of, 240, 241; roots of, 253-78; and state of mind, 254; parental influence and, 255-56, 272, 276; and lack of insight, 255, 256, 276; religion and, 260; education and, 265; a pattern of life, 266, 277; values and, 269, 313

Press: in Europe 45-46; in Latin America, 166; in United States, 325-27; Yiddish, 371, 375; Hebrew, 392, 394, 403, 404, 405

Quotas: 227; and vanishing immigrant, 655, 656, 657-58

Race Relations: 232, 233, 235-36, 237, 240, 244, 245, 246-47, 250, 251; contact and, 239-41, 258-60

Religious Freedom: 209-15, 218; no religious test for public office, 221, 224ff

Restrictive Covenants: 192, 198, 246; social, 227-28, 299

Riesman, David, 182, 183

Ruppin, Arthur, 9, 13, 427, 721

Ribalow, Harold, 322ff.

Ribalow, Menahem, 404, 409

Roosevelt, Franklin Delano, 429ff.

Samuel, Maurice, 11

Sartre, Jean-Paul, 181

Scapegoat: 251, 254, 268-69, 273; projection and, 270; inferiority and, 271, 317

Secular Humanism: 208, 219, 220; and rights of man, 595ff.

Segregation: 192, 205, 227-28; in South, 229, 233, 238; attack on, 241, 245, 246; campaign against, 247

Security: 224-40; lack of, 31, 229, 245, 304, 306, 317

Self-hatred, 205-6

Separation of Church and State, 194, 201, 207-23, 226

Sephardim: 10; in Latin America, 140-41, 169; in Argentina, 156, 158, 160, 167; in United States, 483, 485, 486

Sharett, Moshe, 429

Sherman, C. Bezalel, 196, 198

Sholom Aleichem, 11, 371, 433, 630

Shtetl, 10, 11, 433

Slawson, John H., 177n., 197, 203, 226, 733

Soviet Union: 9, 11, 12, 14, 91-139; revolution, 93-94; anti-Semitism, 94, 110; minorities in, 106; nationalist policy, 107-9; Jewish religious practice and education curtailed in, 109, 113ff., 115-20 *passim*; Jewish doctors' "plot," 110, 130-31; Cold War and Jews

p. 417
p. 460
p. 466
p. 471
p. 473
p. 473